MANAGING INNOVATION

MANAGING INNOVATION

MANAGING INNOVATION

INTEGRATING TECHNOLOGICAL, MARKET AND ORGANIZATIONAL CHANGE

Second edition

Joe Tidd

Science and Technology Policy Research (SPRU)
University of Sussex

John Bessant

Centre for Research in Innovation Management (CENTRIM)
University of Brighton

Keith Pavitt

Science and Technology Policy Research (SPRU)
University of Sussex

JOHN WILEY & SONS, LTD

Chichester • New York • Weinheim • Brisbane • Singapore • Toronto

Second edition © 2001 by   Joe Tidd, John Bessant and Keith Pavitt

First edition © 1997 by   John Wiley & Sons Ltd
                                    Baffins Lane, Chichester
                                    West Sussex, PO19 1UD, England

| *National* | 01243 779777 |
| *International* | (+44) 1234 779777 |

e-mail (for orders and customer service enquiries): cs-books@wiley.co.uk

Visit our Home Page on http://www.wiley.co.uk

Other Wiley Editorial Offices

John Wiley & Sons, Inc., 605 Third Avenue,
New York, NY 10158-0012, USA

Wiley-VCH Verlag GmbH, Pappelallee 3,
D-69469 Weinheim, Germany

John Wiley & Sons Australia Ltd, 33 Park Road, Milton,
Queensland 4064, Australia

John Wiley & Sons (Asia) Pte Ltd, 2 Clementi Loop #02-01,
Jin Xing Distripark, Singapore 129809

John Wiley & Sons (Canada) Ltd, 22 Worcester Road,
Rexdale, Ontario, M9W 1L1, Canada

Library of Congress Cataloging-in-Publication Data

Tidd, Joseph, 1960–
    Managing innovation : integrating technological, market and organizational change / by Joe Tidd, John Bessant, Keith Pavitt—2nd ed.
      p. cm.
    Includes bibliographical references and index.
    ISBN 0-471-49615-4
    1. Industrial management.   2. Technological innovations.   3. Organizational change. I. Bessant, J. R.   II. Pavitt, Keith.   III. Title.

HD31 .T614 2001
658.5′14—dc21

                                                  2001023386

British Library Cataloguing in Publication Data

A catalogue record for this book is available from the British Library

ISBN 0-471-49615-4
(ISBN 0-471-97076-X 1st edition)

Typeset in 10/12pt Palatino by Dorwyn Ltd, Rowlands Castle, Hants
Printed and bound in Great Britain by Antony Rowe Ltd, Chippenham
This book is printed on acid-free paper responsibly manufactured from sustainable forestry in which at least two trees are planted for each one used for paper production

CONTENTS

Preface   xi
About the authors   xiv

Part I   MANAGING FOR INNOVATION

1 Key Issues in Innovation Management   3
   1.1   Innovation and Competitive Advantage   4
   1.2   Types of Innovation   6
   1.3   Riding Two Horses—the Innovator's Dilemma   14
   1.4   Innovation Is Not Easy   15
   1.5   . . . But It Is Imperative   17
   1.6   How to Innovate?   18
   1.7   New Challenges, Same Old Responses?   20
   1.8   Outline of the Book   30
   Further Reading   32
   References   34

2 Innovation as a Management Process   37
   2.1   Innovation as a Core Business Process   39
   2.2   Evolving Models of the Process   42
   2.3   Consequences of Partial Understanding of the Innovation
          Process   43
   2.4   Can We Manage Innovation?   45
   2.5   Successful Innovation and Successful Innovators   48
   2.6   What Do We Know About Successful Innovation
          Management?   50
   2.7   Blueprints for Success   52
   2.8   Managing Innovation   59
   Further Reading   59
   References   60

Part II   TAKING A STRATEGIC APPROACH

3   Developing the Framework for an Innovation Strategy   69
    3.1   'Rationalist' or 'Incrementalist' Strategies for Innovation?   69
    3.2   Technology and Competitive Analysis   75
    3.3   Assessment of Porter's Framework   77
    3.4   The Dynamic Capabilities of Firms   81
    3.5   Innovation Strategy in Small Firms   81
    3.6   Summary and Further Reading   82
    References   83

4   Positions: The National and Competitive Environment   85
    4.1   National Systems of Innovation   85
    4.2   Coping with Competitors   96
    4.3   Appropriating the Benefits from Innovation   100
    4.4   Positioning of Small Firms   105
    4.5   Summary and Further Reading   106
    References   107

5   Paths: Exploiting Technological Trajectories   111
    5.1   Major Technological Trajectories   112
    5.2   Revolutionary Technologies: Biotechnology, Material and IT   116
    5.3   Developing Firm-specific Competencies   120
    5.4   Technological Paths in Small Firms   129
    5.5   Summary and Further Reading   132
    References   135

6   Processes: Integration for Strategic Learning   137
    6.1   Locating R&D Activities—Corporate versus Divisional   138
    6.2   Locating R&D Activities—Global versus Local   141
    6.3   Allocating Resources for Innovation   145
    6.4   Technology and Corporate Strategy   150
    6.5   Organizational Processes in Small Firms   156
    6.6   Summary and Further Reading   156
    References   158

Part III   ESTABLISHING EFFECTIVE EXTERNAL LINKAGES

7   Learning from Markets   163
    7.1   How Do Technology and Markets Affect
           Commercialization?   163
    7.2   Differentiating Products   166
    7.3   Creating Architectural Products   170
    7.4   Marketing Technological Products   176
    7.5   Commercializing Complex Products   181
    7.6   Forecasting the Diffusion of Innovations   185
    7.7   Summary and Further Reading   194
    References   195

CONTENTS

Preface   xi
About the authors   xiv

Part I   MANAGING FOR INNOVATION

1 Key Issues in Innovation Management   3
   1.1   Innovation and Competitive Advantage   4
   1.2   Types of Innovation   6
   1.3   Riding Two Horses—the Innovator's Dilemma   14
   1.4   Innovation Is Not Easy   15
   1.5   . . . But It Is Imperative   17
   1.6   How to Innovate?   18
   1.7   New Challenges, Same Old Responses?   20
   1.8   Outline of the Book   30
   Further Reading   32
   References   34

2 Innovation as a Management Process   37
   2.1   Innovation as a Core Business Process   39
   2.2   Evolving Models of the Process   42
   2.3   Consequences of Partial Understanding of the Innovation
          Process   43
   2.4   Can We Manage Innovation?   45
   2.5   Successful Innovation and Successful Innovators   48
   2.6   What Do We Know About Successful Innovation
          Management?   50
   2.7   Blueprints for Success   52
   2.8   Managing Innovation   59
   Further Reading   59
   References   60

Part II   TAKING A STRATEGIC APPROACH

3 Developing the Framework for an Innovation Strategy   69
   3.1   'Rationalist' or 'Incrementalist' Strategies for Innovation?   69
   3.2   Technology and Competitive Analysis   75
   3.3   Assessment of Porter's Framework   77
   3.4   The Dynamic Capabilities of Firms   81
   3.5   Innovation Strategy in Small Firms   81
   3.6   Summary and Further Reading   82
   References   83

4 Positions: The National and Competitive Environment   85
   4.1   National Systems of Innovation   85
   4.2   Coping with Competitors   96
   4.3   Appropriating the Benefits from Innovation   100
   4.4   Positioning of Small Firms   105
   4.5   Summary and Further Reading   106
   References   107

5 Paths: Exploiting Technological Trajectories   111
   5.1   Major Technological Trajectories   112
   5.2   Revolutionary Technologies: Biotechnology, Material and IT   116
   5.3   Developing Firm-specific Competencies   120
   5.4   Technological Paths in Small Firms   129
   5.5   Summary and Further Reading   132
   References   135

6 Processes: Integration for Strategic Learning   137
   6.1   Locating R&D Activities—Corporate versus Divisional   138
   6.2   Locating R&D Activities—Global versus Local   141
   6.3   Allocating Resources for Innovation   145
   6.4   Technology and Corporate Strategy   150
   6.5   Organizational Processes in Small Firms   156
   6.6   Summary and Further Reading   156
   References   158

Part III   ESTABLISHING EFFECTIVE EXTERNAL LINKAGES

7 Learning from Markets   163
   7.1   How Do Technology and Markets Affect
        Commercialization?   163
   7.2   Differentiating Products   166
   7.3   Creating Architectural Products   170
   7.4   Marketing Technological Products   176
   7.5   Commercializing Complex Products   181
   7.6   Forecasting the Diffusion of Innovations   185
   7.7   Summary and Further Reading   194
   References   195

8   Learning through Alliances   197
     8.1   Why Collaborate?   197
     8.2   Forms of Collaboration   202
     8.3   Patterns of Collaboration   217
     8.4   Effect of Technology and Organization   221
     8.5   Managing Alliances for Learning   229
     8.6   Summary and Futher Reading   237
     References   238

Part IV   BUILDING EFFECTIVE IMPLEMENTATION MECHANISMS

9   Managing the Internal Processes   243
     9.1   Enabling Scanning   243
     9.2   Enabling Strategy-making   246
     9.3   Enabling Effective Resource Provision   250
     9.4   Enabling Implementaion   254
     9.5   Applying the Approach to Process Innovation   264
     9.6   Enabling Learning   269
     Further Reading   272
     References   273

10   Learning through Corporate Ventures   279
     10.1   What Is a Corporate Venture?   279
     10.2   Reasons for Corporate Venturing   282
     10.3   Managing Corporate Ventures   287
     10.4   Structures for Corporate Ventures   297
     10.5   Learning through Internal Ventures   304
     10.6   Summary and Further Reading   308
     References   308

Part V   CREATING THE INNOVATIVE ORGANIZATION

11   Building the Innovative Organization   313
     11.1   Shared Vision Leadership and the Will to Innovate   315
     11.2   Appropriate Organization Structure   317
     11.3   Key Individuals   325
     11.4   Stretching Training and Development   328
     11.5   High Involvement in Innovation   329
     11.6   Effective Teamworking   334
     11.7   Creative Climate   336
     11.8   External Focus   338
     11.9   Extensive Communication   338
     11.10 The Learning Organization   339
     11.11 Organizational Innovation   340
     Further Reading   342
     References   343

12   Creating Innovative New Firms   349
     12.1   Sources of New Technology-based Firms   349

12.2   University Incubators   351
12.3   Profile of a Technical Entrepreneur   353
12.4   The Business Plan   358
12.5   Growth and Performance of Innovative Small Firms   364
12.6   Summary and Further Reading   368
References   369

Part VI   ASSESSING AND IMPROVING INNOVATION
          MANAGEMENT PERFORMANCE

13   An Integrative Approach to Innovation Management   373
13.1   Key Themes   373
13.2   Learning to Manage Innovation   374
13.3   Measuring Success   376
13.4   Auditing Innovation Management   377
13.5   What Kind of Innovator Is Your Organization?   381
References   381

Index   383

PREFACE

Management research confirms that innovative firms—those that are able to use innovation to improve their processes or to differentiate their products and services—outperform their competitors, measured in terms of market share, profitability, growth or market capitalization.[1] However, the management of innovation is inherently difficult and risky: most new technologies fail to be translated into products and services, and most new products and services are not commercial successes. In short, innovation can enhance competitiveness, but it requires a different set of management knowledge and skills from those of everyday business administration.

This book aims to equip readers with the knowledge to understand, and the skills to manage, innovation at the operational and strategic levels. Specifically, the book aims to integrate the management of market, technological and organizational change to improve the competitiveness of firms and effectiveness of other organizations. The management of innovation is inherently interdisciplinary and multifunctional, but most management texts tend to emphasize a single dimension, such as the management of research and development, production and operations management, marketing management, product development or organizational development. In contrast, we aim here to provide an integrative approach to the management of innovation.

Since the first edition was published in 1997 innovation has become a major driver of success in an increasing number of activities and sectors, and is no longer confined to large manufacturing firms. The impact of the information and communication technologies (ICTs) in logistics, distribution and services has already been significant, and has resulted in a wave of new ventures.[2] The completion of the initial stages of mapping the human genome promises to have a similar impact on the pharmaceutical and health-care sectors in the near future. In both cases there is good reason to believe that the competitive and economic exploitation of these and other emerging technologies has just begun.[3] At the same time, research on the management of innovation has increased in depth and breadth, improving our understanding and challenging our previous assumptions. We estimate the half-life of management research in this field is around 10 years, and therefore in this second edition we have taken the opportunity to update or replace about a fifth of the material. We have also incorporated feedback from readers and users of the first edition, and have improved our coverage of topics such as service innovation, innovation networks, entrepreneurship and new ventures and intellectual property.

The latest management research and the experience of leading practitioners confirm that significant dimensions in the management of innovation are not satisfactorily addressed by management teaching or texts. For example, the management of technological innovation reaches beyond efforts to improve the efficiency of production or research and development, to include the effectiveness of technological development, that is the translation of technology into successful products and services. This suggests a competence- and knowledge-based approach to technology management, which also requires analysis of organizational structures and processes. The management of organizational innovation has shifted from an emphasis on 'change management' of structure and culture, to the design and improvement of internal processes, such as knowledge management, and external linkages and networks. In market innovation there has been a shift in emphasis from crude market segmentation and analysis of consumer behaviour, to relationship and networked marketing that demands fine targeting of product development and closer linkages with lead customers.

All this suggests that it is not sufficient to focus on a single dimension of innovation: technological, market and organizational change interact. Better management of research and development may improve the efficiency or productivity of technological innovation, but is unlikely to contribute to product effectiveness, and therefore cannot guarantee commercial or financial success. Even the most expensive and sophisticated market research will fail to identify the potential for radically new products and services. Flat organizational structures and streamlined business processes may improve efficiency of delivering today's products and services, but will not identify or deliver innovative products and services, and may become redundant due to technological or market change.

In this book we aim to provide a coherent framework to integrate the management of technological, market and organizational change. We reject the 'one best way' school of management, and instead seek to identify the links between the structures and processes which support innovation, and the opportunity for, and constraints on, innovation in specific technological and market environments. We shall argue that the process of innovation management is essentially generic, although organization-, technological- and market-specific factors will constrain choices and actions. We present a number of processes that contribute to the successful management of innovation, which are based on internal knowledge and competencies, but at the same time fully exploit external sources of know-how. Contingencies such as firm size, technological complexity and environmental uncertainty will influence the precise choice of processes; for example, complexity requires increased participation in networks of suppliers and users, whereas uncertainty demands vigilance in scanning the external technological and market environment.[4]

This book is written with the needs of postgraduate and other management students in mind, specifically those studying MBA electives or options on the management of innovation and technology, or M.Sc. courses dedicated to technology and operations management. It is also relevant to managers charged with the management of research and development, product development or organizational change. Where possible, we provide examples of good, and not so good practice, drawn from a range of sectors and countries. However, the book is designed to encourage and support organization-specific experimentation and learning, and not to substitute for it. Our analysis and prescriptions are based on the systematic analysis of the latest management research, and our own research, consulting and teaching experiences at Imperial College Management School (ICMS), University of London, the Centre for Research in Innovation Management (CENTRIM) at the University of Brighton, and SPRU—Science and Technology Policy Research, at the University of Sussex, UK, as well as our experience in the USA, Europe and Asia. We acknowledge the formal and informal contributions of our colleagues, in particular Roberto Fontana, Jonathan Sapsed, Mike Hobday and Kim Thorns.

In 1998 we created a joint venture, the Innovation Club, to act as a mechanism to exchange research and practice between member firms and academics. Members include BT, Ove Arup, Procter and Gamble and Rolls-Royce. We organize regular workshops and seminars, and in addition members have formed special interest groups, on subjects such as knowledge management, design and corporate venturing. For further information please contact Charlotte Huggett at c.m.hugget@sussex.ac.uk. In 2002 SPRU and CENTRIM co-locate in the £12m. purpose-built Freeman Centre at Sussex University, to create one of the greatest concentrations of researchers in the field of technology and innovation and management and policy. For details of our current teaching and research please visit us at www.sussex.ac.uk/spru and www.centrim.bus.bton.ac.uk. We would appreciate your feedback.

Joe Tidd
John Bessant
Keith Pavitt
Brighton, Sussex, UK, January 2001

References

1   Tidd, J. (2000) *From Knowledge Management to Strategic Competence: Measuring technological, market and organizational innovation.* Imperial College Press, London.
2   *International Journal of Innovation Management* (2000) Special Issue on Innovation in Services, **4** (4), December.
3   Schwartz, P. (2000) *The Long Boom.* Orion Business, London.
4   Tidd, J. (2001) 'Innovation management in context: environment, organization and performance', *International Journal of Management Reviews*, **3** (3).

ABOUT THE AUTHORS

Joe Tidd
Joe Tidd is a physicist with subsequent degrees in technology policy and business administration. He is Professor of Technology and Innovation Management at SPRU (Science & Technology Policy Research), University of Sussex, and Visiting Professor at Imperial College Management School, University of London. He has worked as policy adviser to the CBI (Confederation of British Industry), and for the Massachusetts Institute of Technology (MIT), and on projects for consultants Arthur D. Little, CAP Gemini and McKinsey, and firms such as BT, Marconi, National Power and Nortel Networks. He is the winner of the Price Waterhouse Urwick Medal for contribution to management teaching and research, and the Epton Prize from the R&D Society. He has written three books and more than 60 papers on the management of technology and innovation, and is managing editor of the *International Journal of Innovation Management.* Contact: j.tidd@sussex.ac.uk.

John Bessant
John Bessant is Professor of Technology Management at the University of Brighton in the UK. His areas of special interest include human resource and organizational development for innovation, inter-firm learning and enabling the emergence of agile enterprises. He was responsible for establishing the University's Centre for Research in Innovation Management (CENTRIM) in 1987 and was its Director until 2000. Originally a chemical engineer, Professor Bessant has been active in the field of research and consultancy in technology and innovation management for over 25 years. He is the author of 12 books and many articles on the topic and has lectured widely around the world. He has been a fellow of SPRU at the University of Sussex since 1983 and holds visiting appointments at a number of overseas universities. He has extensive consulting experience with both private enterprises and international bodies including the United Nations, The World Bank and the OECD. Contact: j.bessant@brighton.ac.uk.

Keith Pavitt
Keith Pavitt is R. M. Phillips Professor of Science and Technology Policy at the University of Sussex, UK. He studied engineering, industrial management, and economics at Cambridge (UK) and Harvard (USA), and then worked at the Organization for Economic Co-operation and Development (OECD) in Paris. During his 30 years at the Science Policy Research Unit, he has published widely on the management of technology, and science and technology policy. His central research interests include: corporate and public strategies for technical innovation; the nature and measurement of technology; the reasons why countries, companies and sectors differ in their rates and directions of technical change; the usefulness of basic research; the links between public science and private technology in a period of globalization; and the co-evolution of technology and organization. Professor Pavitt advises numerous bodies on policies for technical change. He has been a Visiting Lecturer at Princeton University, Visiting Professor at the Universities of Reading, Strasbourg (Louis Pasteur), Padua, Nice, Aalborg, Lyon-Lumiere, Paris 13 and Paris-Dauphine, and Visiting Scholar at Stanford University. He is a main editor of *Research Policy.* Contact: k.pavitt@britishlibrary.net.

Part I

MANAGING FOR INNOVATION

Chapter 1

KEY ISSUES IN INNOVATION MANAGEMENT

'A slow sort of country' said the Red Queen. 'Now here, you see, it takes all the running you can do to keep in the same place. If you want to get somewhere else, you must run at least twice as fast as that!'

(Lewis Carroll, *Alice through the Looking Glass*)

The enormous growth of the Internet has fuelled a demand for high-speed broadband connection—and this has in turn created new opportunities for firms able to offer the technology to provide such links. In 1986 Charles McGregor founded a firm called Fibernet to provide such high-speed networks and has seen the company value grow from £37m. in 1986 to £800m. in 2000. Its current order book includes major provision for national telecoms in Germany involving some 3300 km of fibre optic-based broadband cable.

Supplying the cable to firms like Fibernet is Bookham Technologies, a firm founded on the back of doctoral research by Andrew Rickman who saw that his ideas for high-volume manufacturing of integrated optical circuits in silicon could have real commercial potential. Bookham Technologies has spent the past 10 years developing a range of components based on its unique optical communications (ASOC) technology that can manipulate the optical signal to enable various functions to be performed. These components have developed so that homes and businesses can gain access to information more quickly and efficiently over fibre optic networks. Shares in the company soared when it was floated on the Stock Exchange, and whilst there have been some ups and downs in market sentiment towards technology stocks the long-term future seems strong given the growing commitment to rolling out a broadband communications network in countries around the world.

At the other end of the technological scale there is scope for improvement on an old product—the humble eyeglass. A chance meeting took place between an Oxford physics professor developing his own new ophthalmic lens technology (and with an interest in applying it in the developing world) and someone with a great deal of knowledge of the developing world. This has led to a new technology with the potential to transform the lives of hundreds of millions of people in the developing world—a pair of spectacles with lenses that can be adjusted by the wearer to suit their visual needs. No sight tests by opticians are required, the special lenses can be simply adjusted to accurately correct the vision of large numbers of people. Mass production of the spectacles will soon be under way, with manufacturing designed to give high quality at low cost. In the developing world, where a severe shortage of opticians is a real problem, this innovation is likely to have an impact on a larger number of people than the celebrated wind-up radio.

Innovation is of course not confined to manufactured products; examples of turnaround through innovation can be found in services and in the public and private sector.[1] For example, the Karolinska Hospital in Stockholm has managed to make radical improvements in the speed, quality and effectiveness of its care services—such as cutting waiting lists by 75% and cancellations by 80%—through innovation.[2] In banking the UK First Direct organization became the most competitive bank, attracting around 10 000 new customers each month by offering a telephone banking service backed up by sophisticated IT. A similar approach to the insurance business—Direct Line—has radically changed the basis of that market and led to widespread imitation by all the major players in the sector. A series of Internet-based retailing actors such as Amazon.com have changed the ways in which products as diverse as books, music and travel are sold, whilst firms like e-Bay and QXL have brought the auction house into many living rooms.

1.1 Innovation and Competitive Advantage

What these organizations have in common is that their undoubted success derives in large measure from innovation. Whilst competitive advantage can come from size, or possession of assets, etc. the pattern is increasingly coming to favour those organizations which can mobilize knowledge and technological skills and experience to create new products, processes and services.[3]

Innovation contributes in several ways. For example, research evidence suggests a strong correlation between market performance and new products.[4, 5] New products help capture and retain market shares, and increase profitability in those markets. In the case of more mature and established products, competitive sales growth comes not simply from being able to offer low prices but also from a variety of non-price factors—design, customization and quality.[6] And in a world of shortening product life cycles—where, for example, the life of a particular model of television set or computer is measured in months, and even complex products like motor cars now take less than three years to develop— being able to replace products frequently with better versions is increasingly important.[7] 'Competing in time' reflects a growing pressure on firms not just to introduce new products but to do so faster than competitors.[8]

At the same time new product development is an important capability because the environment is constantly changing. Shifts in the socio-economic field (in what people believe, expect, want and earn) create opportunities and constraints. Legislation may open up new pathways, or close down others—for example, increasing the requirements for environmentally friendly products. Competitors may introduce new products which represent a major threat to existing market positions. In all these ways firms need the capability to respond through product innovation.

Whilst new products are often seen as the cutting edge of innovation in the marketplace, *process innovation* plays just as important a strategic role. Being able to make something no one else can, or to do so in ways which are better than anyone else is a powerful source of advantage. For example, the Japanese dominance in the late twentieth century across several sectors—cars, motorcycles, shipbuilding, consumer electronics—owed a great deal to superior abilities in manufacturing—something which results from a consistent pattern of process innovation. The Toyota production system and its equivalent in Honda and Nissan led to performance advantages of around two to one over average car makers across a range of quality and productivity indicators.[9, 10] One of the main reasons for the ability of relatively small firms like Oxford Instruments or Quantel to survive in highly competitive global markets is the sheer complexity of what they make and the huge difficulties a new entrant would encounter in trying to learn and master their technologies.

Similarly, being able to offer better service—faster, cheaper, higher quality—has long been seen as a source of competitive edge. Citibank was the first bank to offer the ATM-type of service and developed a strong market position as a technology leader on the back of this process innovation. Benetton is one of the world's most successful retailers, largely due to its sophisticated IT-led production network, which it innovated over a 10-year period.[11] Southwest Airlines achieved an enviable position as the most effective airline in the USA despite being much smaller than its rivals; its success was due to process innovation in areas like reducing airport turnaround times.[12]

With the rise of the Internet the scope for service innovation has grown enormously—not for nothing is it sometimes called 'a solution looking for problems'. As Evans and Wurster point out, the traditional picture of services being either offered as a standard to a large market (high 'reach' in their terms) or else highly specialized and customized to a particular individual able to pay a high price (high 'richness') is 'blown to bits' by the opportunities of web-based technology. Now it becomes possible to offer both richness and reach at the same time—and thus to create totally new markets and disrupt radically those which exist in any information-related businesses.[13]

The challenge which the Internet poses is not only one for the major banks and retail companies, although those are the stories which hit the headlines. It is also an issue—and quite possibly a survival one—for thousands of small businesses. Think about the local travel agent and the cosy way in which it used to operate. Racks full of glossy brochures through which people could browse, desks at which helpful sales assistants sort out the details of selecting and booking a holiday, procuring the tickets, arranging insurance and so on. And then think about how all of this can be accomplished at the click of a mouse from the comfort of home—and that it can potentially be done with more choice and at lower cost. Not surprisingly, one of the biggest growth areas in dot.com start-ups has been in the travel sector with names like lastminute.com and Expedia establishing themselves as mainstream players.

Not everyone wants to shop online and there will probably be scope for the high-street travel agent in some form—specializing in personal service, acting as a gateway to the Internet-based services for those who are uncomfortable with computers, etc. But whatever the future there will be winners—and the one thing we can be certain of is that they will be the ones who have changed their products and processes.

Table 1.1 indicates some of the ways in which enterprises can obtain strategic advantage through innovation.

1.2 Types of Innovation

Before we go too much further it will be worth defining our terms. What do we mean by 'innovation'? Essentially we are talking about *change*, and our focus in this book is particularly upon technological change. Change of this kind can take two forms—in the things (products/services) which an organization offers, and change in the ways in which they are created and delivered. (Traditionally these are termed 'product' and 'process' innovation, although these terms can sometimes be confusing.)

For example, a new design of car, a new insurance package for accident-prone babies and a new home entertainment system would all be examples of product innovation. And change in the manufacturing methods and equipment used to produce the car or the home entertainment system, or in the office procedures and sequencing in the insurance case, would be examples of process innovation.

Sometimes the dividing line is somewhat blurred—for example, a new jet-powered sea ferry is both a product and a process innovation. Services represent a particular case of this where the product and process aspects often merge—for example, is a new holiday package a product or process change? We should also be aware that innovation can take place by repositioning the perception of an established product or process. For example, an old-established product in the UK is Lucozade—originally developed as a glucose-based drink to help children and invalids in convalescence. These associations with sickness were abandoned by the brand owners, SmithKline Beecham, when they relaunched the product as a health drink aimed at the growing fitness market where it is now presented as a performance-enhancing aid to healthy exercise.

A second dimension to change is the *degree* of novelty involved. Clearly, updating the styling on our car is not the same as coming up with a completely new concept car which has an electric engine and is made of new composite materials as opposed to steel and glass. Similarly, increasing the speed and accuracy of a lathe is not the same thing as replacing it with a computer-controlled laser forming process. There are degrees of novelty in these, running from minor, incremental improvements right through to radical changes which transform the way we think about and use them. Sometimes these changes are common to a particular sector or activity, but sometimes they are so radical and far-reaching that they change the basis of society—for example the role played by steam

TABLE 1.1   Strategic advantages through innovation.

Mechanism	Strategic advantage	Examples
Novelty in product or service	Offering something no one else can	Introducing the first . . . Walkman, fountain pen, camera, dishwasher . . . to the world
Novelty in process	Offering it in ways others cannot match—faster, lower cost, more customized, etc.	Pilkington's float glass process, Bessemer's steel process, Internet banking, on-line bookselling, etc.
Complexity	Offering something which others find it difficult to master	Rolls-Royce and aircraft engines—only a handful of competitors can master the complex machining and metallurgy involved
Legal protection of intellectual property	Offering something which others cannot do unless they pay a licence or other fee	Blockbuster drugs like Zantac, Prozac, etc.
Add/extend competitive factors	Move basis of competition—e.g. from price of product to price and quality, or price, quality, choice, etc.	Japanese car manufacturing, which systematically moved the competitive agenda from price to quality, to flexibility and choice, to shorter times between launch of new models, and so on—each time not trading these off against each other but offering them all
Timing	First-mover advantage—being first can be worth significant market share in new product fields	Amazon.com and Yahoo—others can follow, but the advantage 'sticks' to the early movers
	Fast follower advantage—sometimes being first means you encounter many unexpected teething problems, and it makes better sense to watch someone else make the early mistakes and move fast into a follow-up product	Palm Pilot and other personal digital assistants (PDAs) which have captured a huge and growing share of the market. In fact the concept and design was articulated in Apple's ill-fated Newton product some five years earlier—but problems with software and especially handwriting recognition meant it flopped
Robust design	Offering something which provides the platform on which other variations and generations can be built	Boeing 737—over 30 years' old, the design is still being adapted and configured to suit different users—this is the most successful aircraft in the world in terms of sales
Rewriting the rules	Offering something which represents a completely new product or process concept—a different way of doing things—and makes the old ones redundant	Typewriters vs. computer word processing, ice vs refrigerators, electric vs gas or oil lamps
Reconfiguring the parts	Rethinking the way in which bits of the system work together—e.g. building more effective networks, outsourcing and co-ordination of a virtual company, etc.	Benetton in clothing, Dell in computers, Toyota in its supply chain management
Others?	Innovation is all about finding new ways to do things and to obtain strategic advantage—so there will be room for new ways of gaining and retaining advantage	Napster? This firm began by writing software which would enable music fans to swap their favourite pieces via the Internet—the Napster program essentially connects person to person (P2P) by providing a fast link. Its potential to change the architecture and mode of operation of the Internet is much greater, and this may be responsible for a whole new generation of programs and services

power in the Industrial Revolution or the ubiquitous changes resulting from today's communications and computing technologies.

As far as managing the innovation process is concerned, these differences are important. The ways in which we approach incremental, day-to-day change will differ from those used occasionally to handle a radical step change in product or process. But we should also remember that it is the *perceived* degree of novelty which matters; novelty is very much in the eye of the beholder. For example, in a giant, technologically advanced organization like Shell or IBM advanced networked information systems are commonplace, but for a small car dealership or food processor even the use of a simple PC to connect to the Internet may still represent a major challenge.

We can plot these two dimensions of innovation as a simple matrix which defines the space which has to be managed (Figure 1.1).

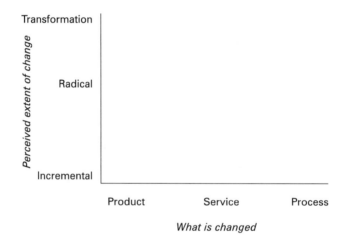

FIGURE 1.1   Dimensions of innovation space.

Variations on the Innovation Theme

Innovation takes place in a number of different ways and it will be useful to consider some of the key themes here.

Continuous and discontinuous change   The desire to create, at least for a time, an advantage through offering something no one else can leads firms to investigate not only innovations which deploy existing technological knowledge but also those which offer opportunities for changing the rules of the game. Extensive studies have shown the power of such innovation in creating and transforming industry structures—for example, in the case of the typewriter, the computer and the automobile.[14]

What we learn from studies of industries which have been transformed are important messages for managing innovation. First, such transformations happen relatively often—no industry is immune (see Box 1.1 for an example). Second, they can be triggered by technological development—and when they are it is generally the new entrant firms which make a success of riding the new wave. This effect is a consequence of their being smaller, able to take decisions quickly and above all because they are not encumbered with the physical and mental baggage associated with the old technology. (The example of the firms which successfully exploited the transistor in the early 1950s is a good case in point—many were new ventures, sometimes started by enthusiasts in their garage, yet they rose to challenge major players in the electronics industry like Raytheon.)

BOX 1.1 The dimming of the light bulb.

In the Beginning . . .

God said let there be light. And for a long time this came from a rather primitive but surprisingly effective method—the oil lamp. From the early days of putting simple wicks into congealed animal fats, through candles to more sophisticated oil lamps people have been using this form of illumination. Archaeologists tell us this goes back at least 40 000 years so there has been plenty of scope for innovation to improve the basic idea! Certainly by the time of the Romans domestic illumination—albeit with candles—was a well-developed feature of civilized society.

Not a lot changed until the late eighteenth century when the expansion of the mining industry led to experiments with uses for coal gas—one of which was as an alternative source of illumination. One of the pioneers of research in the coal industry—Humphry Davy—invented the carbon arc lamp and ushered in a new era of safety within the mines—but also opened the door to alternative forms of domestic illumination and the era of gas lighting began.

But it was not until the middle of the following century that researchers began to explore the possibilities of using a new power source and some new physical effects. Experiments by Joseph Swann in England and Farmer in the USA (amongst others) led to the development of a device in which a tiny metal filament enclosed within a glass envelope was heated to incandescence by an electric current. This was the first electric light bulb—and it still bears more than a passing resemblance to the product found hanging from millions of ceilings all around the world.

By 1879 it became clear that there was significant commercial potential in such lighting—not just for domestic use. Two events occurred during that year which were to have far-reaching effects on the emergence of a new industry. The first was that the city of Cleveland—although using a different lamp technology (carbon arc)—introduced the first public street lighting. And the second was that patents were registered for the incandescent filament light bulb by Joseph Swann in England and one Thomas Edison in the USA.

Needless to say the firms involved in gas supply and distribution and the gas lighting industry were not taking the threat from electric light lying down, and they responded with a series of improvement innovations which helped retain gas lighting's popularity for much of the late nineteenth century. Much of what happened over the next 30 years is a good example of what is sometimes called the 'sailing ship effect'. That is, just as in the shipping world the invention of steam power did not instantly lead to the disappearance of sailing ships but instead triggered a whole series of improvements in that industry, so the gas lighting industry consolidated its position through incremental product and process innovations.

But electric lighting was also improving and the period 1886–1920 saw many important breakthroughs and a host of smaller incremental performance improvements. In a famous and detailed study (carried out by an appropriately named researcher called Bright) there is evidence to show that little improvements in the design of the bulb and in the process for manufacturing it led to a fall in price of over 80% between 1880 and 1896.[15] Examples of such innovations include the use of gas instead of vacuum in the bulb (1913 Langmuir) and the use of tungsten filament.

Innovation theory teaches us that after an invention there is a period in which all sorts of designs and ideas are thrown around before finally a 'dominant design' settles out and the industry begins to mature. So it was with the light bulb; by the 1920s the basic configuration of the product—a tungsten filament inside a glass gas-filled bulb—was established and the industry began to consolidate. It is at this point that the major players with whom we associate the industry—Philips, General Electric (GE), Westinghouse—became established.

Technological Alternatives

Although the industry then entered a period of stability in the marketplace there was still considerable activity in the technology arena. Back in the nineteenth century Henri Becquerel invented the fluorescent lamp and in 1911 Claude invented the neon lamp—both inventions which would have far-reaching effects in terms of the industry and its segmentation into different markets.

The neon lamp started a train of work based on forming different glass tubes into shapes for signs and in filling them with a variety of gases with similar properties to neon but which gave different colours.

The fluorescent tube was first made commercially by Sylvania in the USA in 1938 following extensive development work by both GE and Westinghouse. The technology had a number of important features including low power consumption and long life—factors which led to their widespread use on office and business environments although less so in the home. By the 1990s this product had matured alongside the traditional filament bulb and a range of compact and shaped fittings were available from the major lighting firms.

Meanwhile, in Another Part of the World . . .

Whilst neon and fluorescent tubes were variations on the same basic theme of lights, a different development began in a totally new sector in the 1960s. In 1962 work on the emerging solid-state electronics area led to the discovery of a light emitting diode—LED—a device which would, when a current passed through it, glow in red or green colour. These lights were bright and used little power; they were also part of the emerging trend towards miniaturization. They quickly became standard features in electronic devices and today the average household will have hundreds of LEDs in orange, green or red to indicate whether devices such as TV sets, mobile phones or electric toothbrushes are on and functioning.

Development and refinement of LEDs took place in a different industry for a different market and in particular one line of work was followed in a small Japanese chemical company supplying LEDs to the major manufacturers like Sony. Nichia Chemical began a programme of work on a type of LED which would emit blue light—something much more difficult to achieve and requiring complex chemistry and careful process control. Eventually they were successful and in 1993 produced a blue LED based on gallium arsenide technology. The firm then committed a major investment to development of both product and process technology, amassing around 300 patents along the way. Their research culminated in the development in 1995 of a white light LED—using the principle that white light is made up of red, green and blue light mixed together.

So what? The significance of Shuji Nakamura's invention may not be instantly apparent—and at present the only products which can be bought utilizing it are small high power torches. But think about the significance of this discovery. White LEDs offer the following advantages:

- 85% less power consumption
- 16 times brighter than normal electric lights
- Tiny size
- Long life—tests suggest the life of an LED could be 100 000 hours—about 11 years
- Can be packaged into different shapes, sizes and arrangements
- Will follow the same economies of scale in manufacturing that led to the continuing fall in the price of electronic components so will become very cheap very quickly

If people are offered a low-cost, high-power, flexible source of white light they are likely to adopt it—and for this reason the lighting industry is feeling some sense of threat. The likelihood is that the industry as we know it will be changed dramatically by the emergence of this new light source—and whilst the names may remain the same they will have to pay a high price for licensing the technology. They may try and get around the patents—but with 300 already in place and the experience of the complex chemistry and processing which go into making LEDs Nichia have a long head start.

Things are already starting to happen. Many major cities are now using traffic lights which use the basic technology to make much brighter green and red lights since they have a much longer life than conventional bulbs. One US company, Traffic Technology Inc., has even offered to give away the lights in return for a share of the energy savings the local authority makes! Consumer products like torches are finding their way into shops and online catalogues, whilst the automobile industry is looking at the use of LED white light for interior lighting in cars.

Finally—and most worrying—the source of the technology which destabilizes an industry often comes from outside that industry. So even those large incumbent firms which take time and resources to carry out research to try and stay abreast of developments in their field may find that they are wrong-footed by the entry of something which has been developed in a different field. The massive changes in insurance and financial services which have characterized the shift to online and telephone provision were largely developed by IT professionals often working outside the original industry. In extreme cases we find what is often termed the 'not invented here'—NIH—effect, where a firm finds out about a technology but decides against following it up because it does not fit with their perception of the industry or the likely rate and direction of its technological development. Famous examples of this include Kodak's rejection of the Polaroid process or Western Union's dismissal of Bell's telephone invention.

This suggests strongly that managing innovation is about developing both the ability to scan for signals about change and a readiness to move into new areas— and let go of old ones. Above all it suggests that the primary task is one of managing knowledge—developing and building distinctive competence in particular fields, adapting and absorbing new and different knowledge sets when it becomes necessary and moving out of particular knowledge areas when they become redundant.

Building business through innovation   It is possible to think of products and processes having 'life cycles', in which they are seen to go through some form of development, from being new (either to the world or at least to a particular marketplace), through development and maturity towards a notional end-point where a new generation emerges. Different stages in this life cycle imply different emphasis on innovation; for example, early phases may be characterized by rapid and frequent product innovation, with a proliferation of variety. Later stages might be characterized by a relatively stable product concept with only incremental change, and with more emphasis on process innovation, concerned with cost reduction.[14, 16] At the level of individual product or process technologies the ability to recognize the position of current and potential future generations in terms of such a model is a potential source of competitive advantage.[17]

Architecture and component innovation   Another important concept is the idea of new products as stand-alone elements, or as components in broader systems or architectures. For example, a new type of disk drive represents a product innovation at the component level, but it also makes a contribution to the larger computer system of which it is part. Innovation at the integrated system level usually takes place less frequently than at the component level, and has greater impact. Similarly, in services a new addition to the range of financial services may represent a component product innovation, but its impacts are likely to be less far-reaching (and the attendant risks of its introduction lower) than a complete shift in the nature of the service package—for example, the shift to direct-line systems instead of offering financial services through intermediaries.[18]

Technology fusion   A variation on this theme comes in the field of 'technology fusion', where different technological streams converge, such that products which used to have a discrete identity begin to merge into new architectures. An example here is the home automation industry, where the fusion of technologies like computing, telecommunications, industrial control and elementary robotics is enabling a new generation of housing systems with integrated entertainment, environmental control (heating, air conditioning, lighting, etc.) and communication possibilities.[19]

Incremental innovation   Whilst emphasis is often placed on the dramatic, radical form of innovation it is important not to neglect the potential of sustained incremental change. Studies of incremental process development (such as Hollander's famous study of Du Pont rayon plants) suggest that the cumulative gains in efficiency are often much greater over time than those which come from occasional radical changes.[20] Other examples include Tremblay's studies of paper mills and Figueredo's of steel plants.[21, 22] Continuous improvement of this kind has received considerable attention in recent years as part of the 'total quality management' movement, reflecting the significant gains which Japanese manufacturers have been able to make in improving quality and productivity through sustained incremental change.[23]

Robust design   In addition the ability to modify and develop a basic design has considerable value; much depends on being able to establish a strong basic platform or family which can be extended. Rothwell and Gardiner give several examples of such 'robust designs' which can be stretched and otherwise modified to extend the range and life of the product, including Boeing airliners and Rolls-Royce jet engines.[24] In processes much has been made of the ability to enhance and improve performance over many years from the original design concepts—in fields like steel making and chemicals, for example.

Intangible innovation   One last point to make is that innovation involves deployment of knowledge—but this is not always embodied in a product or a piece of equipment. We associate innovation with physical change, but much change is of a less tangible kind, for example in the development of new methods or techniques. A good illustration of this was the transformation of the Western car, electronics and other industries by the adoption of so-called Japanese production techniques. Grouped together under the label of 'lean manufacturing', these represent new ways of managing and organizing the same basic items of equipment and process stages which dominated manufacturing industry since the days of Henry Ford. But systematic and widespread application of this 'disembodied' knowledge across, for example, the Japanese car industry led to a production advantage which meant that in the early 1980s Japanese cars could be made, shipped and landed in the USA at a cost of around $2000 less than it would take to build them in Detroit.

In general most firms will work on a portfolio of innovations, some of which represent incremental developments and improvements on existing and proven products and processes, whilst others will focus on more radical change. One of the key skills in effective innovation management is balancing the composition of this portfolio and matching it to the firm's competencies and capabilities in technology and markets.

This book is concerned with exploring some of the generic management issues which are associated with trying to deal with the different kinds of innovation represented in Figure 1.1—and with the particular solutions which different organizations have found to work well under different contingencies.

1.3 Riding Two Horses—the Innovator's Dilemma

Whilst a portfolio approach sounds good in theory, making it happen in practice is not simple. Firms tend to structure their innovation management systems and processes around a kind of 'steady state' of change, in which innovation does happen but generally in the direction of 'doing what we do better'. This leads to closer interactions with customers to help identify and implement a series of incremental product improvements, and a close monitoring of process parameters to move ever closer to optimum conditions for quality, speed, costs, etc. Such innovation—which by its nature tends to be more incremental in nature—is essential for the survival of the business. But there are also conditions where—either as a result of unexpected market shifts or the emergence of new technological possibilities—disruptive, discontinuous change takes place. Examples might include the rapid deregulation of markets in many utilities like telecommunications and energy, or the emergence of new technological fields like genetic engineering or the Internet which offer dramatic performance improvements over previous generations. These are conditions in which innovation becomes about 'doing something radically new'—and needs a different set of organizational conditions for its management.

This theme has been picked up on by many writers, but it has been researched in depth by Clayton Christensen with a detailed study of the US hard disk drive industry.[25] His reason for selecting this as a case study is that the electronics industry and its components offer a chance to study many generations of radical innovations in a reasonably short space of time. In this case there have been a number of points in the history of the industry where the product and process technologies have undergone dramatic shifts in performance parameters—for example, drives have become much smaller whilst their capacity and access times have rocketed.

His prime observation confirms the earlier work of Utterback and others that incumbents in a particular industry do not do well when that industry changes dramatically; the balance of advantage shifts to the newcomers.[14] But his studies suggest that this phenomenon occurs in large measure because the organization is set up for steady-state innovation—what he terms sustaining technologies—and is not able to pick up or respond well to weak signals about disruptive change. In other words, firms tend to do what the business schools preach as good practice—stay close to their (existing) customers and develop close interactive relationships with them to create a stream of innovations. This is good for sustaining today's business—but under certain circumstances this may not be the best approach. By contrast the signals about the new generation of products come as weak signals from the fringes of the current market, from a new group of users with radically different performance/price expectations and with the potential to create demand to exploit a step change in technological potential.

As he demonstrates in a number of examples, the likelihood of most organizations being able to respond favourably to the latter is low. Structures for picking up market and technology signals and translating them to innovations are likely to favour variations on an established theme and find the relevance or challenge of the new picture difficult to see or interpret, still less to respond to.

The challenge is to find some way of resolving the innovator's dilemma which gives the title of his influential book. How can firms build structures and processes which allow them to ride both horses? It is not simply a matter—as suggested by Hamel, Peters and others—of going all out for radical change because 'continuous improvement is no longer enough'.[26, 27] Firms need to learn to manage both the steady state 'doing what we already do better' kind of innovation and the radically new generations.

1.4 Innovation Is Not Easy

Although innovation is increasingly seen as a powerful way of securing competitive advantage and a more secure approach to defending strategic positions, success is by no means guaranteed. The history of product and process innovations is littered with examples of apparently good ideas which failed—in some cases with spectacular consequences. For example:

1. In 1952 Ford engineers began working on a new car to counter the mid-size models offered by GM and Chrysler—the 'E' car. After an exhaustive search for a name involving some 20000 suggestions the car was finally named after Edsel Ford, Henry Ford's only son. It was not a success; when the first Edsels came off the production line Ford had to spend an average of $10000 per car (twice the vehicle's cost) to get them roadworthy. A publicity plan was to have 75 Edsels drive out on the same day to local dealers; in the event the firm only managed to get 68 to go, whilst in another live TV slot the car failed to start. Nor were these teething troubles; by 1958 consumer indifference to the design and concern about its reputation led the company to abandon the car—at a cost of $450m. and 110847 Edsels.[28]
2. During the latter part of the Second World War it became increasingly clear that there would be a big market for long-distance airliners, especially on the transatlantic route. One UK contender was the Bristol Brabazon, based on a design for a giant long-range bomber which was approved by the Ministry of Aviation for development in 1943. Consultation with BOAC, the major customer for the new airliner, was 'to associate itself closely with the layout of the aircraft and its equipment' but not to comment on issues like size, range and payload! The budget rapidly escalated, with the construction of new facilities to accommodate such a large plane and, at one stage, the demolition of an entire village in order to extend the runway at Filton, near Bristol. Project control was weak and many unnecessary features were included—for example, the mock-up contained 'a most magnificent ladies' powder room with wooden aluminium-painted mirrors and even receptacles for the various lotions and powders used by the modern young lady'. The prototype took six and a half years to build and involved major technical crises with wings and engine design; although it flew well in tests the character of the post-war aircraft market was very different from that envisaged by the technologists. Consequently in 1952, after flying less than 1000 miles, the project was abandoned at considerable cost to the taxpayer. The parallels with the Concorde project, developed by the same company on the same site a decade later, are hard to escape.[29]

3. During the late 1990s revolutionary changes were going on in mobile communications involving many successful innovations—but even experienced players can get their fingers burned. Motorola launched an ambitious venture which aimed to offer mobile communications from literally anywhere on the planet—including the middle of the Sahara Desert or the top of Mount Everest! Achieving this involved a $7bn project to put 88 satellites into orbit, but despite the costs Iridium—as the venture was known—received investment funds from major backers and the network was established. The trouble was that, once the novelty had worn off, most people realized that they did not need to make many calls from remote islands or at the North Pole and that their needs were generally well met with less exotic mobile networks based around large cities and populated regions. Worse, the handsets for Iridium were large and clumsy because of the complex electronics and wireless equipment they had to contain—and the cost of these hi-tech bricks was a staggering $3000! Call charges were similarly highly priced.

   Despite the incredible technological achievement which this represented the take-up of the system never happened, and in 1999 the company filed for Chapter 11 bankruptcy. Its problems were not over—the cost of maintaining the satellites safely in orbit was around $2m. per month. Motorola who had to assume the responsibility had hoped that other telecoms firms might take advantage of these satellites, but after no interest was shown they had to look at a further price tag of $50m. to bring them out of orbit and destroy them safely! Even then the plans to allow them to drift out of orbit and burn up in the atmosphere were criticized by NASA for the risk they might pose in starting a nuclear war, since any pieces which fell to earth would be large enough to trigger Russian anti-missile defences since they might appear not as satellite chunks but Moscow-bound missiles! The current picture is that a number of firms are bidding for the satellites—but even if the prices offered of around $50–80m. are paid the venture represents a huge loss to Motorola and its partners.

4. Studies of product innovation consistently point to a high level of failure to progress from original idea to successful product in the marketplace is consistently reported. Actual figures range from 30% to as high as 95%; an accepted average is 38%.[30]

5. A survey of 14000 organizations purchasing computer software carried out for the UK Department of Trade and Industry suggested that between 80 and 90% of projects fail to meet their performance goals, around 80% are delivered late and over budget, around 40% fail or are abandoned and only 10–20% fully meet their success criteria.

6. Whilst the Internet is seen as a seedbed for an enormous number of new ventures, the experience of the 'dotcoms' has not all been rosy. Some firms like Amazon and Yahoo! saw their share prices surge upwards on initial flotation—but for them and many others the bubble has burst. Some—like boo.com, an Internet site aimed at meeting fashion needs—failed completely whilst others, like lastminute.com, a travel services site launched in a blaze of publicity in early 2000, found its share price plummeting by the end of the year.

Of course, not all failures are as dramatic or as complete as these; for most organizations the pattern is one of partial success but with problems. This is not surprising—after all, innovation is by its nature a risky business and like omelettes eventual success will involve broken eggs. And we need to remember that there is a great deal of uncertainty in innovation, made up of technical, market, social, political and other factors, with the result that the odds are not too good for success unless the process is managed carefully. Even the best-managed firms still make mistakes—for example, the success story of 3M's 'Post-it' notes is actually a somewhat chequered history where the innovation might have failed at several points.[31–33]

The key point is to ensure that experiments are well designed and controlled so as to minimize the incidence of failure and to ensure that where it does occur lessons are learned to avoid falling into the same trap in the future.

1.5 . . . But It Is Imperative

Faced with what is clearly a risky and uncertain process many organizations could be forgiven for deciding not to innovate, even though the possible rewards are attractive. However, that approach—of doing nothing—is rarely an option, especially in turbulent and rapidly changing sectors of the economy. In essence, unless organizations are prepared to renew their products and processes on a continuing basis, their survival chances are seriously threatened.

In the mid-1980s a study by Shell suggested that the average corporate survival rate for large companies was only about half as long as that of a human being. Since then the pressures on firms have increased enormously from all directions—with the inevitable result that life expectancy is reduced still further. If we take any 10-year period from about 1970 onwards and look at the Fortune 500—by definition the largest and best resourced firms in the world—we find that between a third and a half have disappeared by the end of that period. Of the list in 1970 over 60% have been acquired or have gone under. Of the top 12 companies which made up the Dow Jones index in 1900 only one—General Electric—survives today. Even apparently robust giants like IBM, GM or Kodak can suddenly display worrying signs of mortality, whilst for small firms the picture is often considerably worse since they lack the protection of a large resource base.

Some firms have had to change dramatically to stay in business. For example a company, founded in the early nineteenth century which had wellington boots and toilet paper amongst its product range, is now one of the largest and most successful in the world in the telecommunications business. Nokia began life as a lumber company, making the equipment and supplies needed to cut down forests in Finland. It moved through into paper and from there into the 'paperless office' world of IT—and from there into mobile telephones.

Another mobile phone player—Vodafone Airtouch—grew to its huge size by merging with a firm called Mannesman which, since its birth in the 1870s, has been more commonly associated with the invention and production of steel tubes! Preussag is the company which now owns Thomson the travel group in the UK, and is the largest European travel and tourism services company. Its origins, however, lie in the mines of old Prussia, where in the nineteenth century it began making transport wagons to move the coal and iron around.

Nor is this only a problem for individual firms; as Utterback's study indicates, whole industries can be undermined and disappear as a result of radical innovation which rewrites the technical and economic rules of the game. Two worrying conclusions emerge from his work; first, that many innovations which destroy the existing order originate from newcomers and outsiders to a particular industry, and second, that a significant number of the original players survive such transformations.[14]

So the question is not one of whether or not to innovate but rather of *how* to do so successfully. What lessons can we learn from research and experience about success and failure, and is there any pattern to these which might be used to guide future action? (See Figure 1.2.)

New response needed

Placid environments and stable industrial structures which new entrants can exploit through technological change to 're-write the rules of the game'. Examples include telephone banking and insurance	Fast changing environments—e.g. IT, biotechnology, etc. where major re-drawing of industry structure is taking place. Innovation is essential for old players to survive, but new opportunities also emerging

Low uncertainty ——————————————————— High uncertainty

Placid environments where need for innovation may not be perceived as high. Stable conditions and market structures may provide a sense of false security since new technology or other changes can bring about industry transformation. Risk is that by the time the need for change has been identified it may be too late for existing players to react	Fast changing environments where it appears that existing players can continue to dominate through applying proven—for responses. Risk of being caught out by this approach example, IBM with the shift to networks and decline of mainframes, and the 'Big 3' US car makers in the face of Japanese competition

Old response appropriate

FIGURE 1.2 Environmental uncertainty and organizational response.

1.6 How to Innovate?

In a process as uncertain and complex as innovation, luck plays a part. There are cases where success comes by accident—and sometimes the benefits arising from one lucky break are enough to cover several subsequent failures. But real success lies in being able to repeat the trick—to manage the process consistently so that success, whilst never guaranteed, is more likely. And this depends on understanding and managing the process such that little gets left to chance. Research suggests that success is based on the ability to learn and repeat these behaviours; it is similar to the golfer Gary Player's comment that 'the more I practise, the luckier I get . . .'

So what do we have to manage? We suggest that innovation is a core process concerned with renewing what the organization offers (its products and/or services) and the ways in which it generates and delivers these. Whether the organization is concerned with bricks, bread, banking or baby care, the underlying challenge is still the same. How to obtain a competitive edge through innovation—and through this survive and grow? (This is as much a challenge for non-profit organizations—in police work, in health care, in education the competition is still there, and the role of innovation still one of getting a better edge to dealing with problems of crime, illness or illiteracy.)

At this generic level we suggest that organizations have to manage four phases making up the innovation process. They have to:

- Scan and search their environments (internal and external) to pick up and process signals about potential innovation. These could be needs of various kinds, or opportunities arising from research activities somewhere, or pressures to conform to legislation, or the behaviour of competitors—but they represent the bundle of stimuli to which the organization must respond
- Strategically select from this set of potential triggers for innovation those things which the organization will commit resources to doing. Even the best resourced organization cannot do everything, so the challenge lies in selecting those things which offer the best chance of developing a competitive edge
- Resource the option—providing (either by creating through R&D or acquiring through technology transfer) the knowledge resources to exploit it. This might be a simple matter of buying off the shelf, or exploiting the results of research already carried out—or it might require extensive search to find the right resources. It is also not just about embodied knowledge, but about the surrounding bundle of knowledge—often in tacit form—which is needed to make the technology work
- Implement the innovation, growing it from an idea through various stages of development to final launch—as a new product or service in the external marketplace or a new process or method within the organization
- A fifth—optional—phase is to reflect upon the previous phases and review experience of success and failure—in order to learn about how to manage the process better, and to capture relevant knowledge from the experience

Of course there are countless variations on this basic theme in terms of how organizations actually carry this out. And much depends on where they start from—their particular contingencies. For example, large firms may structure the process much more extensively than smaller firms who work on an informal basis. And firms in knowledge-intensive sectors like pharmaceuticals will concentrate more on formal R&D—often committing sizeable amounts of their income back to this activity—whereas others like clothing will emphasize closer links with their customers as a source of innovation. Non-profit organizations may be more concerned with reducing costs and improving quality, whereas private-sector firms may worry about market share. Networks of firms may have to operate complex co-ordination arrangements to ensure successful completion of joint projects—and to devise careful legal frameworks to ensure that intellectual property rights are respected.

But at heart the process is the same basic sequence of activity. Innovation management is about learning to find the most appropriate solution to the problem of consistently managing this process, and doing so in the ways best suited to the particular circumstances in which the organization finds itself. Therefore particular solutions to the general problem of managing this core process will be firm-specific.

We suggest that there are two key questions in innovation management which form the basis of this book:

1. How do you structure the innovation process appropriately?
2. How do you develop effective behavioural patterns (routines) which define how it operates on a day-to-day basis?

Much of the research on the management of innovation has attempted to identify some 'best practice', but most studies have been based on the experience of particular sectors. For example, the dominant models of technology management are derived from the experience of US high-technology firms, whereas many of the 'rules' for product development are based on research on the practice of Japanese manufacturers of consumer durables. However, there is unlikely to be 'one best way' to manage innovation, as industries differ in terms of technological and market opportunity, and firm-specific features constrain management options.

Therefore in this book we reject the 'one best way' school of management, and instead seek to explore the links between the structures, processes and culture of an organization, the opportunity for and characteristics of technological innovation, and the competitive and market environment in which the organization operates.

1.7 New Challenges, Same Old Responses?

> Constant revolutionising of production, uninterrupted disturbance of all social conditions, everlasting uncertainty . . . all old-established national industries have been destroyed or are daily being destroyed. They are dislodged by new industries . . . whose products are consumed not only at home, but in every quarter of the globe. In place of old wants satisfied by the production of the country, we find new wants . . . the intellectual creativity of individual nations become common property
> (K. Marx and F. Engels, *The Manifesto of the Communist Party*, 1848).

The quote demonstrates that uncertainty, globalization and innovation are not new, and that the only certainty about tomorrow's environment is that it will be just as uncertain as today's. This flash of the blindingly obvious reminds us of a major difficulty in managing innovation—the fact that we are doing so against a constantly shifting backdrop. And it is clear that some trends in the current environment are converging to create conditions which many see as rewriting the rules of the competitive game.

Certainly there are big changes taking place in the environment in which we have to try and manage innovation, and in this final section we will look briefly at some of the major forces underpinning such change. Our view is, however, that whilst there is no room for complacency, we should also not be in a hurry to throw away the basic principles on which this book is based—they will certainly need adapting and configuring to dramatically new circumstances but underneath the innovation management puzzle is what it always was—a challenge to accumulate and deploy knowledge resources in strategically effective fashion.

Living with Discontinuous Change

What happens under these conditions is that the rules appear to break down. Consider the case of publishing. On the one hand we have an industry which was, until recently, based on very physical technologies and a complex network of specialist suppliers who contributed their particular parts of the complex puzzle of publishing. For example, copy—words or pictures—would be generated by a specialist journalist or photographer. He/she would then pass this on to various editors who would check, make choices about design and layout, etc. Next would come typesetting where the physical materials for printing would be made—hot metal would be cast into letters and grouped into blocks to form words and sentences within special frames. Pictures and other items would be transferred on to printing plates. The type frames or printing plates would then be fixed to presses, these would be inked and some test runs made. And finally the printed version would appear—and pass on to someone else to distribute and publish it.

Such a method might still be recognizable by Messrs Caxton and Gutenberg—the pioneers of the printing industry. But it is likely that they would not have much idea about the way in which publishing operates today—with its emphasis on IT. Now the process has changed such that a single person could undertake the whole set of operations—create text on a word processor, design and lay it out on a page formatting program, integrate images with text and when satisfied print to either physical media or—increasingly—publish it worldwide in electronic form.

There are plenty of examples of firms which have exploited this or related opportunities. For example, Adplates is—or was until recently—a small firm in north London specializing in the production of printing plates for the advertising industry (hence the name). They used to be a small link in a long chain which began with a client and an advertising agency agreeing about an advertisement. The photo shoot and copy lines would be created and eventually the material would arrive at Adplates who would carry out the task of preparing a printing plate—which they would then pass on to a printer to use. In other words they were a small link in a long chain.

But technology has changed all that for them. They began to challenge the boundaries of the operation in which they were part—why, for example, could they not move upstream to deal directly with the client? Of course this required new skills and technology in areas like design and image and text preparation—but all of this is available on a PC. Equally, since printing has moved from hot metal to a largely digital process, they could invest in the skills and equipment to move downstream. And why should they leave it to a publisher to disseminate the material when the market and the technology in this end of the industry is changing so rapidly and opening up so many opportunities? Adplates now offers a complete service to clients from initial idea through to printing and even has its own stable of magazines and thriving Web publishing operation.

The challenge of disruption has prompted many others to rethink the business models which operate—and to try and rewrite the rules of the game. The author Stephen King, for example, has made a number of attempts to move beyond the traditional relationships between writers and publishers and particularly to publish directly via the Internet. In his latest venture he has taken this a step further; his new book is being written chapter by chapter and will only appear if enough people ask for it. He has moved from the traditional model of writing in the hope of readers to the point where he is effectively writing on demand—much like a factory nowadays often operates on a make-to-order basis only.

There are winners in this game but also losers. People still think of the *Encyclopaedia Britannica* as a household name and the repository of useful reference knowledge which can be trusted. It is a well-established product—in fact the original idea came from three Scottish printers back in 1768! The brand is fine—but the business has gone through dramatic shifts and is still under threat. From a peak of sales in 1990 of around $650m. its sales have collapsed—for example, in the USA by up to 80%. The problem is not the product but the way in which it is presented—all the hard copy encyclopedias have suffered a similar fate at the hands of the CD-ROM-based versions like Encarta (which is often bundled in as part of a PC purchase).[13]

We could go on looking at the publishing industry but the point is clear—when technology shifts dramatically it opens up major opportunities but also poses major threats to players in the industry and to those who might want to enter from outside. Under these conditions simply being an established player—even with a centuries-old brand name and an excellent product—is not enough. Indeed—as firms like Amazon.com have shown—it is at times like these that coming from outside and starting fresh may offer significant advantages.

What is going on here is clearly not conforming to a stable, big-is-beautiful model, nor is it about historically important emphasis on core competence. The foundations of a business like publishing become shaken and many of the famous names disappear whilst other unknown upstarts become major industry players—in some cases overnight! (Amazon.com was at one time worth more than double the market value of established businesses like British Airways.) Turbulence like this throws a challenge to established models of managing—not only is it a question of urgently needing to change but the very models of change management on which many traditional players rely may not be sufficient or appropriate.

Experience and theory tell us that (a) this kind of discontinuous change happens regularly—often at the level of a sector or branch, less so at the level of the whole economy, and that (b) when it does the old incumbent players are often not very successful at making the transition. New entrants tend to thrive partly because they are small and fast moving (and have little to lose) and partly because they do not come encumbered with the baggage of their past experience. They only have to learn new tricks whereas old players have to unlearn old ones as well.

But it is not just a form of corporate Darwinism in which the thrusting young players overturn the old order; history suggests that a significant number of older players do survive and prosper through discontinuity. And we should not forget that we hear about the few small new firms which enter successfully, but conveniently ignore the large number of failures amongst this size range. (The high fallout from the initial dotcom start-up firms is an indicator of this problem; small businesses are easy to start but also very vulnerable to even minor infections.)

History suggests that under discontinuous conditions there are strategies and responses which can help. Although the technological and market shifts are dramatic the basic innovation management issues remain. In particular:

1. Impacts vary, from niches where the rules change through to sectors through to—very occasionally—the whole economy. It is important to be clear about what is going on and its implications—and this means that firms will need sensitive antennae and a strong future orientation. If anything, effective management of the scanning phase becomes even more critical.

    Utterback and others show that a variation of the product cycle happens in technology—discontinuity does and will continue to happen. And when it does new entrants are better equipped to survive—because they carry little baggage, because they are small and fast decision-makers, etc. But this does not mean that large firms are always likely to fail—rather, they need to adapt and move to take advantage of their greater capabilities in riding the new wave. This places enormous emphasis on managing the knowledge aspects of the business—something which we will discuss in more detail in the next section. Once again the importance of effective management of scanning and of strategy-making emerges strongly.

2. Knowledge is becoming central to competitiveness. It is becoming clear that under current competitive conditions in many sectors protectable competitive advantage comes increasingly from knowledge—because what firms know and have is hard to copy and requires others to go through a similar learning process.[34-37] The problem under conditions of discontinuity is that some knowledge assets become redundant and others need to be acquired quickly. This places emphasis on strategic management of the knowledge base, and of developing effective mechanisms for resourcing technological knowledge. In the latter case it is likely that the generation of relevant knowledge will increasingly take place outside the firm and will need capabilities to ensure that technology transfer can be absorbed and deployed quickly and effectively (see Box 1.2).

3. Change—whilst dramatic—may not affect the entire business. The concept of component and architectural innovation[18] is relevant here—firms need to develop the ability to see which parts of their activity are affected by technological change and to react accordingly. In some cases change at the component level opens up new opportunities—for example, new materials or propulsion systems like fuel cells may open up new options for vehicle assemblers but will not necessarily challenge their core operations. But the shift to MP3 (Box 1.3) as an alternative way of creating and distributing music via the Internet poses challenges to the whole system of music production and publishing and may require a much more significant response.

BOX 1.2 Changing competencies at Kodak.

Founded around 100 years ago the basis of the business was the production and processing of film and the sales and service associated with mass-market photography. Whilst the latter set of competencies are still highly relevant (even though camera technology has shifted) the move away from wet physical chemistry in the dark (coating emulsions on to film and paper) to digital imaging represents a profound change for the firm. It needs—across a global operation and a workforce of thousands—to let go of old competencies which are unlikely to be needed in the future whilst at the same to rapidly acquire and absorb cutting edge new technologies in electronics and communication.

BOX 1.3 The changing nature of the music industry.

One of the less visible but highly challenging aspects of the Internet is the impact it has had—and is having—on the entertainment business. This is particularly the case with music. At one level its impacts could be assumed to be confined to providing new 'e-tailing' channels through which you can obtain the latest CD of your preference—for example from Amazon.com or CD-Now or 100 other websites. These innovations increase the choice and tailoring of the music purchasing service and demonstrate some of the 'richness/reach' economic shifts of the new Internet game.

But beneath this updating of essentially the same transaction lies a more fundamental shift—in the ways in which music is created and distributed and in the business model on which the whole music industry is currently predicated. In essence the old model involved a complex network in which songwriters and artists depended on A&R (artists and repertoire) to select a few acts, production staff who would record in complex and expensive studios, other production staff who would oversee the manufacture of physical discs, tapes and CDs and marketing and distribution staff who would ensure the product was publicized and disseminated to an increasingly global market.

Several key changes have undermined this structure and brought with it significant disruption to the industry. Old competencies may no longer be relevant whilst acquiring new ones becomes a matter of urgency. Even well-established names like Sony find it difficult to stay ahead whilst new entrants are able to exploit the economics of the Internet. At the heart of the change is the potential for creating, storing and distributing music in digital format—a problem which many researchers have worked on for some time. One solution, developed by one of the Fraunhofer Institutes in Germany, is a standard based on the Motion Picture Experts Group (MPEG) level 3 protocol—MP3. MP3 offers a powerful algorithm for managing one of the big problems in transmitting music files—that of compression. Normal audio files cover a wide range of frequencies and are thus very large and not suitable for fast transfer across the Internet—especially with a population who may only be using relatively slow modems. With MP3 effective compression is achieved by cutting out those frequencies which the human ear cannot detect—with the result that the files to be transferred are much smaller.

As a result MP3 files can be moved across the Internet quickly and shared widely. Various programs exist for transferring normal audio files and inputs—such as CDs—into MP3 and back again.

What does this mean for the music business? In the first instance aspiring musicians no longer need to depend on being picked up by A&R staff from major companies who can bear the costs of recording and production of a physical CD. Instead they can use home recording software and either produce a CD themselves or else go straight to MP3—and then distribute the product globally via newsgroups, chatrooms, etc. In the process they effectively create a parallel and much more direct music industry which leaves existing players and artists on the sidelines.

Such changes are not necessarily threatening. For many people the lowering of entry barriers has opened up the possibility of participating in the music business —for example, by making and sharing music without the complexities and costs of a formal recording contract and the resources of a major record company. There is also scope for innovation around the periphery—for example in the music publishing sector where sheet music and lyrics are also susceptible to lowering of barriers through the application of digital technology. Journalism and related activities become increasingly open—now music reviews and other forms of commentary become possible via specialist user groups and channels on the Web, whereas before they were the province of a few magazine titles. Compiling popularity charts—and the related advertising—is also opened up as the medium switches from physical CDs and tapes distributed and sold via established channels to new media such as MP3 distributed via the Internet.

As if this were not enough, the industry is also challenged from another source— the sharing of music between different people connected via the Internet. Although technically illegal this practice of sharing between people's record collections has always taken place—but not on the scale which the Internet threatens to facilitate. Much of the established music industry is concerned with legal issues—how to protect copyright and how to ensure that royalties are paid in the right proportions to those who participate in production and distribution. But when people can share music in MP3 format and distribute it globally, the potential for policing the system and collecting royalties becomes extremely difficult to sustain.

It has been made much more so by another technological development—that of person-to-person or P2P networking. Sean Fanning, an 18-year-old student with the nickname 'the Napster', was intrigued by the challenge of being able to enable his friends to 'see' and share between their own personal record collections. He argued that if they held these in MP3 format then it should be possible to set up some kind of central exchange program which facilitated their sharing.

The result—the Napster.com site—is sophisticated software which enables P2P transactions. The Napster server does not actually hold any music on its files—but every day millions of swaps are made by people around the world exchanging their music collections. Needless to say this posed a huge threat to the established music business since it involved no payment of royalties. A number of high-profile lawsuits have followed, but whilst Napster's activities have been curbed the problem will not go away. There are now many other sites emulating and extending

> what Napster started—sites such as Gnutella take the P2P idea further and enable exchange of many different file formats—text, video, etc. In Napster's own case the phenomenally successful site has concluded a deal with entertainment giant Bertelsman which will pave the way for some kind of subscription-based service which can provide some revenue stream to deal with the royalty issue.

4. A further consideration is the extent to which disruption is seen as a technology-driven event. As Christensen points out, we neglect the market aspects at our peril.[25] There is a need to look for weak signals about potentially disruptive change in market demand as much as in technological opportunity. Once again this places emphasis in innovation management on building effective scanning mechanisms—and for ensuring that the signals generated get heard within the organization and not filtered out because they conflict with the established view—the 'not-invented here' problem.

In other words, even under conditions of high uncertainty and apparent rewriting of the rules, the basic themes around which this book is structured remain constant. Successful innovation depends on being able to look widely and ahead and develop strategic approaches based on an understanding of the knowledge aspects.

In the following pages we look at three of the powerful forces shaping the competitive environment and arguably rewriting the rules of the game. These are:

- Globalization of markets and technology supply
- The rise of networking as a business model
- The emergence of technologies enabling a 'virtual' mode of working

Innovation in a Global Environment

A key challenge in the current environment is that the stage on which the innovation game is played out has expanded enormously. Whereas technological development was confined to a few nations in the early twentieth century it has expanded to the point where it is generated and used globally—and where the challenges become those of being a global player. This has always been the theme of innovation strategy in multi-national corporations, but it now becomes the issue for small enterprises. Even a local firm is no longer insulated; increasingly, large firms are looking to source components, handle administrative processes and manage distribution on a global basis. For example, in the automobile industry components for a car made in Germany may be sourced from as far afield as Brazil or South Africa, whilst in the airline business most of the data processing required to handle reservations and billing is done in the West Indies. Software production for Citibank is handled by a 'software factory' in Bangalore, India.

One of the key enablers of this distribution is information and communications technology (ICT) which—as we saw above—radically changes the balance of richness and reach involved in all kinds of information-based businesses. In the case of design, for example, a firm like IBM can now work on a 24-hour day by mobilizing design teams in the UK, the USA and Japan with each team handing over after its 'shift' to the next time zone where the work will be continued. This has two effects—first it radically compresses the time in which the design of new components or equipment takes place, and second it brings to bear different and complementary knowledge sets. But in order to make such systems work a new form of network/global management is required, one which addresses some of the underlying national cultural characteristics as well as the departmental or functional ones.[38, 39]

The major challenge to innovation management is one of managing the same basic principles but on a much bigger stage. With trade liberalization and the opening of markets has come a massive upsurge in overall activity and the number of players in the game. (It is estimated, for example, that the entire volume of world trade which took place during 1950 is now transacted in a single day!) Competition has intensified and much of it is being driven by innovation in products, services and processes. The response of successful firms is increasingly likely to involve some measure of networking and collaboration.

Innovation in a Virtual World

One of the defining symbols of the early twenty-first-century environment for innovation is the Internet. Born out of informal exchanges and a desire amongst scientists to share and collaborate more effectively, this has grown into a framework for change which bears comparison with the advent of the railways in the nineteenth century.[40] It has fuelled—and been fuelled by—the rise in the power and versatility of ICT, and it has generated an enormous user base—estimates vary, but from a figure of around 35 million users in the late 1990s there are now probably over 1 billion people with access to the Internet around the world.

Such developments—and their parallel and complementary versions inside organizations, across private networks and using different media—wireless, cable, satellite, etc.—create a communications and participation revolution which, one might expect, has all the characteristics of a discontinuous shift in the innovation environment. Yet if we analyse this we can see the same forces for innovation at work as were operating centuries ago. On the 'technology push' side the range of opportunity created by ICT developments is enormous—it has become 'a solution looking for problems'. But similar characteristics were present when steam power first became widely available and reliable. And—as the glut of failed Internet start-ups demonstrates—simply having the technological means is no guarantee of business success—innovation, as always, is about effective coupling of needs and means within a strategic framework.

Similarly on the demand side, there are forces at work which are acting to pull innovations through and to shape and direct the pace and nature of change. Not surprisingly, much of the impact has come in areas which are essentially information rich in terms of their content and delivery—for example, services like banking and insurance have been heavily hit by new developments. Two useful concepts in this connection are those of 'richness' and 'reach'—terms coined by the Boston Consulting Group to help think about where the impacts of the e-revolution are likely to be felt. Richness refers to the content of an information service—how customized and deep it is, whereas reach refers to the extent to which it can be offered to a population. Normally there is a trade-off—you can have rich services but they tend to be high price and reach only a few people with the means to access them—for example, a personalized bank or a tailored travel package via a personal consultant. Equally, low-cost services with high reach tend to be characterized by a 'one size fits all' mentality and to compete on the basis of low cost. What the ICT revolution does is shift the balance between these two so that rich services are available but with global reach—and a new economics emerges.[13, 41]

This is a seductive argument and there are certainly good examples where industries or sectors have been transformed by the new balance of richness and reach—in addition to banking and insurance we can think of travel (last-minute.com), publishing (Amazon), retailing (QXL, e-Bay) and many others.

But there are clear limits to the extent to which even revolutionary changes in the availability of service delivery options will lead to discontinuity. Not all sectors are information rich and consumers still consume goods as well as services. For much of the retail end of the e-revolution there is still the problem of the 'last mile'—getting the physical goods delivered to particular households. These goods have to be manufactured and although the co-ordination and control may become increasingly subject to ICT innovation, it will still be necessary to store and move physical goods around.

In other words, the innovation management picture remains surprisingly constant. Yes, there will be differences—for example, we will need to consider:

- Very high velocity interactions
- Very rich potential connectivity involving many different players
- Global orientation where distance becomes irrelevant

But the underlying problem remains one of picking up—and making sense of—signals about triggers for innovation, and then managing the process of change effectively. It may be that the challenge is more marked—how to pick up weak signals about new opportunities or the ways in which a traditional industry may be disrupted by ICT's combination of richness and reach. But underneath the same basic set of questions need answering—and the good news is that the technological revolution has also brought into play new tools (see Box 1.4).

No Firm is an Island—the Challenge of Networking

Innovation could be seen as having been the province first of heroic individuals who pioneered ideas into action—and certainly many of the great nineteenth-century names conform to this stereotype. Of course, even then it was actually a linked system with sources of finance, of marketing, etc. being part of the puzzle. But the twentieth century—as Freeman observed—was essentially the era of organized R&D and the rise of the firm as the unit of innovation—and again we can think of particular names and innovations—3M, Pilkington, Ford, Hewlett-Packard. Here the role of champions is still important, but the stage at which they act is essentially defined by the firm.[42] But as we move into the twenty-first

BOX 1.4 'New' economy meets 'old' economy.

Although much of the discussion of the Internet and innovation focuses on new services and processes enabled by the network, we should not forget the new opportunities opened up around the edge of this phenomenon. Much potential exists for innovation in the products and technologies sustaining the network itself—for example, the fibre optics, switches, routers, etc. which make the Internet physically possible. One of the problems posed by the Internet revolution, especially in the area of online retailing, is the so-called 'last mile' question. Even for conventional mail or telephone order shopping, one problem is the fact that you need to be at home or arrange for someone to sign for/receive/store your package of books, computer parts, CDs or whatever. And very often the suppliers will not commit themselves to a definite time for the delivery but only to at best a time window.

This market need has prompted a number of ingenious innovations which offer solutions. One is from a firm called e-stops which is looking to develop a network of around 500 delivery/collection points which will act a little like drive through McDonald's, where you can drive in and pick up your goods outside of normal working hours. The brainchild of Brendan Flood, the first four drive-through points will open in 2001 in Manchester, Birmingham and London. Each will be able to handle a wide range of products including chilled and frozen foods. His company, e-shop, will involve a network of participating retailers to whom you can specify this as your preferred mode of delivery and give your personal e-shop number. E-shop then notify you when your item is ready for collection and you drive through next time you are near the e-stop, key in or swipe your e-shop card number and it will be processed and packed into your car for you within a few minutes. The service will be free to customers although a 'rent' of £2 will be charged if the item is not collected within 48 hours. Major retailers like Tesco, Kingfisher, Boots and Dixons have shown interest in the scheme.

Another is the Bear Box concept where people can have a safe-like box outside their homes which can only be opened by an access code which is given to you and the supplier when the goods are ordered. The scheme started trials in London in late 2000 and—although it does not yet cater for large items or for chilled and frozen foods etc.—has attracted attention of major mail order firms. A variant is also planned—the Bear Bank—where a set of boxes are to be sited at major centres such as filling stations or railway forecourts.

In the USA a company called Streamline has been pursuing a similar approach in Boston for the past four years, although their boxes are larger and will cater for frozen and chilled foods.

Whether these ideas work out in practice is hard to tell, but they do demonstrate the potential for innovation which accompanies innovation in services like retailing over the Internet.

century so the locus has shifted again and innovation is increasingly the product of networked activity. It conforms to Rothwell's fifth-generation model—and has arrived at this point because of a number of trends.[43] First, the increase in the complexity in many products and services means that no firm however well endowed can do it all—and it makes sense to collaborate and build on complementary strengths.

Second, there is the division of labour effect whereby firms increasingly question their core competencies and purpose and configure networks accordingly. For example, one of the most successful firms of the twentieth century—General Electric—reconfigured its business in aircraft engines by thinking about 'selling power by the hour'—and as a result moved away from manufacturing activities like grinding turbine blades and into outsourcing these areas of competence. It increasingly became a co-ordinator and began to explore how it could provide financing and other necessary support services—with the result that it is now largely a service business offering a turnkey package to airlines who equally see their needs as buying power for lifting their aircraft rather than shopping for jet engines.

Similar examples include the running shoe firm Nike which sees its competencies in design and marketing rather than in manufacturing, and Dell which has built a business out of configuring computers to individual needs but which makes extensive use of outsourcing and the management of complementary networks.

Third, there is a recognition that networks may not simply be one end of the traditional spectrum between doing everything in-house (vertical integration) and of outsourcing everything to suppliers (with the consequent transaction costs of managing them).[44] It is possible to argue for a third way which builds on the theory of systems and that networks have emergent properties—the whole is greater than the sum of the parts. This does not mean that the benefits flow without effort—on the contrary, unless participants in a network can solve the problems of co-ordination and management they risk being suboptimal. But there is growing evidence of the benefits of networking as a mode of operation in innovation.[45-47] We pick up this theme in more detail in Chapter 8.

The importance of such networking is not simply firm to firm—it is also about building rich linkages within the national system of innovation. Government policy to support innovation is increasingly concerned with enabling better connections between elements—for example, between the many small firms with technological needs and the major research and technology institutes, universities, etc. which might be able to meet these needs.[48]

The implications for innovation management are again that the underlying questions remain the same—how to identify triggers and develop coherent strategic responses—the difference is that the unit to be managed is now a co-operative federation of players. The levers will need to be different and the routines may need to evolve—a major challenge but one with potentially high pay-offs.

1.8 Outline of the Book

The layout of the book is as follows. Chapter 2 looks at the core process of innovation and at variations in the way in which different organizations handle it in response to different contingencies. It also looks at the question of how organizations manage the operation of that process—and the behavioural patterns (routines) which they learn and develop to do so effectively. Drawing on research on success and failure in innovation the chapter provides a framework for categorizing these behaviour patterns into four clusters of enabling routines.

Part II explores the first of these clusters—the creation of a strategic context for innovation. Chapter 3 considers the significance of an innovation strategy in conditions of complexity, continuous change and consequent uncertainty, and contrasts the rational and incrementalist approaches. It develops the three elements of innovation strategy proposed by David Teece and Gary Pisano: market and national *positions,* technological *paths* and organizational *processes.* In Chapter 4 we address the question of how the firm's national and market environment shapes its innovation strategy, in particular the effects of the home country, competencies, economic inducements and institutions. In Chapter 5 we show that marked differences amongst sectors are also central to corporate choices about technological trajectories, firm-specific competencies and innovation strategies, and identify five broad technological trajectories that firms can follow, each of which has distinct implications for the tasks of innovation strategy. We also identify three key technologies (biotechnology, materials and IT) where rapid advances lead to major shifts in technological trajectories, and where it is increasingly important to distinguish the microelectronics revolution (making and using electronic chips) from the more important information revolution (making and using software).

Part III is concerned with the enabling routines for building effective linkages outside the organization. Innovation does not take place in a vacuum, and research has consistently shown that successful organizations understand and work with different actors in their environment. Chapter 7 focuses particularly on the market-related linkages, looking at how markets are defined, explored and understood—and how this knowledge is communicated and updated through-out the organization. It also looks at how understanding of buyer behaviour can be used to support the launch of innovations—whether to an external market (for example, in launching a new consumer product) or an internal market (for example, managing the change process associated with introducing new machinery or systems). Chapter 8 looks at linkages of a different kind, associated with developing collaborations, networks and strategic alliances.

Part IV is concerned with the mechanisms for enabling and implementing innovation. These include the particular structures for decision-making through-out the life of an innovation project, the arrangements for project monitoring and management and the mechanisms whereby change is planned and introduced to the organization. Every organization needs to do these things as part of manag-ing innovation; research indicates that some do it better than others. Chapter 9 explores the different ways in which organizations operationalize these aspects of innovation.

Chapter 10 looks at the special case of starting up an innovative new venture, building on the growing research base of work in this field. It highlights the ways in which organizations can move beyond their current range of technologies, products and processes, and the learning processes involved in doing so effec-tively. In particular the chapter focuses on internal corporate ventures and on the establishment of new technology-based firms.

In Part V the emphasis shifts to exploring the organizational context in which innovation takes place. Much is written about the need for loose, organic and flexible organizations—typified by Tom Peters' concept of 'skunk works'—which offer considerable individual freedom to innovate. But there is a need to balance these models with some element of formality and control, and to ensure a clear sense of strategic direction. Chapter 11 looks at the different elements which influence the way in which innovation takes place, and the choices available to manage under different conditions. Issues explored include organizational structures, teamworking, participation, training and development, motivation and the development of a creative climate within the organization. The chapter also looks briefly at how these different elements can contribute to some form of corporate learning process which helps develop and accumulate competence—the 'learning organization'. A key theme in this chapter is that there is no 'best' model for organizing innovation; the key task is to find the most appropriate fit for a particular set of contingencies. Chapter 12 examines the special case of building a new organization for innovation, looking at the example of innovative small firms.

The book concludes by bringing together key themes. In particular we argue that success in innovation management is not a matter of doing one or two things exceptionally well but one of good all-round performance in the areas highlighted above. But there are also no simple and standard solutions to the problem of how to do this; organizations are like people and come in widely varying shapes, sizes and personalities. As we argue throughout the book, there is a need for each organization to find its own particular answers to the general puzzle of innovation management. There are general recipes available which can be adapted, and the discussion in the body of the book provides an indication of how this can be and has been done to advantage.

Innovation is particularly about learning, both in the sense of acquiring and deploying knowledge in strategic fashion and also in acquiring and reinforcing patterns of behaviour which help this competence-building learning to happen. Managing innovation is particularly about identifying and enabling the development of behaviour patterns—routines—which make such learning possible.

One important aspect of learning is structured reflection on the organization's current position as an input into its next strategic development. Taking stock—auditing—can be a powerful aid to organizational development, and the final chapter looks at the ways in which what we know about innovation management can be integrated into an audit framework.

Further Reading

Few other texts cover the technological, market and organizational aspects of innovation. Peter Drucker's *Innovation and Entrepreneurship* (Harper & Row, 1985) provides a more accessible introduction to the subject, but perhaps relies more on intuition and experience than on empirical research. Since we published the first edition in 1997 a number of interesting texts have been published. Paul Trott's *Innovation Management and New Product Development* (Pitman, 1998), which focuses on the management of product development, and Brockhoff *et al.*[49] which provides a European view; John Etllie's *Managing Technological Innovation* (Wiley, 2000), is based on the experience of American firms, mainly from manufacturing, as is Mascitelli's broad overview[50] and Mark Dodgson's *The Management of Technological Innovation* (Oxford, 2000), which has a strong historical and international perspective. We would encourage you to read these. The review by Paul Adler (1989) 'Technology strategy: a guide to the literatures', in Rosenbloom, R. and Burgelman, R. A. (eds), *Research on Technological Innovation, Management and Policy*, Vol. 4 (JAI Press) provides a competent, albeit a little dated, account of the main issues in the management of innovation. Brian Twiss, *Managing Technological Innovation* (Longman, London, 1992), covers the main themes in technology management, but does not adequately cover organizational or market innovation. The largest edited compilation to date is *Strategic Management of Technology* (2nd edn, Irwin, Homewood, 1995) edited by Robert Burgelman, R. Maidique and Steven Wheelwright, but it is heavily biased towards the experience of the US manufacturing sector. Two more digestible compilations of best papers are Rothwell and Dodgson's *Handbook of Industrial Innovation*[11] and J. Henry and D. Walker, *Managing Innovation* (Sage, London, 1991).

A good selection of case histories of major innovations can be found in Nayak and Ketteringham's *Breakthroughs* (Mercury, London, 1986), whilst Baden-Fuller and Pitt in *Strategic Innovation* (Routledge, London, 1996) supply some company examples of strategic innovation and its management. Leifer *et al.*'s *Radical Innovation* (2000) and Kanter's *Innovation—Breakthrough thinking at 3M, DuPont, GE, Pfizer and Rubbermaid* (1997) supply case studies of a variety of large US firms and particular innovations.[33, 51] Internet-related innovation is well covered in two 'practitioner'-based books—*Blown to Bits* and *Clicks and Mortar*. [13, 41]

Most other texts tend to focus on a single dimension of innovation management. In the 'The nature of the innovative process', in G. Dosi *et al. Technical Change and Economic Theory* (Pinter, London, 1988), Giovani Dosi adopts an evolutionary economics perspective and identifies the main issues in the management of *technological* innovation. On the subject of organizational innovation, Jay Galbraith and E. Lawler summarize recent thinking on organizational structures and processes in *Organizing for the Future* (Jossey-Bass, 1993), although a more critical account is provided by Wolfe (1994) in 'Organizational innovation: review, critique and suggested research', *Journal of Management Studies*, **31** (3), 405–432. For a review of the key issues and leading work in the field of organizational change and learning see M. D. Cohen and L. S. Sproull (eds), *Organizational Learning* (Sage, London, 1996).

Most marketing texts fail to cover the specific issues related to innovative products and services, although a few specialist texts exist which examine the more narrow problem of marketing so-called 'high-technology' products.[52] The best attempts to date to tackle the issues are to be found in the chapter, 'Securing the future' in Gary Hamel and C. K. Prahalad's *Competing for the Future* (Harvard Business School Press, 1994) and the chapter 'Learning from the market', in Dorothy Leonard's *Wellsprings of Knowledge* (Harvard Business School Press, 1995).

The Minnesota Innovation Project (Angle and Van de Ven, 'Research on the management of innovation') also provides a good overview of the field and the key research themes contained within it.[53]

References

1 Wagstyl, S. (1996) 'Innovation zealots a cut above the rest', in *Financial Times*. London.
2 Kaplinsky, R., F. den Hertog and B. Coriat (1995) *Europe's Next Step*. Frank Cass, London.
3 Kay, J. (1993) *Foundations of Corporate Success: How business strategies add value*. Oxford University Press, Oxford, p. 416.
4 Souder, W. and J. Sherman (1994) *Managing New Technology Development*. McGraw-Hill, New York.
5 Luchs, B. (1990) 'Quality as a strategic weapon', *European Business Journal*, **2** (4), 34–47.
6 Baden-Fuller, C. and M. Pitt (1996) *Strategic Innovation*. Routledge, London.
7 Walsh, V. *et al.* (1992) *Winning by Design: Technology, product design and international competitiveness*. Basil Blackwell, Oxford.
8 Stalk, G. and T. Hout (1990) *Competing against Time: How time-based competition is reshaping global markets*. Free Press, New York.
9 Monden, Y. (1983) *The Toyota Production System*. Productivity Press, Cambridge, Mass.
10 Womack, J., D. Jones and D. Roos (1991) *The Machine that Changed the World*. Rawson Associates, New York.
11 Dodgson, M. and R. Rothwell (eds) (1995) *The Handbook of Industrial Innovation*. Edward Elgar, London.
12 Pfeffer, J. (1994) *Competitive Advantage through People*. Harvard Business School Press, Boston, Mass.
13 Evans, P. and T. Wurster (2000) *Blown to Bits: How the new economics of information transforms strategy*. Harvard Business School Press, Boston, Mass.
14 Utterback, J. (1994) *Mastering the Dynamics of Innovation*. Harvard Business School Press, Boston, Mass., p. 256.
15 Bright, A. (1949) *The Electric Lamp Industry: Technological change and economic development from 1800 to 1947*. Macmillan, New York.
16 Sahal, D. (1981) *Patterns of Technological Innovation*. Addison-Wesley, Reading, Mass.
17 Foster, R. (1986) *Innovation—the Attacker's Advantage*. Pan Books, London.
18 Henderson, R. and K. Clark (1990) 'Architectural innovation: the reconfiguration of existing product technologies and the failure of established firms', *Administrative Science Quarterly*, **35**, 9–30.
19 Tidd, J. (1994) *Home Automation: Market and technology networks*. Whurr Publishers, London.
20 Hollander, S. (1965) *The Sources of Increased Efficiency: A study of Dupont rayon plants*. MIT Press, Cambridge, Mass.
21 Tremblay, P. (1994) *Comparative Analysis of Technological Capability and Productivity Growth in the Pulp and Paper Industry in Industrialised and Industrialising Countries*. Ph.D. thesis, University of Sussex.
22 Figuereido, P. (2000) *Technological Learning in Steel Plants in Brazil*. Ph.D. thesis, University of Sussex.
23 Robinson, A. (1991) *Continuous Improvement in Operations*. Productivity Press, Cambridge, Mass.
24 Rothwell, R. and P. Gardiner (1985) 'Invention, innovation, re-innovation and the role of the user', *Technovation*, **3**, 167–186.
25 Christenson, C. (1997) *The Innovator's Dilemma*. Harvard Business School Press, Cambridge, Mass.
26 Hamel, G. (2000) *Leading the Revolution*. Harvard Business School Press, Boston, Mass.
27 Peters, T. (1997) *The Circle of Innovation*. Coronet, London.
28 Bryson, B. (1994) *Made in America*. Minerva, London.
29 Gilbert, J. (1975) *The World's Worst Aircraft*. Coronet, London.
30 Crawford, C. (1991) *New Products Management*, 3rd edn. Irwin, Homewood, Ill.
31 Henry, J. and D. Walker (1990) *Managing Innovation*. Sage, London.
32 Nayak, P. and J. Ketteringham (1986) *Breakthroughs: How leadership and drive create commercial innovations that sweep the world*. Mercury, London.

33   Leifer, R. *et al.* (2000) *Radical Innovation*. Harvard Business School Press, Boston, Mass.

34   Teece, D. (1998) 'Capturing value from knowledge assets: the new economy, markets for know-how, and intangible assets', *California Management Review*, **40** (3), 55–79.

35   Porter, M. (1997) 'Location, knowledge creation and competitiveness', in *Knowledge Capitalism: Competitiveness re-evaluated*. Academy of Management, Boston, Mass.

36   Quinn, J. (1992) *Intelligent Enterprise: A knowledge and service-based paradigm for industry*. Free Press, New York.

37   Quintas, P., P. Lefrere and G. Jones (1997) 'Knowledge management: a strategic agenda'. *Long Range Planning*, **13** (3), 387.

38   Hale, S. (2000) *Incorporating Cultural Sensitivity into Technological Change'*. Ph.D. thesis, Centre for Research in Innovation Management. University of Brighton.

39   Hofstede, G. (1984) *Culture Consequences*. Sage, London.

40   Berners-Lee, T. (2000) *Weaving the Web: The original design and ultimate destiny of the World Wide Web by its inventor*. Harper Business, New York.

41   Pottruck, D. and T. Pearce (2000) *Clicks and Mortar*. Jossey-Bass, San Francisco.

42   Freeman, C. (1982) *The Economics of Industrial Innovation*, 2nd edn. Frances Pinter, London.

43   Rothwell, R. and J. Bessant (1992) 'Fifth generation innovation and fifth wave manufacturing', in *Technology Transfer International*. Conference Proceedings, EPSRC and the Teaching Company Directorate, London.

44   Williamson, O. (1975) *Markets and Hierarchies*. Free Press, New York.

45   Danish Technological Institute (1991) *Network Co-operation—Achieving SME Competitiveness in a Global Economy*. Danish Technological Institute, Aarhus.

46   Grandori, A. and G. Soda (1995) 'Inter-firm networks: antecedents, mechanisms and forms', *Organization Studies*, **16** (2), 183–214.

47   Harland, C. (1995) *Networks and Globalisation*. Engineering and Physical Sciences Research Council, Swindon.

48   Bessant, J. (1999) 'The rise and fall of 'Supernet': a case study of technology transfer policy for smaller firms', *Research Policy*, **28** (6), 601–614.

49   Brockhoff, K., A. Chakrabarti and J. Hauschildt (eds) (1999) *The Dynamics of Innovation*. Springer, Heidelberg.

50   Mascitelli, R. (1999) *The Growth Warriors. Creating Sustainable Global Advantage for America's Technology Industries*. Technology Perspectives, Northridge, Calif.

51   Kanter, R. (ed.) (1977) *Innovation: Breakthrough thinking at 3M, DuPont, GE, Pfizer and Rubbermaid*. Harper Business, New York.

52   Jolly, V. (1997) *Commercialising New Technologies: Getting from mind to market*. Harvard Business School Press, Boston, Mass.

53   Van de Ven, A., H. Angle and M. Poole (1989) *Research on the Management of Innovation*. Harper and Row, New York.

Chapter 2

INNOVATION AS A MANAGEMENT PROCESS

One of America's most successful innovators was Thomas Alva Edison who during his life registered over 1000 patents. Products for which his organization was responsible include the light bulb, 35 mm cinema film and even the electric chair. Edison appreciated better than most that the real challenge in innovation was not invention—coming up with good ideas—but in making them work technically and commercially. His skill in doing this created a business empire worth, in 1920, around $21.6bn. He put to good use an understanding of the interactive nature of innovation, realizing that both technology push (which he systematized in one of the world's first organized R&D laboratories) and demand pull need to be mobilized.

His work on electricity provides a good example of this; Edison recognized that although the electric light bulb was a good idea it had little practical relevance in a world where there was no power point to plug it into. Consequently, his team set about building up an entire electricity generation and distribution infrastructure, including designing lamp stands, switches and wiring. In 1882 he switched on the power from the first electric power generation plant in Manhattan and was able to light up 800 bulbs in the area. In the years that followed he built over 300 plants all over the world.[1]

As Edison realized, innovation is more than simply coming up with good ideas; it is the *process* of growing them into practical use. Definitions of innovation may vary in their wording, but they all stress the need to complete the development and exploitation aspects of new knowledge, not just its invention. Box 2.1 gives some examples.

BOX 2.1 What *is* innovation?

One of the problems in managing innovation is variation in what people under-stand by the term, often confusing it with invention. In its broadest sense the term comes from the Latin *innovare*, meaning 'to make something new'. Our view, shared by the following writers, assumes that innovation is a process of turning opportunity into new ideas and of putting these into widely used practice.

'Industrial innovation includes the technical, design, manufacturing, management and commercial activities involved in the marketing of a new (or improved) prod-uct or the first commercial use of a new (or improved) process or equipment'—Chris Freeman (1982) *The Economics of Industrial Innovation*, 2nd edn. Frances Pinter, London.

'. . . Innovation does not necessarily imply the commercialization of only a major advance in the technological state of the art (a radical innovation) but it includes also the utilisation of even small-scale changes in technological know-how (an improvement or incremental innovation)'—Roy Rothwell and Paul Gardiner (1985) 'Invention, innovation, re-innovation and the role of the user', *Technovation*, **3**, 168.

'Innovation is the specific tool of entrepreneurs, the means by which they exploit change as an opportunity for a different business or service. It is capable of being presented as a discipline, capable of being learned, capable of being practised'—Peter Drucker (1985) *Innovation and Entrepreneurship*, Harper & Row, New York.

'Companies achieve competitive advantage through acts of innovation. They approach innovation in its broadest sense, including both new technologies and new ways of doing things'—Michael Porter (1990) *The Competitive Advantage of Nations*, Macmillan, London.

'Successful exploitation of new ideas'—UK DTI Innovation Unit definition, 1994

If we only understand part of the innovation process, then the behaviours in managing it are also likely to be only partially helpful—even if well intentioned and executed. For example, innovation is often confused with invention—but the latter is only the first step in a long process of bringing a good idea to widespread and effective use. Being a good inventor is—to contradict Emerson—no guaran-tee of commercial success and no matter how good the better mousetrap idea, the world will only beat a path to the door if attention is also paid to project man-agement, market development, financial management, organizational behaviour, etc.* Box 2.2 gives some examples which highlight the difference between inven-tion and innovation.

---

* Ralph Waldo Emerson, 'If a man has good corn, or wood, or boards, or pigs to sell, or can make better chairs or knives, crucibles or church organs than anybody else, you will find a broad-beaten road to his home, though it be in the woods.'

BOX 2.2 Invention and innovation.

In fact, some of the most famous inventions of the nineteenth century were invented by men whose names are forgotten; the names which we associate with them are of the entrepreneurs who brought them into commercial use. For example, the vacuum cleaner was invented by one J. Murray Spengler and originally called an 'electric suction sweeper'. He approached a leather goods maker in the town who knew nothing about vacuum cleaners, but had a good idea of how to market and sell them—one W. H. Hoover. Similarly, a Boston man called Elias Howe produced the world's first sewing machine in 1846. Unable to sell his ideas despite travelling to England and trying there, he returned to the USA to find one Isaac Singer had stolen the patent and built a successful business from it. Although Singer was eventually forced to pay Howe a royalty on all machines made, the name which most people now associate with sewing machines is Singer not Howe. And Samuel Morse, widely credited as the father of modern telegraphy, actually invented only the code which bears his name; all the other inventions came from others. What Morse brought was enormous energy and a vision of what could be accomplished; to realize this he combined marketing and political skills to secure state funding for development work, and to spread the concept of something which for the first time would link up people separated by vast distances on the continent of America. Within five years of demonstrating the principle there were over 5000 miles of telegraph wire in the USA, and Morse was regarded as 'the greatest man of his generation'.[1]

2.1 Innovation as a Core Business Process

Chapter 1 set out a view of innovation as the core process within an organization associated with renewal—with refreshing what it offers and how it creates and delivers that offering. Viewed in this way innovation is a generic activity associated with survival and growth. And at this level of abstraction we can see the underlying process as common to all firms. It essentially involves:

- Scanning the environment (internal and external) for, and processing relevant signals about, threats and opportunities for change
- Deciding (on the basis of a strategic view of how the enterprise can best develop) which of these signals to respond to
- Obtaining the resources to enable the response (through creating something new through R&D, acquiring something from elsewhere via technology transfer, etc.)
- Implementing the project (developing the technology and the internal or external market) to respond effectively

In addition, enterprises have the opportunity to learn from progressing through this cycle so that they can build their knowledge base and can improve the ways in which the process is managed.

All firms are trying to find a way of organizing and managing this process in such a way as to provide a good solution to the problem of renewal. Different circumstances lead to many different solutions—for example, large science-based firms like the pharmaceutical companies will tend to create solutions which have heavy activities around formal R&D, patent searching, etc. whilst small engineering subcontractors will emphasize rapid implementation capability. Retailers may have relatively small R&D commitments in the formal sense but stress scanning the environment to pick up new consumer trends, and they are likely to place heavy emphasis on marketing. Consumer goods producers may be more concerned with rapid product development and launch, often with variants and repositioning of basic product concepts. Heavy engineering firms involved in products like power plant are likely to be design intensive, and critically dependent on project management and systems integration aspects of the implementation phase.

Despite these variations the underlying pattern of phases in innovation remains constant. In this chapter we want to explore the process nature of innovation in more detail, and to look at the kinds of variations on this basic theme.

But we also want to suggest that there is some commonalty around the things which are managed—the key enablers—in successful innovation. Once again, how these enablers are actually put together varies between firms, but they represent particular solutions to the general problem of managing innovation. Exploring these enablers in more detail forms the bulk of the rest of the book.

Central to our view is that innovation management is a *learned* capability. Although there are common issues to be confronted and a common set of recipes for dealing with them, each firm must find its own particular solution and develop this in its own context. Simply copying ideas from elsewhere is not enough; these must be adapted and shaped to suit particular circumstances.

Variations on a Theme

Innovations vary widely, in scale, nature, degree of novelty and so on—and so do innovating organizations. But at this level of abstraction it is possible to see the same basic process operating in each case. For example, developing a new consumer product will involve picking up signals about potential needs and new technological possibilities, developing a strategic concept, coming up with options and then working those up into new products which can be launched into the marketplace.

In similar fashion deciding to install a new piece of process technology also follows this pattern. Signals about needs—in this case internal ones, such as problems with the current equipment—and new technological means are processed and provide an input to developing a strategic concept. This then requires identifying an existing option, or inventing a new one which must then be developed to such a point that it can be implemented, i.e. launched, by users within the enterprise—effectively a group of internal customers. The same principles of needing to understand their needs and to prepare the marketplace for effective launch will apply as in the case of product innovation.

Services may appear different because they are often less tangible—but the same underlying model applies. The process whereby an insurance or financial services company launches a new product will follow a path of signal processing, strategic concept, product and market development and launch. What is developed may be less tangible than a new television set, but the underlying structure to the process is the same.[2]

Complex product systems represent an interesting case, involving the kind of technological system which brings together many different elements into an integrated whole, often involving different firms, long timescales and high levels of technological risk.[3] Although such projects may appear very different from the core innovation process associated with, for example, producing a new soap powder for the mass market, the underlying process is still one of careful understanding of user needs and meeting those. The involvement of users throughout the development process, and the close integration of different perspectives will be of particular importance, but the overall map of the process is the same.

An increasing number of authors draw attention to the need to take the degree of novelty in an innovation into account. Where the concern is essentially around 'doing what we do better' emphasis is placed upon structures and processes which enable improvements to products and processes.[4] By contrast the arrangements needed within the organization to deal with doing totally new things, often involving radical technological and/or market change, are often very different. This point is made by, amongst others, Peters, Hamel and Leifer *et al.*, all of whom argue that under turbulent conditions firms need to develop capabilities for managing both aspects of innovation.[5-7] Perhaps the most detailed review of this problem has been that of Christensen whose in-depth studies of the hard disk drive industry have helped provide a perspective on disruptive and sustaining technological change.

Prescriptions for structuring the process abound; for example, one of the most cited models for product innovation is due to Booz Allen and Hamilton.[8] Many variations exist on this theme—for example, Robert Cooper's work suggests a slightly extended view with 'gates' between stages which permit management of the risks in the process.[9] There is also a British Standard (BS 7000) which sets out a design-centred model of the process.[2]

Of course, in practice this apparently straightforward linear process rarely emerges. Most innovation is messier, involving false starts, recycling between stages, dead ends, jumps out of sequence, etc. Various authors have tried different metaphors—for example, seeing the process as a railway journey with the option of stopping at different stations, going into sidings or even, at times, going backwards—but most agree that there is still some sequence to the basic process.[10, 11]

In an important programme of case study based research looking at widely different innovation types, van de Ven and colleagues explored the limitations of simple models of the process. They drew attention to the complex ways in which innovations actually evolve over time, and derived some important modifiers to the basic model:

- Shocks trigger innovations—change happens when people or organizations reach a threshold of opportunity or dissatisfaction
- Ideas proliferate—after starting out in a single direction, the process proliferates into multiple, divergent progressions

- Setbacks frequently arise, plans are overoptimistic, commitments escalate, mistakes accumulate and vicious cycles can develop
- Restructuring of the innovating unit often occur through external intervention, personnel changes or other unexpected events
- Top management plays a key role in sponsoring—but also in criticizing and shaping—innovation
- Success criteria shift over time, differ between groups and make innovation a political process
- Innovation involves learning, but much of their outcomes are due to other events which occur as the innovation develops—making learning often 'superstitious' in nature

They suggest that the underlying structure can be represented by the metaphor of an 'innovation journey', which has key phases of initiation, development and implementation/termination. But the progress of any particular innovation along this will depend on a variety of contingent circumstances; depending on which of these apply, different specific models of the process will emerge.

Table 2.1 lists some variables which shape the general context in which the innovation process takes place.

TABLE 2.1   How context affects innovation management.

Context variable	Modifiers to the basic process	Example references discussing these
Sector	Different sectors have different priorities and characteristics—for example, scale-intensive, science-intensive	12
Size	Small firms differ in terms of access to resources, etc. and so need to develop more linkages	13, 14
National systems of innovation	Different countries have more or less supportive contexts in terms of institutions, policies, etc.	15
Life cycle (of technology, industry, etc.)	Different stages in life-cycle emphasize different aspects of innovation—for example, new technology industries versus mature established firms	16–18
Degree of novelty	'More of the same' improvement innovation requires different approaches to organization and management to more radical forms. At the limit firms may need to split into different entities to enable advantage to be taken of disruptive technologies	4, 6, 7

2.2 Evolving Models of the Process

The importance of understanding innovation as a process is that this understanding shapes the way in which we try and manage it. This has changed a great deal over time. Early models (both explicit and, more important, the implicit mental models whereby people managed the process) saw it as a linear sequence of functional activities. Either new opportunities arising out of research gave rise to applications and refinements which eventually found their way to the market-place ('technology push') or else the market signalled needs for something new which then drew through new solutions to the problem ('need pull', where necessity becomes the mother of invention).

The limitations of such an approach are clear; in practice innovation is a coupling and matching process where interaction is the critical element.[19–21] Sometimes the 'push' will dominate, sometimes the 'pull', but successful innovation requires interaction between the two. The analogy to a pair of scissors is useful here; without both blades it is difficult to cut.

Rothwell provides a useful historical perspective on this, suggesting that our appreciation of the nature of the innovation process has been evolving from such simple linear models (characteristic of the 1960s) through to increasingly complex interactive models (Table 2.2). His 'fifth-generation innovation' concept sees innovation as a multi-actor process which requires high levels of integration at both intra- and inter-firm levels and which is increasingly facilitated by IT-based networking.[22] Whilst his work did not explicitly mention the Internet, it is clear that the kinds of innovation management challenge posed by the emergence of this new form fit well with the model. Although such fifth-generation models appear complex, they still involve the same basic process framework.

TABLE 2.2   Rothwell's five generations of innovation models.

Generation	Key features
First/second	Simple linear models—need pull, technology push
Third	Coupling model, recognizing interaction between different elements and feedback loops between them
Fourth	Parallel model, integration within the firm, upstream with key suppliers and downstream with demanding and active customers, emphasis on linkages and alliances
Fifth	Systems integration and extensive networking, flexible and customized response, continuous innovation

2.3 Consequences of Partial Understanding of the Innovation Process

Failure to understand fully the process nature of innovation leads in practice to what might be termed 'one-dimensional management', that is, focusing only on those parts which are perceived as important. Examples here include:

- Seeing innovation as a linear 'technology push' process (in which case all the attention goes into funding R&D with little input from users) or one in which the market can be relied upon to pull through innovation
- Seeing innovation simply in terms of major 'breakthroughs'—and ignoring

the significant potential of incremental innovation. In the case of electric light bulbs, the original Edison design remained almost unchanged in concept, but incremental product and process improvement over the 16 years from 1880 to 1896 led to a fall in price of around 80% [23]
- Seeing innovation as a single isolated change rather than as part of a wider system (effectively restricting innovation to component level rather than seeing the bigger potential of architectural changes)[24]
- Seeing innovation as product or process only, without recognizing the inter-relationship between the two

Table 2. 3 provides an overview of the difficulties which arise if we take a partial view of innovation. From this it becomes clear that we need to ensure that the way we structure the generic innovation process:

TABLE 2.3   Problems of partial views of innovation.

If innovation is only seen as . . .	. . . the result can be
Strong R&D capability	Technology which fails to meet user needs and may not be accepted
The province of specialists in white coats in the R&D laboratory	Lack of involvement of others, and a lack of key knowledge and experience input from other perspectives
Meeting customer needs	Lack of technical progression, leading to inability to gain competitive edge
Technology advances	Producing products which the market does not want or designing processes which do not meet the needs of the user and which are opposed
The province only of large firms	Weak small firms with too high a dependence on large customers
Only about 'breakthrough' changes	Neglect of the potential of incremental innovation. Also an inability to secure and reinforce the gains from radical change because the incremental performance ratchet is not working well
Only associated with key individuals	Failure to utilize the creativity of the remainder of employees, and to secure their inputs and perspectives to improve innovation
Only internally generated	The 'not invented here' effect, where good ideas from outside are resisted or rejected
Only externally generated	Innovation becomes simply a matter of filling a shopping list of needs from outside and there is little internal learning or development of technological competence
Only concerning single firms	Excludes the possibility of various forms of inter-organizational networking to create new products, streamline shared processes, etc.

- Represents a complete, not a partial model
- Reflects the particular operating contingencies as well as the generic nature of the process

2.4 Can We Manage Innovation?

It would be hard to find anyone prepared to argue against the view that innovation is important and likely to be more so in the coming years. But that still leaves us with the big question of whether or not we can manage the process.

There is certainly no easy recipe for success. Indeed, at first glance it might appear that it is impossible to manage something so complex and uncertain. There are problems in developing and refining new basic knowledge, problems in adapting and applying it to new products and processes, problems in convincing others to support and adopt the innovation, problems in gaining acceptance and long-term use and so on. Since so many people with different disciplinary backgrounds, varying responsibilities and basic goals are involved, the scope for differences of opinion and conflicts over ends and means is wide. In many ways the innovation process represents the place where Murphy and his associated band of lawmakers hold sway, where if anything can go wrong, there's a very good chance that it will!

But despite the uncertain and apparently random nature of the innovation process, it *is* possible to find an underlying pattern of success. Not every innovation fails, and some firms (and individuals) appear to have learned ways of responding and managing it such that, while there is never a cast-iron guarantee, at least the odds in favour of successful innovation can be improved.

It is important also to see this as a *management* question, in the sense that there are choices to be made about resources and their disposition and co-ordination. (It is important to note the distinction here between 'management' and managers. We are not arguing here about who is involved in taking decisions or directing activity, but rather about what has to be done.) Close analysis of many technological innovations over the years reveals that although there are technical difficulties—bugs to fix, teething troubles to be resolved and the occasional major technical barrier to surmount—the majority of failures are due to some weakness in the way the process is managed. Success in innovation appears to depend upon two key ingredients—technical resources (people, equipment, knowledge, money, etc.) *and* the capabilities in the organization to manage them.

This brings us back to the concept of *routines*, mentioned in Chapter 1. Organizations develop particular ways of behaving which become 'the way we do things around here' as a result of repetition and reinforcement. These patterns reflect an underlying set of shared beliefs about the world and how to deal with it, and form part of the organization's culture—'the way we do things in this organization'. They emerge as a result of repeated experiments and experience around what appears to work well—in other words, they are learned. Over time the pattern becomes more of an automatic response to particular situations, and the behaviour becomes what can be termed a 'routine'.

This does not mean that it is necessarily repetitive, only that its execution does not require detailed conscious thought. The analogy can be made with driving a car; it is possible to drive along a stretch of motorway whilst simultaneously talking to someone else, eating or drinking, listening to, and concentrating on, something on the radio or planning what to say at the forthcoming meeting. But driving is not a passive behaviour; it requires continuous assessment and adaptation of responses in the light of other traffic behaviour, road conditions, weather and a host of different and unplanned factors. We can say that driving represents a behavioural routine in that it has been learned to the point of being largely automatic.

In the same way an organizational routine might exist around how projects are managed, or new products researched. For example, project management involves a complex set of activities such as planning, team selection, monitoring and execution of tasks, replanning, coping with unexpected crises and so on. All of these have to be integrated—and which offer plenty of opportunities for making mistakes. Project management is widely recognized as an organizational skill, which experienced firms have developed to a high degree but which beginners can make a mess of. Firms with good project management routines are able to codify and pass them on to others via procedures and systems. Most important, the principles are also transmitted into 'the way we run projects around here' by existing members passing on the underlying beliefs about project management behaviour to new recruits.

Over time organizational behaviour routines create and are reinforced by various kinds of artefacts—formal and informal structures, procedures and processes which describe 'the way we do things around here', and symbols which represent and characterize the underlying routines. It could be in the form of a policy—for example, 3M is widely known for its routines for regular and fast product innovation. They have enshrined a set of behaviours around encouraging experimentation into what they term 'the 15% policy' in which employees are enabled to work on their own curiosity-driven agenda for up to 15% of their time.[25-27] These routines are firm-specific—for example, they result from an environment in which the costs of product development experimentation are often quite low.

Levitt and March describe routines as involving established sequences of actions for undertaking tasks enshrined in a mixture of technologies, formal procedures or strategies, and informal conventions or habits. Importantly, routines are seen as evolving in the light of experience that works—they become the mechanisms that 'transmit the lessons of history'. In this sense, routines have an existence independent of particular personnel—new members of the organization learn them on arrival, and most routines survive the departure of individual routines.[28] Equally, they are constantly being adapted and interpreted such that formal policy may not always reflect the current nature of the routine—as Augsdorfer points out in the case of 3M.[29]

For our purposes the important thing to note is that routines are what makes one organization different from another in how they carry out the same basic activity. We could almost say they represent the particular 'personality' of the firm. Each enterprise learns its own particular 'way we do things around here' in answer to the same generic questions—how it manages quality, how it manages

BOX 2.3 Fashion statements versus behavioural change in organizations.

The problem with routines is that they have to be learned—and learning is difficult. It takes time and money to try new things, it disrupts and disturbs the day-to-day working of the firm, it can upset organizational arrangements and require efforts in acquiring and using new skills. Not surprisingly most firms are reluctant learners—and one strategy which they adopt is to try and short-cut the process by borrowing ideas from other organizations.

Whilst there is enormous potential in learning from others, simply copying what seems to work for another organization will not necessarily bring any benefits and may end up costing a great deal and distracting the organization from finding its own ways of dealing with a particular problem. The temptation to copy gives rise to the phenomenon of particular approaches becoming fashionable—something which every organization thinks it needs in order to deal with its particular problems.

Over the past 20 years we have seen many apparent panaceas for the problems of becoming competitive. Organizations are constantly seeking new answers to old problems, and the scale of investment in the new fashions of management thinking have often been considerable. Examples include:

- Advanced manufacturing technology (AMT—robots, flexible machines, integrated computer control, etc.)[30, 31]
- Total quality management (TQM)[32]
- Business process re-engineering (BPR)[33]
- Benchmarking best practice[34]
- Quality circles[35, 36]
- Networking/clustering

The *original* evidence for the value of these tools and techniques was strong, with case studies and other reports testifying to their proven value within the context of origin. But there is also extensive evidence to suggest that these changes do not always work, and in many cases lead to considerable dissatisfaction and disillusionment. For example:

- Studies in the 1990s on AMT suggested failure rates of over 50%, with disappointment being expressed by the majority of users
- Failure rates of TQM programmes running as high as 80% one year after inception
- BPR projects being abandoned

What is going on here demonstrates well the principles behind behavioural change in organizations. It is not that the original ideas were flawed or that the initial evidence was wrong. Rather it was that other organizations assumed they could simply be copied, without the need to adapt them, to customize them, to modify and change them to suit their circumstances. In other words, there was no learning, and no progress towards making them become routines, part of the underlying culture within the firm. Chapter 3 picks up this theme in the context of thinking about strategy.

people, etc. 'How we manage innovation around here' is one set of routines which describes and differentiates the responses which organizations make to the question of structuring and managing the generic model described above.

It follows that some routines are better than others in coping with the uncertainties of the outside world, in both the short and the long term. And it is possible to learn from others' experience in this way; the important point is to remember that routines are firm-specific and must be learned. Simply copying what someone else does is unlikely to help, any more than watching someone drive and then attempting to copy them will make a novice into an experienced driver. There may be helpful clues which can be used to improve the novice's routines, but there is no substitute for the long and experience-based process of learning. Box 2.3 gives some examples where change has been introduced without this learning perspective.

Successful innovation management routines are not easy to acquire. Because they represent what a particular firm has learned over time, through a process of trial and error, they tend to be very firm-specific. Whilst it may be possible to identify the kinds of thing which 3M, Toyota, Hewlett-Packard or others have learned to do, simply copying them will not work. Instead each firm has to find its own way of doing these things—in other words, developing its own particular routines.

In the context of innovation management we can see the same hierarchical relationship in developing capability as there is in learning to drive. Basic skills are behaviours associated with things like planning and managing projects or understanding customer needs. These simple routines need to be integrated into broader abilities which taken together make up an organization's capability in managing innovation. Table 2.4 gives some examples.

One last point concerns the negative side of routines. They represent, as we have seen, embedded behaviours which have become reinforced to the point of being almost second nature—'the way we do things around here'. Therein lies their strength, but also their weakness. Because they represent ingrained patterns of thinking about the world, they are resilient—but they can also become barriers to thinking in different ways. Thus core capabilities can become core rigidities— when the 'way we do things round here' becomes inappropriate, but when the organization is too committed to the old ways to change.[37] (We return to this theme in Chapter 5, in the context of strategy.)

So it becomes important, from the standpoint of innovation management, not only to build routines but also to recognize when and how to destroy them and allow new ones to emerge.

Our argument in this book is that successful innovation management is primarily about building and improving effective routines. Such learning comes from recognizing and understanding effective routines (whether developed in-house or observed in another enterprise) and facilitating their emergence across the organization.

2.5 Successful Innovation and Successful Innovators

Before we move to look at examples of successful routines for innovation management, we should pause for a moment and define what we mean by 'success'.

TABLE 2.4 Core abilities in managing innovation.

Basic ability	Contributing routines
Recognizing	Searching the environment for technical and economic clues to trigger the process of change
Aligning	Ensuring a good fit between the overall business strategy and the proposed change—not innovating because it is fashionable or as a knee-jerk response to a competitor
Acquiring	Recognizing the limitations of the company's own technology base and being able to connect to external sources of knowledge, information, equipment, etc. Transferring technology from various outside sources and connecting it to the relevant internal points in the organization
Generating	Having the ability to create some aspects of technology in-house—through R&D, internal engineering groups, etc.
Choosing	Exploring and selecting the most suitable response to the environmental triggers which fit the strategy and the internal resource base/external technology network
Executing	Managing development projects for new products or processes from initial idea through to final launch Monitoring and controlling such projects
Implementing	Managing the introduction of change—technical and otherwise—in the organization to ensure acceptance and effective use of innovation
Learning	Having the ability to evaluate and reflect upon the innovation process and identify lessons for improvement in the management routines
Developing the organization	Embedding effective routines in place—in structures, processes, underlying behaviours, etc.

We have already seen that one aspect of this question is the need to measure the overall process rather than its constituent parts. Many successful inventions fail to become successful innovations, even when well planned.[24, 38-40]

Equally, innovation alone may not always lead to business success. Although there is strong evidence to connect innovation with performance, success depends on other factors as well. If the fundamentals of the business are weak, then all the innovation in the world may not be sufficient to save it. This argues for strategically focused innovation as part of a 'balanced scorecard' of results measurement.[41-43]

We also need to consider the time perspective. The real test of innovation success is not a one-off success in the short term but sustained growth through continuous invention and adaptation. It is relatively simple to succeed once with a lucky combination of new ideas and receptive market at the right time—but it is quite another thing to repeat the performance consistently. Some organizations clearly feel able to do the latter to the point of presenting themselves as innovators, for example, 3M, Sony, IBM, Samsung and Philips, all of whom currently use the term in their advertising campaigns and stake their reputations on their ability to innovate consistently.

In our terms, success relates to the overall innovation process and its ability to contribute consistently to growth.

2.6 What Do We Know About Successful Innovation Management?

The good news is that there is a knowledge base on which to draw in attempting to answer this question. Quite apart from the wealth of experience (of success and failure) by organizations involved with innovation, there is a growing pool of knowledge derived from research. Over the past 50 years or so there have been many studies of the innovation process, looking at many different angles. Different innovations, different sectors, firms of different shapes and sizes, operating in different countries, etc. have all come under the microscope and been analysed in a variety of ways. Table 2.5 gives a few examples of the research which underpins what we know about successful innovation management.

From this knowledge base it is clear that there are no easy answers and that innovation varies enormously—by scale, type, sector, etc. Nonetheless, there does appear to be some convergence around our two key points:

- Innovation is a process, not a single event, and needs to be managed as such
- The influences on the process can be manipulated to affect the outcome—that is, it *can* be managed

Most important, the research base highlights the concept of success routines which are learned over time and through experience. For example, successful innovation correlates strongly with how a firm selects and manages projects, how it co-ordinates the inputs of different functions, how it links up with its customers, etc. Developing an integrated set of routines is strongly associated with successful innovation management, and can give rise to distinctive competitive ability—for example, being able to introduce new products faster than anyone else,[56–58] or being able to use new process technology better.[59, 60]

The other critical point to emerge from research is that innovation needs managing in an integrated way; it is not enough just to manage or develop abilities in some of these areas. There are many examples of firms which have highly developed abilities for managing part of the innovation process but which fail because of a lack of ability in others. For example, there are many with an acknowledged strength in R&D and the generation of technological innovation—but which lack the abilities to relate these to the marketplace or to end-users. Others may lack the ability to link innovation to their business strategy; for example, many firms invested in robots during the 1980s, but most surveys suggest that only half of these investments really paid off. For the other half the problem was an inability to match the 'gee whiz' nature of a glamorous technology to their particular needs, and the result was what might be called 'technological jewellery'—visually impressive but with little more than a decorative function.

The concept of capability in innovation management also raises the question of how it is developed over time. This must involve a learning process. It is not sufficient simply to have experiences (good or bad); the key lies in evaluating and

TABLE 2.5   Examples of innovation studies.

Study name	Key focus	Further reference
Project SAPPHO	Success and failure factors in matched pairs of firms, mainly in chemicals and scientific instruments	22
Wealth from knowledge	Case studies of successful firms—all were winners of the Queen's Award for Innovation	44
Post-innovation performance	Looked at these cases 10 years later to see how they had fared	45
Project Hindsight TRACES	Historical reviews of US government-funded work within the defence industry. Main aims were to identify sources of successful innovation and management factors influencing success.	46
Industry and technical progress	Survey of UK firms to identify why some were apparently more innovative than others in the same sector, size range, etc. Derived a list of managerial factors which comprised 'technical progressiveness'	47
Minnesota studies	Detailed case studies over an extended period of 14 innovations. Derived a 'road map' of the innovation process and the factors influencing it at various stages	11
Project NEWPROD	Long-running survey of success and failure in product development	9, 48–50
Stanford Innovation Project	Case studies of (mainly product) innovations, emphasis on learning	51
Lilien and Yoon	Literature review of major studies of innovation success/failure	39
Rothwell	25-year retrospective review of studies and models of innovation process	22
MIT studies	Five major industry-level cases	17
Sources of innovation	Case studies examining different levels of user involvement	52
Revolutionizing product development	Case studies of NPD practices	53
Winning by design	Case studies of product design and innovation	54
Innovation audit framework	Review of studies to generate an innovation audit	
Radical innovation project (Rensselaer Polytechnic)	Review of mature businesses and their use of innovation to create advantage	7
Rejuvenating the mature business (European studies)		55

reflecting upon them and then developing the organization in such a way that the next time a similar challenge emerges the response is ready. Such a cycle of learning is easy to prescribe but very often missing in organizations—with the result that there often seems to be a great deal of repetition in the pattern of mistakes, and a failure to learn from the misfortunes of others. For example, there is often no identifiable point in the innovation process where a post-mortem is carried out, taking time to try and distil useful learning for next time. In part this is because the people involved are too busy, but it is also because of a fear of blame and criticism. Yet without this pause for thought the odds are that the same mistakes will be repeated.[61, 62] (We will return to this theme in Chapter 9.)

2.7 Blueprints for Success

Successful innovators acquire and accumulate technical resources and managerial capabilities over time; there are plenty of opportunities for learning—through doing, using, working with other firms, asking the customers, etc.—but they all depend upon the readiness of the firm to see innovation less as a lottery than as a process which can be continuously improved.

From the various studies of success and failure in innovation it is possible to construct a checklist and a crude blueprint for effective innovation management. A number of models for auditing innovation have been developed in recent years, which provide a framework against which to assess performance in innovation management. Some of these involve simple checklists, others deal with structures, others with the operation of particular subprocesses.[54, 63]

We can map some of these routines on to the model indicated in Figure 2.1.

Scanning Phase

The first phase in innovation involves detecting signals in the environment about potential for change. These could take the form of new technological opportunities, or changing requirements on the part of markets; they could be the result of legislative pressure or competitor action. Most innovations result from the interplay of several forces, some coming from the need for change pulling through innovation and others from the push which comes from new opportunities.

Given the wide range of signals it is important for successful innovation management to have well-developed mechanisms for identifying, processing and selecting information from this turbulent environment. Chapter 9 explores enabling routines associated with successful signal processing.

Strategy Phase

Innovation is inherently risky, and even well-endowed firms cannot take unlimited risks. It is thus essential that some selection is made of the various market and technological opportunities, and that the choices made fit with the overall business strategy of the firm, and build upon established areas of technical and marketing competence. The purpose of this phase is to resolve the inputs into an

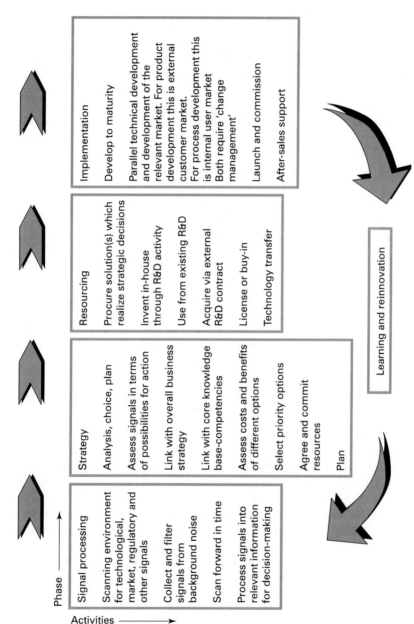

FIGURE 2.1   Routines underlying the process of innovation management.

innovation concept which can be progressed further through the development organization. (We discuss this theme in detail in the following section.)

Three inputs feed this phase. The first is the flow of signals about possible technological and market opportunities available to the enterprise. The second input concerns the current technological base of the firm—its distinctive technological competence.[64] By this we mean what it knows about terms of its product or service and how that is produced or delivered effectively. This knowledge may be embodied in particular products or equipment, but is also present in the people and systems needed to make the processes work. The important thing here is to ensure that there is a good fit between what the firm currently knows about and the proposed changes it wants to make.

This is not to say that firms should not move into new areas of competence; indeed there has to be an element of change if there is to be any learning. But rather there needs to be a balance and a development *strategy*. This raises the third input to this phase—the fit with the overall business. At the concept stage it should be possible to relate the proposed innovation to improvements in overall business performance. Thus if a firm is considering investing in flexible manufacturing equipment because the business is moving into markets where increased customer choice is likely be critical, it will make sense. But if it is doing so in a commodity business where everyone wants exactly the same product at the lowest price, then the proposed innovation will not underpin the strategy—and will effectively be a waste of money. Getting close alignment between the overall strategy for the business and the innovation strategy is critical at this stage.[60, 65]

In similar fashion many studies have shown that product innovation failure is often caused by firms trying to launch products which do not match their competence base.[48] Box 2.4 provides an illustration of such a mismatch.

BOX 2.4 The case of the jug kettle.

Trying to make and market something new involves risks and these increase significantly if the firm has no prior experience. Walker *et al.* discuss the case of the plastic jug kettle which has now become a common item of household equipment and forms part of a market worth around £500m. per year. Redring, a subsidiary of GEC, was the only company to move forward with what was for its time a radical innovation but their potential high market share was eroded not least because of difficulties in manufacturing and marketing the product. An engineering firm specializing in heat exchangers, they lacked the competence in plastics processing technology and in consumer product marketing; by the time they had climbed the learning curves needed to acquire these competencies, other players had entered the market and Redring's market position was reduced to a relatively small niche.[66]

Competency need not be contained within the firm; it is also possible to build upon competencies held elsewhere. The requirement here is to develop the relationships needed to access the necessary complementary knowledge, equipment, resources, etc. Strategic advantage comes when a firm can mobilize a set of internal and external competencies—what Teece calls 'the appropriability regime'—which make it difficult for others to copy or enter the market.[67] (This theme is picked up in more depth in Chapter 4.)

Chapter 9 explores key routines associated with strategy development.

Resourcing

This phase involves combining new and existing knowledge (available within and outside the organization) to offer a solution to the problem. It involves both generation of technological knowledge (via R&D carried out within and outside the organization) and technology transfer (between internal sources or from external sources). As such it represents a first draft of a solution, and is likely to change considerably in its development. The output of this stage in the process is both forward to the next stage of detailed development, and back to the concept stage where it may be abandoned, revised or approved.

'Invention' is used here to denote the first combination of ideas around a concept; the concept may be one articulated by market research, triggered by competitor action or emerging from R&D work in-house or externally. The key point is that it is here that the innovation moves from a collection of ideas, conscious or unconscious, to some physical reality. Much depends at this stage on the nature of the new concept. If it involves an incremental modification to an existing design, there will be little activity within the invention stage. By contrast, if the concept involves a totally new concept, there is considerable scope for creativity.

Whilst individuals may differ in terms of their preferred creative style, there is strong evidence to support the view that everyone has the latent capability for creative problem-solving.[68] Unfortunately, a variety of individual inhibitions and external social and environmental pressures combine and accumulate over time to place restrictions on the exercise of this creative potential. The issue in managing this stage is thus to create the conditions under which this can flourish and contribute to effective innovation.

Another problem with this phase is the need to balance the open-ended environmental conditions which support creative behaviour with the somewhat harsher realities involved elsewhere in the innovation process. As with concept testing and development, it is worth spending time exploring ideas and potential solutions rather than jumping on the first apparently workable option.

The challenge in effective R&D is not simply one of putting resources into the system; it is how those resources are used. Effective management of R&D requires a number of organizational routines, including clear strategic direction, effective communication and 'buy-in' to that direction, and integration of effort across different groups.

But not all firms can afford to invest in R&D; for many smaller firms the challenge is to find ways of using technology generated by others or to complement internally generated core technologies with a wider set drawn from outside (see Chapter 8). This places emphasis on the strategy system discussed above—the need to know which to carry out where and the need for a framework to guide policy in this area. Firms can survive even with no in-house capability to generate technology—but to do so they need to have a well-developed network of external sources which can supply it, and the ability to put that externally acquired technology to effective use.

It also requires abilities in finding, selecting and transferring technology in from outside the firm. This is rarely a simple shopping transaction although it is often treated as such; it involves abilities in selecting, negotiating and appropriating the benefits from such technology transfer.[69] Chapter 9 explores some key routines which are associated with enabling resourcing of innovation.

Implementation

This phase forms the heart of the innovation process. Its inputs are a clear strategic concept and some initial ideas for realizing the concept. Its outputs are both a developed innovation and a prepared market (internal or external), ready for final launch.

One way of representing the development stage is as a funnel, moving gradually from broad exploration to narrow focused problem-solving and hence to final (and successful) innovation. Unfortunately the apparent rational progress implied in this model is often not borne out in practice; instead various problems emerge, such as the lack of input (or sometimes too much input) from key functions, lack of communication between functions, conflicting goals, etc.

It is during this stage that most of the time, costs and commitment are incurred, and it is characterized by a series of problem-solving loops dealing with expected and unexpected difficulties in the technical and market areas. Although we can represent it as a parallel process, in practice effective management of this stage requires close interaction between marketing-related and technical activities. For example, product development involves a number of functions, ranging from marketing, through design and development to manufacturing, quality assurance and finally back to marketing. Differences in the tasks which each of these functions performs, in the training and experience of those working there and in the timescales and operating pressures under which they work all mean that each of these areas becomes characterized by a different working culture. Functional divisions of this kind are often exaggerated by location, where R&D and design activities are grouped away from the mainstream production and sales operations—in some cases on a completely different site.

Separation of this kind can lead to a number of problems in the overall development process. Distancing the design function from the marketplace can lead to inappropriate designs which do not meet the real customer needs, or which are 'over-engineered', embodying a technically sophisticated and elegant solution which exceeds the actual requirement (and may be too expensive as a consequence). This kind of phenomenon is often found in industries which have a tradition of defence contracting, where work has been carried out on a cost-plus basis involving projects which have emphasized technical design features rather than commercial or manufacturability criteria.

Similarly, the absence of a close link with manufacturing means that much of the information about the basic 'make-ability' of a new design either does not get back to the design area at all or else does so at a stage too late to make a difference or to allow the design to be changed. There are many cases in which manufacturing has wrestled with the problem of making or assembling a product which requires complex manipulation, but where minor design change—for example, relocation of a screw hole—would considerably simplify the process. In many cases such an approach has led to major reductions in the number of operations necessary—simplifying the process and often, as an extension, making it more susceptible to automation and further improvements in control, quality and throughput.

In similar fashion, many process innovations fail because of a lack of involvement on the part of users and others likely to be affected by the innovation. For example, many IT systems, whilst technically capable, fail to contribute to improved performance because of inadequate consideration of current working patterns which they will disrupt, lack of skills development amongst those who will be using them, inadequately specified user needs and so on.

Although services are often less tangible, the underlying difficulties in implementation are similar. Different knowledge sets need to be brought together at key points in the process of creating and deploying new offerings. For example, developing a new insurance or financial service product requires technical input on the part of actuaries, accountants, IT specialists, etc.—but this needs to be combined with information about customers and key elements of the marketing mix—the presentation, the pricing, the positioning, etc. of the new service. Knowledge of this kind will lie particularly with marketing and related staff—but their perspective must be brought to bear early enough in the process to avoid creating a new service which no one actually wants to buy.

The 'traditional' approach to this stage was a linear sequence of problem-solving, but much recent work in improving development performance (especially in compressing the time required) involves attempts to do much of this concurrently or in overlapping stages. Useful metaphors for these two approaches are the relay race and the rugby team.[70] These should be seen as representing two poles of a continuum; as we shall see (in Chapter 5 and again in Chapter 9) the important issue is to choose an appropriate level of parallel development.

In parallel with the physical problem-solving associated with developing an innovation, there is also a set of activities associated with preparing the market into which it will be launched. Whether this market is a group of retail consumers or a set of internal users of a new process, the same requirement exists for developing and preparing this market for launch, since it is only when the target market makes the decision to adopt the innovation that the whole innovation process is completed.

The process is again one of sequentially collecting information, solving problems and focusing efforts towards a final launch. In particular it involves collecting information on actual or anticipated customer needs and feeding this into the product development process, whilst simultaneously preparing the marketplace and marketing for the new product. It is essential throughout this process that a dialogue is maintained with other functions involved in the development process, and that the process of development is staged via a series of 'gates' which control progress and resource commitment.

A key aspect of the marketing effort involves anticipating likely responses to new product concepts and using this information to design the product and the way in which it is launched and marketed. This process of analysis builds upon knowledge about various sources of what Thomas calls 'market friction'.[57]

Buyer behaviour is a complex subject, but there are several key guidelines which emerge to help shape market development for a new product. The first is the underlying process of adoption of something new; typically this involves a sequence of awareness, interest, trial, evaluation and adoption. Thus simply making people aware, via advertising, etc. of the existence of a new product, will not be sufficient; they need to be drawn into the process through the other stages. Converting awareness to interest, for example, means forging a link between the new product concept and a personal need (whether real or induced via advertising). Chapter 7 deals with this issue in greater depth.

Successful implementation of internal (process) innovations also requires skilled change management. This is effectively a variation on the marketing principles outlined above, and stresses communication, involvement and intervention (via training, etc.) to minimize resistance to change—again essentially analogous to Thomas's concept of 'market friction'. Chapter 7 discusses this theme in greater detail, whilst Chapter 9 presents some key enabling routines for the implementation phase.

Learning and Reinnovation

One outcome of the launch of an innovation is the creation of new stimuli for restarting the cycle. If the product or process fails, this offers valuable information about what to change for next time. A more common scenario is what Rothwell and Gardiner call 're-innovation'; essentially building upon early success but improving the next generation with revised and refined features. In some cases, where the underlying design is sufficiently 'robust' it becomes possible to stretch and reinnovate over many years and models.[71, 72]

Amongst the main requirements in this stage is the willingness to learn from completed projects. Projects are often reviewed and audited, but these reviews may often take the form of an exercise in 'blame accounting' and in trying to cover up mistakes and problems. The real need is to capture all the hard-won lessons, from both success and failure, and feed these through to the next generation.[61] Nonaka and Kenney provide a powerful argument for this perspective in their comparison of product innovation at Apple and at Canon.[73] Much of the current discussion around the theme of knowledge management represents growing concern about the lack of such 'carry-over' learning—with the result that organizations are often 'reinventing the wheel' or repeating previous mistakes.

Learning can be in terms of technological lessons learned—for example, the acquisition of new processing or product features—which add to the organization's technological competence. But learning can also be around the capabilities and routines needed for effective product innovation management. In this connection some kind of structured audit framework or checklist is useful.

Chapter 9 explores some key routines for enabling learning.

2.8 Managing Innovation

The preceding discussion has provided an extended overview of the behaviours which are associated with successful innovation management. Whilst extensive, these routines tend to cluster around four key themes, and we shall use these in structuring the remainder of the book. Our view is that successful innovation management involves:

- Taking a strategic approach to innovation and the problem of its management
- Developing and using effective implementing mechanisms and structures
- Developing and extending a supporting organizational context for innovation
- Building and maintaining effective external linkages

These four clusters of routines can be superimposed on the process model which we described earlier (Figure 2.2). In this the arrow represents the 'what' which must be managed in any innovation process, whilst the circle contains the 'how' question. We will now move on to looking at each quadrant of the circle in more detail, beginning with the question of strategy.

FIGURE 2.2   Four components of the innovation process which must be managed.

Further Reading

Good overviews of innovation as a process to be managed can be found in references 74–78. Case studies provide a good lens through which this process can be seen and there are several useful collections including references 3, 7, 26, 55, 79–83. Many books and articles focus on particular aspects of the process—for example, on technology strategy,[84, 85] on product development,[52, 86] on process innovation [87, 88], on technology transfer, on implementation,[89–91] and on learning. [37, 92, 93]

For a good review and critique from the academic standpoint which raises a number of issues concerned with managing innovation see references 11, 76, 94.

References

1   Bryson, B. (1994) *Made in America*. Minerva, London.

2   Hollins, G. and W. Hollins (1990), *Total Design*. Pitman, London.

3   Miller, R. *et al.* (1995) 'Innovation in complex systems industries: the case of flight simulation', *Industrial and Corporate Change*, **4** (2).

4   Christenson, C. (1997) *The Innovator's Dilemma*. Harvard Business School Press, Cambridge, Mass.

5   Peters, T. (1997) *The Circle of Innovation*. Coronet, London.

6   Hamel, G. (2000) *Leading the Revolution*. Harvard Business School Press, Boston, Mass.

7   Leifer, R. *et al.* (2000) *Radical innovation*. Harvard Business School Press, Boston, Mass.

8   Booz, A. a. H. C. (1982) *New Product Management for the 1980s*. Booz, Allen and Hamilton Consultants.

9   Cooper, R. (1994) 'Third-generation New Product Processes', *Journal of Product Innovation Management*, **11** (1), 3–14.

10 Souder, W. and J. Sherman (1994) *Managing New Technology Development*. McGraw-Hill, New York.

11 Van de Ven, A., H. Angle and M. Poole (1989) *Research on the Management of Innovation*. Harper and Row, New York.

12 Pavitt, K. (1984) 'Sectoral patterns of technical change; towards a taxonomy and a theory', *Research Policy*, **13**, 343–373.

13 Rothwell, R. (1978) 'Small and medium sized firms and technological innovation', *Management Decision*, **16** (6).

14 Hoffman, K. *et al.* (1998) Small firms, R&D, technology and innovation: a literature review. *Technovation*, **18** (1).

15 Lundvall, B. (1990) *National Systems of Innovation: Towards a theory of innovation and interactive learning*. Frances Pinter, London.

16 Abernathy, W. and J. Utterback (1978) 'Patterns of industrial innovation'. *Technology Review*, **80**, 40–47.

17 Utterback, J. (1994) *Mastering the Dynamics of Innovation*. 1994, Harvard Business School Press, Boston, Mass., p. 256.

18 Tushman, M. and P. Anderson (1987) 'Technological discontinuities and organizational environments', *Administrative Science Quarterly*, **31** (3), 439–465.

19 Freeman, C. (1982) *The Economics of Industrial Innovation*, 2nd edn. Frances Pinter, London.

20 Von Hippel, E. (1988) *The Sources of Innovation*. MIT Press, Cambridge, Mass.

21 Coombs, R., P. Saviotti and V. Walsh (1985) *Economics and Technological Change*. Macmillan, London.

22 Rothwell, R. (1992) 'Successful industrial innovation: Critical success factors for the 1990s'. *R&D Management*, **22** (3), 221–239.

23 Bright, A. (1949) *The Electric Lamp Industry: Technological change and economic development from 1800 to 1947*. Macmillan, New York.

24 Henderson, R. and K. Clark (1990) 'Architectural innovation: The reconfiguration of existing product technologies and the failure of established firms', *Administrative Science Quarterly*, **35**, 9–30.

25 Gundling, E. (2000) *The 3M way to Innovation: Balancing people and profit*. Kodansha International, New York.

26 Kanter, R. (ed.) (1997) *Innovation: Breakthrough thinking at 3M, DuPont, GE, Pfizer and Rubbermaid*. Harper Business, New York.

27 Mitchell, R. (1991) 'How 3M keeps the new products coming', in Henry, J. and Walker, D. (eds) *Managing Innovation*, Sage, London.

28 Levitt, B. and J. March (1988) 'Organisational learning', *Annual Review of Sociology*, **14**, 319–340.

29 Augsdorfer, P. (1996) *Forbidden Fruit*. Avebury, Aldershot.

30 Ettlie, J. (1988) *Taking Charge of Manufacturing*. Jossey-Bass, San Francisco.

31 Bessant, J. (1991) *Managing Advanced Manufacturing Technology: The challenge of the fifth wave*. NCC-Blackwell, Oxford/Manchester.

32 Povey, B. (1996) *Business Process Improvement*. University of Brighton.

33 Grover, V. and S. Jeong (1995) 'The implementation of business process re-engineering', *Journal of Management Information Systems*, **12** (1), 109–144.

34 Camp, R. (1989) *Benchmarking—the Search for Industry Best Practices that Lead to Superior Performance*. Quality Press, Milwaukee, Wis.

35 Dale, B. and S. Hayward (1984) *A Study of Quality Circle Failures*. UMIST, Manchester.

36 Lillrank, P. and N. Kano (1990) *Continuous Improvement: Quality control circles in Japanese industry*. University of Michigan Press, Ann Arbor.

37 Leonard-Barton, D. (1995) *Wellsprings of Knowledge: Building and sustaining the sources of innovation*. Harvard Business School Press, Boston, Mass., p. 335.

38 Robertson, A. (1974) *The Lessons of Failure*. Macdonald, London.

39 Lilien, G. and E. Yoon (1989) 'Success and failure in innovation—a review of the literature'. *IEEE Transactions on Engineering Management*, **36** (1), 3–10.

40 Bessant, J. (1993) 'The lessons of failure—learning to manage new technology'. *International Journal of Technology Management*, **8** (3), 197–215.

41 Voss, C. (1994) *Made in Britain*, London Business School.

42 Voss, C. *et al.* (1999) *Made in Europe 3: The small company study*. London Business School/IBM Consulting, London.

43 Kaplan, R. and D. Norton (1996) 'Using the balanced scorecard as a strategic management system'. *Harvard Business Review*, January–February.

44 Langrish, J. *et al.* (1972) *Wealth from Knowledge*. Macmillan, London.

45 Georghiou, L. *et al.* (1986) *Post-innovation Performance*. Macmillan, Basingstoke.

46 Isenson, R. (1968) *Technology in Retrospect and Critical Events in Science (Project TRACES)*. Illinois Institute of Technology/National Science Foundation, Chicago.

47 Carter, C. and B. Williams (1957) *Industry and Technical Progress*. Oxford University Press, Oxford.

48 Cooper, R. and E. Kleinschmidt (1990) *New Products: The key factors in success*. American Marketing Association, Chicago.

49 Cooper, R. *et al.* (1994) 'What distinguishes the top performing new products in financial services?', *Journal of Product Innovation Management*, **11** (4), 281–300.

50 Cooper, R. (1999) 'The invisible success factors in product innovation'. *Journal of Product Innovation Management*, **16** (2).

51 Maidique, M. and B. Zirger (1985) 'The New Product Learning Cycle', *Research Policy*, **14** (6), 299–309.

52 Wheelwright, S. and K. Clark (1992), *Revolutionising Product Development*. Free Press, New York.

53 Walsh, V. *et al.* (1992) *Winning by Design: Technology, product design and international competitiveness*. Basil Blackwell, Oxford.

54 Chiesa, V., P. Coughlan and C. Voss (1996) 'Development of a technical innovation audit', *Journal of Product Innovation Management*, **13** (2), 105–136.

55 Baden-Fuller, C. and M. Pitt (1996) *Strategic Innovation*. Routledge, London.

56 Johne, A. and P. Snelson (1988) *Successful New Product Development*. Blackwell, Oxford.

57 Thomas, R. (1993) *New Product Development: Managing and forecasting for strategic success*. Wiley, New York.

58 Smith, P. and D. Reinertsen (1991) *Developing Products in Half the Time*. Van Nostrand Reinhold, New York.

59 Tidd, J. (1989) *Flexible Automation*. Frances Pinter, London.

60 Brown, S. *et al.* (2000) *Strategic Operations Management*. Butterworth Heinemann, Oxford.

61 Rush, H., T. Brady and M. Hobday (1997) *Learning between Projects in Complex Systems*. Centre for the Study of Complex Systems, CENTRIM, University of Brighton.

62 Leonard-Barton, D. (1992) 'The organisation as learning laboratory'. *Sloan Management Review*, **34** (1), 23–38.

63 Johne, A. and P. Snelson (1988) 'Auditing product innovation activities in manufacturing firms', *R&D Management*, **18** (3), 227–233.

64 Prahalad, C. and G. Hamel (1994) *Competing for the Future*. Harvard University Press, Boston, Mass.

65 Hill, T. (1993) *Manufacturing Strategy*, 2nd edn. Macmillan, London, p. 230.

66 Walker, D. (1986) *The Redring Jug Kettle Case*, Open University Design and Innovation Course.

67 Teece, D. (1998) 'Capturing value from knowledge assets: the new economy, markets for know-how, and intangible assets', *California Management Review*, **40** (3), 55–79.

68 Kirton, M. (1980) 'Adaptors and innovators', *Human Relations*, **3**, 213–224.

69 Dodgson, M. and J. Bessant (1996) *Effective Innovation Policy*. International Thomson Business Press, London.

70 Clark, K. and T. Fujimoto (1992) *Product Development Performance*. Harvard Business School Press, Boston, Mass.

71 Rothwell, R. and P. Gardiner (1985) 'Invention, innovation, re-innovation and the role of the user', *Technovation*, **3**, 167–186.

72 Rothwell, R. and P. Gardiner (1989) 'The strategic management of re-innovation', *R&D Management*, **19** (2), 147–159.

73 Nonaka, I. and M. Kenney (1991) 'Towards a new theory of innovation management', *Journal of Engineering and Technology Management*, **8**, 67–83.

74 Brockhoff, K., A. Chakrabarti and J. Hauschildt (eds) (1999) *The Dynamics of Innovation*. Springer, Heidelberg.

75 Jelinek, M. and J. Litterer (1994) 'Organising for technology and innovation, in Souder, W. and Sherman, J. (eds), *Managing New Technology Development*, McGraw-Hill, New York.

76 Loveridge, R. and M. Pitt (1990) *The Strategic Management of Technological Innovation*. Wiley, Chichester.

77 Trott, P. (1998) *Innovation*. FT-Pitman, London.

78 Ettlie, J. (1999) *Managing Innovation*. Wiley, New York.

79 Van de Ven, A. and G. Raghu (1993) 'Innovation and industry development: the case of cochlear implants', in Burgelman, R. and Rosenbloom, R. (eds), *Research on Technological Innovation, Management and Policy*. Jai Press, Greenwich, Conn.

80 Belussi, F. (1989) 'Benetton—a case study of corporate strategy for innovation in traditional sectors', in Dodgson, M. (ed.), *Technology Strategy and the Firm*. Longman, London.

81 Rothwell, R. and P. Gardiner (1984) 'Invention and re-innovation—the case of the hovercraft', *R&D Management*, **14** (3).

82 Gallagher, M. and S. Austin (1997) *Continuous Improvement Casebook*. Kogan Page, London.

83 Saad, M. (1996) 'Development of learning capabilities via the transfer of advanced manufacturing technology: the case of two Algerian firms', *Science, Technology and Development*, **14** (1), 21–35.

84 Dodgson, M. (ed.) (1989) *Technology Strategy and the Firm*. Longman, Harlow.

85 Ford, D. and M. Saren (1996) 'Technology Strategy for Business', in Bessant, J. and Preece, D. (eds), *Management of Technology and Innovation*, International Thomson Business Press, London.

86 Cooper, R. (1988) *Winning at New Products*. Kogan Page, London.

87 Pisano, G. (1996) *The Development Factory: Unlocking the potential of process innovation*. Harvard Business School Press, Boston, Mass.

88 Davenport, T. (1992) *Process Innovation: Re-engineering work through information technology*. Harvard University Press, Boston, Mass., p. 326.

89 Leonard-Barton, D. (1988) 'Implementation as mutual adaptation of technology and organization', *Research Policy*, **17**, 251–267.

90 Rhodes, E. and D. Wield (1994) *Implementing New Technologies*. Basil Blackwell, Oxford.
91 Voss, C. (1986) 'Implementation of advanced manufacturing technology', in Voss, C. (ed.), *Managing Advanced Manufacturing Technology*. IFS Publications, Kempston.
92 Cohen, W. and D. Levinthal (1990) 'Absorptive capacity: a new perspective on learning and innovation'. *Administrative Science Quarterly*, **35** (1), 128–152.
93 Boisot, M. (1995) 'Is your firm a creative destroyer? Competitive learning and knowledge flows in the technological strategies of firms'. *Research Policy*, **24**, 489–506.
94 King, N. (1992) 'Modelling the innovation process: an empirical comparison of approaches'. *Journal of Occupational and Social Psychology*, **65**, 89–100.

Part II

TAKING A STRATEGIC APPROACH

A great deal of business success depends on generating new knowledge and on having the capabilities to react quickly and intelligently to this new knowledge. . . . I believe that strategic thinking is a necessary but overrated element of business success. If you know how to design great motorcycle engines, I can teach you all you need to know about strategy in a few days. If you have a PhD in strategy, years of labor are unlikely to give you the ability to design great new motorcycle engines. (Richard Rumelt, 1996, *California Management Review*, **38**, 110, on the continuing debate about the causes of Honda's success in the US motorcycle market).

The above quotation from a distinguished professor of strategy appears on the surface not to be a strong endorsement of his particular trade. In fact, it offers indirect support for the central propositions of this section of our book:

1. Firm-specific knowledge—including the capacity to exploit it—is an essential feature of competitive success.
2. An essential feature of corporate strategy should therefore be an innovation strategy, the purpose of which is deliberately to accumulate such firm-specific knowledge.
3. An innovation strategy must cope with an external environment that is complex and ever-changing, with considerable uncertainties about present and future developments in technology, competitive threats and market (and non-market) demands.
4. Internal structures and processes must continuously balance potentially conflicting requirements:
   (a) to *identify* and *develop* specialized knowledge *within* technological fields, business functions and product divisions;
   (b) to *exploit* this knowledge through integration across technological fields, business functions and product divisions.

In Chapter 3, we address the question, 'What is the appropriate framework for understanding innovation strategy?' Given complexity, continuous change and consequent uncertainty, we conclude that the so-called rational approach to inno-vation strategy is less likely to be effective than the incrementalist approach that stresses continuous adjustment in the light of new knowledge and learning. We also conclude that the approach pioneered by Michael Porter correctly identifies the nature of the competitive threats and opportunities that emerge from advances in technology, and rightly stresses the importance of developing and protecting firm-specific technology in order to enable firms to position them-selves against the competition. But it underestimates the power of technology to change the rules of the competitive game by modifying industry boundaries, developing new products and shifting barriers to entry. It also overestimates the capacity of corporate management to identify and predict the important changes outside the firm, and to implement radical changes in competencies and organi-zational practices within the firm. We therefore adopt the three elements of inno-vation strategy proposed by David Teece and Gary Pisano: market and national *positions,* technological *paths* and organizational *processes.*

In Chapter 4, we address the question, 'How does the firm's national and market environment shape its innovation strategy?' We first show that the *home country* positions of even global firms have a strong influence on their innovation strategies. The national influences can be grouped into three categories: *com-petencies* (workforce education, research), *economic inducement mechanisms* (local demand and input prices, competitive rivalry) and *institutions* (methods of fund-ing, controlling and managing business firms). However, managements still have ample influence over their firms' innovation strategies, and firms can benefit from foreign systems of innovation through a variety of market mechanisms.

We also show that firms can obtain information to position themselves compared to their competitors through an increasing range of sources (including so-called benchmarking). *Information* about what competitors are doing must be clearly distinguished from the *competence* to keep up with competitors, which requires a much greater corporate investment in R&D and reverse engineering activities. Firms maintain their innovative leads over their competitors through a variety of often complementary mechanisms, the relative importance of which varies from industry to industry: for example, patent protection is recognized as a more effective means of protection against imitators in the drug industry than in the paper and pulp industry.

In Chapter 5, we address the question, 'How does the nature of technology shape the firm's innovation strategy?' We show that marked differences amongst sectors are also central to corporate choices about *technological trajectories, firm-specific competencies* and *innovation strategies.* We identify five broad technological trajectories that firms can follow, each of which has distinct implications for the tasks of innovation strategy. We also identify three key technologies (bio-technology, materials and IT) where rapid advances lead to major shifts in technological trajectories, and where it is increasingly important to distinguish the microelectronics revolution (making and using electronic chips) from the more important information revolution (making and using software).

C. K. Prahalad and Gary Hamel have had a major influence on management thinking by showing that the capacity to open up new product markets requires distinctive core competencies, coupled with methods of corporate organization and evaluation that explicitly recognize the importance of these competencies, and top management visions that identify future opportunities. Experience shows that, along some technological trajectories, the opportunities for product diversification are abundant but uncertain, whilst along others they hardly exist at all. It also shows that companies also need background competencies to co-ordinate and integrate changes coming from outside the firm, and that corporate visions can be wrong.

In Chapter 6, we address the question 'What are the linkages across functional areas that are essential for a successful innovation strategy?' We identify three areas where continuous flows of information and knowledge across functional boundaries are crucial. First, the problems of deciding the organizational and geographical *location of R&D activities* reflect conflicting needs: (1) the advantages of concentration—geographical for costly programmes to develop and launch major innovations, and organizational to orchestrate networks with public (including university) research activities; (2) the advantages of decentralization, in order to be responsive to the demands of specific product or geographic markets.

Second, links between the corporate technical function and the corporate *resource allocation function* should be developed to ensure that resource allocation decisions reflect the dual nature of corporate investments in R&D: as a *business investment*, and as an *investment in learning* or *strategic positioning*. For the latter, conventional financial techniques are not appropriate, and effective decisions depend on success in mobilizing a range of professional and functional competencies from across the corporation.

Third, different *corporate strategic* styles—defined along two dimensions: the relative importance *of financial control versus entrepreneurship*, and of *centralization versus decentralization*—are appropriate for different technologies, depending on the range of opportunities that they open, and the costs of experimentation. In other words, corporate technological competencies not only serve corporate strategy, they often determine its main directions.

This section of the book has more to say about large firms, where deliberate innovation strategies are of great importance. However, positions, paths and processes also matter in small firms, and they are therefore discussed towards the end of Chapters 4–6. The purpose of innovation strategy in small firms is the same as in large ones: to create a firm-specific innovative advantage. But the balance of advantages and disadvantages is very different. Small firms in general have the organizational advantages of ease of communication, rapid decision-making and flexibility. They also have the disadvantage of either narrow or shallow technological competencies, and a greater reliance for innovation on suppliers and customers, and for strategies and competencies on the experience and qualifications of their senior managers. As with large firms, small firms vary greatly in their technological trajectories and innovation strategies. Unfortunately, most research attention has been devoted to the minority of small firms who emerge from high-technology opportunities and sometimes become very big. We know very little about innovation strategies in the rest, except that they are nearly all now trying to cope with IT.

Chapter 3

DEVELOPING THE FRAMEWORK FOR AN INNOVATION STRATEGY

Innovation plays an important and dual role, as both a major source of uncertainty and change in the environment, and a major competitive resource within the firm. In this chapter, we develop what we think is the most useful framework for defining and implementing corporate innovation strategy.

We begin by summarizing the well-known debate in corporate strategy between 'rationalist' and 'incrementalist' approaches to the characteristics of technological innovation; we conclude that the latter approach is more useful, given the inevitable complexities and uncertainties in the innovation process. We then describe and evaluate Michael Porter's pioneering framework that links innovation strategy to overall corporate strategy; we conclude that its major strength is in linking the firm's technology strategy to its market and competitive position. But it both underestimates the power of technological change to upset established market and competitive conditions, and overestimates the influence that managers actually have over corporate choice in technology strategy. For this reason, we propose that the most useful framework so far is the one developed by David Teece and Gary Pisano. It gives central importance to *the dynamic capabilities of firms*, and distinguishes three elements of corporate innovation strategy: (1) competitive and national *positions*; (2) technological *paths*; (3) organizational and managerial *processes*. These will then be discussed in detail in the subsequent three chapters.

3.1 'Rationalist' or 'Incrementalist' Strategies for Innovation?

The long-standing debate between 'rational' and 'incremental' strategies is of central importance to the mobilization of technology and to the purposes of corporate strategy. We begin by reviewing the main terms of the debate, and conclude that the supposedly clear distinction between strategies based on 'choice' or on 'implementation' breaks down when firms are making decisions in complex and fast-changing competitive environments. Under such circumstances, formal strategies must be seen as part of a wider process of continuous learning from experience and from others to cope with complexity and change.

Notions of corporate strategy first emerged in the 1960s. A lively debate has continued since then amongst the various 'schools' or theories. Here we discuss the two most influential: the 'rationalist' and the 'incrementalist'. The main protagonists are Ansoff[1] of the rationalist school and Mintzberg[2] amongst the incrementalists. An excellent summary of the terms of the debate can be found in Whittington,[3] and a face-to-face debate between the two in the *Strategic Management Journal* in 1991.

Rationalist Strategy

'Rationalist' strategy has been heavily influenced by military experience, where strategy (in principle) consists of the following steps: (1) describe, understand and analyse the environment; (2) determine a course of action in the light of the analysis; (3) carry out the decided course of action. This is a 'linear model' of rational action: appraise, determine and act. The corporate equivalent is SWOT: the analysis of corporate strengths and weaknesses in the light of external opportunities and threats. This approach is intended to help the firm to:

- Be conscious of trends in the competitive environment
- Prepare for a changing future
- Ensure that sufficient attention is focused on the longer term, given the pressures to concentrate on the day-to-day
- Ensure coherence in objectives and actions in large, functionally specialized and geographically dispersed organizations

However, as John Kay has pointed out, the military metaphor can be misleading.[4] Corporate objectives are different from military ones: namely, to establish a distinctive competence enabling them to satisfy customers better than the competition—and not to mobilize sufficient resources to destroy the enemy. Excessive concentration on the 'enemy' (i.e. corporate competitors) can result in strategies emphasizing large commitments of resources for the establishment of monopoly power, at the expense of profitable niche markets and of a commitment to satisfying customer needs.

More important, as Box 3.1 shows, professional experts, including managers, have difficulties in appraising accurately their real situation, essentially for two reasons. First, their external environment is both *complex,* involving competitors, customers, regulators and so on, and *fast-changing,* including technical, economic, social and political change. It is therefore difficult enough to understand the essential features of the present, let alone to predict the future. Second, managers in large firms disagree on their firms' strengths and weaknesses in part because their knowledge of what goes on *inside* the firm is imperfect.

BOX 3.1 'Strategizing in the real world' by William Starbuck.[5]

'The war in Vietnam is going well and will succeed.' (R. MacNamara, 1963)
'I think there is a world market for about five computers.' (T. Watson, 1948)
'Gaiety is the most outstanding feature of the Soviet Union.' (J. Stalin, 1935)
'Prediction is very difficult, especially about the future.' (N. Bohr)
'I cannot conceive of any vital disaster happening to this vessel.'

(Captain of *Titanic*, 1912)

The above quotes are from the paper by Starbuck,[5] in which he criticizes formal strategic planning:

> 'First, formalization undercuts planning's contributions. Second, nearly all managers hold very inaccurate beliefs about their firms and market environments. Third, no-one can forecast accurately over the long term. . . . However, planners can make strategic planning more realistic and can use it to build healthier, more alert and responsive firms. They can make sensible forecasts and use them to foster alertness; exploit distinctive competencies, entry barriers and proprietary information; broaden managers' horizons and help them develop more realistic beliefs; and plan in ways that make it easier to change strategy later.' (p. 77)

As a consequence, internal corporate strengths and weaknesses are often difficult to identify before the benefit of practical experience, especially in new and fast-changing technological fields. For example:

- In the 1960s, the oil company Gulf defined its distinctive competencies as producing energy, and so decided to purchase a nuclear energy firm. The venture was unsuccessful, in part because the strengths of an oil company in finding, extracting, refining and distributing oil-based products, i.e. geology and chemical processing technologies, logistics, consumer marketing, were largely irrelevant to the design, construction and sale of nuclear reactors, where the key skills are in electromechanical technologies and in selling to relatively few, but often politicized electrical utilities[6]
- In the 1960s and 1970s, many firms in the electrical industry bet heavily on the future of nuclear technology as a revolutionary breakthrough that would provide virtually costless energy. Nuclear energy failed to fulfil its promise, and firms only recognized later that the main revolutionary opportunities and threats for them came from the virtually costless storage and manipulation of information provided by improvements in semiconductor and related technologies[7]
- In the 1980s, analysts and practitioners predicted that the 'convergence' of computer and communications technologies through digitalization would lower the barriers to entry of mainframe computer firms into telecommunications equipment, and vice versa. Many firms tried to diversify into the other

market, often through acquisitions or alliances, e.g. IBM bought Rohm, AT&T bought NCR. Most proved unsuccessful, in part because the software requirements in the telecommunications and office markets were so different[8]

- The 1990s have similarly seen commitments in the fast-moving fields of ICT (information and communication technology) where initial expectations about opportunities and complementarities have been disappointed (see Box 3.2). For example, the investments of major media companies in the Internet in the late 1990s have not yet proved profitable: problems remain in delivering products to consumers and in getting paid for them, and advertising remains ineffective[9]. There have been similar disappointments so far in development of 'e-entertainment'[10]

BOX 3.2 The limits of rational strategizing.

Jonathan Sapsed's thought-provoking analysis of corporate strategies of entry into new digital media[11] concludes that the rationalist approach to strategy in emerging industries is prone to failure. Because of the intrinsic uncertainty in such an area, it is impossible to forecast accurately and predict the circumstances on which rationalist strategy, e.g. as recommended by Porter will be based. Sapsed's book includes case studies of companies that have followed the classical rational approach and subsequently found their strategies frustrated.

An example is Pearson, the large media conglomerate, which conducted a SWOT (identify strengths, weaknesses, opportunities, threats) analysis in response to developments in digital media. The strategizing showed the group's strong assets in print publishing and broadcasting, but perceived weaknesses in new media. Having established its 'gaps' in capability Pearson then searched for an attractive multimedia firm to fill the gap. It expensively acquired Mindscape, a small Californian firm. The strategy failed with Mindscape being sold for a loss of £212m. four years later, and Pearson announcing exit from the emerging market of consumer multimedia.

The strategy failed for various reasons. Firstly, unfamiliarity with the technology and market, secondly, a misjudged assessment of Mindscape's position and thirdly, a lack of awareness of the multimedia activities already within the group. The formal strategy exercises that preceded action were prone to misinterpretation and misinformation. The detachment from operations recommended by rationalist strategy exacerbated the information problems. The emphasis of rational strategy is not on assessing information arising from operations, but places great credence in detached, logical thought.

Sapsed argues that whilst formal strategizing is limited in what it can achieve, it may be viewed as a form of therapy for managers operating under uncertainty. It can enable disciplined thought on linking technologies to markets, and direct attention to new information and learning. It focuses minds on products, financial flows and anticipating options in the event of crisis or growth. Rather than determining future action, it can prepare the firm for unforeseen change.

Incrementalist Strategy

Given these conditions, 'incrementalists' argue that the complete understanding of complexity and change is impossible: our ability both to comprehend the present and to predict the future is therefore inevitably limited. As a consequence, successful practitioners—engineers, doctors and politicians, as well as business managers—do not, in general, follow strategies advocated by the rationalists, but incremental strategies which explicitly recognize that the firm has only very imperfect knowledge of its environment, of its own strengths and weaknesses, and of the likely rates and directions of change in the future. It must therefore be ready to adapt its strategy in the light of new information and understanding, which it must consciously seek to obtain. In such circumstances the most efficient procedure is to:

1. Make deliberate steps (or changes) towards the stated objective.
2. Measure and evaluate the effects of the steps (changes).
3. Adjust (if necessary) the objective and decide on the next step (change).

This sequence of behaviour goes by many names, such as incrementalism, trial and error, 'suck it and see', muddling through and learning. When undertaken deliberately, and based on strong background knowledge, it has a more respectable veneer, such as:

*   Symptom $\rightarrow$ diagnosis $\rightarrow$ treatment $\rightarrow$ diagnosis $\rightarrow$ adjust treatment $\rightarrow$ cure (for medical doctors dealing with patients)
*   Design $\rightarrow$ development $\rightarrow$ test $\rightarrow$ adjust design $\rightarrow$ retest $\rightarrow$ operate (for engineers making product and process innovations)

   Corporate strategies that do not recognize the complexities of the present, and the uncertainties associated with change and the future, will certainly be rigid, will probably be wrong, and will potentially be disastrous if they are fully implemented. But this is not a reason for rejecting analysis and rationality in innovation management. On the contrary, under conditions of complexity and continuous change, it can be argued that 'incrementalist' strategies are more rational (that is, more efficient) than 'rationalist' strategies. Nor is it a reason for rejecting all notions of strategic planning. The original objectives of the 'rationalists' for strategic planning—set out above—remain entirely valid. Corporations, and especially big ones, without any strategies will be ill-equipped to deal with emerging opportunities and threats: as Pasteur observed '. . . chance favours only the prepared mind'.[12]

Implications for Management

This debate has two sets of implications for managers. The first concerns the practice of corporate strategy, which should be seen as a form of corporate *learning, from analysis and experience, how to cope more effectively with complexity and change.* The implications for the processes of strategy formation are the following:

- Given uncertainty, explore the implications of a *range* of possible future trends
- Ensure broad participation and informal channels of communication
- Encourage the use of multiple sources of information, debate and scepticism
- Expect to change strategies in the light of new (and often unexpected) evidence

The second implication is that *successful management practice is never fully reproducible.* In a complex world, neither the most scrupulous practising manager nor the most rigorous management scholar can be sure of identifying—let alone evaluating—all the necessary ingredients in real examples of successful management practice. In addition, the conditions of any (inevitably imperfect) reproduction of successful management practice will differ from the original, whether in terms of firm, country, sector, physical conditions, state of technical knowledge, or organizational skills and cultural norms.

Thus, in conditions of complexity and change—in other words, the conditions for managing innovation—there are no easily applicable recipes for successful management practice. This is one of the reasons why there are continuous swings in management fashion (see Box 3.3). Useful learning from the experience and analysis of others necessarily requires the following:

1. *A critical reading of the evidence underlying any claims to have identified the factors associated with management success.* Compare, for example, the explanations for the success of Honda in penetrating the US motorcycle market in the 1960s, given (1) by the Boston Consulting Group: exploitation of cost reductions through manufacturing investment and production learning in deliberately targeted and specific market segments;[13] and (2) by Richard Pascale: flexibility in product-market strategy in response to unplanned market signals, high-quality product design, manufacturing investment in response to market success.[14] The debate has recently been revived, although not resolved, in the *California Management Review.*[15]
2. A careful comparison of the context of successful management practice, with the context of the firm, industry, technology and country in which the practice might be reused. For example, one robust conclusion from management research and experience is that major ingredients in the successful implementation of innovation are effective linkages amongst functions within the firm, and with outside sources of relevant scientific and marketing knowledge. Although very useful to management, this knowledge has its limits. As we shall show later in Chapter 5, conclusions from a drug firm that the key linkages are between university research and product development are profoundly misleading for an automobile firm, where the key linkages are amongst product development, manufacturing and the supply chain. And even within each of these industries, important linkages may change over time. In the drug industry, the key academic disciplines are shifting from chemistry to include more biology. And in automobiles, computing and associated skills have become important for the development of 'virtual prototypes', and for linkages between product development, manufacturing and the supply chain.[16]

The management tools and techniques described in this book represent only very imperfectly the complexities and changes of the real world. As such, they can be no more than aids to systematic thinking, and to collective learning based on analysis and experience. Especially in conditions of complexity and change, *tacit knowledge* of individuals and groups (i.e. know-how that is based on experience, and that cannot easily be codified and reproduced) is of central importance, whether in the design of automobiles and drugs, or in the strategic management of innovation.

BOX 3.3 Swings in management fashion.

'Upsizing. After a decade of telling companies to shrink, management theorists have started to sing the praises of corporate growth.' (Feature title from *The Economist*, 10 February 1996, p. 81)

'Fire and forget? Having spent the 1990s in the throes of restructuring, re-engineering and downsizing, American companies are worrying about corporate amnesia.' (Feature title from *The Economist*, 20 April 1996, pp. 69–70)

Above are two not untypical examples of swings in management fashion and practice that reflect the inability of any recipe for good management to reflect the complexities of the real thing, and to put successful experiences in the past in the context of the function, firm, country, technology, etc. More recently, a survey of 475 global firms by Bain and Co. showed that the proportion of companies using management tools associated with *business process re-engineering, core competencies* and *total quality management* has been declining since the mid-1990s. But they still remain higher than the more recently developed tools associated with *knowledge management*, which have been less successful, especially outside North America. ('Management fashion: fading fads', *The Economist*, 22 April 2000, pp. 72–73)

3.2 Technology and Competitive Analysis

In the early 1980s, Michael Porter made a major contribution to the analysis of innovation in corporate strategy, by explicitly linking technology to the 'five forces' driving industry competition, and to the choice amongst a number of 'generic strategies' that must be made by the firm. His approach situates the firm's technological activities in a wider context of industry competition, and he develops a systematic SWOT analysis, based on competitive forces and firms' internal choices. His approach has been very influential, and it illustrates both the strengths and the weaknesses of the 'rationalist' approach to technology strategy, which is why we shall discuss it now.

The 'Five Forces' Driving Industry Competition

For Porter, the unit of analysis is the *industry* producing similar products. Profitable opportunities are fewer in mature industries. There are five forces driving industry competition, each of which generates opportunities and threats:

1. Relations with suppliers.
2. Relations with buyers.
3. New entrants.
4. Substitute products.
5. Rivalry amongst established firms.

According to Porter, '(t)he goal of competitive strategy . . . is to find a position in an industry where a company can best defend itself against these competitive forces or can influence them in its favour'.[17] Technological change can influence all the five forces, as is shown in Box 3.4.

Generic Innovation Strategies for Firms

According to Porter, there are also four generic market strategies from which firms must choose:

1. Overall cost leadership.
2. Product differentiation.
3. Cost focus.
4. Differentiation focus.

BOX 3.4 Threats and opportunities from changes in technology in Porter's competitive analysis.

Potential Entrants and Substitute Products

- Threats of new entrants can be *increased* through reduced economies of scale (e.g. telecommunications, publishing), and through substitute products (e.g. mini-computers, aluminium for steel cans)
- They can be *decreased* through 'lock-in' to technological standards (e.g. Microsoft), and through patent and other legal protection (e.g. most major ethical drugs)

Power of Suppliers over Buyers

- Can be *increased* by innovations that are more essential to the firm's inputs (e.g. microprocessors into computers)
- Can be *decreased* by innovations that reduce technological dependence on suppliers (engineering materials)

Rivalry amongst Established Firms

- Rival firms can *establish* a monopoly position through innovation (e.g. Polaroid in instant photography), or *destroy* a monopoly position through imitation (US General Electric in Brain Scanners)

As is shown in Table 3.1, the choice of product strategy has direct and obvious implications for the choice of technology strategy, in particular for priorities in product and process development. Thus, in consumer durable goods markets like automobiles, consumer electronics and 'white (kitchen) goods', we can observe a range of products with different trade-offs between performance and price, with each aiming at specific market segments, and each requiring different choices in the balance between product and process innovation. Porter insists on the importance of these choices: he argues that firms that get 'stuck in the middle' between cost and product quality will have low profits.

Innovation 'Leadership' versus 'Followership'

Finally, according to Porter, firms must also decide between two market strategies:

1. Innovation 'leadership'—where firms aim at being first to market, based on technological leadership. This requires a strong corporate commitment to creativity and risk-taking, with close linkages both to major sources of relevant new knowledge, and to the needs and responses of customers.
2. Innovation 'followership'—where firms aim at being late to market, based on imitating (learning) from the experience of technological leaders. This requires a strong commitment to competitor analysis and intelligence, to reverse engineering (i.e. testing, evaluating and taking to pieces competitors' products, in order to understand how they work, how they are made and why they appeal to customers), and to cost cutting and learning in manufacturing.

TABLE 3.1   Porter's generic technnology strategies.

	Cost leadership	Differentiation	Cost focus	Differentiaion focus
Product development	Lower material inputs	Enhance quality	Minimum features	Niche market
		Enhance features		
	Ease of manufacture			
		Deliverability		
	Improve logistics			
Process development	Learning curve	Precision	Minimize costs	Precision
	Economies of scale	Quality control		Quality control
		Response time		Response time

3.3 Assessment of Porter's Framework

The strengths of Porter's framework are precisely those we should expect from someone whose initial training was in industrial economics: a deep understanding of the competitive environment in which the business firm operates, and in which it must consciously try to *position* itself in its innovation strategy, as well as in other dimensions of corporate policy. Competitive rivalry provides the essential incentive for innovation. Technology can help give a firm a distinctive competence, enabling it to provide goods and services better than competitors. However, technology can never be completely monopolized. Knowledge always leaks out, and competencies can always be imitated, unless they are continually renewed. A distinctive competence must be sustainable over the long term. This can be decided by the firm only after a careful analysis of competitors and the market conditions in which it is embedded. In later analysis Porter also identifies the major influence of home country conditions on the innovation strategies of firms in global markets.[18] The main elements of the strategic task of *positioning* corporate technology strategy in the context of competition and markets will be discussed in Chapter 4.

Porter also argues that innovation strategy should aim to repel competitive threats, both from incumbents in the industry and potential new entrants, including new and substitute products based on new technological opportunities. Box 3.5 describes such a case: how radical change in semiconductor technology completely transformed the structure and competitive conditions in the US computer industry, over a period of 20 years, from a few integrated oligopolistic firms supplying essentially the office machinery market, to a disintegrated structure with many new entrants and a few remaining incumbents.

BOX 3.5 Technological change in the computer industry since 1970.[19]

The experience over the past 25 years of the US computer industry is a spectacular example of the power of technological change to transform completely the structure and competitive conditions in an industry. In the early 1970s, the industry was dominated by a few mainframe producers, some of whom were fully vertically integrated from basic circuitry through to distribution. Barriers to entry were high, suppliers relatively weak and customers had a limited range of choice. By the early 1990s, the industry had literally disintegrated, with independent firms (most of whom are new entrants since the 1970s) competing at each stage from basic circuitry to distribution. The main destabilizing factor has been the rapid rate of technical improvement in the microprocessor—the computer on a chip. This has drastically reduced the costs of computing, thereby lowering barriers to entry to the users of microprocessors and opening a whole range of potential applications outside mainframes (of which the personal computer is one of the most spectacular), and thereby creating a whole range of new opportunties for firms in systems and applications software.

However, this example also reveals the essential weaknesses of Porter's framework for analysis and action. As Martin Fransman has pointed out, technical personnel in firms like IBM in the 1970s were well aware of trends in semiconductor technology, and their possible effects on the competitive position of mainframe producers.[20] IBM in fact made at least one major contribution to developments in the revolutionary new technology: RISC microprocessors. Yet, in spite of this knowledge, none of the established firms proved capable over the next 20 years of achieving the primary objective of strategy, as defined by Porter: '. . . to find a position . . . where a company can best defend itself against these competitive forces or can influence them in its favour'.

Like many mainstream industrial economics, Porter's framework underestimates the power of technological change to transform industrial structures, and over-estimates the power of managers to decide and implement innovation strategies. Or, to put it another way, it underestimates the importance of *technological trajectories,* and of the firm-specific *technological and organizational competencies* to exploit them. Large firms in mainframe computers could not control the semiconductor trajectory. Although they had the necessary technological com-petencies, their organizational competencies were geared to selling expensive products in a focused market, rather than a proliferating range of cheap products in an increasing range of (as yet) unfocused markets.

These shortcomings of Porter's framework in its treatment of corporate tech-nology and organization lead it to underestimate the constraints on individual firms in choosing their innovation strategies. In particular:

- Firm *size* influences the choice between 'broad front' and 'focused' technologi-cal strategies. Large firms typically have 'broad front' strategies whilst small firms are 'focused'
- The firm's *established product base* and related technological competencies will influence the range of technological fields and industrial sectors in which it can hope to compete in future. Chemical-based firms do not diversify into making electronic products, and vice versa. It is very difficult (if not impos-ible) for a firm manufacturing traditional textiles to have an innovation strategy to develop and make computers[21]
- The *nature of its products and customers* will strongly influence its degree of choice between quality and cost. Compare food products, where there are typically a wide range of qualities and prices, with ethical drugs and passenger aeroplanes where product quality (i.e. safety) is rigidly controlled. Food firms therefore have a relatively wide range of potential innovation strategies to be chosen from amongst those described by Porter. The innovation strategies of drug and aircraft firms, on the other hand, inevitably require large-scale expenditures on product development and rigorous testing

In addition, technological opportunities are always emerging from advances in knowledge, so that:

- Firms and technologies do not fit tidily into preordained and static industrial structures. In particular, firms in the chemical and electrical–electronic indus-tries are typically active in a number of product markets, and also create new ones, like personal computers
- Technological advances can increase opportunities for profitable innovation

in so-called mature sectors. See, for example, the opportunities generated over the past 15 years by applications of IT in marketing, distribution and co-ordination in such firms as Benetton and Hotpoint.[22] See also the increasing opportunities for technology-based innovation in traditional service activities like banking, following massive investments in IT equipment and related software competencies[23]

- Firms do not become stuck in the middle as Porter predicted. John Kay has shown that firms with medium costs and medium quality compared to the competition achieve higher returns on investment than those with either low–low or high–high strategies.[24] Furthermore, some firms achieve a combination of high quality and low cost compared to competitors and this reaps high financial returns. These and related issues of product strategy will be discussed in Chapter 7

There is also little place in Porter's framework for the problems of *implementing* a strategy:

- Organizations which are large and specialized must be capable of learning and changing in response to new and often unforeseen opportunities and threats. This does not happen automatically, but must be consciously managed. In particular, the continuous transfer of knowledge and information across functional and divisional boundaries is essential for successful innovation
- Elements of Porter's framework (Box 3.3) have been contradicted as a result of organizational and related technological changes. The benefits of non-adversarial relations with both suppliers and customers have become apparent. Instead of bargaining in what appears to be a zero-sum game, co-operative links with customers and suppliers can increase competitiveness, by improving both the value of innovations to customers, and the efficiency with which they are supplied.[25] According to a survey of innovation strategies in Europe's largest firms, just over 35% replied that the technical knowledge they obtain from their suppliers and customers is very important for their own innovative activities.[26] The role of collaboration will be discussed more fully in Chapter 8

Finally, Porter returned to the subject of strategy in the mid-1990s.[27] He finally recognizes the importance of the path dependent nature of corporate activity by stressing the importance of 'fit' (i.e. coherence and balance) between the various elements of what firms have done in the past, and what they plan to do in the future (e.g. in their customers, products, forms of organization). He also makes a more questionable distinction between 'operational effectiveness' (i.e. doing things better) and 'strategy' (i.e. doing things that others cannot do), arguing that the latter is always essential. He has nothing to say about the contemporary problems of adopting business methods based on radical improvements in ICT technology (e.g. IT-based supply chains or accounting methods) that are necessary for corporate survival, but which will by themselves never be a source of sustainable competitive advantage. More generally, Porter seems uncomfortable in dealing with the inevitably high level of uncertainty found in emerging industries.

3.4 The Dynamic Capabilities of Firms

David Teece and Gary Pisano[28] integrate the various dimensions of innovation strategy identified above into what they call the 'dynamic capabilities' approach to corporate strategy, which underlines the importance of dynamic change and corporate learning:

> This source of competitive advantage, dynamic capabilities, emphasizes two aspects. First, it refers to the shifting character of the environment; second, it emphasizes the key role of strategic management in appropriately adapting, integrating and re-configuring internal and external organisational skills, resources and functional competencies towards a changing environment (p. 537).

> To be strategic, a capability must be honed to a user need (so that there are customers), unique (so that the products/services can be priced without too much regard for the competition), and difficult to replicate (so that profits will not be competed away) (p. 539).

> We advance the argument that the strategic dimensions of the firm are its managerial and organisational *processes,* its present *position,* and the *paths* available to it. By managerial *processes* we refer to the way things are done in the firm, or what might be referred to as its 'routines', or patterns of current practice and learning. By *position,* we refer to its current endowment of technology and intellectual property, as well as its customer base and upstream relations with suppliers. By *paths* we refer to the strategic alternatives available to the firm, and the attractiveness of the opportunities which lie ahead (pp. 537–541, our italics).

The role of position, paths and processes in the strategic management of innovation is examined in the next three chapters.

3.5 Innovation Strategy in Small Firms

Much of the above analysis has been directed to the problems of managing innovation in large, complex organizations where deliberate management action is necessary to co-ordinate or integrate specialized resources and skills. Like their large counterparts, small firms also need to concern themselves with their market position, their technological trajectories and competence-building, and their organizational processes. However, the challenges to management present themselves in somewhat different ways. In this section we summarize the key differences between innovation in small and large firms. At the end of the three subsequent chapters, we shall explore their implications for the strategic management of small firms in defining their positions, paths and processes. The discussion of small firms will necessarily be short, given the lack of systematic research on the majority of firms that are not particularly innovative, but which must necessarily cope with changing technology that impacts their business, as IT does today.

As Table 3.2 shows, debates about the role of small firms (<500 employees) in technological innovation excite strong opinions based on weak empirical evidence. The evidence also shows that, compared to large innovating firms, small innovating firms have the following characteristics:

- Similar *objectives—to develop* and combine technological and other competencies to provide goods and services that satisfy customers better than alternatives, and that are difficult to imitate

- Organizational strengths—ease of communication, speed of decision-making, degree of employee commitment and receptiveness to novelty. This is why small firms often do not need the formal strategies that are used in large firms to ensure communication and co-ordination
- Technological weaknesses—specialized range of technological competencies, inability to develop and manage complex systems, inability to fund long-term and risky programmes
- *Different* sectors—small firms make a greater contribution to innovation in certain sectors, such as machinery, instruments and software, than in chemicals, electronics and transport

TABLE 3.2   Misleading assertions about innovation in small firms.

Misleading assertions	*What the evidence shows*
'Small firms make most of the major innovations'	It depends on the product and the technology
'Small firms make few innovations since they do so little R&D'	They do lots of 'informal', 'part-time' and non-measured R&D, and produce a share of total innovations roughly proportionate to their output and employment
'Small firms are much more innovative than large firms, since they account for a higher share of innovations than of R&D'	Not if you include unmeasured, 'part-time' R&D
'New small firms create a lot of employment'	They also lose a lot, since they have high birth *and* death rates

We shall discuss the implications of these and other characteristics of small firms[29] for innovation strategy in subsequent chapters.

3.6 Summary and Further Reading

Innovation involves complexity and change, whether in the firm's technology, its organization or its economic environment. As a consequence, technological opportunities and threats are often difficult to identify, innovation strategies difficult to define, and outcomes difficult to predict. There are therefore no management *recipes* and tools that guarantee success. In all cases a capacity to learn from experience and analysis is essential. None the less, both research and experience point to three essential ingredients in corporate innovation strategies:

1. The *position* of the firm, compared to its competitors, in terms of its product, processes and technologies; and in terms of the national system of innovation in which it is embedded.
2. The technological *paths* open to the firm, given its accumulated competencies, and the emerging opportunities that these enable it to exploit.
3. The organizational *processes* followed by the firm, in order to integrate strategic learning across functional and divisional boundaries.

Two streams of literature are relevant to innovation and strategy. The first, from mainstream strategic management, is in general weak with respect to innovation, but a few writers consider some of the issues. For example, Porter's paper 'The technological dimension of competitive strategy' in *Research on Technological Innovation, Management and Policy*, Vol. 1 (UAI Press, London, 1983) epitomizes the rational planning approach to strategy, whereas the case for incrementalism is made by Henry Mintzberg's 'Rethinking strategic planning' in *Long Range Planning*, **27** (3), 12–30 (1994). Richard Whittington's *What is Strategy and Does it Matter?* (Routledge, London, 1994) presents both cases. Chapter 21 of John Kay's book *Foundations of Corporate Success: How businesses add value* (OUP, Oxford, 1993) is a masterly survey of the strengths and weaknesses of the strategic management literature. More recent contributions include C. Baden-Fuller and M. Pitt, *Strategic Innovation* (Routledge, 1996), A. Chandler, P. Hagstrom and O. Solvell, *The Dynamic Firm* (OUP, 1998), and R. Stacey, *Strategic Management and Organizational Dynamics: The challenge of complexity* (Prentice Hall, 3rd edn, 2000).

Second, there is a growing literature on technology strategy. Three books of edited papers contain excellent contributions: Mark Dodgson (ed.) *Technology Strategy and the Firm: Management and public* policy (Longman, Harlow, 1989); Mel Horwitch (ed.) *Technology and the Modern Corporation: A strategic perspective* (Pergamon, 1986); and Ray Loveridge and Martyn Pitt (eds) *The Strategic Management of Technological Innovation* (Wiley, Chichester, 1990). Paul Adler provides a comprehensive, but now dated review in 'Technology strategy: a guide to the literatures', in Rosenbloom, R. and Burgelman, R.A. (eds) *Research on Technological Innovation, Management and Policy* (Vol. 4, JAI Press, 1989, pp. 25–80), Goodman and Lawless, and Dussuage, Hart and Ramanantsoa identify a number of useful frameworks in *Technology and Strategy* (OUP, 1994) and *Strategic Technology Management* (Wiley, Chichester, 1994) respectively. UMIST maintains a website of tools and techniques for technology strategy at http://info.mcc.ac.uk/UMIST-CROMTEC/itm/itm.htm. More recent contributions include R. Burgelman, M. Maidique and S. Wheelwright, *Strategic Management of Technology and Innovation*, (Irwin, 2nd edn, 1996); M. Tushman and P. Anderson (eds) *Managing Strategic Innovation and Change: A collection of readings* (OUP, 1997); M. Dodgson, *The Management of Technological Innovation* (OUP, 2000); and K. Pavitt and E. Steinmueller, 'Technology in corporate strategy: change, continuity and the information revolution', chapter in Pettigrew, A. Thomas, H. and Whittington, R. (eds) *Handbook of Strategy and Management* (Sage Publications, 2001).

References

1   Ansoff, I. (1965) 'The firm of the future', *Harvard Business Review*, Sept.–Oct., 162–178.
2   Mintzberg, H. (1987) 'Crafting strategy', *Harvard Business Review*, July–August, 66–75. See also the interview with Mintzberg in *The Academy of Management Executive* (2000), **14** (3), 31–42.
3   Whittington, R. (1994) *What is Strategy and Does it Matter?* Routledge, London.
4   Kay, J. (1993) *Foundations of Corporate Success: How business strategies add value*. Oxford University Press, Oxford.
5   Starbuck, W. H. (1992) 'Strategizing in the real world', *International Journal of Technology Management*, special publication on 'Technological foundations of strategic management', **8** (1/2), 77–85.
6   Howard, N. (1983) 'A novel approach to nuclear fusion', *Dun's Business Month (dmi)*, **123**, 72, 76, November.
7   Berton, L. (1974) 'Nuclear energy stocks, set to explode', *Financial World (two)*, **141** (16 Jan.), 8–11; Freeman, C. (1984) Prometheus unbound', *Futures*, **16**, 495–507.

8   Duysters, G. (1995) *The Evolution of Complex Industrial Systems: The dynamics of major IT sectors.* MERIT, University of Maastricht, Maastricht; *The Economist* (1996) 'Fatal attraction: why AT&T was led astray by the lure of computers', management brief, 23 March; von Tunzelmann, N. (1997) 'Technological accumulation and corporate change in the electronics industry', in Gambardella, A. and Malerba, F. (eds) *The Organization of Scientific and Technological Research in Europe,* Cambridge University Press (1999).

9   See 'The failure of new media', *The Economist,* 19 August 2000: 59–60

10 See 'A survey of e-entertainment' *The Economist,* 7 October 2000.

11 Sapsed, J. (2001) *Restricted Vision: Strategizing under Uncertainty.* Imperial College Press, London.

12 Pasteur, L. (1854) Address given on the inauguration of the Faculty of Science, University of Lille, 7 December. Reproduced in *Oxford Dictionary of Quotations.* Oxford University Press.

13 Boston Consulting Group (1975) *Strategy Alternatives for the British Motorcycle Industry.* HMSO, London.

14 Pascale, R. (1984) 'Perspectives on strategy: the real story behind Honda's success', *California Management Review,* **26,** 47–72.

15 Mintzberg, H., R. Pascale, M, Goold and R. Rumelt (1996) 'The "Honda effect" revisited', *California Management Review,* **38,** 78–117.

16 Lee, G. (1995) 'Virtual prototyping on personal computers', *Mechanical Engineering,* **117** (July), 70–73.

17 Porter, M. (1980) *Competitive Strategy.* Free Press, New York.

18 Porter, M. (1990) *The Competitive Advantage of Nations.* Macmillan, London.

19 Manasian, D. (1993) 'The computer industry: reboot system and start again', Computer Industry Survey. *The Economist,* 27 February. *The Economist* (1993) 'What went wrong at IBM', 16 January, 23–25; Snell, I. (1994) 'R&D configurational strategies in the M-form: the case of Hewlett Packard', M.Sc. dissertation, Science Policy Research Unit, University of Sussex, UK; Steinmueller, E. (1995) 'The US software industry: an interpretative history', in Mowery, D. (ed.), *The International Computer Software Industry.* Oxford University Press, Oxford, pp. 15–52.

20 Fransman, M. (1994) 'Information, knowledge, vision and theories of the firm', *Industrial and Corporate Change,* **3,** 713–757.

21 Patel, P. and K. Pavitt (1998) 'The wide (and increasing) spread of technological competencies in the world's largest firms: a challenge to conventional wisdom', in Chandler, A., Hagstrom, P. and Solvell, O. (eds), *The Dynamic Firm,* Oxford University Press, Oxford.

22 Baden-Fuller, C. and J. Stopford, (1994) *Rejuvenating the Mature Business: The competitive challenge,* Harvard Business School Press, Boston, Mass.; Belussi, F. (1989) 'Benetton—a case study of corporate strategy for innovation in traditional sectors', in Dodgson, M. (ed.), *Technology Strategy and the Firm: Management and public policy.* Longman, London, pp. 116–133.

23 Barras, R. (1990) 'Interactive innovation in financial and business services: the vanguard of the service revolution', *Research Policy,* **19,** 215–238.

24 Kay, J. (1996) 'Oh Professor Porter, whatever did you do?', *Financial Times,* 10 May: 17.

25 Lamming, R. (1993) *Beyond Partnership,* Prentice-Hall, Hemel Hempstead.

26 Arundel, A., G. van de Paal and L. Soete (1995) *Innovation Strategies of Europe's Largest Industrial Firms.* PACE Report, MERIT, University of Limbourg, Maastricht.

27 Porter, M. (1996) 'What is strategy?', *Harvard Business Review,* Nov.–Dec., 61–78.

28 Teece, D. and G. Pisano (1994) 'The dynamic capabilities of firms: an introduction', *Industrial and Corporate Change,* **3,** 537–556.

29 Rothwell, R. and M. Dodgson (1990) 'Innovation and size of firm', in *The Handbook of Industrial Innovation,* Elgar, Aldershot. MERIT, University of Maastricht, Maastricht; *The Economist* (1996) 'Fatal attraction: why AT&T was led astray by the lure of computers', management brief, 23 March; von Tunzelmann, N. (1997) 'Technological accumulation and corporate change in the electronics industry', in Gambardella, A. and Malerba, F. (eds) *The Organization of Scientific and Technological Research in Europe,* Cambridge University Press (1999).

Chapter 4

POSITIONS: THE NATIONAL AND COMPETITIVE ENVIRONMENT

Two features of the firm's environment have a major influence on its innovation strategy: first, the *national system of innovation* in which the firm is embedded, and which in part defines its range of choices in dealing with opportunities and threats; and second, its *market position* compared to *competing firms,* which in part defines the innovation-based opportunities and threats that it faces.

4.1 National Systems of Innovation

On 14 May 1990, the cover story in *Business Week* was entitled 'The stateless corporation'. The main thrust of the analysis was that global firms now rely hardly at all on their home—or any other one—country for their operations, since they compete and increasingly produce in global markets. On the other hand, analysts like Porter[1] and his colleagues[2] have shown that business firms—and even the largest ones competing in global markets—are strongly influenced in their choice of technological strategies by the conditions existing in their home countries. This is because even global firms draw on mainly one—or perhaps two—countries for their strategic skills and expertise in formulating and executing their innovation strategies. As we shall see in Chapter 6, only about 12% of the innovative activities of the world's largest 500, technologically active firms were located outside their home countries in the 1990s, compared to about 25% of their production and much larger shares of sales (see Chapter 6).[3] As a consequence, we find that the technological strengths and weaknesses of countries are reflected in their major firms.

In Table 4.1 we see that, in the 1990s, the largest numbers of European firms amongst the technical leaders were to be found in the technological fields of industrial and fine chemicals, and defence-related technologies (i.e. aerospace), which are fields of national technological strength, whilst the reverse is the case

TABLE 4.1   Nationalities of top 20 firms patenting in the USA in 1992–96.

Broad technological field	Europe	USA	Japan	South Korea	Canada
Industrial chemicals	9	9	2		
Defence-related technologies	9	11	0		
Fine chemicals	7	12	1		
Telecommunications	6	6	7		1
Mechanical engineering	5	9	6		
Composite materials	4	9	7		
Motor vehicles	4	4	12		
Electrical machinery	4	7	8	1	
Raw material-related technologies	4	16	0		
Electronic capital goods & components	2	8	9	1	
Electronic consumer goods	2	3	14	1	

Source: P. Patel, *Large Firm Database*, SPRU, University of Sussex. Based on data provided by the US Patent Office.

in electronic capital and consumer goods. Japanese firms predominate in consumer electronics and motor vehicle technologies, and US firms in fine chemicals and in raw materials-based (i.e. oil, gas and food) and defence-related technologies, again reflecting the technological strengths of their home countries.

The strategic importance to corporations of home countries' technological competencies would matter little if they were all more or less the same. But Table 4.1 and other data[4] show that they are not. Patterns of sectoral specialization differ greatly: for example, the Japanese pattern of strengths and weaknesses is almost the opposite of that in the USA. In addition, Table 4.2 illustrates that countries differ in both the level and the rate of increase in the resources devoted by business firms to innovative activities. It shows, for selected OECD countries, trends over 31 years in business-funded R&D as a share of GDP (gross domestic product). As we have already seen, R&D captures corporate innovative activities only imperfectly. But it is one of the best available indicators of aggregate innovative investments, and international differences significantly influence national economic growth and trade performance.[5]

Three major conclusions emerge from Table 4.2. First, and contrary to what many observers continue to assume, Europe and Japan did not progressively and smoothly catch up with the USA, which was the technological leader in the period after the Second World War. Switzerland has always been amongst the leaders and remains so. As early as 1971, Germany and Japan overtook the USA and progressively increased their lead until the late 1980s. This was reflected in the relative performance in R&D and sales growth of the large firms based in these countries.[6] Since then, the trend has changed, with the shares of business-funded R&D in GDP stabilizing in Japan, declining in Germany, and increasing in the USA. At the same time, the three Scandinavian countries have continued to increase their shares, with the growth of major firms in pharmaceuticals and telecommunications.

Second, the other early leaders of the late 1960s—the UK and the Netherlands—have not reacted to the growing competition like the USA in the 1990s.

TABLE 4.2 Trends in business-funded R&D as percentage of GDP.

	1967	1971	1975	1979	1983	1987	1991	1995	1996	1997	1998
Switzerland	1.78	1.67	1.67	1.74	1.67	1.92	1.79		1.80		
USA	0.99	0.97	0.98	1.05	1.31	1.37	1.60	1.54	1.65	1.71	1.80
Japan	0.83	1.09	1.12	1.19	1.59	1.82	2.13	1.90	1.99	2.06	
Germany	0.94	1.13	1.11	1.32	1.48	1.80	1.58	1.36	1.35	1.38	1.42
Sweden	0.71	0.80	0.96	1.11	1.45	1.73	1.69	2.32		2.56	
Denmark	0.34	0.39	0.41	0.42	0.53	0.66	0.86	0.88	0.99	1.00	
Finland	0.30	0.44	0.44	0.53	0.73	0.99	1.10	1.33		1.67	
Canada	0.40	0.38	0.33	0.39	0.46	0.57	0.58	0.68	–	0.73	0.75
UK	1.00	0.81	0.80	0.82	0.86	1.02	0.99	0.92	0.88	0.87	
Netherlands	1.12	1.02	0.97	0.86	0.89	1.11	0.91	0.86	0.94		

Source: OECD.

The share of business-funded R&D in GDP in both countries declined considerably in the 1970s, and has not recovered to earlier levels.

Third, the rate of increase in corporate commitment to R&D in a country is not closely related to its industrial structure. Compare Finland and Canada, both of whose economies rely heavily on natural resources; Finland's R&D expenditures have increased even more rapidly than Japan's as a share of GDP, whilst Canada's increased only slightly.

Thus, the national systems of innovation in which a firm is embedded matter greatly, since they strongly influence both the direction and the vigour of its own innovative activities. Several approaches have been taken on the nature and impact of such national systems.[7] Our own is to identify the main national factors that influence the rate and direction of technological innovation in a country: more specifically, the national market *incentives and pressures* to which firms have to respond, their *competencies in production and research*, and the *institutions of corporate governance*.[8] We shall now discuss each of these in turn.

Incentives and Pressures: National Demand and Competitive Rivalry

Patterns of national demands Those concerned to explain international patterns of innovative activities have long recognized the important influence of local demand and price conditions on patterns of innovation in local firms.[9] Strong local 'demand pull' for certain types of product generates innovation opportunities for local firms, especially when the demand depends on face-to-face interactions with customers.

In Table 4.3 we identify the main factors that influence local demands for innovation, and give some examples. In addition to the obvious examples of local buyers' tastes, we identify:

- Local (private and public) investment activities, which create innovative opportunities for local suppliers of machinery and production inputs, where competence is accumulated mainly through experience in designing, building and operating machinery

TABLE 4.3   Factors influencing national demands for innovation.

Factors in	Examples
Local buyers' tastes	• Quality food and clothing in France and Italy • Reliable machinery in Germany
Private investment activities	• Automobile and other downstream investments stimulating innovation in computer-aided design and robots in Japan, Italy, Sweden and Germany
Public investment activities	• Railways in France • Medical instruments in Sweden • Coal-mining machinery in the UK (<1979)
Input prices	• Labour-saving innovations in the USA • Europe–USA differences in automobile technology • Environmental technology in Scandinavia • Synthetic fertilizers in Germany
Local natural resources	• Innovations in oil and gas, mineral ores, and food and agriculture in North America, Scandinavia and Australia

- Local production input prices, where international differences can help generate very different pressures for innovation (e.g. the effects of different petrol prices on the design and related competencies in automobiles in the USA and Europe). High prices can also generate pressure for substitute products, like synthetic fertilizers in Germany at the beginning of the twentieth century
- Local natural resources, which create opportunities for innovation in both upstream extraction and downstream processing

Competitive rivalry   Innovation is always difficult and often upsetting to established interests and habits, so that local demands by themselves do not create the necessary conditions for innovation. Both case studies and statistical analysis show that competitive rivalry stimulates firms to invest in innovation and change, since their very existence will be threatened if they do not.[10] A comparison by Lacey Thomas of public policies towards the pharmaceutical industries in Britain and France has shown that the former was more successful in creating a demanding local competitive environment conducive to the emergence of British firms amongst the world leaders.[11] German strength in chemicals is based on three large and technologically dynamic firms, BASF, Bayer and Hoechst, rather than on one super-large firm. Similarly, Table 4.1 shows that Japanese strength in consumer electronics is based on numerous technologically active firms rather than a few giants. Relatively smaller size also reduces the severity of the task of management to maintain corporate entrepreneurship. This is because managers can spend more time familiarizing themselves with the innovative potentialities of the various businesses, and can thereby avoid the dangers of managing divisions purely through financial indicators (see Chapter 6).

Thus although corporate policy-makers in large firms might often be tempted in the short term to avoid strong competition—and to reap extra monopoly profits—by merging with their competitors, the long-term costs could be considerable. Public policy-makers should be persuaded by the evidence that creating gigantic firms does not increase innovation, quite the contrary, and therefore take countervailing measures. Lack of competitive rivalry makes firms less fit to compete on global markets through innovation.

Competencies in Production and Research

Local demand opportunities and competitive pressures will not result in innovation unless firms have the competencies that enable them to respond. Corporate and national competencies in *production* and in *research* are essential.

There are significant differences amongst apparently similar European countries in the level of *production* competencies. In the 1980s and 1990s, Professor Prais and his colleagues made detailed comparisons of the level of education of the workforce in five European countries (France, the Federal Republic of Germany, the Netherlands, Switzerland and the UK). Although similar at the top of the educational pyramid, the differences amongst countries in the proportion without any qualifications were particularly striking, varying from less than about a quarter in Germany and Switzerland to nearly two-thirds in Britain. More detailed case studies comparing British and German firms show that these differences in skills make an important competitive difference, with productivity in the German firms being as much as twice as high, with equal or superior product quality, because German workers are more skilled in repairs and in learning new techniques more quickly.[12]

Behind the differences in vocational skills are important international differences in basic education, which will become critical with the growth of the knowledge economy. These have recently been revealed in an OECD survey, some of the results of which are summarized in Table 4.4. The first three columns compare three major dimensions of literacy and the fourth gives the share of the population with only rudimentary levels of skills, judged inadequate for coping in modern society. A number of conclusions emerge from this table and related sources:

- The survey confirms the higher level of skills in Germany than in the UK, but not to such a striking extent, probably because the survey includes inhabitants of the old German Democratic Republic, who are not as well educated as their West German counterparts, who were the subject of the earlier studies by Prais
- In spite of a well-developed system of higher education, the US ranking is not the highest, in part because of a relatively large share of the population with Level 1 (i.e. lowest level) skills. The same is true of the UK
- The Czech Republic and (to a lesser degree) Hungary have skills comparable to those in Western European countries which, combined with their currently low salary levels, may help explain their attractiveness to international investors
- The Scandinavian countries have the highest levels of skills, and the smallest proportions of the population with lowest level skills, which may partly explain their relatively high levels of adoption of Internet-related technologies[13]

TABLE 4.4   Rankings in international literacy survey* (population aged 16–64, 1994–98).

Country	Prose skills* (USA = 100)	Document skills* (USA = 100)	Quantitative skills* (USA = 100)	% of population with quantitative skills at level 1†
Sweden	110	113	111	7.5
Denmark	100	110	108	9.6
Czech Republic	98	106	108	15.7
Norway	105	111	108	8.5
Germany	101	106	107	14.4
Netherlands	103	107	105	10.5
Finland	105	108	104	10.4
Canada	102	104	102	16.6
USA	100	100	100	20.7
Hungary	88	93	98	33.8
UK	97	100	97	21.8
Ireland	97	97	96	22.6
Portugal	81	82	84	48.0
Chile	81	82	76	50.1

*Literacy: Understanding and employing printed information in daily activities at work, at home, and in the community, and developing knowledge and potential.
*Prose: Understanding text.
*Document: Locating and using written information.
*Quantitative: Applying arithmetic operations to numbers in written material.
Country rankings: Sorted according to Quantitative Index. USA = 100.
†Level 1 skills: Lowest on five-point scale. Considered insufficient for coping with modern society.
Source: *Literacy in the Information Age: Final report of the International Adult Literacy Survey*, Paris, OECD, 2000, Tables 2.1 and 2.2.

National competencies in *research* are also an important input into firms' technological capabilities. Especially in large firms, R&D laboratories actively seek support, knowledge and skills from national basic research activities, especially in universities. The knowledge they seek is mainly tacit and person-embodied, which explains why language and distance are real barriers to co-operation and why the firms generally prefer to deal with domestic universities.[14] It also explains why the differing national levels of production of basic research, measured in Table 4.5 as the number of papers per head of population, are similar to the national levels of investment in technology, measured in Table 4.2. This is because technology in dynamic business firms demands high-quality investment in national basic research. The apparent exception is Japan, but this simply reflects the lag in the basic research system, which is now expanding rapidly—in quantity and quality—in response to the world frontier technological investments by business firms.[15]

These differences in national endowments of research and production competencies influence managers in their search to identify technological fields and related product markets where specific national systems of innovation are likely to be most supportive to corporate innovative activities. For example, firms in the UK and USA are particularly strong in software and pharmaceuticals, both of which require strong basic research and graduate skills, but few production skills; they are therefore particularly well matched to local skill structures. Similarly, Japanese strength in consumer electronics and automobiles is particularly well matched to its local strength in production skills, as are the German strengths in mechanical engineering.

TABLE 4.5   Comparative performance of national systems of basic research.

Country	Papers per 1000 population in 1993
Switzerland	1.471
Sweden	1.297
Denmark	1.074
Finland	0.964
Netherlands	0.962
UK	0.912
USA	0.886
Norway	0.817
Ireland	0.631
France	0.621
Germany	0.569
Singapore	0.452
Japan	0.416
Italy	0.362
Spain	0.329
Taiwan	0.225
Portugal	0.121
South Korea	0.068
India	0.016

Source: Lattimore, R. and J. Ravesz (1996) *Australian Science: Performance from published papers*. Bureau of Industry Economics, Report 96/3, Australian Government Printing Office, Canberra. Table 4.10. Based on data provided by the Institute of Scientific Information.

In many countries, national advantages in natural resources and traditional industries have been fused with related competencies in broad technological fields that then become the basis for technological advantage in new product fields. Figure 4.1 illustrates how this happened in Denmark, Sweden and Switzerland. It shows, with some inevitable simplification, how strong technological competencies emerged over time in specific fields in the three countries. In all cases, linkages with established fields of strength were the basis of local technological accumulation. This accumulation reinforced corporate and national competencies and created the potential for entry and competitiveness in new product fields. Firm-specific investments in technology and related basic research and training in universities led to the mastery of broad technological fields with multiple potential applications: metallurgy and materials in Sweden, machinery in Switzerland and Sweden, and chemistry and (more recently) biology in Switzerland and Denmark.[16] Another example is the development of chemical engineering in the USA, in response to the challenges and opportunities of refining petrol.[17]

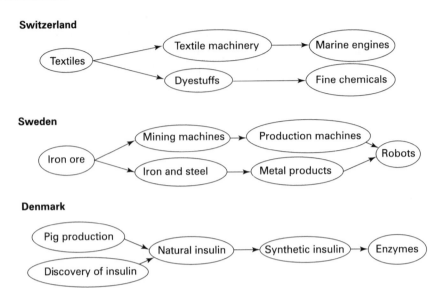

FIGURE 4.1   Technological accumulation in three countries.

Institutions: Finance, Management and Corporate Governance

Firms' innovative behaviours are strongly influenced by the competencies of their managers and the ways in which their performance is judged and rewarded (and punished). Methods of judgement and reward vary considerably amongst countries, according to their national systems of *corporate governance*: in other words, the systems for exercising and changing corporate ownership and control. In broad terms, we can distinguish two systems: one practised in the USA and UK, and the other in Japan, Germany and its neighbours, such as Sweden and Switzerland. In his book *Capitalism against Capitalism,* Michel Albert calls the first the 'Anglo-Saxon' and the second the 'Nippon–Rhineland' variety.[18] A lively debate continues about the essential characteristics and performance of the two systems, in terms of innovation and other performance variables. Table 4.6 is based on a variety of sources, and tries to identify the main differences that affect innovative performance.

In the UK and the USA, corporate ownership (shareholders) is separated from corporate control (managers), and the two are mediated through an active stock market. Investors can be persuaded to hold shares only if there is an expectation of increasing profits and share values. They can shift their investments relatively easily. On the other hand, in countries with governance structures like those of Germany or Japan, banks, suppliers and customers are more heavily locked into the firms in which they invest. Until the 1990s, countries strongly influenced by German and Japanese traditions persisted in investing heavily in R&D in established firms and technologies, whilst the US system has since been more effective in generating resources to exploit radically new opportunities in IT and biotechnology.

TABLE 4.6 The effects of corporate governance on innovative activities.

Characteristics	Anglo-Saxon	Nippon–Rhineland
Ownership	Individuals, pension funds, insurers	Companies, individuals, banks
Control	Dispersed, arm's length	Concentrated, close and direct
Management	Business schools (USA), accountants (UK)	Engineers with business training
Evaluation of R&D investments	Published information	Insider knowledge
Strengths	• Responsive to radically new technological opportunities • Efficient use of capital	• Higher priority to R&D than to dividends for shareholders • Remedial investment in failing firms
Weaknesses	• Short-termism • Inability to evaluate firm-specific intangible assets	• Slow to deal with poor investment choices • Slow to exploit radically new technologies

During the 1980s, the Nippon–Rhineland model seemed to be performing better. As we saw in Table 4.2, aggregate R&D expenditures were on a healthy upward trend, and so were indicators of aggregate economic performance. Since then, there have been growing doubts. The aggregate technological and economic indicators have been performing less well. Japanese firms have proved unable to repeat in telecommunications, software, microprocessors and computing their technological and competitive successes in consumer electronics.[19] German firms have been slow to exploit radically new possibilities in IT and biotechnology,[20] and there have been criticisms of expensive and unrewarding choices in corporate strategy, like the entry of Daimler Benz into aerospace.[21] At the same time, US firms appear to have learned important lessons, especially from the Japanese in manufacturing technology, and to have reasserted their eminence in IT and biotechnology. The 1990s have also seen sustained increases in productivity in US industry. According to *The Economist* in 1995, in a report entitled 'Back on top?', one professor at the Harvard Business School believed that people will look back at this period as 'a golden age of entrepreneurial management in the USA'.[22]

However, some observers have concluded that the strong US performance in innovation cannot be satisfactorily explained simply by the combination of entrepreneurial management, a flexible labour force, and a well-developed stock exchange. The US experience has not been repeated in the other Anglo-Saxon country with apparently similar characteristics—the UK (see Tables 4.2, 4.4 and 4.5). They argue that the groundwork for US corporate success in exploiting IT and biotechnology was laid initially by the US Federal Government, with the large-scale investments by the Defense Department in California in electronics, and by the National Institutes of Health in the scientific fields underlying biotechnology.[23] In addition, we should not write off Germany and Japan too soon. The former is now dealing with the dirt and inefficiency of the former East Germany[24] (the inclusion of which in official statistics is one reason for the German decline in the 1990s in business R&D as a share of GDP in Table 4.2). Japanese firms like Sony are world leaders in exploiting in home electronics the opportunities opened up by advances in digital technology. And Scandinavian countries are now well ahead of the rest of the world (including the USA) in mobile tele-phony,[25] as well as in more general indicators of skills and knowledge (see Tables 4.2, 4.4 and 4.5 above). The jury is still out.

Learning from Foreign Systems of Innovation

Firms have at least three reasons for monitoring and learning from the develop-ment of technological, production and organizational competencies of national systems of innovation other than those in which they are embedded themselves, and especially from those that are growing and strong:

1. They will be the sources of firms with a strong capacity to compete through innovation. For example, beyond Japan, other East Asian countries are de-veloping strong innovation systems. In particular, business firms in South Korea and Taiwan now spend more than 2% of GDP on R&D, which puts them up with the advanced OECD countries. By the early 1990s, Taiwan was granted more patents in the USA than Sweden, and together with South Korea, is catching up fast with Italy, the Netherlands and Switzerland. Other Asian countries like Malaysia are also developing strong technological competencies. Following the collapse of the Russian Empire, we can also anticipate the re-emergence of strong systems of innovation in the Czech Republic and Hungary (see Table 4.4).
2. They are also potential sources of improvement in the corporate management of innovation, and in national systems of innovation. However, as we shall see below, understanding, interpreting and learning general lessons from foreign systems of innovation is a difficult task. Effectiveness in innovation has become bound up with wider national and ideological interests, which makes it more difficult to separate fact from belief. Both the business press and business education are dominated by the English language and Anglo-Saxon examples: very little is available in English on the management of innovation in Germany; and much of the information about the management of innova-tion in Japan has been via interpretations of researchers from North America.
3. Finally, firms can benefit more specifically from the technology generated in foreign systems of innovation. Table 4.7 shows that a high proportion of large European firms attach great importance to foreign sources of technical knowl-edge, whether obtained through affiliated firms (i.e. direct foreign investment) and joint ventures, links with suppliers and customers, or reverse engineer-ing. In general, they find it is more difficult to learn from Japan than from North America and elsewhere in Europe, probably because of greater dis-tances—physical, linguistic and cultural. Perhaps more surprising, European firms find it most difficult to learn from foreign publicly funded research. This is because effective learning involves more subtle linkages than straightfor-ward market transactions: for example, the membership of informal pro-fessional networks. This public knowledge is often seen as a source of

TABLE 4.7 Outside sources of technical knowledge for large European firms: percentage judging the source as very important.

	Home country	Other Europe	North America	Japan
Affiliated firms	48.9	42.9	48.2	33.6
Joint ventures	36.6	35.0	39.7	29.4
Independent suppliers	45.7	40.3	30.8	24.1
Independent customers	51.2	42.2	34.8	27.5
Public research	51.1	26.3	28.3	12.9
Reverse engineering	45.3	45.9	40.0	40.0

Source: Arundel, A., G. van der Paal and L. Soete (1995) *Innovation Strategies of Europe's Largest Industrial Firms*. PACE Report, MERIT, University of Limbourg, Maastricht. Reproduced by permission of Anthony Arundel.

potential world innovative advantage, and we shall see in Chapter 6 that firms are increasingly active in trying to access foreign sources. In contrast, knowledge obtained through market transactions and reverse engineering enables firms to catch up, and keep up, with competitors. East Asian firms have been very effective over the past 25 years in making these channels an essential feature of their rapid technological learning (see Box 4.1)

BOX 4.1 Technology strategies of latecomer firms in East Asia.

The spectacular modernization in the past 25 years of the East Asian 'dragon' countries—Hong Kong, South Korea, Singapore and Taiwan—has led to lively debate about its causes. Michael Hobday has provided important new insights into how business firms in these countries succeeded in rapid learning and technological catch-up, in spite of underdeveloped domestic systems of science and technology, and of lack of technologically sophisticated domestic customers.

Government policies provided the favourable general economic climate: export orientation; basic and vocational education, with strong emphasis on industrial needs; and a stable economy, with low inflation and high savings. However, of major importance were the strategies and policies of specific business firms for the effective assimilation of foreign technology.

The main mechanism for catching up was the same in electronics, footwear, bicycles, sewing machines and automobiles, namely the 'OEM' (original equipment manufacture) system. OEM is a specific form of subcontracting, where firms in catching-up countries produce goods to the exact specification of a foreign transitional company (TNC) normally based in a richer and technologically more advanced country. For the TNC, the purpose is to cut costs, and to this end offers assistance to the latecomer firms in quality control, choice of equipment, and engineering and management training.

OEM began in the 1960s, and became more sophisticated in the 1970s. The next stage in the mid-1980s was ODM (own design and manufacture), where the latecomer firms learned to design products for the buyer. The last stage was OBM (own brand manufacture) when latecomer firms market their own products under their own brand name (e.g. Samsung, Acer) and compete head-on with the leaders.

For each stage of catching up, the company's technology position must be matched with a corresponding market position, as is shown below:

Stage	Technology position	Market position
1.	Assembly skills Basic production Mature products	Passive importer pull Cheap labour Distribution by buyers
2.	Incremental process change Reverse engineering	Active sales to foreign buyer Quality and cost-based
3.	Full production skills Process innovation Product design	Advanced production sales International marketing department Markets own design
4.	R&D Product innovation	Product marketing push Own brand product range and sales
5.	Frontier R&D R&D linked to market needs Advanced innovation	Own brand push In-house market research Independent distribution

Source: Hobday, M. (1995) *Innovation in East Asia: The challenge to Japan*. Elgar, Guildford.

4.2 Coping with Competitors

In defining their innovation strategies, firms must be in a position to answer four questions about their competitors' innovative resources compared to their own:

- How do they compare in terms of size and composition?
- How efficiently are they used?
- How effectively do we learn from their knowledge and experience?
- How do we maintain our own innovative advantages?

In this context, it is important to distinguish knowledge of what technological developments are being undertaken by competitors, from knowledge of how the innovations can be made to work in practice. As we shall now see, the former can be obtained relatively quickly through *information-gathering* activities, whilst the latter requires extensive investments of resources and time in *benchmarking* and *learning* activities. Finally, in the light of the evidence available to it, corporate management must evaluate the market *position* of its innovation strategy in the light of intentions and competencies of competitors, and of the characteristics of its innovations: in particular, should it aim at innovation leadership or followership?

Large firms are surprisingly well informed about the technological activities of their competitors. According to a study by Mansfield, large US firms typically know about rivals' product development characteristics and plans within 6–12 months.[26] There are numerous methods of obtaining information about competitors' innovative strategies, all of which are imperfect, and some of which are of doubtful morality or legality. The sources based on publicly available literature are summarized in Table 4.8. The range and ease of access to these and other sources has been increasing rapidly with development of the Internet.

TABLE 4.8   Public information sources on corporate innovative activities.

Nature of information	Sources	Strengths	Limits
Corporate R&D expenditures	• Company Annual Reports • *R&D Scoreboard* (June each year. UK firms and international comparisons) www.innovation.gov.uk/ finance/ • European Commission (1997) *Second European Report on S&T Indicators*, EUR 17639	• Easy access	• No detail of projects • Misses innovative activities outside R&D
Corporate patents and scientific publications	• US Patent Office (USPO) www.almaden.ibm.com/cs/ ibm_pat_srvr/homepage.html www.uspto.gov/web/offices/ ac/ido/oecp/taf/tafp.html • European Patent Office www.Austria.EU.net/epo/ • Private consultants (CHI, Derwent) www.chiresearch.com/ • Patel and Vega (1998), *Technology Strategies of Large European Firms*, P.R.Patel@sussex.ac.uk • Web of Science (Science Citation Index) wos.mimas.ac.uk	• Comparisons possible in great detail • Identifies possible entrants as well as incumbents • Citations and joint authorship identify networks and alliances	• Choosing relevant patent classes • Dealing with firms with several names • Non-patented innovations
Public announcements and press analysis	• Conferences • Media • Trade press	• Direct and detailed signal of corporate intentions	• Distortions for financial or marketing reasons

Comparisons of Effectiveness through Benchmarking

'Benchmarking' goes beyond the routine collection of publicly available information. It consists of comparisons amongst competitor companies on specific dimensions of corporate performance—beyond financial performance—with the purpose of identifying and catching up with best practice. The approach started in the 1980s, when US firms found that their loss of market share to Japanese firms reflected underlying deficiencies in both manufacturing and product development. A pioneer was Xerox, who made systematic comparisons with Japanese competitors and found huge deficiencies in performance, as measured by the frequency of assembly line rejects, defects per machine, and the costs and time required for product development.[27] The improvement resulting from conscious policies to overcome these deficiencies has led to both higher customer satisfaction and higher financial returns on assets.

In some cases, groups of firms have funded academics and consultants to make the inter-firm comparisons. Probably the best known and most influential has been the International Motor Vehicle Programme at MIT. Its favourable conclusions in the late 1980s about production efficiency in Japanese automobile companies, compared to US and European counterparts, had major effects, both in mobilizing laggard firms to do better, and in developing new concepts—such as *lean production* compared to mass production—which are now common currency amongst both managers and academics. A similar approach to benchmarking has been applied to the semiconductor industry in a programme of studies at Berkeley.[28]

In Europe, periodic surveys of performance and problems in manufacturing have been undertaken since the 1980s.[29] And after 1993, Chris Voss and his colleagues at London Business School made detailed and comprehensive benchmarking surveys of manufacturing and design in companies in Britain and other European countries. Some of their findings are summarized in Box 4.2.

BOX 4.2 Britain's manufacturing and design, according to Chris Voss and colleagues.[30]

- Only 2% of the manufacturing sites can be said to be truly world class—but another 42% have most of the practices in place to become world class
- The food industry is very strong, particularly in its logistics; aerospace/automotive industry sites, on the other hand, consistently lag in terms of both practice and performance
- Purchasing power can be a force for good: companies which supply certain types of large organization (such as food retailers and the computer industry) have significantly better practice and/or performance
- Leaders (the top 10% of companies on the scale) are eight times more likely to use external benchmarks to improve their business than laggards (the lower 10%)
- There are no quick fixes—the leading companies are better than the laggards because they have adopted best practices and improved their performance at every level
- Compared to firms in Britain, those in Germany made higher investments and had higher productivity growth, but not enough to achieve lower costs than British plants
- In manufacturing practice and performance both British and German leaders rank with the best in the world, but Britain has a long tail of low achievers
- However, design in the British firms consistently lags the German firms

---

According to another British survey of benchmarking by Coopers & Lybrand, managers claim that benchmarking is practised in 78% of the top 1000 companies, and achieves positive results.[31] It is more common in customer-facing areas (customer service, marketing and sales, logistics) than in manufacturing, and is least common in product development and R&D. This balance probably reflects the greater degree of difficulty in obtaining accurate information on competitors' performance in the manufacturing and R&D functions. Customer satisfaction can be assessed by surveys, and some of them are in the public domain (e.g. the surveys of US automobile users by J.D. Power Associates; consumer journals like *Which?*). In quality management various awards have long been established which allow firms to benchmark their quality systems, such as the European Quality Award, the Baldridge Award in the USA and the Deming Prize in Japan. More recently, specialized organizations have now emerged to collect and compare performance indicators in manufacturing and product development.

Whatever the corporate function concerned, all companies stress the importance of being willing to commit substantial corporate resources to benchmarking activities. This is because, as we shall now see, imitation and learning are neither cheap nor easy.

Learning and Imitating

Whilst information on competitors' innovations is relatively cheap and easy to obtain, corporate experience shows that knowledge of how to replicate competitors' product and process innovations is much more costly and time-consuming to acquire. Such imitation typically costs between 60 and 70% of the original, and typically takes three years to achieve.[32]

These conclusions are illustrated by the examples of Japanese and Korean firms, where very effective imitation has been sustained by heavy and firm specific investments in education, training and R&D.[33] They are confirmed by a large-scale survey of R&D managers in US firms in the 1980s. As Table 4.9 shows, these managers reported that the most important methods of learning about competitors' innovations were independent R&D, reverse engineering and licensing, all of which are expensive compared to reading publications and the patent literature. Useful and usable knowledge does not come cheap. A similar and more recent survey of innovation strategy in more than 500 large European firms also found that nearly half reported the great importance, for their own innovative activities, of the technical knowledge they accumulated through the reverse engineering of competitors' products.[34]

TABLE 4.9   The effectiveness of methods of learning about competitors' innovations in large US firms.

Method of learning	*Overall sample means**	
	Processes	*Products*
Independent R&D	4.76	5.00
Reverse engineering	4.07	4.83
Licensing	4.58	4.62
Hiring employees from innovating firm	4.02	4.08
Publications or open technical meetings	4.07	4.07
Patent disclosures	3.88	4.01
Consultations with employees of the innovating firm	3.64	3.64

*Range: 1 = not at all effective; 7 = very effective.
Source: Levin, R., A. Klevorick, R., Nelson and S. Winter (1987) 'Appropriating the returns from industrial research and development', *Brookings Papers on Economic Activity*, 3, 783–820. Reproduced by permission of The Brookings Institution.

4.3 Appropriating the Benefits from Innovation

Technological leadership in firms does not necessarily translate itself into economic benefits.[35] Table 4.10 reproduces some examples of technology leaders and followers, some of which in each category turned out to be competitive winners and others losers. David Teece argues that the capacity of the firm to appropriate the benefits of its investment in technology depends on two factors: (i) the firm's capacity to translate its technological advantage into commercially viable products or processes; (ii) the firm's capacity to defend its advantage against imitators. Thus, effective patent protection enabled Pilkington to defend its technological breakthrough in glass-making, and stopped Kodak imitating Polaroid's instant photography. Lack of commitment of complementary assets in production and marketing resulted in the failure of EMI and Xerox to reap commercial benefits from their breakthroughs in medical scanning and personal computing technologies (see also Chapter 7). De Havilland's pioneering Comet jet passenger aircraft paid the price of revealing the effects of metal fatigue on high-altitude flight, the details of which were immediately available to all competitors. In video recorders, Matsushita succeeded against the more innovative Sony in imposing its standard, in part because of a more liberal licensing policy towards competitors.

TABLE 4.10   Technological leaders and followers: competitive outcomes.

	Technology leaders	Technology followers
Competitive winners	Pilkington (float glass)	Matsushita (VHS) IBM (personal computer?)
Competitive losers	EMI (scanner) Xerox (PC) De Havilland (Comet)	Kodak (instant photos)

Source: Based on Teece (1986).[35] Reprinted with kind permission of Elsevier Science-NL, Sara Burgerhartstraat 25, 1055 KV Amsterdam, The Netherlands.

Some of the factors that enable a firm to benefit commercially from its own technological lead can be strongly shaped by its management: for example, the provision of complementary assets to exploit the lead. Other factors can be influenced only slightly by the firm's management, and depend much more on the general nature of the technology, the product market and the regime of intellectual property rights: for example, the strength of patent protection. We identify below nine factors which influence the firm's capacity to benefit commercially from its technology:

1. Secrecy.
2. Accumulated tacit knowledge.
3. Lead times and after-sales service.
4. The learning curve.
5. Complementary assets.
6. Product complexity.

7.   Standards.
8.   Pioneering radical new products.
9.   Strength of patent protection.

We begin with those over which management has some degree of discretion for action, and move on to those where its range of choices is more limited.

1. *Secrecy* is considered an effective form of protection by industrial managers, especially for process innovations. However, it is unlikely to provide absolute protection, because some process characteristics can be identified from an analysis of the final product, and because process engineers are a professional community, who talk to each other and move from one firm to another, so that information and knowledge inevitably leak out.[36]

2. *Accumulated tacit knowledge* can be long and difficult to imitate, especially when it is closely integrated in specific firms and regions. Examples include product design skills, ranging from those of Benetton and similar Italian firms in clothing design, to those of Rolls-Royce in aircraft engines.

3. *Lead times and after-sales service* are considered by practitioners as major sources of protection against imitation, especially for product innovations. Taken together with a strong commitment to product development, they can establish brand loyalty and credibility, accelerate the feedback from customer use to product improvement, generate learning curve cost advantages (see below) and therefore increase the costs of entry for imitators. Based on the survey of large European firms, Table 4.11 shows that there are considerable differences amongst sectors in product development lead times, reflecting differences both in the strength of patent protection and in product complexity.

4. *The learning curve* in production generates both lower costs, and a particular and powerful form of accumulated and largely tacit knowledge that is well recognized by practitioners. In certain industries and technologies (e.g. semi-conductors, continuous processes), the first-comer advantages are potentially large, given the major possibilities for reducing unit costs with increasing cumulative production. However, such 'experience curves' are not automatic, and require continuous investment in training, and learning.

5. *Complementary assets.* The effective commercialization of an innovation very often depends on assets (or competencies) in production, marketing and after-sales to complement those in technology. As we have seen above, EMI did not invest in them to exploit its advances in electronic scanning. On the other hand, Teece argues that strong complementary assets enabled IBM to catch up in the personal computer market.[37]

6. *Product complexity.* However, Teece was writing in the mid-1980s, and IBM's performance in personal computers has been less than impressive since then. Previously, IBM could rely on the size and complexity of their mainframe computers as an effective barrier against imitation, given the long lead times required to design and build copy products. With the advent of the micro-processor and standard software, these technological barriers to imitation disappeared and IBM was faced in the late 1980s with strong competition from IBM 'clones', made in the USA and in East Asia. Boeing and Airbus

TABLE 4.11   Inter-industry differences in product development lead times.

Industry	% of firms noting >5 years for development and marketing of alternative to a significant product innovation
All	11.0
Pharmaceuticals	57.5
Aerospace	26.3
Chemicals	17.2
Petroleum products	13.6
Instruments	10.0
Automobiles	7.3
Machinery	5.7
Electrical equipment	5.3
Basic metals	4.2
Utilities	3.7
Glass, cement and ceramics	0
Plastics and rubber	0
Food	0
Telecommunications equipment	0
Computers	0
Fabricated metals	0

Source: Arundel et al. (1995).[34] Reproduced by permission of Anthony Arundel.

have faced no such threat to their positions in large civilian aircraft, since the costs and lead times for imitation remain very high (see Table 4.11). Product complexity is recognized by managers as an effective barrier to imitation.

7. *Standards.* The widespread acceptance of a company's product standard widens its own market and raises barriers against competitors. Carl Shapiro and Hal Varian have written the standard (so far) text on the competitive dynamics of the Internet economy,[38] where standards compatibility is an essential feature of market growth, and 'standards wars' an essential feature of the competitive process (see Box 4.3). However, they point out that such wars have been fought in the adoption of each new generation of radically new technology: for example, over the width of railway gauges in the nineteenth century, the provision of electricity through direct or alternating current early in the twentieth, and rival technical systems for colour television more recently. Amongst other things they conclude that the marker leader normally has the advantage in a standards war, but this can be overturned through radical technological change, or a superior response to customers' needs. Competing firms can adopt either 'evolutionary' strategies minimizing switching costs for customers (e.g. backward compatibility with earlier generations of the product), or 'revolutionary' strategies based on greatly superior performance–price characteristics, such that customers are willing to accept higher switching costs. Standards wars are made less bitter and dramatic when the costs to the losers of adapting to the winning standard are relatively small (see Box 4.3).

BOX 4.3 Standards and 'winner takes all' industries.

Charles Hill has gone so far as to argue that standards competition creates 'winner takes all industries'.[39] This results from so-called 'increasing returns to adoption', where the incentive for customers to adopt a standard increases with the number of users who have already adopted it, because of the greater availability of complementary and compatible goods and services (e.g. content programmes for video recorders, and computer application programs for operating systems). While the experiences of Microsoft and Intel in personal computers give credence to this conclusion, it does not always hold. The complete victory of the VHS standard has not stopped the loser (Sony) from a successful business in the video market, based on its rival's standard.[40] Similarly, IBM has not benefited massively (some would say at all), compared to its competitors, from the success of its own personal computer standard.[41] In both cases, rival producers have been able to copy the standard and to prevent 'winner takes all', because the costs to producers of changing to other standards have been relatively small. This can happen when the technology of a standard is licensed to rivals, in order to encourage adoption. It can also happen when technical differences between rival standards are relatively small. When this is the case (e.g. in TV and mobile phones) the same firms will often be active in many standards.

---

8. *Pioneering radical new products.* It is not necessarily a great advantage to be a technological leader in the early stages of the development of radically new products, when the product performance characteristics, and features valued by users, are not always clear, either to the producers or to the users themselves. Especially for consumer products, valued features emerge only gradually through a process of dynamic competition, that involves a considerable amount of trial, error and learning by both producers and users. New features valued by users in one product can easily be recognized by competitors and incorporated in subsequent products. This is why market leadership in the early stages of the development of personal computers was so volatile, and why pioneers are often displaced by new entrants.[42] In such circumstances, product development must be closely coupled with the ability to monitor competitors' products and to learn from customers. According to research by Tellis and Golder, pioneers in radical consumer innovations rarely succeed in establishing long-term market positions. Success goes to so-called 'early entrants' with the vision, patience and flexibility to establish a mass consumer market.[43]

9. *Strength of patent protection* can, as we have already seen in the examples described above, be a strong determinant of the relative commercial benefits to innovators and imitators. Table 4.12 summarizes the results of the surveys of the judgements of managers in large European and US firms about the strength of patent protection. The firms' sectors are ordered according to the first column of figures, showing the strength of patent protection for product innovations for European firms. On the whole, European firms value patent

protection more than their US counterparts. However, with one exception (cosmetics), the variations across industry in the strength of patent protection are very similar in Europe and the USA. Patents are judged to be more effective in protecting product innovations than process innovations in all sectors except petroleum refining, probably reflecting the importance of improvements in chemical catalysts for increasing process efficiency. It also shows that patent protection is rated more highly in chemical-related sectors (especially drugs) than in other sectors. This is because it is more difficult in general to 'invent round' a clearly specified chemical formula than round other forms of invention.

Radically new technologies are now posing new problems for the protection of intellectual property, including the patenting system. The number of patents granted to protect software technology is growing in the USA, and so are the numbers of financial institutions getting involved in patenting for the first time.[44] Debate and controversy surround important issues, such as the possible effects of digital technology on copyright protection,[45] the validity of patents to protect living organisms, and the appropriate breadth of patent protection in biotechnology.[46]

TABLE 4.12   Inter-industry differences in the effectiveness of patent protection, according to large European and US firms.*

Industry	Products		Processes	
	Europe	USA	Europe	USA
Drugs	4.8	4.6	4.3	3.5
Plastic materials	4.8	4.6	3.4	3.3
Cosmetics	4.6	2.9	3.9	2.1
Plastic products	3.9	3.5	2.9	2.3
Motor vehicle parts	3.9	3.2	3.0	2.6
Medical instruments	3.8	3.4	2.1	2.3
Semiconductors	3.8	3.2	3.7	2.3
Aircraft and parts	3.8	2.7	2.8	2.2
Communications equipment	3.6	2.6	2.4	2.2
Steel mill products	3.5	3.6	3.5	2.5
Measuring devices	3.3	2.8	2.2	2.6
Petroleum refining	3.1	3.1	3.6	3.5
Pulp and paper	2.6	2.4	3.1	1.9

* Range: 1 = not at all effective; 5 = very effective.
Note: Some industries omitted because of lack of Europe–USA comparability.
Sources: Arundel *et al.* (1995) and Levin *et al.* (1987). Reproduced by permission of Anthony Arundel.

Finally, we should note that firms can use more than one of the above nine factors to defend their innovative lead. Some of the methods are mutually exclusive: for example, secrecy precludes patenting, which requires disclosure of information, although it can precede patenting. However, firms typically deploy all the useful means available to them to defend their innovations against imitation.[47]

4.4 Positioning of Small Firms

Even more than in large firms, the opportunities for innovation in small firms are strongly influenced by the 'system of innovation' in which they are embedded. Table 4.13, which is based on a comprehensive survey in France, shows that the frequency of innovation in firms with fewer than 100 employees is much lower than in larger firms. They also rely more heavily in-house on informal rather than formal R&D. Smaller firms also make less frequent use of outside sources of knowledge (R&D and licences) than larger firms, reflecting their limited capacity to absorb outside knowledge. Above all, small firms depend more than others for their innovations on their suppliers of machinery and materials, in which the innovations are embodied.

TABLE 4.13   Frequency and sources of innovation, by firm size (France, 1993/94).

Firm size	Innovating firms (%)	Sources of innovation(%)					
		Own R&D	Part-time R&D	Outside R&D	Licences	Machine suppliers	Material suppliers
20–49	55	16	25	10	5	26	18
50–99	66	19	25	10	5	23	16
100–199	70	21	25	11	5	22	16
200–499	80	24	24	12	6	20	15
500–1999	86	26	23	13	6	19	14
2000+	96	25	21	14	6	18	14

Sources: 'L'innovation technologique', Min. de l'Industrie (1994); Kaminski, P. (1994) 'Le cas particulier de la micro-entreprise', INSEE, France.

These conclusions are reinforced and extended by a survey in Canada,[48] covering 1500 small industrial firms distinguished by their strong growth performance (their average annual sales were $6.6m., and their average employment 44 people). According to their managers:

- Only 9.3% performed their own R&D, 10.4% introduced their product innovations and 5.4% their own process innovations
- The three major sources of innovation were customers, suppliers and internal management—formal R&D was considered much less important
- About 55% of firms introduced innovations from one of these sources
- The main factors contributing to growth are the skills in management, labour and marketing
- Their distinctive competence is in product quality, flexibility and customer services

Thus, the opportunities for innovation in small firms are strongly influenced by the innovativeness of their suppliers. We shall also see in Chapter 5 that small firms in some important sectors (like machinery) are also strongly influenced by the innovativeness of their customers. In both cases personal contacts with, and close geographical proximity to, suppliers and customers reinforce and augment the effectiveness of innovation in small firms. So do the quality and skills of the local labour force. As a consequence, a small firm's innovativeness is strongly conditioned by the national and regional context in which it finds itself embedded. Examples of the regional concentration of innovative small firms include not only Silicon Valley in northern California, but also the small machinery firms linked to large firms like Robert Bosch and Daimler Benz in Baden-Württemberg, and the 'industrial districts' producing textiles in Italy.[49] In addition, small-firm clusters are now emerging in the provision of software-based services.

4.5 Summary and Further Reading

In formulating and executing their innovation strategies, business firms cannot ignore the national systems of innovation in which they are embedded. Through their strong influences on demand and competitive conditions, the provision of human resources, and forms of corporate governance, national systems of innovation both open opportunities and impose constraints on what firms can do.

However, although firms' technological strategies are *influenced* by their own national systems of innovation, they are not *determined* by them. In an analysis of more than 400 of the world's largest firms, only part of the variance between firms in their share of corporate resources devoted to innovative activities could be explained by their products and by their country of origin: a considerable share of the differences reflects the discretionary decisions by managers on the proportion of corporate resources to be devoted to innovative activities.[50]

In deciding how to cope with competitors' technology, there are a variety of useful and accessible public sources of information on firms' innovative activities. Benchmarking is more rewarding, since it makes detailed comparisons between specific firms and identifies specific factors for improvement. It is also more difficult and costly, given problems of access, comparability and interpretation. Learning (i.e. assimilating knowledge) from competitors is both essential for the firm's own innovative activities, and costly since it requires extensive investment in R&D, reverse engineering and related training. There are no readily applicable recipes for translating a technological lead into commercial success. This depends in part on what management itself does, by way of investing in complementary assets in production, marketing and after-sales. It also depends on a variety of factors that make the pioneering innovation more or less difficult to imitate, and over which management can sometimes have very little influence.

There are a number of texts which describe and compare different systems of national innovation policy, including *National Innovation Systems* (Oxford University Press, 1993), edited by Richard Nelson; *National Systems of Innovation* (Pinter, London, 1992) edited by B.-A. Lundvall; and *Systems of Innovation: Technologies, Institutions and Organisations* (Pinter, 1997) edited by Charles Edquist. The former is stronger on US policy, the other two on European, but all have an emphasis on public policy rather than corporate strategy. Bo Carlsson (ed.) and his colleagues have developed the notion of sectoral systems of innovation in *Technological Systems and Economic Performance: The case of factory automation* (Kluwer, 1995); Michael Porter's *The Competitive Advantage of Nations* (Macmillan, London, 1990) provides a useful framework in which to examine the direct impact on corporate behaviour of innovation systems. At the other extreme, David Landes' *Wealth and Poverty of Nations* (Little Brown, 1998), takes a broad (and stimulating) historical view of the subject.

The literature on analysing and benchmarking competitors' innovative capability is less well developed. One of the pioneering texts is Camp's (1989) *Benchmarking: The search for industry best practices that lead to superior performance* (Quality Press, Milwaukee, 1989), and more recent are the excellent series of publications by Chris Voss and his colleagues, M. Zairi *Benchmarking for Best Practice* (Butterworth-Heinemann, 1996) and J. Tidd (ed.) *From Knowledge Management to Strategic Competence: Measuring technological, market and organizational innovation* (Imperial College Press, 2000). Published comparisons of corporate innovative activities are becoming increasingly frequent, for example the annual comparisons of *The R&D Scoreboard* (Table 4.8).

The best analysis of the strategic advantages of being a technological leader or follower remains Teece's 1986 paper. The surveys by Arundel, Levin and their colleagues are rich sources of information on corporate experience in assimilating technological knowledge and on how to maintain innovative leads.

Finally there has been a recent spate of papers and books on the implications of the Internet (and of ICT more generally) for corporate market positioning strategies. On product development and market positioning, these include M. Iansiti, 'Mastering the rapids: managing product development in turbulent environments', *California Management Review*, **38** (1), Fall 1995, 37–58; D. B. Yoffie and M. A. Cusumano: 'Judo strategy. The competitive dynamics of Internet time', *Harvard Business Review*, Jan.–Feb. 1999, 71–81; M. Iansiti and A. MacCormack, 'Developing products on internet time', *Harvard Business Review*, Sept.–Oct. 1997, 108–117; *The Economist*, 25 May 1996, 'Survey of the software industry'; M. A. Cusumano, Y. Mylonadis and R. S. Rosenbloom: 'Strategic manoeuvring and mass-market dynamics: the triumph of VHS over Beta', *Business History Review*, **66**, Spring 1992, 51–94.

On open source software: J. B. De Long and A. H. Froomkin: 'Beating Microsoft at its own game', *Harvard Business Review*, Jan.–Feb. 2000, 159–164, *The Economist*, 12 June 1999, 'Business: venture communism: open-source software: the next high-tech listings', 92–94; *The Economist*, 11 July 1998, 'Business: revenge of the hackers: the software is free', 81–84; R. Garud and A. Kumaraswary, 'Changing competitive dynamics in networks industries. An exploration of Sun Microsystems' open source strategy', *Strategic Management Journal*, **14** (5), July 1993, 351.

References

1 Porter, M. (1990) *The Competitive Advantage of Nations*. Macmillan, London.
2 Nelson, R. (ed.) (1993) *National Innovation Systems*. Oxford University Press, Oxford.
3 Cantwell, J. (1992) 'The internationalisation of technological activity and its implications for competitiveness', in Granstrand, O., Hakanson, L. and Sjolander, S. (eds) *Technology Management and International Business*, John Wiley, Chichester, 75–95; Patel, P. (1995) 'The localised production of global technology', *Cambridge Journal of Economics*, **19**, 141–153.
4 Patel, P. and K. Pavitt (1994) 'Uneven (and divergent) technological accumulation amongst advanced countries: evidence and a framework of explanation', *Industrial and Corporate Change*, **3**, 759–787.

5 Fagerberg, J. (1987) 'A technology gap approach to why growth rates differ', in Freeman, C. (ed.), *Output Measurement in Science and Technology: Essays in honour of Y. Fabian*. North-Holland, Amsterdam, pp. 33–45; Fagerberg, J. (1988) 'International competitiveness', *Economic Journal*, **98**, 355–374.

6 Franko, L. (1989) 'Global corporate competition: who's winning, who's losing, and the R&D factor as one reason why', *Strategic Management Journal*, **10**, 449–474.

7 Freeman, C. (1988) 'Japan: a new national system of innovation?', in Dosi, G., Freeman, C., Nelson, R., Silverberg, G. and Soete, L. (eds), *Technical Change and Economic Theory*, Pinter, London, pp. 330–348; Nelson, R. (ed.) (1993) *National Innovation Systems*. Oxford University Press, Oxford; Lundvall, B.-A. (ed.) (1992) *National Systems of Innovation*. Pinter, London.

8 Patel, P. and K. Pavitt (1994) 'National innovation systems: why they are important, and how they might be measured and compared', *Economics of Innovation and New Technology*, **3**, 77–95.

9 Vernon, R. (1966) 'International investment and international trade in the product cycle', *Quarterly Journal of Economics*, **80**, 190–207; Dunning, J. (1980) 'Towards an eclectic theory of international production: some empirical tests', *Journal of International Business Studies*, **1**, 9–31.

10 Patel, P. and K. Pavitt (1994) 'National innovation systems: why they are important, and how they might be measured and compared', *Economics of Innovation and New Technology*, **3**, 77–95; Porter, M. (1990) *The Competitive Advantage of Nations*. Macmillan, London.

11 Thomas, L. (1994) 'Implicit industrial policy: the triumph of Britain and the failure of France in global pharmaceuticals' *Industrial and Corporate Change*, **3**, 451–489.

12 Prais, S. (1993) 'Economic performance and education: the nature of Britain's deficiencies', *Proceedings of the British Academy*, **84**, 151–207.

13 See OECD (2000) *Internet Technology Outlook, 2000: ICTs, E-commerce and the information economy*. Paris, www.oecd.org/dsti/sti/stat-ana/

14 Faulkner, W. and J. Senker (1995) *Knowledge Frontiers*. Clarendon Press, Oxford; Hicks, D. (1995) 'Published papers, tacit competencies and corporate management of the public/private character of knowledge', *Industrial and Corporate Change*, **4**, 401–424; Jaffe, A. (1989) 'Real effects of academic research', *American Economic Review*, **79**, 957–970; Narin, F., K. S. Hamilton and D. Olivastro (1998) 'The increasing linkage between U.S. technology and public science', *Research Policy*, **26**, 317.

15 Martin, B. (1992) 'The position of British science', *Nature*, **355**, 760; and 'Struggling to keep up appearances', *New Scientist*, 7 November; Nathan, R. (1996) 'Japan hints at a shift to the life sciences', *Nature*, **383**, 7.

16 Carlsson, B. and S. Jacobsson (1994) 'Technological systems and economic policy: the diffusion of factory automation in Sweden', *Research Policy*, **23**, 235–248; Laursen, K. (1997) 'Horizontal diversification in the Danish national system of innovation: the case of pharmaceuticals', *Research Policy*, **25**, 1121.

17 Landau, R. and N. Rosenberg (1992) 'Successful commercialisation in the chemical process industries', in Rosenberg, N., Landau, R. and Mowery, D. (eds), *Technology and the Wealth of Nations*. Stanford University Press, Stanford, pp. 73–119.

18 Albert, M. (1992) *Capitalism against Capitalism*. Whurr, London.

19 Fransman, M. (1995) *Japan's Computer and Communications Industry*. Oxford University Press, Oxford.

20 Albach, H. (1996) 'Global competitive strategies for scienceware products', in Koopmann, G. and Scharrer, H. E. (eds), *The Economics of High Technology Competition and Co-operation in Global Markets*. Nomos, Baden-Baden, pp. 203–217.

21 *The Economist* (1995) 'Dismantling Daimler-Benz', 18 November, 99–100.

22 *The Economist* (1995) 'Back on top. A survey of American business', 16 September.

23 Gordon, P. L. (1996) 'Industrial districts and the globalisation of innovation: regions and networks in the new economic space', in Vence-Deza, X. and Metcalfe, J. (eds), *Wealth from Diversity*. Kluwer, Dordrecht, pp. 103–134; Computer Science and Telecommunications Board (1999) *Funding a Revolution: Government support for computing research*, National Research Council, Washington, DC.

24 Harding, R. and W. Paterson (eds) (2000) *The Future of the German Economy: an end to the miracle?*, Manchester University Press, Manchester.

25 See *The Economist* (1999) 'The world in your pocket: a survey of telecommunications', 9 October.

26 Mansfield, E. (1985) 'How rapidly does new industrial technology leak out?', *Journal of Industrial Economics*, **34**, 217–223.

27 Camp, R. (1989) *Benchmarking—the Search for Industry Best Practices That Lead to Superior Performance*. Quality Press, Milwaukee, Wis.

28 Altshuler, A., M. Anderson, D. Jones, D. Roos and J. Womack (1984) *The Future of the Automobile: The report of MIT's international automobile program*. MIT Press, Cambridge, Mass.; Womack, J., D. Jones and D. Roos (1990) *The Machine that Changed the World*. Macmillan, New York; Leachman, R. and D. Hodges (1996) 'Benchmarking semiconductor manufacturing', *IEEE Transactions on Semiconductor Manufacturing*, **9**, 158–169.

29 De Meyer, A. and B. Pycke (1997) 'Separating the fads from the facts: trends in manufacturing action programmes and competitive priorities from 1986 till 1996', in Miller, J., A. de Meyer and J. Nakane (eds), *Benchmarking Global Manufacturing: Understanding international suppliers, customers, and competitors*. Irwin, Ill.

30 Voss, C. and K. Blackmon (1996) 'The impact of national and parent company origin on world-class manufacturing: findings from Britain and Germany', *International Journal of Operations and Production Management*, **16**, 96–112; Hanson, P. and C. Voss (1993) *Made in Britain*. IBM Consulting, London; P. Hanson, C. Voss, K. Blacken and T. Claxton (1996) *Made in Europe 2*. IBM Consulting, London.

31 Coopers & Lybrand (1994) *Survey of Benchmarking in the UK: Executive summary*. London.

32 Levin, R., A. Klevorick, R. Nelson and S. Winter. (1987) 'Appropriating the returns from industrial research and development', *Brookings Papers on Economic Activity*, **3**, 783–820; Mansfield, E., M. Schwartz and S. Wagner (1981) 'Imitation costs and patents: an empirical study', *Economic Journal*, **91**, 907–918.

33 Kim, L. (1993) 'National system of industrial innovation: dynamics of capability building in Korea', and Odagiri, H. and A. Goto (1993) 'The Japanese system of innovation: past, present and future', in Nelson, R. (ed). *National Innovation Systems*, Oxford University Press, Oxford, 357–383, 76–114.

34 Arundel, A., G. van de Paal and L. Soete (1995) *Innovation Strategies of Europe's Largest Industrial Firms* (PACE Report). MERIT, University of Limbourg, Maastricht.

35 Teece, D. (1986) 'Profiting from technological innovation: implications for integration, collaboration, licensing and public policy', *Research Policy*, **15**, 285–305.

36 Von Hippel, E. (1987) 'Co-operation between rivals: informal know-how training', *Research Policy*, **16**, 291–302.

37 Teece, D. (1986) 'Profiting from technological innovation: implications for integration, collaboration, licensing and public policy', *Research Policy*, **15**, 285–305.

38 Shapiro, C. and H. Varian (1998) *Information Rules: A strategic guide to the network economy*. Harvard Business School Press, Boston, Mass.

39 Hill, C. (1997) 'Establishing a standard: competitive strategy and technological standards in winner-take-all industries', *Academy of Management Executive*, **11**, 7–25.

40 Rosenbloom, R. and M. Cusumano (1987) 'Technological pioneering and competitive advantage: the birth of the VCR industry', *California Management Review*, **24**, 51–76.

41 Chesbrough, H. and D. Teece (1996) 'When is virtual virtuous? Organizing for innovation', *Harvard Business Review*, Jan.–Feb., 65–73.

42 Steffens, J. (1994) *Newgames: Strategic competition in the PC revolution*. Pergamon Press, Oxford.

43 Tellis, G. and P. Golder (1996) 'First to market, first to fail? Real causes of enduring market leadership', *Sloan Management Review*, Winter, 65–75.

44 *The Economist* (2000) 'The knowledge monopolies: patent wars', 8 April, 95–99; (1996) 'A dose of patent medicine', 10 February, 93–94.

45 *The Economist* (1999) 'Digital rights and wrongs', 17 July, 99–100.

46 Mazzolini R. and R. Nelson (1998) 'The benefits and costs of strong patent protection: a contribution to the current debate', *Research Policy*, **26**, 405.

47 Bertin, G. and S. Wyatt (1988) *Multinationals and Industrial Property: The control of the world's technology*. Harvester-Wheatsheaf, Hemel Hempstead.

48 Baldwin, K. (1994) *Innovation: The key to success in small firms*. Statistics Canada, Ottawa.

49 Cooke, P. and K. Morgan (1997) *The Associational Economy: Firms, regions and innovation*. Oxford University Press, Oxford.

50 Patel, P. and K. Pavitt (1998) 'The wide (and increasing) spread of technological competencies in the world's largest firms: a challenge to conventional wisdom', in Chandler, A., Hagstrom P. and Solvell, O. (eds), *The Dynamic Firm*. Oxford University Press, Oxford.

Chapter 5

PATHS: EXPLOITING TECHNOLOGICAL TRAJECTORIES

Firms' strategies are strongly constrained by their current position and by the specific opportunities open to them in future: in other words, they are path-dependent.[1] At any point in time, two sets of constraints make path-dependency in corporate innovation strategy inevitable: those of the present and likely future state of technological knowledge, and those of the limits of corporate competence.

Critics of technological determinism notwithstanding, pure technological development does have its own internal logic, which helps define where firms will find innovative opportunities. Thus, we can marvel at the rapid rate of improvement in the performance–price ratio of the electronic chip and at the economic and social changes it has made possible. But we can also be frustrated that our personal computers can rarely be made to run independently for more than three hours, or that battery-driven cars are so heavy, limited in range and slow to be refuelled: in spite of extensive private investments, existing knowledge of battery technology has not enabled us to do much better. The energy density of gasoline fuel (i.e. energy generated per unit weight) remains 100 times higher than electric batteries.[2] Similarly, we can speculate that a set of technologies that could convert deep-mined coal into oil and gas at the same price, and with lesser adverse environmental consequences than existing supplies, would have economic, social and political effects at least equal to those of the microchip. But it will remain speculation, since the present state of knowledge does not enable it to be done.[3]

In addition to the constraints of knowledge, there are those of competence: in other words, of what specific firms are capable of learning and exploiting. As we have seen in Chapter 3, innovation requires improvements and changes in the operation of complex technical and organizational systems. This involves trial, error and learning. Learning tends to be incremental, since major step changes in too many parameters both increases uncertainty and reduce the capacity to learn. As a consequence, firms' learning processes are path-dependent, with the directions of search strongly conditioned by the competencies accumulated for the development and exploitation of their existing product base.[4] Moving from one path of learning to another can be costly, even impossible, given cognitive limits—think of the problems of learning a foreign language from scratch.

Furthermore, firms cannot easily jump from one major path to another through hiring individuals with the required competencies. Corporate competencies are rarely those of an individual, and most often those of specialized, interdependent and co-ordinated groups, where tacit technical and organizational knowledge accumulated through experience are of central importance. This is why firms perform most of their innovative activities in-house.[5] And even when competencies come from outside the firm as part of a corporate acquisition, different practices and cognitive structures may make their assimilation costly or impossible. For example, it is no accident that electrical firms find it much easier to master and exploit semiconductor technology than chemical firms: the fields of technological competencies required are much closer.[6]

From the fact of path dependency has emerged the notion of technological trajectory, first proposed by Nelson and Winter[7] and later extended by Dosi.[8] As we have seen above, it can be applied equally to a technology, constrained by knowledge limits, and to a firm, constrained by limits in competence. In Chapter 4, we have shown that it can also be applied to a country, which will often have more than one trajectory. These overlapping categories are inevitable, since technologies develop in firms, which themselves are situated in sectors and countries.

5.1 Major Technological Trajectories

We focus here on firms and broad technological trajectories. This is because firms and industrial sectors differ greatly in their underlying technologies. For example, designing and making an automobile is not the same as designing and making a therapeutic drug, or a personal computer. We are dealing not with one *technology*, but with several *technologies*, each with its historical pattern of development, skill requirements and strategic implications. It is therefore a major challenge to develop a framework, for integrating changing technology into strategic analysis, that deals effectively with corporate and sectoral diversity. We describe below the framework that one of us has developed over the past 10 or more years to encompass diversity.[9] It has been strongly influenced by the analyses of the emergence of the major new technologies over the past 150 years by Chris Freeman and his colleagues,[10] and by David Mowery and Nathan Rosenberg.[11]

A number of studies have shown marked, similar and persistent differences amongst industrial sectors in the sources and directions of technological change. They can be summarized as follows:

- *Size of innovating firms:* typically *big* in chemicals, road vehicles, materials processing, aircraft and electronic products; and *small* in machinery, instruments and software
- *Type of product made:* typically *price sensitive* in bulk materials and consumer products; and *performance sensitive* in ethical drugs and machinery

- *Objectives of innovation:* typically *product* innovation in ethical drugs and machinery; *process* innovation in steel; and *both* in automobiles
- *Sources of innovation: suppliers* of equipment and other production inputs in agriculture and traditional manufacture (like textiles); *customers* in instrument, machinery and software; *in-house* technological activities in chemicals, electronics, transport, machinery, instruments and software; and *basic research* in ethical drugs
- *Locus of own innovation: R&D laboratories* in chemicals and electronics; *production engineering departments* in automobiles and bulk materials; *design offices* in machine-building; and *Systems Departments* in service industries (e.g. banks and supermarket chains)

Five Major Technological Trajectories

In the face of such diversity there are two opposite dangers. One is to generalize about the nature, source, directions and strategic implications of innovation on the basis of experience in one firm or in one sector. In this case, there is a strong probability that many of the conclusions will be misleading or plain wrong. The other danger is to say that all firms and sectors are different, and that no generalizations can be made. In this case, there can be no cumulative development of useful knowledge. In order to avoid these twin dangers, one of us distinguished five major technological trajectories, each with its distinctive nature and sources of innovation, and with its distinctive implications for technology strategy and innovation management. This was done on the basis of systematic information on more than 2000 significant innovations in the UK, and of a reading of historical and case material. In Table 5.1 we identify for each trajectory its typical core sectors, its major sources of technological accumulation and its main strategic management tasks.

Thus, in *supplier-dominated firms*, technical change comes almost exclusively from suppliers of machinery and other production inputs. This is typically the case in both agriculture and textiles, where most new techniques originate in firms in the machinery and chemical industries. Firms' technical choices reflect input costs, and the opportunities for firm-specific technological accumulation are relatively modest, being focused on improvements and modifications in production methods and associated inputs. *The main task of innovation strategy* is therefore to use technology from elsewhere to reinforce other competitive advantages. Over the past 10 years, advances elsewhere in IT have opened up radical new applications in design, distribution, logistics and transactions, thereby making production more responsive to customer demands. But, since these revolutionary changes are available from specialized suppliers to all firms, it is still far from clear whether they can be of a lasting advantage for firms competing in supplier-dominated sectors.

In *scale-intensive firms*, technological accumulation is generated by the design, building and operation of complex production systems and/or products. Typical core sectors include the extraction and processing of bulk materials, automobiles and large-scale civil engineering projects. Given the potential economic advantages of increased scale, combined with the complexity of products and/or production systems, the risks of failure associated with radical but untested changes are

TABLE 5.1 Five major technological trajectories.

	Supplier-dominated	Scale-intensive	Science-based	Information-intensive	Specialized suppliers
Typical core products	• Agriculture • Services • Traditional manufacture	• Bulk materials • Consumer durables • Automobiles • Civil engineering	• Electronics • Chemicals	• Finance • Retailing • Publishing • Travel	• Machinery • Instruments • Software
Main sources of technology	• Suppliers • Production learning	• Production engineering • Production learning • Suppliers • Design offices	• R&D • Basic research	• Software and systems departments • Suppliers	• Design • Advanced users
Main tasks of innovation strategy					
1. Positions	1. Based on non-technological advantages	1. Cost-effective and safe complex products and processes	1. Develop technically related products	1. New products and services	1. Monitor and respond to user needs
2. Paths	2. Use of IT in finance and distribution	2. Incremental integration of new knowledge (e.g. virtual prototypes, new materials, B2B*)	2. Exploit basic science (e.g. molecular biology)	2. Design and operation of complex information processing systems	2. Matching changing technologies to users' needs
3. Processes	3. Flexible response to user	3. Diffusion of best practice in design, production and distribution	3. Obtain complementary assets. Redefine divisional boundaries	3. To match IT-based opportunities with user needs	3. Strong links with lead users

*B2B = business to business.

potentially very costly. Process and product technologies therefore develop incrementally on the basis of earlier operating experience, and improvements in components, machinery and subsystems. The main sources of technology are in-house design and production engineering departments, operating experience, and specialized suppliers of equipment and components. In these circumstances, *the main tasks of innovation strategy* are the incremental improvement of technological improvements in complex products or production systems, and the diffusion throughout the firm of best-practice methods in design and production. Recent advances in the techniques of large-scale computer simulation and modelling now offer considerable opportunities for saving time and money in the building and testing of prototypes and pilot plant.

In *science-based firms*, technological accumulation emerges mainly from corporate R&D laboratories, and is heavily dependent on knowledge, skills and techniques emerging from academic research. Typical core sectors are chemicals and electronics: fundamental discoveries (electromagnetism, radio waves, transistor effect, synthetic chemicals, molecular biology) open up major new product markets over a wide range of potential applications. The major directions of technological accumulation in the firm are horizontal searches for new and technologically related product markets. As a consequence, the *main tasks of innovation strategy* are to monitor and exploit advances emerging from basic research, to develop technologically related products and acquire the complementary assets (e.g. production and marketing) to exploit them, and to reconfigure the operating divisions and business units in the light of changing technological and market opportunities.

Information-intensive firms have begun to emerge only in the past 10–15 years, particularly in the service sector: finance, retailing, publishing, telecommunications and travel. See, for example, the surveys in *The Economist*, on *retailing* (4 March 1995) and *online finance* (20 May 2000). The main sources of technology are in-house software and systems departments, and suppliers of IT hardware and of systems and applications software. The main purpose is to design and operate complex systems for processing information, particularly in distribution systems that make the provision of a service or a good more sensitive to customer demands. The *main tasks of innovation strategy* are the development and operation of complex information processing systems, and the development of related and often radically new services.

Specialized supplier firms are generally small, and provide high-performance inputs into complex systems of production, of information processing and of product development, in the form of machinery, components, instruments and (increasingly) software. Technological accumulation takes place through the design, building and operational use of these specialized inputs. Specialized supplier firms benefit from the operating experience of advanced users, in the form of information, skills and the identification of possible modifications and improvements. Specialized supplier firms accumulate the skills to match advances in technology with user requirements, which—given the cost, complexity and interdependence of production processes—put a premium on reliability and performance, rather than on price. The *main tasks of innovation strategy* are keeping up with users' needs, learning from advanced users and matching new technologies to users' needs.

Knowledge of these major technological trajectories can improve analysis of particular companies' technological strategies, by helping answer the following questions:

- Where do the company's technologies come from?
- How do they contribute to competitive advantage?
- What are the major tasks of innovation strategy?
- Where are the likely opportunities and threats, and how can they be dealt with?

Although the above taxonomy has held up reasonably well to subsequent empirical tests,[12] it inevitably simplifies.[13] For example, we can find 'supplier-dominated' firms in electronics and chemicals, but they are unlikely to be technological pace-setters. In addition, firms can belong in more than one trajectory.

In particular, large firms in all sectors have capacities in *scale-intensive* (mainly mechanical and instrumentation) technologies, in order to ensure efficient production. Software technology is beginning to play a similarly pervasive role across all sectors.

5.2 Revolutionary Technologies: Biotechnology, Materials and IT

Firm-specific technological trajectories change over time as improvements in the knowledge base open up new technological opportunities. Since the beginning of the 1980s, biotechnology, new materials and IT have been widely identified by corporate R&D directors as the three fields with the greatest promise. This is confirmed by data showing that the number of the world's largest firms with competencies in these fields has increased greatly since then.[14]

Third-generation biotechnology has not yet had such widespread effects, but is beginning to change methods of product development in drugs and agricultural products (see Box 5.1). Materials technology has been advancing steadily with a strengthening science base (see Box 5.2)

However, it is *information technology* that has had, so far, the most revolutionary effects, and is likely to continue to do so in the foreseeable future. As in the midst of all revolutions, the signals are incomplete, confusing and sometimes misleading, so that information and experience must be interpreted with particular care. In the 1970s, the so-called *microelectronics revolution* was associated with the spectacular achievements in semiconductor technology: in particular, the microprocessor and the capacity to store and manipulate vast quantities of information on a small and increasingly cheap electronic chip. Thereafter, the phrase *IT revolution* has come into increasing use, reflecting similar advances in the capacity to transmit information, culminating in the Internet.

Perhaps even more important, we have seen the spectacular advance in *software* technology (i.e. techniques for manipulating information), which had previously been developed and closely controlled by manufacturers of computer hardware. The steep reduction in hardware costs and the emergence of cheap standard products (such as personal computers) have resulted in the emergence of two other major sources of software technology: independent software suppliers (e.g. Microsoft) and operators of large-scale systems (e.g. banks, retail chains, airlines). As a result, the technological trajectories of firms and countries in the development of software have progressively become decoupled from their trajectories in computer hardware.

Table 5.2 compares and contrasts the characteristics of the two trajectories, which can be summarized as follows:

- The microelectronics revolution is about designing and producing electronic chips, and the IT revolution about producing software
- The former (microelectronics) is located firmly in manufacturing, and principally involves the highly sophisticated and demanding design and manufacturing of hardware. It opens up technological opportunities mainly for firms in—or close to—the electronics industry

BOX 5.1 Post-war developments in biotechnology.

'Biotechnology has been defined many times. . . . The OECD definition "the application of scientific and engineering principles to the processing of materials by biological agents" has been widely adopted and encompasses the use and application of a series of skills drawn from biology, biochemistry, genetics, microbiology, biochemical engineering and separations processing.

The development of biotechnology over the past forty years has been a continuous process. The discovery of the structure of DNA, the genetic material, in the 1950s, the detailed analysis of protein synthesis in the 1960s, and the study of bacteriophage genetics in the basis of antibiotic resistance in the 1970s, laid the foundations for the scientific breakthrough of recombinant DNA (rDNA) in the 1970s. For the first time, a gene sequence could be cut and a foreign DNA sequence from another organism inserted and expressed. . . .

. . . Since then the science underpinning developments in biotechnology has progressed very rapidly. Gene therapy, antisense technology, automated gene sequencing and gene discovery now present new technological opportunities to develop and apply technology. Moreover, genome analysis or genomics in particular has placed new emphasis and value on information which can be widely exploited by industry . . . biotechnology can now be regarded as an expanding series of enabling technologies. . . .

. . . To date, the greatest impact of these technologies has been on the R&D programmes of companies in the pharmaceutical and agro-food sectors, where it has led to major investments by existing companies and the foundation of specialist biotechnology companies. Biotechnology is expected to continue to be of critical importance to these sectors, despite the fact that it has not yet delivered the short cuts to profitability hoped for by the pharmaceutical sector. In addition, biotechnology is currently widely used to improve the efficiency of key production processes, particularly in food processing, drinks and detergents. . . .

(m)ajor new applications will emerge in industries such as textiles, leather, paper and pulp, oil refining, metals and mining, printing, environmental services and speciality chemicals. . . .

Creating value through biotechnology depends upon the effective functioning of an "innovation system". This has three main components: . . . (t)he science base, . . . specialist biotech companies, . . . user industries.'

Source: Business Decisions and SPRU, 1996.

- The latter (software) involves not only the design and manufacturing function, but also the administration, co-ordination and distribution functions. It opens up technological opportunities in all sectors in both manufacturing and services
- This reflects major differences in the size of the barriers to entry into the two technologies. In chip manufacture, they are massive, with major investments required in difficult and demanding design and manufacturing activities. The development of chip technology is in fact one of the most concentrated in the

BOX 5.2 The improving science base of materials technology.

The technology of materials is of pervasive importance, across both industry and time. In a number of the *Scientific American* published in 1986, there were separate papers on materials for information and communication, for aerospace, for ground transportation and for energy utilisation. There were also papers on materials that were electronic and magnetic, photonic, and that were advanced metals, advanced ceramics and advanced polymers. Underlying all these applications are the ever closer and more productive links between materials science and materials technology.

'Until very recently the practitioners of materials engineering and materials science remained separated by a wide gulf. Craftsmanship and technology flourished. The selection, modification and processing of materials came to be fundamental elements of human cultures. Yet the science of materials—an attempt to understand their fundamental nature and why particular manipulations of them have particular effects—was slow to develop beyond the level of speculation. It was not until the 19th century that chemistry and to a lesser extent physics began to support the largely empirical efforts of artisans and engineers with applicable theories and novel analytical tools. Within the last half century the collaboration has thrived. The advent of powerful new theories and instrumentation has made investigative science an essential driving force for advances in engineering. . . .

. . . The key contribution of science was the coupling of a material's external properties to its internal structure. Materials were discovered to possess an inner architecture—a hierarchy of several structural levels. The architecture was seen to be complex enough to account for the widely varying behaviour of materials. This recognition in turn implied that the behaviour of a particular material could be predicted from close study of its internal architecture.

Such study has been facilitated by a battery of new instruments and techniques that reveal increasingly fine detail. . . . microscopy was followed by transmission electron microscopy, which reveals details of substructure, and then by scanning electron microscopy, which provides important three-dimensional surface information. X-ray diffraction maps the spatial arrangements of atoms or molecules in a crystal. The very identity of a material's atoms is revealed by various excitation spectroscopies, and bombardment of a material with high energy particles probes the atomic nucleus. . . .

. . . Now, as more becomes known about how processing can modify a material's structure, and thus its properties and ultimately its performance, scientists are becoming more interested in processing and are having more impact on it. Their findings have been translated into improved processes in areas ranging from steel manufacture to the production of pure glass fibres. A striking example of scientific input is the development of ways to grow the very large single crystals of the semiconductor silicon from which integrated circuit chips are made.'

Liedl, G. (1986) 'The science of materials', *Scientific American*, **255** (4), 104–112.

world. In software, they are much lower, with software skills and access to a workstation being all that is required for specialized applications

- Since chip manufacture is a large-scale activity undertaken by well-established manufacturing firms, it is clearly visible in a whole range of published statistics. Software development, on the other hand, is often hidden away either in small and specialized firms in the service sector, or embedded in large organizations in sectors like retailing and finance, and is therefore hardly visible in established statistics. Perhaps the most important comprehensive statistic so far is buried in the periodic US reports *Science and Engineering Indicators* (National Science Foundation, Washington) and shows that the number of qualified scientists and engineers employed in US manufacturing was overtaken by the number employed in services in 1989, and that in finance and retailing a high proportion are software specialists

TABLE 5.2   Which technological revolution?

Description	'Microelectronic'	'Information technology'
Location	Producing electronic chips	Producing software
Key corporate functions	• Design • Production	• Design • Production • Administration • Co-ordination • Distribution
Sectors	• Electronics	• Manufacturing • Services
Pervasiveness of production	Low	High
Barriers to entry	High	Low
Visibility in available statistics	High	Low

It is particularly difficult during a period of revolutionary technological change to distinguish what is important from what is not. Fads and fashions flourish:

- *In financial markets*—see the rapid rise and fall of the so-called dot.com companies in the spring of 2000
- *Amongst economics journalists*—see the debatable emergence of the so-called 'New Economy', when we know that revolutionary technologies—like electricity and IT—not only create the new, but transform the old. See *The Economist's Survey of the New Economy*, 23 September 2000
- *Amongst management consultants*—see the emergence of so-called 'knowledge management', which sometimes assumes that 'knowledge' is an easily recognized, homogeneous and manipulable commodity.

We shall nonetheless risk identifying three features of the IT revolution that we think will be increasingly important for innovation strategies in future:

1. The increasingly *systemic* nature of economic and technological activities, resulting from the digitalization and interconnection of previously separate activities: for example, home electronics; logistics, sales and distribution in

retailing; management information systems in large organizations. This is increasing the importance of interface technologies, and of competencies in systems integration, and is one of the factors behind the growth of external technological alliances (see Chapter 8).

2. The decreasing cost of product development through the use of simulations and virtual prototypes. For example, Paul Nightingale has shown how improvements in simulation technology have been combined with radical improvements in fundamental biomedical knowledge to begin to revolutionize the process of drug discovery.[15]

3. Given the growing importance of software technology in distribution activities, the traditional distinction between hi-tech, medium-tech and low-tech is becoming even less useful.[16] For example, does it still make sense to describe as 'traditional, low-tech' distribution-intensive activities such as banking, retailing, and the export of Dutch tulips, [17] and Australian fresh fruit?[18]

5.3 Developing Firm-specific Competencies

The ability of firms to track and exploit the technological trajectories described above depends on their specific technological and organizational competencies, and on the difficulties that competitors have in imitating them. The notion of firm-specific competencies has become increasingly influential amongst economists, trying to explain why firms are different, and how they change over time,[19] and also amongst business practitioners and consultants, trying to identify the causes of competitive success. In the 1990s, management began to shift interest from improvements in short-term operational efficiency and flexibility (through 'de-layering', 'downsizing', 'outsourcing' and 'business process re-engineering', etc.), to a concern that—if taken too far—the 'lean corporation' could become the 'anorexic corporation', without any capacities for longer-term change and survival.

Hamel and Prahalad on Competencies

The most influential business analysts promoting and developing the notion of 'core competencies' have been Gary Hamel and C. K. Prahalad.[20] Their basic ideas can be summarized as follows:

1. The sustainable competitive advantage of firms resides not in their products but in their *core competencies*: 'The real sources of advantage are to be found in management's ability to consolidate corporate-wide technologies and production skills into competencies that empower individual businesses to adapt quickly to changing opportunities' (1990, p. 81).[20]

2. Core competencies feed into more than one core products, which in turn feed into more than one business unit. They use the metaphor of the tree:

End products   = Leaves, flowers and fruit
Business units   = Smaller branches
Core products   = Trunk and major limbs
Core competencies = Root systems

Examples of core competencies include Sony in miniaturization, Philips in optical media, 3M in coatings and adhesives and Canon in the combination of the precision mechanics, fine optics and microelectronics technologies that underlie all their products (see Box 5.3). Examples of core products include Honda in lightweight, high-compression engines and Matsushita in key components in video cassette recorders.

3. The importance of associated organizational competencies is also recognized: 'Core competence is communication, involvement, and a deep commitment to working across organisational boundaries' (1990, p. 82).[20]

4. Core competencies require focus: 'Few companies are likely to build world leadership in more than five or six fundamental competencies. A company that compiles a list of 20 to 30 capabilities has probably not produced a list of core competencies' (1990, p. 84).[20]

5. As Table 5.3 shows, the notion of core competencies suggests that large and multidivisional firms should be viewed not only as a collection of strategic business units, but as bundles of competencies that do not necessarily fit tidily in one business unit.

TABLE 5.3   Two views of the corporation: SBUs and core competencies.

	Strategic business unit	Core competencies
Basis for competition	Competitiveness of today's products	Inter-firm competition to build competencies
Corporate structure	Portfolio of businesses in related product markets	Portfolio of competencies, core products and business
Status of business unit	Autonomy: SBU 'owns' all resources other than cash	SBU is a potential reservoir of core competencies
Resource allocation	SBUs are unit of analysis. Capital allocated to SBUs	SBUs and competencies are unit of analysis. Top management allocates capital and talent
Value added of top management	Optimizing returns through trade-offs among SBUs	Enunciating strategic architecture, and building future competencies

According to Hamel and Prahalad, the concept of the corporation based on core competencies should not replace the traditional one, but a commitment to it 'will inevitably influence patterns of diversification, skill deployment, resources allocation priorities, and approaches to alliances and outsourcing' (1990, p. 86).[20] More specifically, the conventional multi-divisional structure may facilitate efficient innovation within specific product markets, but may limit the scope for learning new competencies: firms with fewer divisional boundaries are associated with a strategy based on capabilities-broadening, whereas firms with many divisional boundaries are associated with a strategy based on capabilities-deepening.[22]

BOX 5.3 Core competencies at Canon.

Product	Competencies		
	Precision mechanics	Fine optics	Micro-electronics
Basic camera	×	×	
Compact fashion camera	×	×	
Electronic camera	×	×	
EOS autofocus camera	×	×	×
Video still camera	×	×	×
Laser beam printer	×	×	×
Colour video printer	×		×
Bubble jet printer	×		×
Basic fax	×		×
Laser fax	×		×
Calculator			×
Plain paper copier	×	×	×
Colour copier	×	×	×
Laser copier	×	×	×
Colour laser copier	×	×	×
Still video system	×	×	×
Laser imager	×	×	×
Cell analyser	×	×	×
Mask aligners	×		×
Stepper aligners	×		×
Excimer laser aligners	×	×	×

The above list of competencies and related products in Canon are taken from Prahalad and Hamel.[20] According to Christer Oskarsson:[21]

'In the late 1950s, . . . the time had come for Canon to apply its precision mechanical and optical technologies to other areas [than cameras] . . . such as business machines. By 1964 Canon had begun by developing the world's first 10-key fully electronic calculator . . . followed by entry into the coated paper copier market with the development of an electrofax copier model in 1965, and then into . . . the revolutionary Canon plain paper copier technology unveiled in 1968. . . . Following these successes of product diversification, Canon's product lines were built on a foundation of precision optics, precision engineering and electronics. . . .

The main factors behind . . . increases in the numbers of products, technologies and markets . . . seem to be the rapid growth of information technology and electronics, technological transitions from analogue to digital technologies, technological fusion of audio and video technologies, and the technological fusion of electronics and physics to optronics' (pp. 24–26).

6. The identification and development of a firm's core competencies depend on its *strategic architecture*, defined as:

> ... a road map of the future that identifies which core competencies to build and their constituent technologies. . . . should make resource allocation priorities transparent to the whole organisation. . . . Top management must add value by enunciating the strategic architecture that guides the competence acquisition process (1990, p. 89).[20]

Examples given include:

- NEC   = convergence of computing and communication technologies
- Vickers, USA   = being the best power and motion control company in the world
- Honda   = lightweight, high-compression engines
- 3M   = coatings and adhesives

Assessment of the Core Competencies Approach

The great strength of the approach proposed by Hamel and Prahalad is that it places the cumulative development of firm-specific technological competencies at the centre of the agenda of corporate strategy. Although they have done so by highlighting practice in contemporary firms, their descriptions reflects what has been happening in successful firms in science-based industries since the beginning of the twentieth century. For example, Gottfried Plumpe has shown that the world's leading company in the exploitation of the revolution in organic chemistry in the 1920s—IG Farben in Germany—had already established numerous 'technical committees' at the corporate level, in order to exploit emerging technological opportunities that cut across divisional boundaries.[23] These enabled the firm to diversify progressively out of dyestuffs into plastics, pharmaceutical and other related chemical products.

Other histories of businesses in chemicals and electrical products tell similar stories.[24] In particular, they show that the competence-based view of the corporation has major implications for the organization of R&D, for methods of resource allocation and for strategy determination, to which we shall return in Chapter 6. In the meantime, their approach does have limitations and leaves at least three key questions unanswered.

Differing potentials for technology-based diversification   It is not clear whether the corporate core competencies in all industries offer a basis for product diversification. Compare the recent historical experience of most large chemical and electronics firms, where product diversification based on technology has been the norm, with that of most steel and textile firms, where technology-related product diversification has proved very difficult (see, for example, the unsuccessful attempts to diversify by the Japanese steel industry in the 1980s).[25]

Multi-technology firms Recommendations that firms should concentrate resources on a few fundamental (or 'distinctive') world-beating technological competencies are potentially misleading. Large firms are typically active in a wide range of technologies, in only a few of which do they achieve a 'distinctive' world-beating position.[26] In other technological fields, a *background* technological competence is necessary to enable the firm to co-ordinate and benefit from outside linkages, especially with suppliers of components, subsystems, materials and production machinery. In industries with complex products or production processes, a high proportion of a firm's technological competencies are deployed in such background competencies.[27] In addition, firms are constrained to develop competencies in an increasing range of technological fields (e.g. IT, new materials, biotechnology, see section 5.2 above) in order to remain competitive as products become even more 'multi-technological'.

TABLE 5.4   The strategic function of corporate technological activities.

Strategic functions	Definition	Typical examples
Core or critical functions	Central to corporate competitiveness. Distinctive and difficult to imitate	Technologies for product design and development. Key elements of process technologies
Background or enabling	Broadly available to all competitors, but essential for efficient design, manufacture and delivery of corporate products	Production machinery, instruments, materials, components (software)
Emerging or key	Rapidly developing fields of knowledge presenting potential opportunities or threats, when combined with existing core and background technologies	Materials, biotechnology, ICT-software

Thus, as is shown in Table 5.4, a firm's innovation strategy will involve more than its distinctive core (or critical) competencies. In-house competencies in background (enabling) technologies are necessary for the effective co-ordination of changes in production and distribution systems, and in supply chains. In industries with complex product systems (like automobiles), background technologies can account for a sizeable proportion of corporate innovative activities. Background technologies can also be the sources of revolutionary and disruptive change. For example, given the major opportunities for improved performance that they offer, all businesses today have no choice but to adopt advances in IT technology, just as all factories in the past had no choice but to convert to electricity as a power source. However, in terms of innovation strategy, it is important to distinguish firms where IT is a core technology and a source of distinctive competitive advantage (e.g. CISCO, the supplier of Internet equipment) from firms where it is a background technology, requiring major changes but available to all competitors from specialized suppliers, and therefore unlikely to be a source of distinctive and sustainable competitive advantage (e.g. Tesco, the supermarket chain).

In all industries, emerging (key) technologies can end up having pervasive and major impacts on firms' strategies and operations (e.g. software). A good example of how an emerging/key technology can transform a company is provided by the Swedish telecommunications firm Ericsson. Table 5.5 traces the accumulation of technological competencies, with successive generations of mobile cellular phones and telecommunication cables. In both cases, each new generation required competencies in a wider range of technological fields, and very few established competencies were made obsolete. The process of accumulation involved both increasing links with outside sources of knowledge, and greater expenditures on R&D, given greater product complexity. This was certainly not a process of concentration, but of diversification in both technology and product.

TABLE 5.5   Technology accumulation in Ericsson's product generations.

Product and generation	No. of important technologies				R&D costs (base = 100)	% of technologies acquired externally	Main technological fields (d)	No. of patent classes (e)
	Old (e)	New (b)	Total	Obsolete (c)				
Cellular phones								
1. NMT-450	n.a.	n.a.	5	n.a.	100	12	E	17
2. NMT-900	5	5	10	0	200	28	EPM	25
3. GSM	9	5	14	1	500	29	EPMC	29
Telecoms cables								
1. Coaxial	n.a.	n.a.	5	n.a.	100	30	EPM	14
2. Optical	4	6	10	1	500	47	EPCM	17

n.a. = not applicable.

Notes:
(a) No. of technologies from the previous generation.
(b) No. of new technologies, compared to previous generation.
(c) No. of technologies obsoleted from previous generation.
(d) 'Main' = >15% of total engineering stock. Categories are: E = electrical; P = physics; K = chemistry; M = mechanical; C = computers.
(e) Number of international patent classes (IPC) at four-digit level.
Source: Derived from Granstrand, O., E. Bohlin, C. Oskarsson and N. Sjorberg (1992), 'External technology acquisition in large multi-technology corporations', *R&D Management*, **22**.

For these reasons, the notion of 'core competencies' should perhaps be replaced for technology by the notion of *'distributed* competencies', given that, in large firms, they are distributed:

- Over a large number of *technical fields*
- Over a variety of organizational and physical *locations* within the corporation—in the R&D, production engineering and purchasing departments of the various divisions, and in the corporate laboratory
- Amongst different *strategic objectives* of the corporation, which include not only the establishment of a distinctive advantage in existing businesses (involving both core and background technologies), but also the exploration and establishment of new ones (involving emerging technologies)

Core rigidities   As Dorothy Leonard-Barton has pointed out, 'core competencies' can also become 'core rigidities' in the firm, when established competencies become too dominant.[28] In addition to sheer habit, this can happen because established competencies are central to today's products, and because large numbers of top managers may be trained in them. As a consequence, important new competencies may be neglected or underestimated (e.g. the threat to mainframes from mini- and microcomputers by management in mainframe companies). In addition, established innovation strengths may overshoot the target. In Box 5.4, Leonard-Barton gives the fascinating example from the Japanese automobile industry: how the highly successful 'heavyweight' product managers of the 1980s (see Chapter 9) overdid it in the 1990s. Many examples show that, when 'core rigidities' become firmly entrenched, their removal often requires changes in top management.

BOX 5.4 Heavyweight product managers and fat product designs.

'Some of the most admired features . . . identified . . . as conveying a competitive advantage [to Japanese automobile companies] were: (1) overlapping problem solving among the engineering and manufacturing functions, leading to shorter model change cycles; (2) small teams with broad task assignments, leading to high development productivity and shorter lead times; and (3) using a "heavyweight" product manager—a competent individual with extensive project influence . . . who led a cohesive team with autonomy over product design decisions. By the early 1990s, many of these features had been emulated . . . by US automobile manufacturers, and the gap between US and Japanese companies in development lead time and productivity had virtually disappeared.

However . . . there was another reason for the loss of the Japanese competitive edge—"fat product designs" . . . an excess in product variety, speed of model change, and unnecessary options . . . "overuse" of the same capability that created competitive advantages in the 1980s has been the source of the new problem in the 1990s. The formerly "lean" Japanese producers such as Toyota had overshot their targets of customer satisfaction and overspecified their products, catering to a long "laundry list" of features and carrying their quest for quality to an extreme that could not be cost-justified when the yen appreciated in 1993. . . . Moreover, the practice of using heavyweight managers to guide important projects led to excessive complexity of parts because these powerful individuals disliked sharing common parts with other car models.' (Leonard-Barton, D. *Wellsprings of Knowledge*. Harvard Business School Press, Boston, 1995, p. 33)

Developing and Sustaining Competencies

The final question about the notion of core competencies is very practical: how can management identify and develop them?

Definition and measurement There is no widely accepted definition or method of measurement of competencies, whether technological or otherwise. One possible measure is the level of *functional performance* in a generic product,

---

BOX 5.5 On visions.

In recent years the notion of 'visions' has become popular to describe informal expectations of the future, as distinct from the formally derived forecasting of conventional strategic planning. Jonathan Sapsed's study of vision statements and strategic change argues that visions are essentially tactical devices: internally they serve to announce new directions and close debate, whilst externally they allure investors or signal to competitors.

Examples are the media wars over video-on-demand in the late 1990s. BT (British Telecom) announced plans for full-motion-video to be transmitted through the existing copperwire telephone network, using the then unproven technology ADSL (asymmetric digital subscriber line). This was heavily publicized as BT conducted a high-profile technical and market trial of the interactive service. The vision of consumers dialling up premium movies for instant transmission on their telephone handsets was widely interpreted as a spoiler to investment in the nascent UK cable television industry. It had the effect of lowering market valuations of the struggling cable franchisees. They, in response, revealed their alternative visions and trials of a rival cable-based technical solution, ATM (asynchronous transfer mode). The press quoted both camps expressing scepticism about the viability of the other's technology.

In fact, neither service was eventually introduced to the market, although the technological learning of the trials was redeployed on new applications and product markets. Sapsed shows that visions and strategies are ephemeral and much more volatile than the underlying technological paths. Announcements of visions serve various purposes, but should not be taken to signify genuine strategic intention. They can, however, be extremely important, particularly for start-up firms in new, uncertain technologies who often have nothing more tangible to sell to prospective investors. The stock market valuations of high-tech start-ups are often based on the 'buying' of visions.

Source: Sapsed, J. (2001) *Restricted Vision: Strategizing under uncertainty*. Imperial College Press, London.

---

component or subsystem: in, for example, performance in the design, development, manufacture and performance of compact, high-performance combustion engines. As a strategic technological *target* for a firm like Honda, this obviously makes sense. But its achievement requires the combination of technological competencies from a wide variety of *fields* of knowledge, the composition of which changes (and increases) over time. Twenty years ago, they included mechanics (statics and dynamics), materials, heat transfer, combustion, fluid flow. Today they also include ceramics, electronics, computer-aided design, simulation techniques and software.

Thus, the functional definition of technological competencies bypasses two central tasks of corporate technology strategy: first, to identify and develop the range of disciplines or fields that must be combined into a functioning

BOX 5.6 The overvaluation of technological wonders.

In 1986, Schnaars and Berenson published an assessment of the accuracy of forecasts of future growth markets since the 1960s, with the benefit of 20 or more years of hindsight.[32] The list of failures is as long as the list of successes. Below are some of the failures.

'The 1960s were a time of great economic prosperity and technological advancement in the United States. . . .

One of the most extensive and widely publicized studies of future growth markets was TRW Inc.'s "Probe of the Future". The results . . . appeared in many business publications in the late 1960s. . . . Not all . . . were released. Of the ones that were released, nearly all were wrong! Nuclear-powered underwater recreation centres, a 500 kilowatt nuclear power plant on the moon, 3-D colour TV, robot soldiers, automatic vehicle control on the interstate system, and plastic germproof houses were amongst some of the growth markets identified by this study.

. . . In 1966, industry experts predicted, "The shipping industry appears ready to enter the jet age." By 1968, large cargo ships powered by gas turbine engines were expected to penetrate the commercial market. The benefits of this innovation were greater reliability, quicker engine starts and shorter docking times.

. . . Even dentistry foresaw technological wonders . . . in 1968, the Director of the National Institute of Dental Research, a division of the US Public Health Service, predicted that "in the next decade, both tooth decay and the most prevalent form of gum disease will come to a virtual end". According to experts at this agency, by the late 1970s false teeth and dentures would be "anachronisms" replaced by plastic teeth implant technology. A vaccine against tooth decay would also be widely available and there would be little need for dental drilling.'

technology; second (and perhaps more important) to identify and explore the new competencies that must be added if the functional capability is not to become obsolete. This is why a definition based on the measurement of the combination of competencies in different technological fields is more useful for formulating innovation strategy, and is in fact widely practised in business.[29]

Richard Hall goes some way towards identifying and measuring core competencies.[30] He distinguishes between intangible assets and intangible competencies. Assets include intellectual property rights and reputation. Competencies include the skills and know-how of employees, suppliers and distributors, and the collective attributes which constitute organizational culture. His empirical work, based on a survey and case studies, indicates that managers believe that the most significant of these intangible resources are company reputation and employee know-how, both of which may be a function of organizational culture. Thus organizational culture, defined as the shared values and beliefs of members of an organizational unit, and the associated artefacts, becomes central to organizational learning.

Top management and 'strategic architecture' for the future   The importance given by Hamel and Prahalad to top management in determining the 'strategic architecture' for the development of future technological competencies is debatable. As *The Economist* has argued:[31]

> It is hardly surprising that companies which predict the future accurately make more money than those who do not. In fact, what firms want to know is what Mr. Hamel and Mr. Prahalad steadfastly fail to tell them: how to guess correctly. As if to compound their worries, the authors are oddly reticent about those who have gambled and lost.

The evidence in fact suggests that the successful development and exploitation of core competencies does not depend on management's ability to forecast accurately long-term technological and product developments: as Boxes 5.5 and 5.6 illustrate, the record here is not at all impressive.[33] Instead, the importance of new technological opportunities and their commercial potential emerge not through a flash of genius (or a throw of the dice) from senior management, but gradually through an incremental corporate-wide process of learning in knowledge building and strategic positioning. New core competencies cannot be identified immediately and without trial and error: thus Box 5.3 above neglects to show that Canon failed in electronic calculators and in recording products.[34]

It was through a long process of trial and error that Ericsson's new competence in mobile telephones first emerged.[35] As Box 5.7 shows, it is also how Japanese firms developed and exploited their competencies in opto-electronics.

BOX 5.7 Learning about opto-electronics in Japanese companies.

Using a mixture of bibliometric and interview data, Kumiko Miyazaki traced the development and exploitation of opto-electronics technologies in Japanese firms. Her main conclusions were as follows:

'. . . Competence building is strongly related to a firm's past accomplishments. The notions of path dependency and cumulativeness have a strong foundation. Competence building centres in key areas to enhance a firm's core capabilities.

. . . by examining the different types of papers related to semiconductor lasers over a 13 year period, it was found that in most firms there was a decrease in experimental type papers accompanied by a rise in papers marking "new developments" or "practical applications". The existence of a wedge pattern for most firms confirmed . . . that competence building is a cumulative and long process resulting from trial and error and experimentation, which may eventually lead to fruitful outcomes. The notion of search trajectories was tested using . . . INSPEC and patent data. Firms search over a broad range in basic and applied research and a narrower range in technology development. . . . In other words, in the early phases of competence building, firms explore a broad range of technical possibilities, since they are not sure how the technology might be useful for them. As they gradually learn and accumulate their knowledge bases, firms are able to narrow the search process to find fruitful applications.'

Source: Miyazaki, K. (1994) 'Search, learning and accumulation of technological competencies: the case of optoelectronics', *Industrial and Corporate Change*, **3**, 653.

5.4 Technological Paths in Small Firms

Unlike large firms, small firms tend to be specialized rather than diversified in their technological competencies and product range. However, as with large firms, it is impossible to make robust generalizations about their technological trajectories and innovation strategies. Kurt Hoffman and his colleagues have recently pointed out that relatively little research has been undertaken on innovation in small firms: what research has been done tends to concentrate on the small group of spectacular high-tech successes (or failures) rather than the much more numerous run-of-the-mill small firms coping (say) with the introduction of IT into their distribution systems.[36]

Table 5.6 tries to categorize these differences. Until recently, attention has been focused on the left-hand side of the table—the spectacular and visible successes amongst small innovating firms: in particular, the 'superstars' that became big, and those of the new technology-based firms (NTBFs) that often want to become big. As we have seen earlier in this chapter and in Chapter 4, recent more systematic surveys of innovative activities and of small firms show two other classes of small firm with less spectacular innovation strategies, but of far greater importance to the overall economy: specialized suppliers of production inputs, and firms whose sources of innovation are mainly their suppliers.

Superstars are large firms that have emerged from small beginnings, through high rates of growth based on the exploitation of a major invention (e.g. instant photography, reprography), or a rich technological trajectory (e.g. semiconductors, software), enabling small firms to exploit first-mover advantages like patent protection and learning curves (see Chapter 3). Successful innovators often either accumulated their technological knowledge in large firms before leaving to start their own, or they offered their invention to large firms but were refused (examples: Polaroid, Xerox). Few superstars have emerged either in the chemical industry over the past 50 years, or—contrary to expectations—out of biotechnology firms over the past 15 years, probably because the barriers to entry (in R&D, production, or marketing) remain high.

The examples in Table 5.6 show that many superstars are from the USA, although we can find European and Japanese examples. Experience suggests that one of the main challenges facing the management of superstars is their transition from the original innovator and the original innovation to new management and a new line of products. Beyond the period of spectacular growth, the characteristics behind the original success can become sources of 'core rigidities' (see section 5.3). Successful innovators are often strong characters who do not necessarily encourage diversity in ideas and approaches within the firm. Successful innovations are often well protected by patents and other first-comer advantages, which can blunt the drive for improvement and change. These difficulties have beset companies like DEC, Polaroid and Xerox. One of the most successful in maintaining its innovative performance has been Sony. An interesting exercise is to speculate about the future of today's superstars: what will happen to Microsoft after Bill Gates?

New technology-based firms (NTBFs) are small firms that have emerged recently from large firms and large laboratories in such fields as electronics, software and biotechnology. They are usually specialized in the supply of a key component,

TABLE 5.6   Categories of innovating small firms.

	Superstars: small firms into big since 1950	New technology-based firms (NTBFs)	Specialized suppliers	Supplier-dominated
Examples	Polaroid, DEC, TI, Xerox, Intel, Microsoft, Compaq, Sony, Casio, Benetton	Start-ups in electronics, biotechnology and software	Producer goods (machines, components, instruments, software)	Traditional products (e.g. textiles, wood products, food products) and many services
Sources of competitive advantage	Successful exploitation of major invention or technological trajectory	1. Product or process development in fast-moving and specialized area 2. Privatizing academic research	Combining technologies to meet users' needs	Integration and adaptation of innovations by suppliers
Main tasks of innovation strategy	Preparing replacements for the original invention (or inventor)	1. 'Superstar' or 'specialized supplier?' 2. Knowledge or money?	Links to advanced users and pervasive technologies	Exploiting new IT-based opportunities in design, distribution and co-ordination

subsystem, service or technique to larger firms, who may often be their former employers. Contrary to a widespread belief, most of the NTBFs in electronics and software have emerged from corporate or government laboratories involved in development and testing activities. It is only with the advent of biotechnology (and, more recently software), that university laboratories have become regular sources of NTBFs, thereby strengthening the strong direct links that have always existed between university-based research and the pharmaceutical industry. However, some observers criticize this trend, and fear the 'privatization' of university research in biotechnology will in the long term reduce the rate of scientific progress and innovation and their contribution to economic and social welfare.

The management of NTBFs faces two sets of strategic problems:

1. The first relates to long-term prospects for growth. Very few technology-based small firms can become superstars, since they provide mainly specialized 'niche' products with no obvious or spectacular synergies with other markets. How far the firm will grow, or how long it will survive, will often depend on its ability to negotiate the transition from the first to the second (improved) generation of products, and to develop the supporting managerial competencies.

2. How far the NTBF will grow depends on the second strategic choice: whether the management is aiming to maximize long-term value of the business, or merely seeking an increase in income and independence. Thus, owners of small firms often sell their firms after a few years and live off their invest-

ments. And university researchers set up consultancy firms, either to increase their personal income (the BMW effect), or to find supplementary income for their university-based research and teaching activities in times of increasing financial stringency.

These will be discussed in more detail in Chapter 12.

Specialized supplier firms have already been described earlier in this chapter. They design, develop and build specialized inputs into production, in the form of machinery, instruments and (increasingly) software, and interact closely with their (often large) technically progressive customers. They perform relatively little formal R&D, but are nonetheless a major source of the active development of significant innovations, with major contributions being made by design and production staff.[37]

Finally, most small firms fall into the *supplier-dominated* category, with their suppliers of production inputs as their main sources of new technology. As we saw in Chapter 3, these firms depend heavily on their suppliers for their innovations, and therefore are often unable to appropriate firm-specific technology as a source of competitive advantage. Technology will become more important in future, with the growing range of potential IT applications offered by suppliers, especially in service activities like distribution and co-ordination. An increasing range of small firms will therefore need to obtain the technological competencies to be able to specify, purchase, install and maintain software systems that help increase their competitiveness. Whether these competencies will become distinctive, *core* competencies is less clear, given that they can be adopted by all small firms. Distinctive advantage will emerge only where the software competencies are difficult to imitate, namely in developing and operating complex systems. Amongst small firms, such competencies are less likely to emerge in those *using* software, than amongst those *supplying* software services.

5.5 Summary and Further Reading

In this chapter we have shown how firms are inevitably constrained in their choice of innovation strategies by their accumulated skills, and by the opportunities that they are capable of exploiting. In other words, they are on technological trajectories. We identified five broad technological trajectories, each of which has distinct sources and directions of technical change, and which defines key tasks for innovation strategy. We also identified key technologies that are expected to create major technological opportunities in the future. In particular, we stress the importance of distinguishing between the nature and strategic implications of the microelectronics revolution (i.e. the costly business of making electronic chips) from the IT revolution (i.e. the pervasive possibilities of applying software technology to the corporate functions of R&D, logistics, distribution, transactions and co-ordination, as well as production).

We reviewed the concepts developed by Prahalad and Hamel in strategic management, which are (at last!) giving technological competencies a centrally important role. They show the potential tensions between corporate structures built around into strategic business units, and the requirements to reconfigure organizations and associated competencies to exploit emerging technological opportunities. However, the emphasis on *distinctive* core competencies neglects the wider function of technological competencies in establishing linkages with the outside world, and in exploring future opportunities. Similarly, the emphasis on *strategic architecture* (or *vision*) neglects the inevitable uncertainties in the development of future competencies, and the consequent need for experiment and experience.

Given these uncertainties, management concepts and tools for identifying and developing technological competencies should be kept simple, robust and capable of constant revision of assumptions and inputs in the light of new evidence or insights. Probably the most useful remains the technology–product matrix, where existing competencies can be mapped against products, and technical judgement can explore systematically (see Box 5.8).

In addition the matrix in Box 5.8 can be used to explore the:

- Likely effects of emerging new technical fields on the firm's existing competencies and products
- Possibilities of product diversification based on existing competencies
- Additional competencies that need to be acquired to allow product diversification

There has been a plethora of papers and books on competencies since Prahalad and Hamel published their original article in the *Harvard Business Review* in 1990, ranging from statistical analysis of patents and other technology indicators (see e.g. N. Argyres, 1996, 'Capabilities, technological diversification and divisionalization', *Strategic Management Journal*, **17**, 395–410), through to conceptual papers based on case studies in specific sectors (see e.g. R. Henderson and I. Cockburn, 1995, 'Measuring competence? Exploring firm effects in pharmaceutical research', *Strategic Management Journal*, **15**, Special Issue, 63–84). Despite this, most studies have not been sufficiently critical or robust to provide theoretical or practical insights for managers. The best introduction is still *Competing for the Future* by Prahalad and Hamel (Harvard Business School Press, 1994), followed by *Competence-Based Competition* edited by Gary Hamel (Wiley, Chichester, 1994). Dorothy Leonard-Barton provides a more critical assessment in her book *Wellsprings of Knowledge* (Harvard Business School Press, 1995), and a range of more practical tools and techniques are provided by *Measuring Strategic Competencies: Technological, market and organizational indicators of innovation*, edited by Joe Tidd (Imperial College Press, London, 2000).

The implications of radical new technologies (and especially IT) for corporate strategy are immense, ever-changing and difficult to define with certainty. Good papers on the subject are emerging in management journals, but some of the best descriptive—and analytical—material can be found in business journals like *The Economist*.

On *retailing*, see *The Economist*, 26 Feb., 2001: 42; C. H. Cristensen and R. S. Tedlow, 'Patterns of disruption in retailing', *Harvard Business Review*, Jan.–Feb. 2000, 42–45; N. C. Kim and R. Hamborgne, 'Creating new market space', *Harvard Business Review*, Jan.–Feb. 1999, 83–93; M. Harvey, 'Innovation and competition in UK supermarkets', CRIC Briefing Paper No. 3, June 1999; http://les1.man.ac.uk/cric/Pdfs/BP3.pdf

BOX 5.8 The technology–product matrix.

	Strategic technical area (STA)		
	Product line 1	Product line 2	Product line 3 etc.
Integrated circuit fabrication	×		
Integrated circuit design	×	×	×
System architecture		×	
Software engineering	×	×	×

When he was Director of Planning for GTE Laboratories Incorporated, Graham Mitchell wrote the following:

'. . . the issue which is . . . most frustrating and difficult to resolve concerns the degree to which technical programs should be targeted merely to the support of the existing strategies of the business, as opposed to providing opportunities for significant and sometimes revolutionary change. . . .

. . . For business management, it requires acceptance of an enlarged role for the technologist in the formulation of business goals and strategy. For technical management, it implies that the traditional emphasis on the *management of projects* be extended to include a greater emphasis on the strategically more important issue of the *management of technology*. . . . The underlying situation which gives particular value to the STA (strategic technical area) is that, in many large industrial corporations, similar technical skills and expertise are widely applicable in different parts of the organisation. . . .

The STA/product line, service or business matrix . . . [see above] provides the framework needed to integrate the conflicting approaches to technical strategy.

A review of the distribution of technical effort *vertically*—that is, by product line or organisation—deals directly with the general management question: "Is the technical strategy viable, and to what extent is the distribution of technical resources consistent with the stated strategy of the business?"

A *horizontal* view through the matrix begins to answer the technical managers' question: "Where are the greatest technical opportunities for the corporation?" The horizontal view defines those technical areas which are most important to the corporation in aggregate and, at the same time, identifies the specific present and future business lines which will be the most affected by advances in the underlying technology.'

Source: Mitchell, G. (1986) 'New approaches for the strategic management of technology', in M. Horwich (ed.), *Technology and the Modern Corporation: A strategic perspective*, Pergamon, New York, p. 134.

On *bookselling*, see *The Economist*, 20 November 1999, 108–111; 22 August 1998, 24–25; 10 May 1997, 'Survey of electronic commerce'. On the *music industry*, see *The Economist*, 8 May 1999, 91–92.

Intermediate users: *Pharmaceuticals, Biotech and new Materials*, see *The Economist*, 26 June 1999, 17–29; 21 Feb. 1998, 14–16; 14 Mar. 1998, 123; 3 Jan. 1998, 78–79; 20 Apr. 1996, 96; G. P. Pisano, 'Learning before doing in the development of new process technology', *Research Policy*, **25**, 1996, 1097–1119.

The suppliers, see *The Economist*, 8 Apr. 2000; 6 June 1998, 97–100; 28 Mar. 1998, 98; 12 July 1997, 71–72; 29 Mar. 1997, 14–20.

E-commerce: see N. Venkatraman, 'Five steps to a dot-com strategy: how to find your footing on the Web', *Strategic Management Review*, Spring 2000, 15–28; *The Economist*, 26 Feb. 2000; 6 Nov. 1999, 97–98.

References

1   Teece, D. and G. Pisano (1994) 'The dynamic capabilities of firms: an introduction', *Industrial and Corporate Change*, **3**, 537–556.

2   Prof. J. Meisel, cited in Fluss, J. (1996) 'The Electric Vehicle: Development and potential', MBA dissertation, The Management School, Imperial College, London.

3   Fulkerson, W., R. Judkins and M. Sanghvi (1990) 'Energy from fossil fuels', *Scientific American*, September, 83–89.

4   Patel, P. and K. Pavitt (2000) 'How technological competencies help define the core (not the boundaries) of the Firm', in Dosi, G., Nelson, R. R. and Winter, S. G. (eds), *The Nature and Dynamics of Organizational Capabilities*, Oxford University Press, Oxford, pp. 313–333.

5   Mowery, D. and N. Rosenberg (1989) *Technology and the Pursuit of Economic Growth*. Cambridge University Press.

6   Patel, P. and K. Pavitt (1998) 'The wide (and increasing) spread of technological competencies in the world's largest firms: a challenge to conventional wisdom', in Chandler, A., Hagstrom, P. and Solvell, O. (eds), *The Dynamic Firm*. Oxford University Press, Oxford.

7   Nelson, R. and S. Winter (1977) 'In search of a useful theory of innovation', *Research Policy*, **6**, 36–76.

8   Dosi, G. (1982) 'Technological paradigms and technological trajectories', *Research Policy*, **11**, 147–162.

9   Pavitt, K. (1984) 'Sectoral patterns of technical change: towards a taxonomy and a theory', *Research Policy*, **13**, 343–373; Pavitt, K. (1990) 'What we know about the strategic management of technology', *California Management Review*, **32**, 17–26.

10 Freeman, C., J. Clark and L. Soete (1982) *Unemployment and Technical Innovation: A study of long waves and economic development*. Frances Pinter, London.

11 Mowery, D. and N. Rosenberg (1989) *Technology and the Pursuit of Economic Growth*. Cambridge University Press, Cambridge.

12 Arundel, A., G. van de Paal and L. Soete (1995) *Innovation Strategies of Europe's Largest Industrial Firms*. PACE Report, MERIT, University of Limbourg, Maastricht; Cesaretto, S. and S. Mangano (1992) 'Technological profiles and economic performance in the Italian manufacturing sector, *Economics of Innovation and New Technology*, **2**, 237–256.

13 Coombs, R. and A. Richards (1991) 'Technologies, products and firms' strategies', *Technology Analysis and Strategic Management*, **3**, 77–86, 157–175.

14 Patel, P. and K. Pavitt (1998) 'The wide (and increasing) spread of technological competencies in the world's largest firms: a challenge to conventional wisdom', in Chandler, A., Hagstrom, P. and Solvell, O. (eds), *The Dynamic Firm*. Oxford University Press, Oxford.

15 Nightingale, P. (2000) 'Economies of scale in experimentation: knowledge and technology in pharmaceutical R&D', *Industrial and Corporate Change*, **9**, 315–359.

16 Belussi, F. (1989) 'Benetton—a case study of corporate strategy for innovation in traditional sectors', in Dodgson, M (ed.), *Technology Strategy and the Firm: Management and public policy*.

Longman, London; Barras, R. (1990) 'Interactive innovation in financial and business services: the vanguard of the service revolution', *Research Policy*, **19**, 215–238.

17   Schneider, A. (1986) 'High tech comes to the tulip bed', *Business Week* (Industrial-Technology Edition) Issue 2946, May 12, 72D, 72H.

18   Kennedy, A. (1993) 'Up and comers: all wrapped up in a great gift idea', *BRW* (International Edition), **3**(5), 32–33.

19   Dosi, G., D. Teece and S. Winter (1992) 'Towards a theory of corporate coherence: preliminary remarks', in Dosi, G., Giannetti, R. and Toninelli, P. (eds), *Technology and Enterprise in a Historical Perspective*. Clarendon Press, Oxford.

20   Prahalad, C. K. and G. Hamel (1990) 'The core competencies of the corporation', *Harvard Business Review*, May–June, 79–91; Prahalad, C. K. and Hamel, G. (1994) *Competing for the Future*. Harvard Business School Press, Cambridge, Mass.

21   Oskarsson, C. (1993) *Technology Diversification: The phenomenon, its causes and effects*. Department of Industrial Management and Economics, Chalmers University, Gothenburg.

22   Argyres, N. (1996) 'Capabilities, technological diversification and divisionalization', *Strategic Management Journal*, **17**, 395–410.

23   Plumpe, G. (1995) 'Innovation and the structure of IG Farben', in Caron, F., Erker, P. and Fischer, W. *Innovations in the European Economy between the Wars*. De Gruyter, Berlin.

24   Graham, M. (1986) *RCA and the Videodisc: The business of research*. Cambridge University Press, Cambridge; Hounshell, D. and J. Smith (1988) *Science and Corporate Strategy: Du Pont R&D, 1902–1980*. Cambridge University Press, New York; Reader, W. (1975) *Imperial Chemical Industries, a History*. Oxford University Press, Oxford; Reich, L. (1985) *The Making of American Industrial Research: Science and business at GE and Bell*. Cambridge University, Cambridge. For a discussion of the implications for innovation strategy of these and related studies, see Pavitt, K. & W. Steinmueller (2001) 'Technology in corporate strategy: change, continuity and the information revolution', in Pettigrew, A., Thomas, H. and Whittington, R. (eds), *Handbook of Strategy and Management*, Sage.

25   *The Economist* (1989) 'Japan's smokestack fire-sale', 19 August, 63–64.

26   Granstrand, O., P. Patel and K. Pavitt (1997) 'Multi-technology corporations: why they have "distributed" rather than "distinctive core" competencies', *California Management Review*, **39**, 8–25. Patel, P. and K. Pavitt (1998) 'The wide (and increasing) spread of technological competencies in the world's largest firms: a challenge to conventional wisdom', in Chandler, A., Hagstrom, P. and Solvell, O. (eds), *The Dynamic Firm*. Oxford University Press, Oxford.

27   Prencipe, A. (1997) 'Technological competencies and product's evolutionary dynamics: a case study from the aero-engine industry,' *Research Policy*, **25**, 1261.

28   Leonard-Barton, D. (1995) *Wellsprings of Knowledge*. Harvard Business School Press, Boston.

29   Capon, N. and R. Glazer (1987) 'Marketing and technology: a strategic coalignment', *Journal of Marketing*, **51**, 1–14.

30   Hall, R. (1994) 'A framework for identifying the intangible sources of sustainable competitive advantage', in Hamel, G. and Heene, A. (eds), *Competence-Based Competition*. John Wiley & Sons, Chichester, pp. 149–169.

31   *The Economist* (1994) 'The vision thing', 3 September, 77.

32   Schnaars, S. and C. Berenson (1986) 'Growth market forecasting revisited: a look back at a look forward', *California Management Review*, **28**, 71–88.

33   For more detail, see Schnaars, S. (1989) *Megamistakes: Forecasting and the myth of rapid technological change*. Free Press, New York.

34   Sandoz, P. (1997) *Canon*. Penguin, London.

35   Granstrand, O., E. Bohlin, C. Oskarsson and N. Sjorberg (1992) 'External technology acquisition in large multi-technology corporations', *R & D Management*, **22** (2), 111–133.

36   Hoffman, K., M. Parejo and J. Bessant (1998) 'Small firms, R&D, technology and innovation in the UK: a literature review', *Technovation*, **18**, 39–56.

37   Pavitt, K., M. Robson and J. Townsend (1989) 'Technological accumulation, diversification and organisation in UK companies, 1945–83', *Management Science*, **35**, 81–99.

Chapter 6

PROCESSES: INTEGRATION FOR STRATEGIC LEARNING

Amongst the important dynamic capabilities of the firm, the most critical are the processes that ensure effective *integration* and *learning*.[1] Integration has long been recognized as a major task of management, especially in R&D departments with scientists and engineers from specialized disciplines[2] and in large firms with specialized functions and divisions.[3] And as we have seen many times already, continuous learning is central to the survival and success of firms operating in changing and complex environments.

The trick in innovation strategy is to be able to do both together. Effective learning in innovation requires strong feedback between decisions and their implementation (in other words, between analysis and action), and this often requires the effective integration of information and knowledge across functional and divisional boundaries. In the literature on innovation management, probably the best known and the most studied of these interfaces is between the R&D and marketing functions.[4] This and others closely related to the implementation of innovations will be discussed in Chapter 9.

Here we shall concentrate on three areas where integration and learning are essential for the success of innovation strategy: the location of R&D (and other technological activities) within the corporation; the role of the R&D and related functions in determining the allocation of corporate financial resources; and the links between innovation strategy and corporate strategy. We shall emphasize the nature and the importance of the tasks to be addressed, rather than the specific procedures designed to implement them. At the very least, these will probably require the exchange of information across organizational boundaries within the firm. Given the importance of transferring accumulated tacit knowledge, they will be all the more effective if they involve the mobility of practitioners across organizational boundaries. For a study of Japanese practice in this respect, see Kenney and Florida.[5]

6.1 Locating R&D Activities—Corporate versus Divisional

Building organizations that are responsive to change, i.e. are capable of continuous learning, is one of the major tasks of innovation strategy. The R&D and related technical functions within the firm are central features of this capacity to learn. However, as can be seen in Table 6.1, the nature and purpose of the large firms' technological activities vary greatly. Contrast R&D activities of interest to different parts of the firm:

- *Corporate* level: time horizons are long, learning feedback loops slow, internal linkages weak, linkages to external knowledge sources strong, and projects relatively cheap
- *Business unit* level: time horizons are short, learning feedback loops fast, internal linkages (with production and marketing) strong, and projects expensive

TABLE 6.1   The heterogeneity of large firms' technological activities.[6]

Locus of interest	Time horizon (years)	Focus
Corporate-wide	~ 10	• Monitoring major scientific and technical developments • Knowledge-building • Creating new options • Technology positioning • Technical and human resource development
Group/division	~ 5	• Exploit synergies across business units
Business unit	~ 2–3	Implementing business objectives in product: • Cost • Quality • Development time, etc.

Balancing these various activities is a demanding activity involving choices between (i) R&D (and other technological activities) performed in the operating divisions, and in the corporate laboratory; (ii) R&D (and other technological activities) performed in the home country, and in foreign countries. Until recently, a useful rule of thumb for deciding where R&D should be performed was the following:

- *R&D supporting existing businesses* (i.e. products, processes, divisions) should be located in established divisions
- *R&D supporting new businesses* (i.e. products, processes, divisions) should initially be located in central laboratories, then transferred to divisions (established or newly created) for exploitation
- *R&D supporting foreign production* should be located close to that foreign production, and concerned mainly with adapting products and processes to local conditions

Corporate versus Divisional Laboratories

As we shall now see, the decisions about the location of R&D have become more complicated.[7] Recent experience shows that there are in fact two dimensions in the organizational location of a firm's R&D activities:

- *Physical location*, determined mainly by the importance of the main organizational interface: the corporate laboratory towards the general development of fundamental fields of science and technology, and the divisional laboratories towards present-day businesses
- Its *funding*, determined by where the potential benefits will be captured: by some of the established divisions or by the corporation as a whole

TABLE 6.2   The location and funding of a company's R&D.

	Corporate-level performance:	Divisional-level performance:
	Where important interfaces are with general advances in generic science and technologies	Where important interfaces are with production, customers and suppliers
	Quadrant 1	Quadrant 2
Corporate-level funding:	Scanning external research threats and opportunities	Commercializing radical new technologies
When potential benefits are corporate-wide	Assimilating and assessing radical new technologies	Exploiting interdivisional synergies (e.g. production and materials technologies)
	Quadrant 3	Quadrant 4
Divisional-level funding:	Exploratory development of radical new technologies	Mainstream product and process development
When potential benefits are division-specific	Contract research for specific problem-solving for established divisions	Incremental improvements.

As Table 6.2 shows, this leads to four possible categories of R&D activities in the firm. The two already described are in quadrants 1 and 4: activities funded and performed by corporate-level laboratories (quadrant 1), and those funded and performed by division-level laboratories (quadrant 4). The growth of interest in those in quadrants 2 and 3 reflects a major problem that has emerged in the last 20 years, namely the gap within large firms between the corporate-level and division-level laboratories, at a time when competitive success often depends on rapid product development (see Box 6.1).

Activities in quadrant 3 reflect the attempt to ensure stronger linkages between the central and divisional laboratories by strengthening the financial contribution of the divisions to the corporate laboratory, thereby encouraging the interest of the former in the latter, and the sensitivity of the latter to the former. Activities in quadrant 2 recognize that the full-scale commercial exploitation of radically new technologies does not always fit tidily within established divisional structures, so that central funding and initiative may be necessary.

BOX 6.1 Problems in linking corporate R&D to the rest of the firm.

Corporate R&D became unpopular in US firms in the 1980s, when two specific examples were very influential. First, at RCA, failure in the early 1980s of the *videodisc*—in competition with the then emerging video-cassette recorder—resulted in part from the dominant influence and mistaken technical choices made by the Corporate Laboratories, in opposition to the Consumer Electronics Division.[8]

Second, Xerox's Palo Alto Research Centre (PARC) in the 1970s made major inventions that were subsequently exploited by other companies. Examples in personal computing include 'bit mapped' displays, windows, the mouse and word processing programmes. According to Bro Uttal, Xerox had difficulty translating first-rate research into money-making products for the following reasons:

the process takes time at any large company. . . . Sheer size slows decision-making, and the need to concentrate on existing businesses impairs management's ability to move deftly into small, fast-changing markets. This is a special problem for Xerox, still overwhelmingly a one-product company. . . .

Serious organizational flaws, acknowledged by high Xerox executives, have proved a handicap. PARC had weak ties with the rest of Xerox, and the rest of Xerox had no channel for marketing products based on the researchers' efforts. . . . The company has revamped marketing five times in the last six years . . . disgruntled researchers have left in frustration. These Xeroids, as they call themselves, have showered PARC's concepts—for designing personal computers, office equipment, and other products—on competing companies.[9]

Similar cutbacks in central corporate R&D in the UK have been analysed by Whittington.[10] Writing in the mid-1980s, Margaret Graham concluded the following:

Whether or not corporate R&D organizations continue to generate long-term research in-house, the ability to translate research performed elsewhere into usable technology for a specific firm will almost certainly remain a responsibility internal to the firm. For this purpose, if corporate R&D did not exist in some form, sooner or later it would have to be invented.[11]

The growing interest in the 1990s in 'core competencies' suggests that she was right.

Corporate R&D: Centralization, Decentralization or External Collaboration?

Within this framework, there are no simple rules that tell managers how to strike the right balance between corporate and divisional initiatives in R&D—a situation that is further complicated by the growth of so-called 'strategic alliances' in R&D with organizations external to the firm. The histories of major firms in science-based industries reveals a cyclical pattern, suggesting there is no right answer, and that finding and maintaining the proper balance is not easy (see, for example, the long history and experience of Du Pont[12]). Nonetheless, we can identify four sets of factors that will influence the proper balance:

1. *The firm's main technological trajectory.* This gives strong guidance on the appropriate balance. At one extreme, the corporate initiatives are very important in the chemically based—and particularly the pharmaceutical—industry, where fundamental discoveries at the molecular level are often directly applicable in technological development. At the other extreme, corporate-level laboratories are less important in sectors—like aircraft and automobiles—that are based on complex products and production systems, where the benefits of basic advances are more indirect (e.g. the use of simulation technologies), and the critical interface is between R&D and design, on the one hand, and production, on the other.

2. *The degree of maturity of the technology.* The examples of opto-electronics and biotechnology[13] show that, after the emergence of a fundamental technological breakthrough, extended periods of trial, error and learning are necessary before specific technological opportunities begin to emerge. During the early 'incubation' stage, there are advantages in isolating such learning processes from immediate commercial pressure by locating them in the corporate laboratory, before transfer to a more market-oriented framework in an established division or internal venture group.

3. *Corporate strategic style.* The corporate R&D laboratory will have low importance in firms whose strategies are entirely driven by short-term financial performance in existing products (see section 6.4). Such 'market-led' strategies will concentrate on the bottom row of division-level funding in Table 6.2, and miss the opportunities emerging from the development and exploitation of radical new technologies. Such financially driven strategies became increasingly apparent in US and UK firms in the 1980s,[14] although Rod Coombs and Albert Richards reported a reversal of the trend in some British firms in the 1990s.[15]

4. *Links to 'new science'-based technologies.* New forms of corporate linkages with basic and academic research are emerging in the 'new sciences' that have grown out of recent advances in molecular biology, nanotechnology and IT.[16] Advances in these fields are the basis of the growth of firms spun off from universities, since they have reduced the costs of technical experimentation to a level where university-type laboratories and research methods can make significant technical advances. This has also had the effect of increasing both the range of technological opportunities that large firms can exploit, and the uncertainties surrounding their eventual usefulness. Large firms therefore prefer to explore these opportunities through collaborations until the uncertainties are reduced.[17]

6.2 Locating R&D Activities—Global versus Local

Since the 1980s, some analysts and practitioners have argued that, following the 'globalization' of product markets, financial transactions and direct investment, large firms' R&D activities should also be globalized—not only in their traditional role of supporting local production—but also in order to create interfaces with specialized skills and innovative opportunities at a world level.[18] However, although striking examples of the internationalization of R&D can be found (e.g. the large Dutch firms, particularly Philips[19]), more comprehensive evidence casts doubt on the strength of such a trend. This evidence is based on the countries of origin of the inventors cited on the front page of patents granted in the USA, to nearly 359 of the world's largest, technologically active firms (and which account for about half of all patenting in the USA). This information turns out to be an accurate guide to the international spread of large firms' R&D activities.

TABLE 6.3   Indicators of the geographic location of large firms' innovative activities in the 1990s.

Nationality of large firms (no.) (1)	% share of origin of US patents in 1992–96 (2–3)		% share of foreign-performed R&D expenditure (year) (4)	% share of foreign origin of US patents in 1992–96 (5–8)				% change in foreign origin of US patents, since 1980–84 (9)
	Home	Foreign		USA	Europe	Japan	Other	
Japan (95)	97.4	2.6	2.1 (1993)	1.9	0.6	0.0	0.1	–0.7
USA (128)	92.0	8.0	11.9 (1994)	0.0	5.3	1.1	1.6	2.2
Europe (136)	77.3	22.7		21.1	0.0	0.6	0.9	3.3
Belgium	33.2	66.8		14.0	52.6	0.0	0.2	4.9
Finland	71.2	28.8	24.0 (1992)	5.2	23.5	0.0	0.2	6.0
France	65.4	34.6		18.9	14.2	0.4	1.2	12.9
Germany	78.2	21.8	18.0 (1995)	14.1	6.5	0.7	0.5	6.4
Italy	77.9	22.1		12.0	9.5	0.0	0.6	7.4
Netherlands	40.1	59.9		30.9	27.4	0.9	0.6	6.6
Sweden	64.0	36.0	21.8 (1995)	19.4	14.2	0.2	2.2	–5.7
Switzerland	42.0	58.0		31.2	25.0	0.9	0.8	8.2
UK	47.6	52.4		38.1	12.0	0.5	1.9	7.6
All firms (359)	87.4	12.6	11.0 (1997)	5.5	5.5	0.6	0.9	2.4

Sources: Derived from Patel, P. and K. Pavitt (2000) 'National systems of innovation under strain: the internationalization of corporate R&D' in Barrell, R., G. Mason and M. O'Mahoney (eds), *Productivity, Innovation and Economic Performance*. Cambridge UP; and Patel, P. and M. Vega (1998) *Technology Strategies of Large European Firms*, P.R.Patel@sussex.ac.uk.

Table 6.3 summarizes the available evidence. Column 1 gives the country of origin and number of large firms; columns 2 and 3 the percentage shares of corporate patenting in the USA from inside and outside the home country (2+3=100); column 4 the percentage share of R&D outside the home country (should be similar to column 3); columns 5–8 break down the foreign patenting in column 3 by region (5+6+7+8=3); and column 9 the rate of increase of foreign patenting from the 1980s to the 1990s.

Taken together, this evidence and some further analysis[20] shows that:

- The world's large firms perform about 12% of their innovative activities outside their home country. The equivalent share of production is about 25%
- The most important factor explaining each firm's share of foreign innovative activities is its share of foreign production. Firms from smaller countries in general have higher shares of foreign innovative activities. On average, foreign production is less innovation-intensive than home production
- Most of the foreign innovative activities are performed in the USA and Europe (in fact, Germany). They are *not* 'globalized'
- Since the late 1980s, European firms—and especially those from France, Germany and Switzerland—have been performing an increasing share of their innovative activities in the USA, in large part in order to tap into local skills and knowledge in such fields as biotechnology and IT.

What Should Management Make of 'Techno-globalism'?

Controversy remains both in the interpretation of this general picture, and in the identification of implications for the future. Our own views are as follows:

1. There are major efficiency advantages in the geographic concentration in one place of strategic R&D for *launching major new products and processes* (first model and production line). These are:
   (a) dealing with unforeseen problems, since proximity allows quick, adaptive decisions;
   (b) integrating R&D, production and marketing, since proximity allows integration of tacit knowledge through close personal contacts (see Box 6.2).
2. The nature and degree of international dispersion of R&D will also depend on the company's major technological trajectory, and the strategically important points for integration and learning that relate to it. Thus, whereas automobile firms find it difficult to separate their R&D geographically from production when launching a major new product, drug firms can do so, and instead locate their R&D close to strategically important basic research and testing procedures.
3. In deciding about the internationalization of their R&D, managers must distinguish between:
   (a) becoming part of global *knowledge networks*—in other words, being aware of, and able to absorb—the results of R&D being carried out globally. Practising scientists and engineers have always done this, and it is now easier with modern IT. However, business firms are finding it increasingly useful to establish relatively small laboratories in foreign countries in order to become strong members of local research networks and thereby benefit from the person-embodied knowledge behind the published papers;
   (b) the *launching of major innovations*, which remains complex, costly, and depends crucially on the integration of tacit knowledge. This remains difficult to achieve across national boundaries. Firms therefore still tend to concentrate major product or process developments in one country. They will sometimes choose a foreign country when it offers identifiable

advantages in the skills and resources required for such developments, and/or access to a lead market.[22]

4. Matching global knowledge networks with the localized launching of major innovations will require increasing international mobility amongst technical personnel, and the increasing use of multinational teams in launching innovations.

5. Advances in IT will enable spectacular increases in the international flow of codified knowledge in the form of operating instructions, manuals and software. They may also have some positive impact on international exchanges of tacit knowledge through teleconferencing, but not anywhere near to the same extent. The main impact will therefore be at the second stage of the 'product cycle',[23] when product design has stabilized, and production methods are standardized and documented, thereby facilitating the internationalization of production. Product development and the first stage of the product cycle will still require frequent and intense personal exchanges, and be facilitated by physical proximity. Advances in IT are therefore more likely to favour the internationalization of production than of the process of innovation.

BOX 6.2 Globalization of product development? Lessons from Ford and Chrysler.[21]

'April 20th [1994] . . . Ford's chairman . . . announced a sweeping management reorganization, removing power from regional fiefs and giving it to global teams. Five so-called "platform teams" will work on the basic Ford models to be sold around the world. . . .

Ford's problem is no longer learning to make cars cheaply . . . but also designing them quickly and cheaply enough. Ford's most ambitious attempt at global design, the simultaneous development of the Contour (as it is known in America) and the Mondeo (Europe) is a case in point.

Both cars were based on the same basic chassis. Design teams in Michigan and Cologne were wired into the same computer. Yet the Contour/Mondeo project ran a year late and cost $6 billion. Too many regional managers managed, as before, to get in the way. Now Mr Trotman is giving a small cadre of managers global authority, while, lower down the ladder, local managers will have more freedom to take smaller decisions without referring them to head office. GM's reorganization is likely to follow similar lines.

. . . both Ford and GM managers admit they have learnt something from Chrysler. For the past three years, Chrysler has been concentrating on developing models faster—and stripping out bureaucracy. On April 19th Chrysler unveiled its best-ever quarterly net profit. . . .'

Chrysler is reaping the profits from having already reorganized its designers and engineers into 'platform teams'—as Ford is now doing. Anyone involved in a particular vehicle—from marketing to manufacturing—works out of the same office, eliminating potential design snags, speeding up product development and sharply reducing costs. The Chrysler Cirrus and Dodge Stratus models will come to market this autumn, less than three years after the project won approval (and two years faster than the models they replace). Their development cost of $900m. is less than a sixth of that for Ford's Mondeo.

6.3 Allocating Resources for Innovation

Given their mathematical skills, one might have expected R&D managers to be enthusiastic users of quantitative methods for allocating resources to innovative activities. The evidence suggests otherwise: practising R&D managers have been sceptical for a long time (see Box 6.3). An exhaustive report by practising European managers on R&D project evaluation classifies and assesses more than 100 methods of evaluation and presents 21 case studies on their use.[24] However, it concludes that no method can guarantee success, that no single approach to pre-evaluation meets all circumstances, and that—whichever method is used—the most important outcome of a properly structured evaluation is *improved communication*. These conclusions reflect three of the characteristics of corporate investments in innovative activities:

1. They are uncertain, so that success cannot be assured.
2. They involve different stages that have different outputs that require different methods of evaluation.
3. Many of the variables in an evaluation cannot be reduced to a reliable set of figures to be plugged into a formula, but depend on expert judgements: hence the importance of communication, especially between the corporate functions concerned with R&D and related innovative activities, on the one hand, and with the allocation of financial resources, on the other.

BOX 6.3 A chief executive officer's completely perfect and absolutely quantitative method of measuring his R&D programme.

I multiply your projects by words I can't pronounce,
And weigh your published papers to the nearest half an ounce;
I add a year-end bonus for research that's really pure,
(And if it's also useful, your job will be secure).

I integrate your patent-rate upon a monthly basis;
Compute just what your place in the race to conquer space is;
Your scientific stature I assay upon some scales
Whose final calibration is the Company net-to-sales.

And thus I create numbers where there were none before;
I have lots of facts and figures—and formulae galore—
And these quantitative studies make the whole thing crystal clear.
Our research should cost exactly what we've budgeted this year.

Source: R. Landon, cited in Dr A. Bueche (Vice-President for Research and Development of the US General Electric Company) in 'From laboratory to commercial application: some critical issues'. Paper presented at the 17th International Meeting of the Institute of Management Sciences, London, 2 July 1970.

Uncertainty

Given the complexities involved, the outcomes of investments in innovation are uncertain, so that the forecasts (of costs, prices, sales volume, etc.) that underlie project and programme evaluations can be unreliable. According to Joseph Bower, management finds it easier, when appraising investment proposals, to make more accurate forecasts of reductions in production cost than of expansion in sales, whilst their ability to forecast the financial consequences of new product introductions is very limited indeed.[25] This last conclusion is confirmed by the study by Edwin Mansfield and his colleagues of project selection in large US firms.[26] By comparing project forecasts with outcomes, he showed that managers find it difficult to pick technological and commercial winners:

- Probability of *technical* success of projects (P_t) = 0.80
- Subsequent probability of *commercial* success (P_c) = 0.20
- Combined probability for all stages: $0.8 \times 0.2 = 0.16$.

He also found that managers and R&D workers cannot predict accurately the *development costs, time periods, markets and profits* of R&D projects. On average, costs were greatly *underestimated*, and time periods *overestimated* by 140–280% in incremental product improvements, and by 350–600% in major new products. Other studies have found that:

- About half business R&D expenditures are on *failed* R&D projects. The higher rate of success in *expenditures* than in *projects* reflects the weeding out of unsuccessful projects at their early stages and before large-scale commercial commitments are made to them[27]
- R&D scientists and engineers are often deliberately over-optimistic in their estimates, in order to give the illusion of a high rate of return to accountants and managers[28]

How to Evaluate Learning?

The potential benefits of innovative activities are twofold. First, *extra profits* derived from increased sales and/or higher prices for superior products, and from lower costs and/or increased sales from superior production processes. Conventional project appraisal methods can be used to compare the value of these benefits against their cost. Second, *accumulated firm-specific knowledge* ('learning', 'intangible assets') that may be useful for the development of *future* innovations (e.g. new uses for solar batteries, carbon fibres, robots, word processing). This type of benefit is relatively more important in R&D projects that are more long term, fundamental and speculative.

Conventional techniques cannot be used to assess this second type of benefit, because it is an 'option'—in other words, it creates the *opportunity* for the firm to invest in a potentially profitable investment, but the realization of the benefits still depend on a decision to commit further resources. Conventional project appraisal techniques cannot evaluate options (see Box 6.4).

BOX 6.4 Why conventional financial evaluation methods do not work with investments in technology.

The following text was written by the Professor of Finance at the Sloan School of Management at MIT.[29]

'Suppose a firm invests in a negative NPV (net present value) project in order to establish a foothold in an attractive market. Thus a valuable second-stage investment is used to justify the immediate project. The second stage must depend on the first: if the firm could take the second project without having taken the first, then the future opportunity should have no impact on the immediate decision. . . .

At first glance, this may appear to be just another forecasting problem. Why not estimate cash flows for both stages, and use discounted cash flow to calculate the NPV for the two stages taken together?

You would not get the right answer. The second stage is an option, and conventional discounted cash flow does not value options properly. The second stage is an option because the firm is not committed to undertaking it. It will go ahead if the first stage works and the market is still attractive. If the first stage fails, or if the market sours, the firm can stop after stage 1 and cut its losses. Investing in stage 1 purchases an intangible asset: a call option on stage 2. If the option's present value offsets the first stage's negative NPV, the first stage is justified. . . .

. . . DCF (discounted cash flow) is readily applied to "cash cows"—relatively safe businesses held for the cash they generate. . . . It also works for "engineering investments", such as machine replacements, where the main benefit is reduced cost in a defined activity.

. . . DCF is less helpful in valuing businesses with substantial growth opportunities or intangible assets. In other words, it is not the whole answer when options account for a large fraction of a business's value.

. . . DCF is no help at all for pure research and development. The value of R&D is almost all option value. Intangible assets' value is usually options value.'

How Practising Managers Cope

These two sets of difficulties—in evaluating the potential contributions of technological investments to firm-specific intangible assets, and in dealing with uncertainty—are reflected in how successful managers allocate resources to technological activities. In particular, they:

- Encourage *incrementalism*—step-by-step modification of objectives and resources, in the light of new evidence
- Use *simple rules* models for allocating resources, so that the implications of changes can be easily understood
- Make explicit from the outset criteria for *stopping* the project or programme
- Use *sensitivity analysis* to explore if the outcome of the project is 'robust' (unchanging) to a range of different assumptions (e.g. 'What if the project costs twice as much, and takes twice as long, as the present estimates?')

- Seek the reduction of *key uncertainties* (technical and—if possible—market) before any irreversible commitment to full-scale—and costly—commercialization
- Recognise that *different types* of R&D should be evaluated by *different criteria*

Organizing Resource Allocation to Innovative Activities

In other words, the corporate R&D community recognizes that the successful allocation of resources to innovation depends less on robustness of decision-making techniques than on the organizational processes in which they are embedded. According to Mitchell and Hamilton,[30] there are three (overlapping) categories of R&D that large firms must finance. Each category has different objectives and criteria for selection, the implications of which are set out in Table 6.4.

Knowledge-building   This is the early-stage and relatively inexpensive research for nurturing and maintaining expertise in fields that could lead to future opportunities or threats. It is often treated as a necessary overhead expense, and sometimes viewed with suspicion (and even incomprehension) by senior management obsessed with short-term financial returns and exploiting existing markets, rather than creating new ones.

  With knowledge-building programmes, the central question for the company is: 'What are the potential costs and risks of *not* mastering or entering the field?' Thus, no successful large firm in manufacture can neglect to explore the implications of development in IT, even if IT is not a potential core competence. And no successful firm in pharmaceuticals could avoid exploring recent developments in biotechnology. Decisions about such programmes should be taken solely by R&D staff on the basis of technical judgements, and especially those staff concerned with the longer term. Market analysis should not play any role. Outside financial linkages are likely to be with academic and other specialist groups, and to take the form of a grant.

Strategic positioning   These activities are in between knowledge-building and business investment, and an important—and often neglected—link between them. They involve applied R&D and feasibility demonstration, in order to reduce technical uncertainties, and to build in-house competence, so that the company is capable of transforming technical competence into profitable investment. For this type of R&D, the appropriate question is: 'Is the programme likely to create *an option* for a profitable investment at a later date?' Comparisons are sometimes made with financial 'stock options', where (for a relatively small sum) a firm can purchase the *option* to buy a stock at a specified price, before a specified date—in anticipation of increase in its value in future (see Box 6.4).

  Decisions about this category of R&D programme should involve divisions, R&D directors and the chief executive, precisely because—as their description implies—these programmes will help determine the strategic options open to the company at a later date. At this stage, market analysis should be broad (e.g. where could genetic engineering create new markets for vegetables in a food company?). A variety of evaluation methods may be used (e.g. the

TABLE 6.4   Criteria and procedures for evaluating different types of R&D.

Objective	Technical activity	Evaluation criteria (% of all R&D)	Decision-takers	Market analysis	Nature of risk	Higher volatility	Longer time horizons	Nature of external alliances
Knowledge building	Basic research, monitoring	Overhead cost allocation (2–10%)	R&D	None	Small = cost of R&D	Reflects wide potential	Increases search potential	Research grant
Strategic positioning	Focused applied research, exploratory development	'Options' evaluation (10–25%)	Chief executive R&D division	Broad	Small = cost of R&D	Reflects wide potential	Increases search potential	R&D contract. Equity
Business Investment	Development and production engineering	'Net present value' analysis (70–99%)	Division	Specific	Large = total cost of launching	Uncertainty reduces net present value	Reduces present value	Joint venture. Majority control

product–technology matrix), but they will be more judgemental than rigorously quantitative. Costs will be higher than those of knowledge-building, but much lower than those of full-scale business investment. As with knowledge-building programmes, both high volatility in predictions and expectations, and long time horizons, are *not* unwelcome signs of unacceptably high risk, but welcome signs are rich possibilities and sufficient time to explore them. Outside linkages require tighter management than those related to knowledge-building, probably through a contract or equity participation.

Business investment This is the development, production and marketing of new and better products, processes and services. It involves relatively large-scale expenditures, evaluated with conventional financial tools such as *net present value* (see Box 6.5).

BOX 6.5 Net present value.

Net present value (NPV) $= \sum_{0}^{T} P_t/(1 + i)^t - C$

where P_t = forecast cash flow in time period t;

T = project life;

i = expected rate of return on securities equivalent in risk to project being evaluated;

C = cost of project at time $t = 0$.

In such projects, the appropriate question is: 'What are the potential costs and benefits in continuing with the project?' Decisions should be taken at the level of the division bearing the costs and expecting the benefits. Success depends on meeting the precise requirements of specific groups of users, and therefore depends on careful and targeted marketing. Financial commitments are high, so that volatility in technological and market conditions is unwelcome, since it increases risk. Long time horizons are also financially unwelcome, since they increase the financial burden. Given the size and complexity of development and commercialization, external linkages need to be tightly controlled through majority ownership or a joint venture. Given the scale of resources involved, careful and close monitoring of progress against expectations is essential.

6.4 Technology and Corporate Strategy

In linking technology to corporate strategy, it must be remembered that the links run both ways. Not only does corporate strategy define objectives for technology.

Technology defines opportunities and constraints for corporate strategy. We shall discuss each of these links in turn.

How Technology Contributes to Corporate Strategy

According to a report prepared by practising managers in large European firms, the R&D function should play a central role in the formulation of an innovation strategy, as part of overall corporate strategy:[31]

> It is essential that the R&D function is totally integrated with the company's activities and strategic thinking. This is the most effective way of judging the relevance of technology past, present and future, to the company's fortunes—its strengths, weaknesses, opportunities and threats. R&D management needs to take the initiative in playing a proactive part in strategy formulation and in executing the plan. . . .
>
> For R&D to participate fully, a person with an overall technical awareness of the company's activities, such as the Technical Director, at senior management level is essential. His/her primary functions are:
>
> - to provide a technical awareness within the company and a 'window' on the external world of technology;
> - to ensure the appropriate level of technology for maintaining or regenerating the company's existing business;
> - to provide a technical input into reviews of new business opportunities;
> - to determine the overall technical strategy consistent with corporate requirements.

The relevance of this recommendation is supported by systematic statistical studies in the USA and the UK,[32] showing that a company's commitment to, and performance in, innovation depends in part on the share of top management with training in science and engineering. The EIRMA report also showed that the technical director had influence over corporate strategy in about 60% of the firms.

R&D strategies—defining the contribution of technology to corporate objectives—are developed formally in most European large firms at the level of the division and the corporation. Table 6.5 shows that formal R&D strategies had their greatest impact in the areas of direct responsibility of the R&D director (namely, the volume, composition, and balance of R&D activities). They had less influence on the organizational location and methods of funding R&D—organization, new venture areas, balance between divisions, methods of funding, and on positioning—role in market, technological position, patent and licensing policies.

Compatibility between Corporate Strategy and the Nature of Technological Opportunities

The EIRMA report makes no mention of the compatibility (or otherwise) between the technological opportunities open to the firm, on the one hand, and its organizational structure and strategic style, on the other. One view is that overall corporate strategy should determine both organizational *structure* and

TABLE 6.5 The areas of impact of R&D strategy in large European firms.

Tasks of R&D strategy	% of companies observing impact
Focal R&D areas	91
Volume of R&D expenditures	85
R&D balance—short, medium and long term	83
R&D organization	71
Internal versus external R&D	69
New venture areas	60
R&D balance between divisions	60
Role in the market	59
Technological position	54
Personnel policy	51
Methods of funding	48
Patent policy	37
Licence policy	33

Source: Derived from EIRMA (1986) *Developing R&D Strategies*, Paris.

technology *strategy*. Another view (our own) is that different kinds of technological opportunities requires different kinds of strategies and structures if they are to be exploited effectively.

According to Chandler, large firms' corporate headquarters have two functions: entrepreneurial promotion and administrative control (see Box 6.6).

BOX 6.6 The entrepreneurial and administrative functions of corporate HQ.[33]

'One was *entrepreneurial*, that is to determine strategies to utilise for the long term the firm's organisational skills, facilities and capital to allocate resources—capital and product-specific technical and managerial skills—to pursue these strategies. The second was more *administrative*. It was to monitor the performance of the operating divisions; to check on the use of the resources allocated; and, when necessary, redefine the product lines of the divisions so as to continue to use effectively the firm's organisational capabilities.

. . . there are differences in the ways the two basic economic functions of the corporate office are carried out—the *entrepreneurial* function of planning for the future health and growth of the enterprise and the *administrative* function of controlling the operation of its many divisions.' (Our italics)

Gould and Campbell identify three generic corporate strategic styles that each have a different balance between the entrepreneurial and administrative functions.[34] As Table 6.6 shows, three 'strategic styles' are appropriate for different types of technology and market:

1. *Financial control* strategies are reflected in a strong administrative monitoring function in corporate HQ, and an expectation of high, short-term financial returns. Technological investments in knowledge-building and strategic positioning will be neither understood nor encouraged, but will concentrate instead on low-risk incremental improvements in established businesses. As such, this strategic style is suited to conglomerates in low-technology industries. There will therefore be relatively little organic growth, and in high-tech industries many technology-based opportunities that are missed rather than exploited.

2. *Strategic planning* strategies are reflected in strong central entrepreneurial direction with corporate HQ giving strong encouragement to investments in knowledge-building and strategic positioning, and taking a central role in deciding technological priorities and—more generally—of showing what Leonard-Barton calls 'strategic intent'.[35] As such, this strategic style is most appropriate for high-tech, focused and lumpy businesses, such as automobiles, drugs and petroleum, where experimentation is costly, and customer markets clearly defined.

TABLE 6.6   Strategic styles and technology strategies.

Strategic style	Functions of HQ	Emphasis in HQ	Firm type	Examples	Mismatch
Financial control	Financial monitoring and control of divisions	*Administrative*: Tight control and quick profits	*Low tech*: Low capital intensity	Conglomerates like Hanson	GEC (UK) ITT (USA)
Strategic planning	Heavy influence in divisions' strategic plans	*Entrepreneurial*: Decides new business and costly projects	*High tech*: Lumpy projects, focused markets	Drugs, oil and automobile firms	IBM (1980s) ICI
Strategic control	Strategic plans devolved to divisional HQ	*Entrepreneurial*: But leaves choices to divisions	*High tech*: Pervasive technology, varied markets	3M Consumer electronics firms	Digitalization in consumer electronics firms

3. *Strategic control* strategies also give high priorities to entrepreneurial technological investments, but devolve the formulation and execution of strategies much more to the divisions and business units. Instead of exercising 'strategic intent', the HQ shows 'strategic recognition' in recognizing and reinforcing successful entrepreneurial ventures emerging from the divisions, and which become separate divisions themselves. As such, this style of strategy is best suited to high-tech businesses with pervasive technologies, varied markets and relatively low costs of experimentation. Examples include 3M Corporation, with its widespread applications of adhesives and coatings technologies, and consumer electronics firms.

BOX 6.7 ITT and GEC.[36]

'. . . ITT was the quintessential conglomerate: a collection of hundreds of businesses held together not by the logic of their activities but by the force of their management. Now, . . . the company has decided to split itself into three easier-to-understand firms. . . . The biggest of the three, *ITT Hartford*, will take over *ITT*'s sprawling insurance operations. . . . *ITT Industries* will take in the old *ITT*'s car, defence, electronics and fluid technology businesses. . . . Finally, hotels, entertainment and information-services will go into a "new" *ITT Corporation*.

In the 1960s and 1970s they [conglomerates] were stock analysts' darlings. They were thought to be immune from the vagaries of the business cycle. . . . They were also thought to demonstrate that good management techniques can be applied to any business, however remote from the company's core concerns. . . . At ITT, these management techniques were synonymous with Harold Geenen. . . . Under his . . . stare, ITT, which started out as a Caribbean telephone company, acquired a rag-bag of companies, including Avis, Continental Baking, Rayonier, Sheraton and Hartford Fire Insurance. The ostensible aim . . of this spending spree was to insure against the uncertain future of the telephone business, but the immediate effect was to expand Mr. Geenen's empire. By 1970, he had control of 400 separate companies operating in 70 different countries. . . . To all these businesses, Mr. Geenen applied the same ruthless, financially driven approach.

Today, focus, not size, is the essence of managerial correctness . . . they must decide what they are good at, and get out of non-related businesses. . . . Conglomerates are not on the way out entirely, however. Even Anglo-Saxon capitalism has a place for combative "antique-dealer" conglomerates such as Britain's Hanson, which specialises in buying under-valued companies, polishes them up and then flogging them off.'

'GEC is the creation of one man, Arnold Weinstock—the most impressive British industrialist of his generation. In the 1960s, he mopped up most of Britain's electronics and electrical engineering industry and cornered a fair chunk of its defence budget. A little monopolistic perhaps, but then many of the best businessmen try to be so. Mr. Weinstock was a management pioneer, forcing the companies he acquired to follow strict financial disciplines. . . .

Unfortunately . . . the times have changed and GEC has not. True, Lord Weinstock, as he is now, has continued to add British defence businesses, but he is better known for sitting atop a pile of cash that many shareholders would rather invest for themselves . . . every boss worth his MBA nowadays looks at the books, but the more modern ones also give their managers freedom. . . . The young technology entrepreneurs whom Britain is beginning to produce see GEC as a horrible relic of the past. "We arranged a $1m. contract with them: it went to head office and never came out," complains one.'

Mismatches between a firm's strategic style and its core technology will inevitably cause instability, and can have two causes. First, the imposition of a strong style of financial control in a sector where high technological investments—especially in knowledge-building and strategic positioning—are necessary for long-term survival. Examples include GEC in the UK, which has

progressively reduced its competence in electronic computers and components, and moved out of high-tech sectors with expanding opportunities; and ITT in the USA (see Box 6.7).

Second, the changing nature of technological opportunities, which require a changed strategic style for their effective exploitation. Contemporary examples include:

- The *chemical industry*, where the focus of technical change over the past 30 years has shifted from large-scale process innovations in bulk plastics and synthetic fibres, to product innovation in drugs and other fine chemicals, and smaller-scale developments in speciality chemicals. This raises two questions for corporate strategy: (1) Are there still *technological* synergies between bulk and fine chemicals? If not, should the large chemical companies demerge? (2) Are there *organizational* incompatibilities between bulk chemicals requiring centralized strategic planning, and speciality chemicals requiring decentralized strategic control? (see Box 6.8).

BOX 6.8 Why ICI chose to demerge.[37]

'. . . Imperial Chemical Industries (ICI) sought new sources of growth during the 1980s to offset the sluggish sales of its older products but, in the end, only increased the complexity of its already complicated and hard-to-manage portfolio of businesses. . . . ICI's response . . . was unusual: a merger that split the organisation into two separate companies: new ICI and Zeneca.

The rationale underlying the structure composition and expansion of the old ICI . . . had been technology and vertical integration. Investment in research and development traditionally ensured a flow of new products. . . . Huge chemical complexes grew up around very large plants, such as ethylene crackers, and ICI exploited each by-product stream to develop a new business. . . . in the 1970s . . . the chemical industry began to mature. [In the 1980s] ICI pushed strongly into high-value specialty chemicals, using both in-house development and acquisitions. . . . Such moves did little to reduce the complexity of ICI's businesses.

. . . the key to successful restructuring was recognising a technological fault line with ICI. Pharmaceuticals and other bioscience-related activities fell on one side of the fault line; the traditional chemical businesses fell to the other. The fault line divided two coherent groups of businesses that could be managed as separate companies. Within each group—but not across them—there was the potential for mutual support and interdependence. . . . the demerger . . . preserved the advantages of retaining under a single ownership businesses that shared technical competencies and benefited from common services and informed central direction. Each of the two companies has had to evolve a balance between the centre and the businesses that suits its particular circumstances. The narrower focus and greater homogeneity of the problems that the new head offices handle shorten and sharpen the lines of communication between headquarters and the operating businesses.'

- The *computer industry*, where technological change over the past 20 years has resulted in a revolutionary change from a market requiring the centralized style of strategic planning (selling large and lumpy mainframe computers to large organizations) to one requiring the decentralized style of strategic control (selling a wide range of relatively cheap hardware and software products in a wide range of market applications). Thus, although IBM and other large firms had the *technological* capacity to make the necessary transformations, they did not succeed in making the matching changes in strategic style and organization

These examples shed important new light on the changing nature of the threats posed to established firms by radically new technology. In the past the main threat was considered to be the inability of the established firms to master the new technology (e.g. makers of horse-drawn carriages could not make automobiles). However, large firms today all typically have R&D laboratories that enable them to monitor, assess and (if necessary) master most new technology. The more difficult challenge now is to deal with the *organizational* implications of the new technology, which may require radical and disruptive changes in, for example, products, markets, degree of centralization, the boundaries of corporate divisions, the key internal interfaces and external networks, and the relative power and influence of various professional groups.[38]

6.5 Organizational Processes in Small Firms

In small firms, deliberate organizational processes to integrate the technical function with production, marketing, strategy and resource allocation are of less central importance than in large firms. In general, these functions are less specialized, and less likely to be separated by physical and organizational distance. Table 6.7 tries to contrast the differences between large and small firms in how certain key tasks of innovation strategy are accomplished. In large firms, deliberate organizational design and formal procedures are essential as a means of integrating knowledge, of supporting professional judgements and of getting things done. In small firms, the characteristics of senior managers—their training, experience, responsibilities and external linkages—play a central role. In particular, their level of technical and organizational skills will determine whether or not they will be able to develop and commercially exploit a firm-specific technological advantage.

6.6 Summary and Further Reading

There are no correct recipes for locating R&D and related innovative activities in the firm. Tensions are inevitable between *organizational decentralization* for rapid implementation, and sensitivity to production and customers, on the one hand, and *organizational centralization* for the exploration of radical and long-term opportunities, not linked to current businesses, on the other. There are also inevitable tensions between *geographic dispersion* for adapting to local markets

TABLE 6.7 How tasks of innovation strategy are accomplished in large and small firms.

Strategic tasks	Large firms	Small firms
Integrating technology with production and marketing	• Organizational design • Organizational processes for knowledge flows across boundaries	• Responsibilities of senior managers
Monitoring and assimilating new technical knowledge	• Own R&D and external networks	• Trade and technical journals • Training and advisory services • Consultants • Suppliers and customers
Judging the learning benefits of investments in technology	• Judgements based on formal criteria and procedures	• Judgements based on qualifications and experience of senior management
Matching strategic style with technological opportunities	• Deliberate organizational design	• Qualifications of managers and staff

and integrating local skills, on the one hand, and *geographic concentration* for the effective launching of major innovations, on the other. The important management challenges are therefore:

- Reconciling rapid product development and quick profit returns, with long-term search for major new technological opportunities
- Reconciling effective new product launches, with the assimilation of competencies located in foreign countries

Formal inputs from the corporate technical function into corporate strategy have been strongest in the determination of R&D priorities, but less strong in R&D funding and organization, and in market positioning. In addition:

- Corporate strategic style must be compatible with *the nature of technological opportunities*, if these are to be effectively exploited. Complete emphasis on financial control will discourage innovation. And the appropriate degree of centralization of entrepreneurial initiative will depend on the size of each innovative investment, and on the degree of similarity of user markets
- Failures in established firms to benefit from radical new technologies now arise less from the inability to master them, and more from the inability or unwillingness to deal with their consequences for *organizational change*
- Conventional project appraisal techniques are of *only limited usefulness* for R&D project evaluation and resource allocation, given high uncertainties in outcomes and difficulties in putting a financial value on the technological learning associated with R&D. In particular, in the early stages of R&D, uncertainties are high, costs (and therefore risks) are low, and choices essentially *judgemental*
- Of great importance are the *processes* of resource allocation that recognize the essentially incremental nature of progress in R&D and related innovative activities, and that *integrate* the skills and methods (technical, financial and

other) appropriate to the purpose and nature of three types of innovative activity: knowledge-building, strategic positioning and business investment

For further reading Professor Rubenstein's text *Managing Technology in the Decentralised Firm* (Wiley, Chichester, 1989) covers most of the ground very thoroughly. The journal *R&D Management* is a major source of the latest research results on R&D project evaluation and related subjects. In addition, there are the papers by R. Cooper, S. Edgett and A. Kleinschmidt 'Best practices for managing R&D portfolios' (*Research-Technology-Management*, **41**(1), 1998) and by A. Henricksen, 'A technology assessment primer for management of technology' (*International Journal of Technology Management*, **13**(5), 1997). Also, the European Industrial Research Management Association (EIRMA) has produced two excellent reports by practitioners on R&D Strategy (reference 31) and R&D Evaluation (reference 24). Professor Chandler's books (*The Visible Hand: The managerial revolution in American business*, The Belknap Press of Harvard University Press, 1977; and *Scale and Scope: The dynamics of industrial competition*, Harvard University Press, 1990) are the classic texts on the relationship between corporate strategy and structure. More recently, the implications of radical technical change for established organizational practices have been explored by Clayton Christensen in *The Innovator's Dilemma* (Harvard University Press, 1997). Research results on the internationalization of corporate R&D can be found in O. Granstrand, L. Hakanson and S. Sjolander, *Technology Management and International Business* (John Wiley & Sons, Chichester, 1992), the special numbers of *Research Policy* on 'The internationalization of industrial R&D' (28/2/1999), and of the *Journal of Product Innovation Management* on the 'Internationalization of innovation' (17/5/2000). Finally, a major series of case studies on the problems of managing innovation in an international framework is presented in the book by R. Boutellier, O. Gassman and M. von Zedwitz, *Managing Global Innovation* (Springer, 1999).

Finally, the organizational implications of advances in IT are not obvious, and are still being discovered through experience and experiment. Recent contributions include: K. Werback, 'Syndication: the emerging model for business in the Internet era', *Harvard Business Review*, May–June 2000, 85–93; D. B. Yoffie and M. A. Cusumano: ' Building a company on Internet time: lessons from Netscape', *California Management Review*, **41**(3), Spring 1999, 8–28; *The Economist*, 18 November: 2000 'Survey of E-management'.

References

1   Teece, D. and G. Pisano (1994) 'The dynamic capabilities of firms: an introduction', *Industrial and Corporate Change*, **3**, 537–556.
2   Allen, T. (1977) *Managing the Flow of Technology*. MIT Press, Cambridge, Mass.
3   Lawrence, W. and J. Lorsch (1967) *Organization and Environment: Managing differentiation and integration*. Graduate School of Business Administration, Harvard University, Boston, Mass.
4   Cooper, R. (1983) 'A process model for industrial new product development', *IEEE Transactions on Engineering Management*, EM-30; Rothwell, R. (1977) 'The characteristics of successful innovators and technically progressive firms', *R & D Management*, **7**, 191–206.
5   Kenney, M. and R. Florida (1994) 'The organization and geography of Japanese R&D: results from a survey of Japanese electronics and biotechnology firms', *Research Policy*, **23**, 305–323.
6   Rieck, R. and K. Dickson (1993) 'A model of technology strategy', *Technology Analysis and Strategic*

Management, **5**, 397–412; Mitchell, G. (1986) 'New approaches for the strategic management of technology,' in Horwitch, M. (ed.), *Technology in the Modern Corporation: A strategic perspective'.* Pergamon, New York.

7   Rousell, P., K. Saad and T. Erickson (1991) *Third Generation R & D.* Harvard Business School Press, Boston, Mass.

8   Graham, M. (1986) *RCA and the Videodisc: The business of research*, Cambridge University Press.

9   Uttal, B. (1983) 'The lab that ran away from Xerox', *Fortune*, 5 September.

10 Whittington, R. (1990) 'The changing structures of R&D: from centralisation to fragmentation', in Loveridge, R. and Pitt, M. (eds), *The Strategic Management of Technological Innovation.* John Wiley & Sons, Chichester.

11 Graham, M. (1986) 'Corporate research and development: the latest transformation', in Horwitch, M. (ed.), *Technology in the Modern Corporation: A strategic perspective.* Pergamon, New York.

12 Hounshell, D. and J. Smith (1988) *Science and Corporate Strategy: Du Pont R&D, 1902–1980.* Cambridge University Press, New York; Rubenstein, A. (1989). *Managing Technology in the Decentralised Firm.* John Wiley & Sons, Chichester.

13 Miyazaki, K. (1994) 'Search, learning and accumulation of technological competencies: the case of optoelectronics', *Industrial and Corporate Change*, **3**, 631–654. For a more detailed analysis, see K. Miyazaki (1995) *Building Competencies in the Firm.* Macmillan, Basingstoke; Sharp, M. (1991) 'Technological trajectories and corporate strategies in the diffusion of biotechnology', in Deiaco, E., Hornell, E. and Vickery, G. (eds), *Technology and Investment.* Pinter, London.

14 Graham, M. (1986) 'Corporate research and development: the latest transformation', in Horwitch, M. (ed.), *Technology in the Modern Corporation: A strategic perspective'*, Pergamon, New York; Whittington, R. (1990) 'The changing structures of R&D: from centralisation to fragmentation', in Loveridge, R. and Pitt, M. (eds), *The Strategic Management of Technological Innovation.* John Wiley & Sons, Chichester.

15 Coombs, R. and A. Richards (1993) 'Strategic control of technology in diversified companies with decentralised R&D', *Technology Analysis and Strategic Management*, **5**, 385–396.

16 See, for example, Koumpis, K. and K. Pavitt (1999) 'Corporate activities in speech recognition and natural language: another "New Science"-based Technology', *International Journal of Innovation Management*, **3**, 335–366; Mahdi, S. and K. Pavitt (1997) 'Key national factors in the emergence of computational chemistry firms', *International Journal of Innovation Management*, **1**, 355–386.

17 In biotechnology, see Pisano, G. (1991) 'The governance of innovation: vertical integration and collaborative relationships in the biotechnology industry', *Research Policy*, **20**, 237–249.

18 Ohmae, K. (1990) *The Borderless World: Power and strategy in the interlinked economy'.* Collins, London.

19 Ghoshal, S. and C. Bartlett (1987) 'Innovation processes in multinational corporations', *Strategic Management Journal*, **8**, 425–439.

20 Cantwell, J. (1992) 'The internationalisation of technological activity and its implications for competitiveness', in Granstrand, O., L. Hakanson and S. Sjolander, *Technology Management and International Business*, John Wiley & Sons, Chichester; Patel, P. (1996) 'Are large firms internationalising the generation of technology? Some new evidence', *IEEE Transactions on Engineering Management*, **43**, 41–47; Ariffin, L. and Bell, M. (1999) 'Firms, politics and political economy: patterns of subsidiary–parent linkages and technological capability-building in electronics TNC subsidiaries in Malaysia', in Jomo, K.S., Felker, G. and Rasiah, R. (eds), *Industrial Technology Development in Malaysia: Industry and firm studies*, London and New York, Routledge, 1999;. Hu, Y-S. (1995) 'The international transferability of competitive advantage', *California Management Review*, **37**, 73–88; Senker, J. (1995) 'Tacit knowledge and models of innovation', *Industrial and Corporate Change*, **4**, 425–447; Senker, J., P. Benoit-Joly and M. Reinhard (1996) *Overseas Biotechnology Research by Europe's Chemical-Pharmaceuticals Multinationals: Rationale and implications.* STEEP Discussion Paper No. 33, Science Policy Research Unit, University of Sussex, Brighton;. Niosi, J. (1999) 'The internationalization of industrial R&D', *Research Policy*, **29**, 107.

21 *The Economist* (1994) 'Following Chrysler', 23 April, 86–87.

22 See Gerybadze, A. and G. Reger (1999) 'Globalisation of R&D: recent changes in the management of innovation in transnational corporations', *Research Policy*, **28**, 251–274.

23 See Vernon, R. (1966) 'International investment and international trade in the product cycle', *Quarterly Journal of Economics* **80**, 190–207.

24 EIRMA (European Industrial Research Management Association) (1995) *Evaluation of R&D Projects.* Paris.

25 Bower, J. (1986) *Managing the Resource Allocation Process*. Harvard Business School, Division of Research, Boston, Mass.

26 Mansfield, E., J. Raporport, J. Schnee, S. Wagner and M. Hamburger (1972) *Research and Innovation in the Modern Corporation*. Macmillan, London.

27 Booz Allen and Hamilton (1982) *New Product Management in the 1980s*. New York.

28 Freeman, C. and L. Soete (1997) *The Economics of Industrial Innovation*, 3rd edn. Pinter, London.

29 Myers, S. (1984) 'Finance theory and financial strategy', *Interfaces*, **14**, 126–137.

30 Mitchell, G. and W. Hamilton (1988) 'Managing R&D as a strategic option', *Research-Technology Management*, **31**, 15–22.

31 EIRMA (European Industrial Research Management Association) (1986) *Developing R&D Strategies*. Paris.

32 Scherer, F. and K. Huh (1992) 'Top management education and R&D investment', *Research Policy*, **21**, 507; Bosworth, D. and R. Wilson (1992) *Technological Change: The role of scientists and engineers*. Avebury, Aldershot.

33 Chandler, A. (1991) 'The functions of the HQ unit in the multibusiness firm', *Strategic Management Journal*, **12**, 31–50.

34 Gould, M. and A. Campbell (1987) *Strategies and Styles: The role of the centre in managing diversified corporations*. Blackwell, Oxford.

35 Leonard-Barton, D. (1995) *Wellsprings of Knowledge: Building and sustaining the sources of innovation*. Harvard Business School Press, Boston.

36 *The Economist* (1995) 'The death of the Geneen machine', 17 June, 86–92; *The Economist* (1996) 'Changing of the guard', 7 September, 72; *The Economist* (2000) 'Reinventing Marconi', 2 December, 42–47.

37 Owen, G. and T. Harrison (1995) 'Why ICI chose to demerge', *Harvard Business Review*, March–April, 133–142.

38 Pavitt, K. (2000) 'Innovating routines in the business firm: what matters, what's staying the same, and what's changing?' Keynote speech at Annual Meeting of the Schumpeter Society, Manchester, 1 July, 2000. SPRU Electronic Working Paper No. 45, University of Sussex.

Part III

ESTABLISHING EFFECTIVE EXTERNAL LINKAGES

In Part I we identified a number of generic processes for the management of innovation, which include scanning the environment, resourcing development and implementing innovation. In Part II we discovered how market position, technological paths and organizational processes influence and constrain these generic processes in the development and implementation of an innovation strategy. In this section we are concerned with the enabling routines for building effective linkages outside the organization in order to identify, resource and implement innovations.

Chapter 7 focuses on linkages with customers and markets. As we saw in Chapter 2, much of the early innovation research suggests that 'understanding user needs' and the involvement of 'lead users' improves the likelihood of new product success: involving users in the development process helps firms to acquire knowledge from the users, and encourages the subsequent acceptance of the innovation and commitment to its use. However, there is increasing evidence that the nature of different technologies and markets affects the process of selection and involvement of customers. In short, there is no 'one best way', but rather a range of alternatives. For example, where new products or services are very novel or complex, potential users may not be aware of, or able to articulate, their needs. In such cases traditional methods of market research are of little use, and there will be a greater burden on developers of radical new products and services to 'educate' potential users. Therefore we examine how the novelty and complexity of technologies and markets influence the identification, development and adoption of innovations.

Chapter 8 focuses on linkages with suppliers, competitors and other external sources of knowledge. Organizations collaborate for many reasons, including efficiency and flexibility, but here we are concerned with gaining access to technological and market knowledge. Such relationships may take many forms, ranging from simple licensing agreements, loose coalitions or so-called strategic alliances, to more formal joint ventures. Therefore the technological and market competencies of a specific firm may be a less reliable indicator of innovative potential than its position in a network.

Increasingly, such networks of relationships are the most appropriate unit of analysis for understanding the innovation process. A network is as much a process as a structure, which both constrains firms, and in turn is shaped by firms. In these terms collaboration can be understood as an attempt to cope with the increasing complexity and interrelatedness of different technologies and markets. We examine the technological and market motives for collaboration, and identify the organizational processes necessary to exploit it as an opportunity for knowledge acquisition and learning.

Chapter 7

LEARNING FROM MARKETS

In Chapters 5 and 6 we examined how firms identify their technological competencies and develop the appropriate organizational structures and processes to support these. In this chapter we focus on the identification and development of market innovations. Market innovation includes the identification of market trends and opportunities, the translation of these requirements into new products and services, and the promotion and diffusion of these products and services. In this chapter we examine three issues:

1. How do the *characteristics of an innovation* constrain the options for development and marketing? Most marketing texts focus on relatively mature, simple low-technology products or services, but different factors will be relevant in the case of novel, complex high-technology products or services.
2. In what way do the *characteristics of potential users* affect the development and adoption of innovations? Most research on marketing examines the behaviour of consumers, but industrial and business users demand different relationships.
3. Which *commercialization or diffusion processes* are most effective in promoting the awareness and use of new products and services? The traditional distinction between 'early adopters' and 'laggards' in the take-up of innovations is unhelpful, and we need to understand what factors affect the adoption of novel products and services.

7.1 How do Technology and Markets Affect Commercialization?

Marketing focuses on the needs of the customer, and therefore should begin with an analysis of customer requirements, and attempt to create value by providing products and services that satisfy those requirements.

The marketing mix is the set of variables that are to a large extent controllable by the company, normally referred to as the 'four Ps': product, price, place and promotion. All four factors allow some scope for innovation: product innovation results in new or improved products and services, and may change the basis of competition; product innovation allows some scope for premium pricing, and process innovation may result in price leadership; innovations in logistics may affect how a product or service is made available to customers, including distribution channels and nature of sales points; innovations in media provide new opportunities for promotion.

However, we need to distinguish between strategic marketing, that is whether or not to enter a new market, and tactical marketing, which is concerned mainly with the problem of differentiating existing products and services, and extensions to such products. There is a growing body of research that suggests that factors which contribute to new product success are not universal, but are contingent upon a range of technological and market characteristics. A recent study of 110 development projects found that complexity, novelty and whether the project was for hardware or software development affected the factors that contributed to success.[1] Our own research confirms that different managerial processes, structures and tools are appropriate for routine and novel development projects.[2] For example, in terms of frequency of use, the most common methods used for high novelty projects are segmentation, prototyping, market experimentation and industry experts, whereas for the less novel projects the most common methods are partnering customers, trend extrapolation and segmentation. The use of market experimentation and industry experts might be expected where market requirements or technologies are uncertain, but the common use of segmentation for such projects is harder to justify. However, in terms of usefulness, there are statistically significant differences in the ratings for segmentation, prototyping, industry experts, market surveys and latent needs analysis. Segmentation and market surveys appear to be most effective for routine development projects, and latent needs analysis and prototyping more appropriate for novel projects (Table 7.1).

TABLE 7.1   The effect of product novelty on the tools used for new product and service development.

	High novelty		Low novelty	
	Usage (%)	Usefulness	Usage (%)	Usefulness
Segmentation*	89	3.42	42	4.50
Prototyping*	79	4.33	63	4.08
Market experimentation	63	4.00	53	3.70
Industry experts*	63	3.83	37	3.71
Surveys/focus groups*	52	4.50	37	4.00
Trend extrapolation	47	4.00	47	3.44
Latent needs analysis*	47	3.89	32	3.67
User-practice observation	47	3.67	42	3.50
Partnering customers	37	4.43	58	3.67
User-developers	32	4.33	37	3.57
Scenario development	21	3.75	26	2.80
Role-playing	5	4.00	11	1.00

* Denotes difference in usefulness rating is statistically significant at 5% level ($n = 50$).
Source: Adapted from Tidd, J. and K. Bodley (2001) 'Effect of project novelty on the effectiveness of tools used to support new product development', *R&D Management* (submitted).

Clearly then, many of the standard marketing tools and techniques are of limited utility for the development and commercialization of novel or complex new products or services. A number of weaknesses can be identified:

- *Identifying and evaluating novel product characteristics.* Marketing tools such as conjoint analysis have been developed for variations of existing products or product extensions, and therefore are of little use for identifying and developing novel products or applications
- *Identifying and evaluating new markets or businesses.* Marketing techniques such as segmentation are most applicable to relatively mature, well-understood products and markets, and are of limited use in emerging, ill-defined markets
- *Promoting the purchase and use of novel products and services.* The traditional distinction between consumer and business marketing is based on the characteristics of the customers or users, but the characteristics of the innovation and the relationship between developers and users is more important in the case of novel and complex products and services

Therefore before applying the standard marketing techniques, we must have a clear idea of the maturity of the technologies and markets. Figure 7.1 presents a simple two-by-two matrix, with technological maturity as one dimension, and market maturity as the other. Each quadrant raises different issues and will demand different techniques for development and commercialization:

- *Differentiated.* Both the technologies and markets are mature, and most innovations consist of the improved use of existing technologies to meet a known customer need. Products and services are differentiated on the basis of packaging, pricing and support
- *Architectural.* Existing technologies are applied or combined to create novel products or services, or new applications. Competition is based on serving specific market niches and on close relations with customers. Innovation typically originates or is in collaboration with potential users
- *Technological.* Novel technologies are developed which satisfy known customer needs. Such products and services compete on the basis of performance, rather than price or quality. Innovation is mainly driven by developers
- *Complex.* Both technologies and markets are novel, and co-evolve. In this case there is no clearly defined use of a new technology, but over time developers work with lead users to create new applications. The development of multimedia products and services is a recent example of such a co-evolution of technologies and markets

Assessing the maturity of a market is particularly difficult, mainly due the problem of defining the boundaries of a market. The real rate of growth of a market provides a good estimate of the stage in the product life cycle, and by inference, the maturity of the market. In general high rates of market growth are associated with high R&D costs, high marketing costs, rising investment in capacity and high product margins (Figure 7.2). At the firm level there is a significant correlation between expenditure on R&D, number of new product launches and financial measures of performance such as value-added and market to book value.[3] Generally, profitability declines as a market matures as the scope for product and service differentiation reduces, and competition shifts towards price.

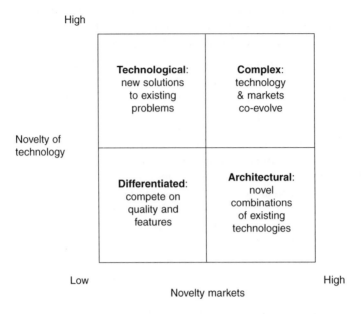

FIGURE 7.1 Technological and market maturity determine the marketing process.

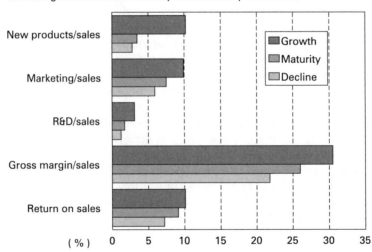

FIGURE 7.2 Market maturity affects the innovation process. Source: Derived from Buzzell, R. D. and B. T. Gale (1987) *The PIMS Principle*. Free Press, New York.

7.2 Differentiating Products

In Chapter 3 we discussed generic corporate strategies based on price leadership or differentiation. Here we are concerned with the specific issue of how to differentiate a product from competing offerings where technologies and markets are relatively stable. It is in these circumstances that the standard tools and techniques of marketing are most useful. We assume the reader is familiar with the basics of marketing, so here we shall focus on product differentiation by quality and other attributes.

Differentiation measures the degree to which competitors differ from one another in a specific market. Markets in which there is little differentiation and no significant difference in the relative quality of competitors are characterized by low profitability, whereas differentiation on the basis of relative quality or other product characteristics is a strong predictor of high profitability in any market conditions. Where a firm achieves a combination of high differentiation and high perceived relative quality, the return on investment is typically twice that of non-differentiated products. Analysis of the Strategic Planning Institute's database of more than 3000 business units helps us to identify the profit impact of market strategy (PIMS):[4]

- *High relative quality is associated with a high return on sales.* One reason for this is that businesses with higher relative quality are able to demand higher prices than their competitors. Moreover, higher quality may also help reduce costs by limiting waste and improving processes. As a result companies may benefit from both higher prices and lower costs than competitors, thereby increasing profit margins
- *Good value is associated with increased market share.* Plotting relative quality against relative price provides a measure of relative value: high quality at a high price represents average value, but high quality at a low price represents good value. Products representing poor value tend to lose market share, but those offering good value gain market share
- *Product differentiation is associated with profitability.* Differentiation is defined in terms of how competitors differ from each other within a particular product segment. It can be measured by asking customers to rank the individual attributes of competing products, and to weight the attributes. Customer weighting of attributes is likely to differ from that of the technical or marketing functions

Analysis of the PIMS data reveals a more detailed picture of the relationships between innovation, value and market performance (Figure 7.3). Process innovation helps to improve relative quality and to reduce costs, thereby improving the relative value of the product. Product innovation also affects product quality, but has a greater effect on reputation and value. Together, innovation, relative value and reputation drive growth in market share. For example, there is an almost linear relationship between product innovation and market growth: businesses with low levels of product innovation, that is having less than 1% of products introduced in the last three years, experience an average real annual market growth of less than 1%, whereas businesses with high levels, that is having around 8% of products introduced in the past three years, experience real annual market growth of around 8%.[5] The compound effect of such differences in real growth can have a significant impact on relative market share over a relatively short period of time. However, in consumer markets maintaining high levels of new product introduction is necessary, but not sufficient. In addition, reputation, or brand

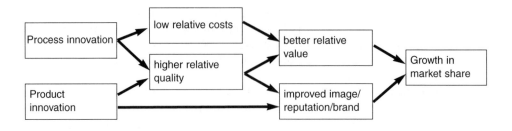

FIGURE 7.3   Relationship between innovation and market performance. Source: Adapted from Clayton, T. and G. Turner (2000) 'Brands, innovation and growth', in Tidd, J. (ed.), *From Knowledge Management to Strategic Competence: Measuring technological, market and organizational innovation.* Imperial College Press, London.

image, must be established and maintained, as without it consumers are less likely to sample new product offerings whatever the value or innovativeness. Witness the rapid and consistent growth of Nokia in the mobile phone market (see Box 7.1).

Quality function deployment (QFD) is a useful technique for translating customer requirements into development needs, and encourages communication between engineering, production and marketing. Unlike most other tools of quality management, QFD is used to identify opportunities for product improvement or differentiation, rather than to solve problems. Customer-required characteristics are translated or 'deployed' by means of a matrix into language which engineers can understand (Figure 7.4). The construction of a relationship matrix—also known as 'the house of quality'—requires a significant amount of technical and market research. Great emphasis must be made on gathering market and user data in order to identify potential design trade-offs, and to achieve the most appropriate balance between cost, quality and performance. The construction of a QFD matrix involves the following steps:[6]

1. Identify customer requirements, primary and secondary, and any major dislikes.
2. Rank requirements according to importance.
3. Translate requirements into measurable characteristics.
4. Establish the relationship between the customer requirements and technical product characteristics, and estimate the strength of the relationship.
5. Choose appropriate units of measurement and determine target values based on customer requirements and competitor benchmarks.

Symbols are used to show the relationship between customer requirements and technical specifications, and weights attached to illustrate the strength of the relationship. Horizontal rows with no relationship symbol indicate that the existing design is incomplete. Conversely, vertical columns with no relationship symbol indicate that an existing design feature is redundant as it is not valued by the customer. In addition, comparisons with competing products, or benchmarks, can be included. This is important because relative quality is more relevant than absolute quality: customer expectations are likely to be shaped by what else is available, rather than some ideal.

In some cases potential users may have latent needs or requirements which they cannot articulate. In such cases three types of user need can be identified: 'must be's', 'one-dimensionals' and attractive features or 'delighters'.[7] Must be's are those features which must exist before a potential customer will consider a product or service. For example, in the case of an executive car it must be relatively large and expensive. One-dimensionals are the more quantifiable features which allow direct comparison between competing products. For example, in the case of an executive car, the acceleration and braking performance. Finally, the delighters which are the most subtle means of differentiation. The inclusion of such features delights the target customers, even if they do not explicitly demand them. For example, delighters in the case of an executive car include ultrasonic parking aids, rain-sensitive windscreen wipers and photochromatic mirrors. Such features are rarely demanded by customers or identified by regular market research. However, indirect questioning can be used to help identify latent requirements.

QFD was originally developed in Japan, and is claimed to have helped Toyota to reduce its development time and costs by 40%. More recently many leading American firms have adopted QFD, including AT&T, Digital and Ford, but results have been mixed: only around a quarter of projects have resulted in any quantifiable benefit.[8] In contrast, there has been relatively little application of QFD by European firms. This is not the result of ignorance, but rather a recognition of the practical problems of implementing QFD.

Clearly, QFD requires the compilation of a lot of marketing and technical data, and more importantly the close co-operation of the development and marketing functions. Indeed, the process of constructing the relationship matrix provides a structured way of getting people from development and marketing to communicate, and therefore is as valuable as any more quantifiable outputs. However, where relations between the technical and marketing groups are a problem, which is too often the case, the use of QFD may be premature. The problem of cross-functional communication in product development will be discussed in more detail in Chapter 9.

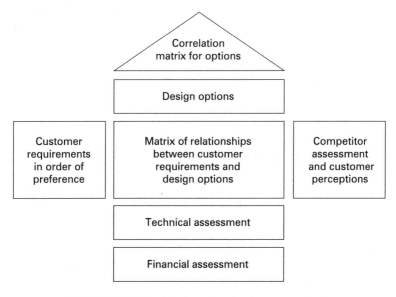

FIGURE 7.4   Quality function deployment matrix.

BOX 7.1 Nokia: Differentiation by design and innovation.

Founded in 1865, Nokia began as a forestry company, and for almost 100 years remained in the pulp and paper industry until a series of unrelated acquisitions in the 1960s. However, in the past decade Nokia has transformed itself from a sprawling conglomerate, with a wide range of mature, low-margin products, to the world's largest manufacturer of mobile phones, with around 30% of the global market for handsets, and 60% share of the industry profits.

When Jorma Ollila, a graduate of the LSE in London, became chief executive in 1992, his strategy consisted of four phrases: 'global', 'telecom-orientated', 'focus' and 'value-added'. In 1993 Ollila told the European Commission that he thought that Europe had lost the computer market to the USA, and consumer electronics to Japan, but could still dominate the emerging telecom market. By 1992 Nokia had become a conglomerate with businesses in aluminium, cables, paper, rubber, televisions, tyres, power generation and real estate. In the mid-1980s Nokia acquired its first interest in the electronics sector, the company Teleste, and in 1991 acquired the British telecoms company Techophone. In 1985 the share of Nokia's revenues derived from telecoms was just 14%, but following disposal of almost all non-telecoms businesses, this share had grown to almost 90% by 1995. Its success has been based on a combination of technological innovation and product design. It has benefited from its early focus on digital and data traffic, rather than analogue and voice, and the co-development of the GSM (global system of mobile communications) standard, but also has developed a strong brand and carefully segmented the market by means of product design.

Annual growth has regularly been some 40%, and in 2000 the company sold more than 400 million phones. Despite the trend towards a high-volume mass market, Nokia achieves product margins of up to 25%, compared to its rivals' 1–3%. The company is now the fifth largest in Europe, employs 44 000 people in 11 countries, almost half of which are Finns. Due to the high rate of growth, half of Nokia's staff has worked for the company for less than three years, and the average age is only 32. It spends around 9% of revenues on R&D, and around a third of its staff work in design or R&D.

7.3 Creating Architectural Products

Architectural products consist of novel combinations of existing technologies that serve new markets or applications. In such cases the critical issue is to identify or create new market segments.

Market share is associated with profitability: on average, market leaders earn three times the rate of return of businesses ranked fifth or less.[9] Therefore the goal is to segment a market into a sufficiently small and isolated segment which can be dominated and defended. This allows the product and distribution channels to be closely matched to the needs of a specific group of customers.

Market or buyer segmentation is simply the process of identifying groups of customers with sufficiently similar purchasing behaviour so that they can be targeted and treated in a similar way. This is important because different groups are likely to have different needs. By definition the needs of customers in the same segment will be highly homogeneous. In formal statistical terms the objective of segmentation is to maximize across-group variance and to minimize within-group variance.

In practice segmentation is conducted by analysing customers' buying behaviour and then using factor analysis to identify the most significant variables influencing behaviour—descriptive segmentation—and then using cluster analysis to create distinct segments which help identify unmet customer needs—prescriptive segmentation. The principle of segmentation applies to both consumer and business markets, but the process and basis of segmentation is different in each case.

Segmenting Consumer Markets

Much of the research on the buying behaviour of consumers is based on theories adapted from the social and behavioural sciences. Utilitarian theories assume that consumers are rational and make purchasing decisions by comparing product utility with their requirements. This model suggests a sequence of phases in the purchasing decision: problem recognition, information search, evaluation of alternatives and finally the purchase. However, such rational processes do not appear to have much influence on actual buying behaviour. For example, in the UK the Consumers' Association routinely tests a wide range of competing products, and makes buying recommendations based on largely objective criteria. If the majority of buyers were rational, and the Consumers' Association successfully identified all relevant criteria, these recommendations would become best-sellers, but this is not the case.

Behavioural approaches have greater explanatory power. These emphasize the effect of attitude, and argue that the buying decision follows a sequence of changing attitudes to a product—awareness, interest, desire and finally action. The goal of advertising is to stimulate this sequence of events. However, research suggests that attitude alone explains only 10% of decisions, and can rarely predict buyer behaviour.

In practice the balance between rational and behavioural influences will depend on the level of customer involvement. Clearly, the decision-making process for buying an aircraft or machine tool is different from the process of buying a toothpaste or shampoo. Many purchasing decisions involve little cost or risk, and therefore low involvement. In such cases consumers try to minimize the financial, mental and physical effort involved in purchasing. Advertising is most effective in such cases. In contrast, in high-involvement situations, in which there is a high cost or potential risk to customers, buyers are willing to search for information and make a more informed decision. Advertising is less effective in such circumstances, and is typically confined to presenting comparative information between rival products.

There are many bases of segmenting consumer markets, including by socio-economic class, life-cycle groupings and by lifestyle or psychographic (psychological–demographic) factors. An example of psychographic segmentation is the Taylor–Nelson classification that consists of self-explorers, social registers, experimentalists, achievers, belongers, survivors and the aimless. Better-known examples include the *Yuppy* (young upwardly mobile professional) and *Dinky* (dual income, no kids), and the more recent *Yappy* (young affluent parent) and *Sitcoms* (single income, two children, oppressive mortgage). There is often a strong association between a segment and particular products and services. For example, the yuppy of the 1980s was defined by a striped shirt and braces, personal organizer, brick-sized mobile phone and, of course, a BMW. Annual sales of Filofax were just £100 000 in the UK in 1980, but the deregulation of the City of London in 1986 created 50 000 new, highly paid jobs. As a result annual sales of Filofax reached a peak of £6m. in 1986, the year before the City crashed.

Such segmentation is commonly used for product development and marketing in fast-moving consumer goods such as foods or toiletries and consumer durables such as consumer electronics or cars (see Box 7.2). It is of particular relevance in the case of product variation or extension, but can also be used to identify opportunities for new products, such as functional foods for the health-conscious, and emerging requirements such as new pharmaceuticals and health-care services for the wealthy elderly.

Segmenting Business Markets

Business customers tend to be better informed than consumers and, in theory at least, make more rational purchasing decisions. Business customers can be segmented on the basis of common buying factors or purchasing processes. The basis of segmentation should have clear operational implications, such as differences in preferences, pricing, distribution or sales strategy. For example, customers could be segmented on the basis of how experienced, sophisticated or price-sensitive they are. However, the process is complicated by the number of people involved in the buying process:

- The actual customer or buyer, who typically has the formal authority to choose a supplier and agree terms of purchase
- The ultimate users of the product or service, who are normally, but not always, involved in the initiation and specification of the purchase
- Gatekeepers, who control the flow of information to the buyers and users
- Influencers, who may provide some technical support to the specification and comparison of products

Therefore it is critical to identify all relevant parties in an organization, and determine the main influences on each. For example, technical personnel used to determine the specification may favour performance, whereas the actual buyer may stress value for money.

The most common basis of business segmentation is by the benefits customers derive from the product, process or service. Customers may buy the same product for very different reasons, and attach different weightings to different product features. For example, in the case of a new numerically controlled machine tool, one group of customers may place the greatest value on the reduction in unit costs it provides, whereas another group may place greater emphasis on potential improvements in precision or quality of the output (see Box 7.3).

BOX 7.2 The marketing of Persil Power.

In 1994 the Anglo-Dutch firm Unilever launched its revolutionary new washing powder 'Persil Power' across Europe. It was heralded as the first major technological breakthrough in detergents for 15 years. Development had taken 10 years and more than £100m. The product contained a manganese catalyst, the so-called 'accelerator', which Unilever claimed washed whiter at lower temperatures. The properties of manganese were well known in the industry, but in the past no firm had been able to produce a catalyst which did not also damage clothes. Unilever believed that it had developed a suitable manganese catalyst, and protected its development with 35 patents. The company had test marketed the new product in some 60 000 households and more than 3 million washes, and was sufficiently confident to launch the product in April 1994. However, reports by Procter and Gamble, Unilever's main rival, and subsequent tests by the British Consumers' Association found that under certain conditions Persil Power significantly damaged clothes. After a fierce public relations battle Unilever was forced to withdraw the product, and wrote off some £300m. in development and marketing costs. What went wrong?

There were many reasons for this, but with the benefit of hindsight two stand out. First, the nature of the test marketing and segmentation. Unilever had conducted most of its tests in Dutch households. Typically, northern Europeans separate their whites from their coloured wash, and tend to read product instructions. In contrast, consumers in the South are more likely to wash whites and dyed fabrics together, and to wash everything on a hot wash irrespective of any instructions to the contrary. The manganese catalyst was fine at low temperatures for whites only, but reacted with certain dyes at higher temperatures. Second, the nature of the product positioning. Persil Power was launched as a broad-base detergent suitable for all fabrics, but in practice was only a niche product effective for whites at low temperatures. Unilever learned a great deal from this product launch, and has since radically reorganized its product development process to improve communication between the research, development and marketing functions. Now product development is concentrated in a small number of innovation centres, rather than being split between central R&D and the product divisions, and the whole company uses the formal new product development process based on the development funnel discussed in Chapter 9.

It is difficult in practice to identify distinct segments by benefit because these are not strongly related to more traditional and easily identifiable characteristics such as firm size or industry classification.[10] Therefore benefit segmentation is only practical where such preferences can be related to more easily observable and measurable customer characteristics. For example, in the case of the machine

BOX 7.3 The marketing of Mondex.

Mondex is a smart card which can be used to store cash credits, in other words, an electronic purse. The card incorporates a chip which allows cash-free transfers of monetary value from consumer to retailer, and from retailer to bank. NatWest bank first conceived of Mondex in 1990. The rationale for development of the system was the huge costs involved in handling small amounts of cash, estimated to be some £4.5bn in the UK each year, and therefore the banks and retailers are the main potential beneficiaries. The benefits to consumers are less clear.

In 1991 NatWest created a venture to franchise the system worldwide, and in the UK entered alliances with Midland Bank and BT. Interviews with customer focus groups were conducted in the UK, USA, France, Germany and Japan to determine the likely demand for the service. The results of this initial market research suggested that up to 80% of potential customers would use Mondex, if available. Therefore internal technical trials went ahead in 1992, based on 6000 staff of NatWest. As a result, minor improvements were made, such as a key fob to read the balance remaining on a card, and a locking facility. Market trials began in Swindon in 1995, chosen for its demographic representativeness. Almost 70% of the town's retailers were recruited to the pilot, although several large multiple retailers declined to participate as they were planning their own cards. Some 14 000 customers of NatWest and Midland applied for a free card, but this represented just 25% of their combined customer base in the town. The main barrier to adoption appeared to be the lack of clear benefits to users, whereas the banks and retailers clearly benefited from reduced handling and security costs.

Nevertheless, in 1996 it was announced that Mondex would be offered to all students of Essex University, and cards were to include a broader range of functions including student identification and library access, as well as being accepted by all the banks, shops and bars on campus. University students are ideal consumers of such innovative services, and the campus environment represents a controllable environment in which to test the attractiveness of the service where universal acceptance is guaranteed. Five other universities were subsequently recruited to the three-year trial.

In 1996 Mondex was spun off from NatWest Bank, and is now owned by a consortium headed by Mastercard International. The main competing products are Visa Cash and Belgium's Proton technology. Only 2 million Mondex cards were in use in 2000, but many millions more are to be used by large credit card companies such as JCB of Japan which plans to replace 15 million credit, debit and loyalty cards over the next few years. In addition, Mondex technology, in particular its well-regarded operating system MultOS, has since successfully licensed its technology in more than 50 countries. In 2000 it was announced that Mondex technology was to be used in the Norwegian national lottery, and Mondex was part of a bid consortium for the UK national lottery. Thus the technology and associated business have evolved from a narrow focus on electronic cash, to the broader issue of smart card applications.

tool, analysis of production volumes, batch sizes, operating margins and value added might help differentiate between those firms which value higher efficiency from those which seek improvements in quality.

This suggests a three-stage segmentation process for identifying new business markets:

1. First, a segmentation based on the functionality of the technology, mapping functions against potential applications.
2. Next, a behavioural segmentation to identify potential customers with similar buying behaviour, for example regarding price or service.
3. Finally, combine the functional and behavioural segmentations in a single matrix to help identify potential customers with relevant applications and buying behaviour.

In addition, analysis of competitors' products and customers may reveal segments not adequately served, or alternatively an opportunity to redefine the basis of segmentation. For example, existing customers may be segmented on the basis of size of company, rather than the needs of specific sectors or particular applications. However, in the final analysis segmentation only provides a guide to behaviour as each customer will have unique characteristics.

There is likely to be a continuum of customer requirements, ranging from existing needs, to emerging requirements and latent expectations, and these must be mapped on to existing and emerging technologies.[11] Whereas much of conventional market research is concerned with identifying the existing needs of customers and matching these to existing technological solutions, in this case the search has to be extended to include emerging and new customer requirements. There are three distinct phases of analysis:

1. Cross-functional teams including customers are used to generate new product concepts by means of brainstorming, morphology and other structured techniques.
2. These concepts are refined and evaluated, using techniques such as QFD.
3. Parallel prototype development and market research activities are conducted. Prototypes are used not as 'master models' for production, but as experiments for internal and external customers to evaluate.

Where potential customers are unable to define or evaluate product design features in-depth interview clinics must be carried out with target focus groups or via antenna shops. In antenna shops market researchers and engineers conduct interactive customer interviews, and use marketing research tools and techniques to identify and quantify perceptions about product attributes.

Product mapping can be used to expose the technological and market drivers of product development, and allows managers to explore the implications of product extensions. It helps to focus development efforts and limit the scope of projects by identifying target markets and technologies. This helps to generate more detailed functional maps for design, production and marketing. An initial product introduction, or 'core' product, can be extended in a number of ways:

- An enhanced product, which includes additional distinctive features designed for an identified market segment
- An 'upmarket' extension. This can be difficult because customers may associate the company with a lower quality segment. Also, sales and support staff may not be sufficiently trained or skilled for the new segments
- A 'downmarket' extension. This runs the risk of cannibalizing sales from the higher end, and may alienate existing customers and dealers
- Custom products with additional features required by a specific customer or distribution channel
- A hybrid product, produced by merging two core designs to produce a new product

In his detailed analysis of the disk drive industry, Clayton Christensen distinguishes between two types of architectural innovation.[12] The first, *sustaining* innovation, which continue to improve existing product functionality for existing customers and markets. The second, *disruptive* innovation, provide a different set of functions which are likely to appeal to a very different segment of the market. As a result, existing firms and their customers are likely to undervalue or ignore disruptive innovations, as these are likely to underperform existing technologies in terms of existing functions in established markets. This illustrates the danger of simplistic advice such as 'listening to customers', and the limitations of traditional management and marketing approaches. Therefore established firms tend to be blind to the potential of disruptive innovation, which is more likely to be exploited by new entrants. Segmentation of current markets and close relations with existing customers will tend to reinforce sustaining innovation, but will fail to identify or wrongly reject potential disruptive innovations. Instead firms must develop and maintain a detailed understanding of potential applications and changing users needs.

7.4 Marketing Technological Products

Technological products are characterized by the application of new technologies in existing products or relatively mature markets. In this case the key issue is to identify existing applications where the technology has a cost or performance advantage.

The traditional literature on industrial marketing has a bias towards relatively low-technology products, and has failed largely to take into account the nature of high-technology products and their markets.

The first and most critical distinction to make is between a technology and a product.[13] Technologists are typically concerned with developing devices, whereas potential customers buy products, which marketing must create from the devices. Developing a product is much more costly and difficult than developing a device. Devices that do not function or are difficult to manufacture are relatively easy to identify and correct compared to an incomplete product offering. A product may fail or be difficult to sell due to poor logistics and branding, or difficult to use because insufficient attention has been paid to customer training or support. Therefore attempting to differentiate a product on the basis of its functionality or the performance of component devices can be expensive and futile.

For example, a personal computer (PC) is a product consisting of a large number of devices or subsystems, including the basic hardware and accessories, operating system, application programs, languages, documentation, customer training, maintenance and support, advertising and brand development. Therefore a development in microprocessor technology, such as RISC (reduced instruction set computing) may improve product performance in certain circumstances, but may be undermined by more significant factors such as lack of support for developers of software and therefore a shortage of suitable application software.

Therefore in the case of high-technology products it is not sufficient to carry out a simple technical comparison of the performance of technological alternatives, and conventional market segmentation is unlikely to reveal opportunities for substituting a new technology in existing applications. It is necessary to identify why a potential customer might look for an alternative to the existing solution. It may be because of lower costs, superior performance, greater reliability, or simply fashion. In such cases there are two stages to identify potential applications and target customers: technical and behavioural.[14]

Statistical analysis of existing customers is unlikely to be of much use because of the level of detail required. Typically technical segmentation begins with a small group of potential users being interviewed to identify differences and similarities in their requirements. The aim is to identify a range of specific potential uses or applications. Next, a behavioural segmentation is carried out to find three or four groups of customers with similar situations and behaviour. Finally, the technical and behavioural segments are combined to define specific groups of target customer and markets that can then be evaluated commercially (Figure 7.5).

Several features are unique to the marketing of high-technology products, and affect buying behaviour:[15]

FIGURE 7.5   Technical and behavioural segmentation for marketing high-technology products.

- *Buyers' perceptions of differences in technology affect buying behaviour.* In general, where buyers believe technologies to be similar, they are likely to search for longer than when they believe there to be significant differences between technologies
- *Buyers' perceptions of the rate of change of the technology affects buying behaviour.* In general, where buyers believe the rate of technological change is high, they put a lot of effort in the search for alternatives, but search for a shorter time. In non-critical areas a buyer may postpone a purchase
- *Organizational buyers may have strong relationships with their suppliers, which increases switching costs.* In general, the higher the supplier-related switching costs, the lower the search effort, but the higher the compatibility-related switching costs, the greater the search effort

Exploiting Intellectual Property

In addition, in some cases technology can be commercialized by licensing or selling the intellectual property rights (IPR), rather than developing products or processes. For example, in 1998 IBM reported licence income of US$1bn, and in the USA the total royalty income from licensing was around US$100bn. There is a range of IPR that can be used to exploit technology, the main types being patents, copyright and design rights and registration.

All industrialized countries have some form of patent legislation, the aim of which is to encourage innovation by allowing a limited monopoly, usually for 20 years, provided certain legal tests are satisfied:

- *Novelty*—no part of 'prior art', including publications, written, oral or anticipation. In most countries the first to file the patent is granted the rights, but in the USA it is the first to invent. The American approach may have the moral advantage, but results in many legal challenges to patents
- *Inventive step*—'not obvious to a person skilled in the art'. This is a relative test, as the assumed level of skill is higher in some fields than others. For example, Genentech was granted a patent for the plasminogen activator t-PA which helps to reduce blood clots, but despite its novelty, a Court of Appeal revoked the patent on the grounds that it did not represent an inventive step because its development was deemed to be obvious to researchers in field
- *Industrial application*—utility test requires the invention to be capable of being applied to a machine, product or process. In practice a patent must specify an application for the technology, and additional patents sought for any additional application. For example, Unilever developed Ceramides and patented their use in a wide range of applications. However, it did not apply for a patent for application of the technology to shampoos, which was subsequently granted to a competitor
- *Patentable subject*—for example, discoveries and formula cannot be patented, and in Europe neither can software (the subject of copyright) nor new organisms, although both these are patentable in the USA. For example, contrast of the mapping of the human genome in the USA and Europe: in the USA the research is being conducted by a commercial laboratory which is patenting

the outcomes, and in Europe by a group of public laboratories which is publishing the outcomes on the Internet

- *Clear and complete disclosure.* Note that a patent provides only certain legal property rights, and in the case of infringement the patent holder needs to take the appropriate legal action. In some cases secrecy may be a preferable strategy. Conversely, national patent databases represent a large and detailed reservoir of technological innovations which can be interrogated for ideas

Copyright is concerned with the expression of ideas, and not the ideas themselves. Therefore the copyright exists only if the idea is made concrete, for example, in a book or recording. There is no requirement for registration, and the test of originality is low compared to patent law, requiring only that 'the author of the work must have used his own skill and effort to create the work'. Like patents, copyright provides limited legal rights for certain types of material for a specific term. For literary, dramatic, musical and artistic works copyright is normally for 70 years after the death of the author, 50 in the USA, and for recordings, film, broadcast and cable programmes 50 years from their creation. Typographical works have 25 years copyright. The type of materials covered by copyright include:

- 'Original' literary, dramatic, musical and artistic works, including software and in some cases databases
- Recordings, films, broadcasts and cable programmes
- Typographical arrangement or layout of a published edition

Design rights are similar to copyright protection, but mainly apply to three-dimensional articles, covering any aspect of the 'shape' or 'configuration', internal or external, whole or part, but specifically excludes integral and functional features, such as spare parts. Design rights exist for 15 years and 10 years if commercially exploited. Design registration is a cross between patent and copyright protection, is cheaper and easier than patent protection, but more limited in scope. It provides protection for up to 25 years, but covers only visual appearance—shape, configuration, pattern and ornament. It is used for designs that have aesthetic appeal, for example, consumer electronics and toys. For example the knobs on top of Lego bricks are functional, and would therefore not qualify for design registration, but were also considered to have 'eye appeal', and therefore granted design rights.[16]

Licensing IPR can have a number of benefits:

- Reduce or eliminate production and distribution costs and risks
- Reach a larger market
- Exploit in other applications
- Establish standards
- Gain access to complementary technology
- Block competing developments
- Convert competitor into defender

Considerations when drafting a licensing agreement include degree of exclusivity, territory and type of end use, period of licence and type and level of payments—royalty, lump sum or cross-licence. Pricing a licence is as much an art as a science, and depends on a number of factors such as the balance of power and negotiating skills. Common methods of pricing licences are:[17]

- Going market rate—based on industry norms, e.g. 6% of sales in electronics and mechanical engineering
- 25% rule—based on licensee's gross profit earned through use of the technology
- Return on investment—based on licensor's costs
- Profit-sharing—based on relative investment and risk. First, estimate total life-cycle profit. Next, calculate relative investment and weight according to share of risk. Finally, compare results to alternatives, e.g return to licensee, imitation, litigation

There is no 'best' licensing strategy, as it depends on the strategy of the organization and the nature of the technology and markets (see Box 7.4). For example, Celltech licensed its asthma treatment to Merck for a single payment of $50m., based on sales projections. This isolated Celltech from the risk of clinical trials and commercialization, and provided a much-needed cash injection. Toshiba, Sony and Matsushita license DVD technology for royalties of only 1.5% to encourage its adoption as the industry standard. Until the recent legal proceedings, Microsoft applied a 'per processor' royalty its OEM (original equipment manufacturer) customers for Windows to discourage its customers from using competing operating systems. The successful exploitation of IPR also incurs costs and risks:

BOX 7.4 ARM Holdings.

ARM Holdings designs and licenses high-performance, low-energy-consumption 16- and 32-bit RISC (reduced instruction set computing) chips, which are used extensively in mobile devices such as cellphones, cameras, electronic organizers and smart cards. ARM was established in 1990 as a joint venture between Acorn Computers in the UK and Apple Computer. Acorn did not pioneer the RISC architecture, but it was the first to market a commercial RISC processor in the mid-1980s. Perhaps ironically, the first application of ARM technology was in the relatively unsuccessful Apple Newton PDA (Personal Digital Assistant). ARM designs but does not manufacture chips, and receives royalties of between 5 cents and US$2.50 for every chip produced under licence. Licensees include Ericsson, Fujitsu, HP, NEC, Nintendo, Sega, Sharp, Sony, Toshiba and 3Com. In 1999 it announced joint ventures with leading chip manufacturers such as Intel and Texas Instruments to design and build chips for the next generation of hand-held devices. It is estimated that ARM-designed processors were used in 10 million devices in 1996, 50 million in 1998 and more than 120 million devices sold in 1999, representing around almost half of the market for mobile devices. In 1998 the company was floated in London and on the Nasdaq in New York, and it achieved a market capitalization of £3bn in December 1999, with an annual revenue growth of 40% to £15.7m. The company employs around 400 staff, 250 of which are based in Cambridge in the UK, and spends almost 30% of revenues on R&D. The company has created 30 millionaires amongst its staff.

- Cost of search, registration and renewal
- Need to register in various national markets
- Full and public disclosure of your idea
- Need to be able to enforce

In most countries the basic registration fee for a patent is relatively modest, but in addition applying for a patent includes the cost of professional agents, such as patent agents, translation for foreign patents, official registration fees in all relevant countries and renewal fees. For example, the lifetime cost for a single non-pharmaceutical patent in the main European markets would be around £80 000, and the addition of the USA and Japan some £40 000 more. Patents in the other Asian markets are cheaper, at up to £5000 per country, but the cumulative cost becomes prohibitive, particularly for lone inventors or small firms. Pharmaceutical patents are much more expensive, up to five times more, due to the complexity and length of the documentation. In addition to these costs, firms must consider the competitive risk of public disclosure, and the potential cost of legal action should the patent be infringed. Some of these issues and most appropriate strategies for dealing with them were discussed in Chapter 4.

7.5 Commercializing Complex Products

Complex products or systems are a special case in marketing because neither the technology nor markets are well defined or understood. Therefore technology and markets co-evolve over time, as developers and potential users interact. Note that technological complexity does not necessarily imply market complexity, or vice versa. For example, the development of a passenger aircraft is complex in a technological sense, but the market is well defined and potential customers are easy to identify. We are concerned here with cases where both technologies and markets are complex, for example telecommunications, multimedia and pharmaceuticals.

The traditional distinction between consumer and industrial marketing in terms of the nature of users, rather than the products and services themselves, is therefore unhelpful. For example, a new industrial product or process may be relatively simple, whereas a new consumer product may be complex. The commercialization process for complex products has certain characteristics common to consumer and business markets:[18]

- Products are likely to consist of a large number of interacting components and subsystems, which complicates development and marketing
- The technical knowledge of customers is likely to be greater, but there is a burden on developers to educate potential users. This requires close links between developers and users
- Adoption is likely to involve a long-term commitment, and therefore the cost of failure to perform is likely to be high
- The buying process is often lengthy and adoption may lag years behind availability and receipt of the initial information

The Nature of Complex Products

Complex products typically consist of a number of components, or subsystems. Depending on how open the standards are for interfaces between the various components, products may be offered as bundled systems, or as subsystems or components. For bundled systems, customers evaluate purchases at the system level, rather than at the component level. For example, many pharmaceutical firms are now operating managed health-care services, rather than simply developing and selling specific drugs. Similarly, robot manufacturers offer 'manufacturing solutions', rather than stand-alone robot manipulators. Bundled systems can offer customers enhanced performance by allowing a package of optimized components using proprietary interfaces of 'firmware', and in addition may provide the convenience of a single point of purchase and after-sales support. However, bundled systems may not appeal to customers with idiosyncratic needs, or knowledgeable customers able to configure their own systems.

The growth of systems integrators and 'turnkey' solutions suggests that there is additional value to be gained by developing and marketing systems rather than components: typically, the value added at the system level is greater than the sum of the value added by the components. There is, however, an important exception to this rule. In cases where a particular component or subsystem is significantly superior to competing offerings, unbundling is likely to result in a larger market.[19] The increased market is due to additional customers who would not be willing to purchase the bundled system, but would like to incorporate one of the components or subsystems into their own systems. For example, Intel and Microsoft have captured the dominant market shares of microprocessors and operating systems respectively, by selling components rather than by incorporating these into their own PCs.

Links between Developers and Users

The development and adoption process for complex products, processes and services is particularly difficult. The benefits to potential users may be difficult to identify and value, and because there are likely to be few direct substitutes available the market may not be able to provide any benchmarks. The choice of suppliers is likely to be limited, more an oligopolistic market than a truly competitive one. In the absence of direct competition, price is less important than other factors such as reputation, performance and service and support.

Innovation research has long emphasized the importance of 'understanding user needs' when developing new products,[20] but in the special case of complex products and services potential users may not be aware of, or may be unable to articulate, their needs. In such cases it is not sufficient simply to understand or even to satisfy existing customers, but rather it is necessary to lead existing customers and identify potential new customers. Conventional market research techniques are of little use, and there will be a greater burden on developers to 'educate' potential users. Hamel and Prahalad refer to this process as *expeditionary marketing*.[21] The main issue is how to learn

as quickly as possible through experimentation with real products and customers, and thereby anticipate future requirements and pre-empt potential
competitors.

The relationship between developers and users will change throughout the
development and adoption process (Figure 7.6). Three distinct processes need to
be managed, each demanding different linkages: development, adoption and
interfacing. Numerous frameworks have been formulated to help structure and
manage the development process, and these will be discussed in the next chapter. The process of diffusion and adoption is examined in section 7.6. However,
relatively little guidance is available for managing the interface between the
developers and adopters of an innovation.

The interface process can be thought of as consisting of two flows, information
flows and resource flows.[22] Developers and adopters will negotiate the inflows
and outflows of both information and resources. Therefore developers should
recognize that resources committed to development and resources committed to
aiding adoption should not be viewed as independent or 'ring-fenced'. Both
contribute to the successful commercialization of complex products, processes
and services. Developers should also identify and manage the balance and
direction of information and resource flows at different stages of the process of
development and adoption. For example, at early stages managing information
inflows may be most important, but at later stages managing outflows of
information and resources may be critical. In addition, learning will require the
management of knowledge flows, involving the exchange or secondment of
appropriate staff.

Two dimensions help determine the most appropriate relationship between
developers and users: the range of different applications for an innovation; and
the number of potential users of each application:[23]

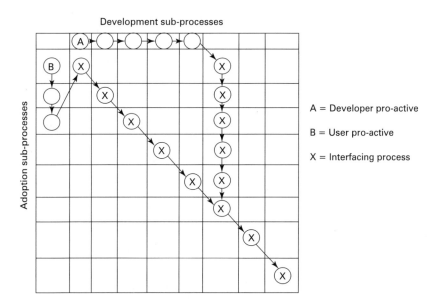

FIGURE 7.6   Developer–adopter relationships for development.[22]

- *Few applications and few users.* In this case direct face-to-face negotiation regarding the technology design and use is possible
- *Few applications, but many users.* This is the classic marketing case, which demands careful segmentation, but little interaction with users
- *Many applications, but few users.* In this case there are multiple stakeholders amongst the user groups, with separate and possibly conflicting needs. This requires skills to avoid optimization of the technology for one group at the expense of others. The core functionality of the technology must be separated and protected, and custom interfaces developed for the different user groups
- *Many applications and different users.* In this case developers must work with multiple archetypes of users and therefore aim for the most generic market possible, customized for no one group

In general, where there are relatively few potential users, as is usually the case with complex products for business customers, customers are likely to demand that developers have the capability to solve their problems, and be able to transfer the solution to them. However, customer expectations vary by sector and nationality. For example, firms in the paper and pulp industry do not expect suppliers to have strong problem-solving capabilities, but do require solutions to be adapted to their specific needs. Conversely, firms in the speciality steel industry demand suppliers to possess strong problem-solving capabilities. Overall, German and Swedish customers expect suppliers to have problem-solving and adaptation capabilities, but British, French and Italian customers appear to be less demanding.[24]

Adoption of Complex Products

The buying process for complex products is likely to be lengthy due to the difficulty of evaluating risk and subsequent implementation. Perceived risk is a function of a buyer's level of uncertainty and the seriousness of the consequences of the decision to purchase. There are two types of risk; the performance risk, that is the extent to which the purchase meets expectations, and the psychological risk associated with how other people in the organization react to the decision. Low-risk decisions are likely to be made autonomously, and therefore it is easier to target decision-makers and identify buying criteria. For complex products there is greater uncertainty, and the consequences of the purchase are more significant, and therefore some form of joint or group decision-making is likely.

If there is general agreement concerning the buying criteria, a process of information gathering and deliberation can take place in order to identify and evaluate potential suppliers. However, if there is disagreement concerning the buying criteria, a process of persuasion and bargaining is likely to be necessary before any decision can be made.

In the case of organizational purchases, the expectations, perceptions, roles and perception of risk of the main decision-makers may vary. Therefore we should expect and identify the different buying criteria used by various decision-makers in an organization. For example, a production engineer may favour the reliability or performance of a piece of equipment, whereas the finance manager is likely to focus on life-cycle costs and value for money (see Box 7.5). Three factors are likely to affect the purchase decision in an organization:[25]

1. *Political and legal environment.* This may affect the availability of, and information concerning, competing products. For example, government legislation might specify the tender process for the development and purchase of new equipment.
2. *Organizational structure and tasks.* Structure includes the degree of centralization of decision-making and purchasing; tasks include the organizational purpose served by the purchase, the nature of demand derived from the purchaser's own business, and how routine the purchase is.
3. *Personal roles and responsibilities.* Different roles need to be identified and satisfied. Gatekeepers control the flow of information to the organization, influencers add information or change buying criteria, deciders choose the specific supplier or brand, and the buyers are responsible for the actual purchase. Therefore the ultimate users may not be the primary target.

7.6 Forecasting the Diffusion of Innovations

A great deal of research has been conducted to try to identify what factors affect the rate and extent of adoption of an innovation. In this section we examine three issues relevant to the marketing of innovations:

1. How the characteristics of an innovation affect adoption.
2. How the process of commercialization and diffusion affects adoption.
3. What techniques are available for forecasting future patterns of adoption.

Characteristics of an Innovation Affecting Diffusion

A number of characteristics of an innovation have been found to affect diffusion:[26]

- Relative advantage
- Compatibility
- Complexity
- Trialability
- Observability

Relative advantage   Relative advantage is the degree to which an innovation is perceived as better than the product it supersedes, or competing products. Relative advantage is typically measured in narrow economic terms, for example cost or financial payback, but non-economic factors such as convenience, satisfaction and social prestige may be equally important. In theory, the greater the perceived advantage, the faster the rate of adoption.

It is useful to distinguish between the primary and secondary attributes of an innovation. Primary attributes, such as size and cost, are invariant and inherent to a specific innovation irrespective of the adopter. Secondary attributes, such as

---

BOX 7.5 The EMI CAT scanner.

In 1972 the British firm EMI launched the first computer-assisted tomography (CAT) scanner for use in medical diagnosis. The CAT scanner converted conventional X-ray information into three-dimensional pictures which could be examined using a monitor. EMI had invented and patented all the key technologies of the CAT scanner. The initial slow scanning speed of early machines meant that they were only suitable for organs with minimal movement, such as the brain. In 1976 EMI introduced a faster machine which had a scan time of only 20 seconds, and therefore could be used for whole body scans. It was generally acknowledged that at that time the EMI CAT scanner provided a scanned image superior to that of competing machines, therefore allowing more detailed diagnosis.

Established suppliers of conventional X-ray equipment such as Siemens in Europe and General Electric in the USA responded by differentiating their CAT scanners from those offered by EMI. They competed with the technically superior machines of EMI by emphasizing the faster scan speed of their machines, which they claimed improved patient throughput times. EMI argued that there was a trade-off between scan time and image quality, and that in any case scan time was insignificant relative to the total consultation time required for a patient. However, in North American hospitals, which were the largest market for such machines, patient throughput was of critical importance. Worse still, early machines provided by EMI were highly complex and proved unreliable, and the company was unable to provide worldwide service and support until much later. Early users unfairly compared the reliability of the CAT scanners to more mature and less complex X-ray machines. As a result, the EMI scanner gained a reputation for being unreliable and slow. The machines supplied by its competitors were technically inferior in terms of scanning quality, but gained market share through clever marketing and better customer support. By 1977 the Medical Division of EMI was making a loss, and in 1979 the company was purchased by the Thorn Group.

EMI had invented the CAT scanner, but failed to identify the requirements of its key customers, and underestimated the technical and marketing response of established firms.

---

relative advantage and compatibility, may vary from adopter to adopter, being contingent upon the perceptions and context of adopters.

Incentives may be used to promote the adoption of an innovation, by increasing the perceived relative advantage of the innovation, subsidizing trials or reducing the cost of incompatibilities.

Compatibility   Compatibility is the degree to which an innovation is perceived to be consistent with the existing values, experience and needs of potential adopters. There are two distinct aspects of compatibility: existing skills and practices; and values and norms. The extent to which the innovation fits the existing skills, equipment, procedures and performance criteria of the potential adopter is important, and relatively easy to assess.

So-called 'network externalities' can affect the adoption process. For example, the cost of adoption and use, as distinct from the cost of purchase, may be influenced by: the availability of information about the technology from other users, of trained skilled users, technical assistance and maintenance, and of complementary innovations, both technical and organizational.

However, compatibility with existing practices may be less important than the fit with existing values and norms.[26] Significant misalignments between an innovation and an adopting organization will require changes in the innovation or organization, or both. In the most successful cases of implementation, mutual adaptation of the innovation and organization occurs.[27]

Complexity   Complexity is the degree to which an innovation is perceived as being difficult to understand or use. In general, innovations which are simpler for potential users to understand will be adopted more rapidly than those which require the adopter to develop new skills and knowledge.

Trialability   Trialability is the degree to which an innovation can be experimented with on a limited basis. An innovation that is trialable represents less uncertainty to potential adopters, and allows learning by doing. Innovations which can be trialed will generally be adopted more quickly than those which cannot. The exception is where the undesirable consequences of an innovation appear to outweigh the desirable characteristics. In general, adopters wish to benefit from the functional effects of an innovation, but avoid any dysfunctional effects. However, where it is difficult or impossible to separate the desirable from the undesirable consequences trialability may reduce the rate of adoption.

Observability   Observability is the degree to which the results of an innovation are visible to others. The easier it is for others to see the benefits of an innovation, the more likely it will be adopted. The simple epidemic model of diffusion assumes that innovations spread as potential adopters come into contact with existing users of an innovation.

Processes of Diffusion

Research on diffusion attempts to identify what influences the rate of adoption of an innovation. The diffusion of an innovation is typically described by an S-shaped (logistic) curve (Figure 7.7). Initially, the rate of adoption is low, and adoption is confined to so-called 'innovators'. Next to adopt are the 'early adopters', then the 'late majority', and finally the curve tails off as only the 'laggards' remain. Such taxonomies are fine with the benefit of hindsight, but provide little guidance for future patterns of adoption.

Hundreds of marketing studies have attempted to fit the adoption of specific products to the S-curve, ranging from television sets to new drugs. In most cases mathematical techniques can provide a relatively good fit with historical data, but research has so far failed to identify robust generic models of adoption. In practice the precise pattern of adoption of an innovation will depend on the interaction of demand-side and supply-side factors:

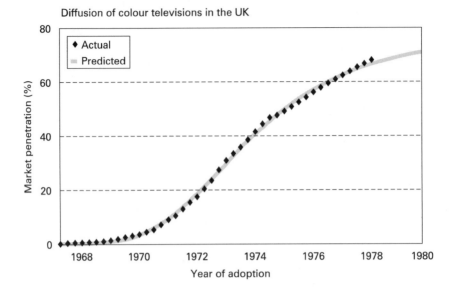

Diffusion of colour televisions in the UK

FIGURE 7.7   Typical diffusion curve for a new product. Source: Data from Meade, N. (1984) 'The use of growth curves in forecasting market development—a review and appraisal', *Journal of Forecasting*, No. 3, 429–451.

1. Demand-side models, mainly statistical:
   (a) epidemic, based on direct contact with or imitation of prior adopters;
   (b) Bass, based on adopters consisting of innovators and imitators;
   (c) Probit, based on adopters with different benefit thresholds;
   (d) Bayesian, based on adopters with different perceptions of benefits and risk.
2. Supply-side models, mainly sociological:
   (a) appropriability, which emphasizes relative advantage of an innovation;
   (b) dissemination, which emphasizes the availability of information;
   (c) utilization, which emphasizes the reduction of barriers to use;
   (d) communication, which emphasizes feedback between developers and users.

The epidemic model was the earliest and is still the most commonly used. It assumes a homogeneous population of potential adopters, and that innovations spread by information transmitted by personal contact and the geographical proximity of existing and potential adopters. This model suggests that the emphasis should be on communication, and the provision of clear technical and economic information. However, the epidemic model has been criticized because it assumes that all potential adopters are similar and have the same needs.

As a result, the Bass model of diffusion is modified to include two different groups of potential adopters: innovators, who are not subject to social emulation; and imitators, for whom the diffusion process takes the epidemic form. This produces a skewed S-curve because of the early adoption by innovators, and suggests that different marketing processes are needed for the innovators and subsequent imitators. The Bass model is highly influential in economics and marketing research.

The Probit model takes a more sophisticated approach to the population of potential adopters. It assumes that potential adopters have different threshold values for costs or benefits, and will only adopt beyond some critical or threshold value. In this case differences in threshold values are used to explain different rates of adoption. This suggests that the more similar potential adopters are, the faster the diffusion.

In the Probit model potential adopters know the value of adoption, but delay adoption until the benefits are sufficient. However, it is unrealistic to assume that adopters will have perfect knowledge of the value of an innovation. Therefore Bayesian models of diffusion introduce lack of information as a constraint to diffusion. Potential adopters are allowed to hold different beliefs regarding the value of the innovation, which they may revise according to the results of trials to test the innovation. Because these trials are private, imitation cannot take place and other potential adopters cannot learn from the trials. This suggests better-informed potential adopters may not necessarily adopt an innovation earlier than the less well informed, which was an assumption of earlier models.[29]

The choice between the four models will depend on the characteristics of the innovation and nature of potential adopters. The simple epidemic model appears to provide a good fit to the diffusion of new processes, techniques and procedures, whereas the Bass model appears to best fit the diffusion of consumer products. However, the mathematical structure of the epidemic and Bass models tends to overstate the importance of differences in adopter characteristics, but tends to underestimate the effect of macroeconomic and supply-side factors. In general, both these models of diffusion work best where the total potential market is known, that is for derivatives of existing products and services, rather than totally new innovations. All demand-side models have limitations:

- Adopters are assumed to be relatively homogeneous, apart from some difference in progressiveness or threshold values. They do not consider the possibility that the rationality and the profitability of adopting a particular innovation might be different for different adopters. For example, local 'network externalities' such as the availability of trained skilled users, technical assistance and maintenance, or complementary technical or organizational innovations are likely to affect the cost of adoption and use, as distinct from the cost of purchase
- The population of potential adopters and the innovation are assumed to be the same at the beginning and at the end of the diffusion period. However, research confirms that many innovations change over the course of diffusion, and that this may change the potential population of adopters, who in turn may lead to subsequent modifications to the innovation
- They focus almost exclusively on the adopters' or demand side of the diffusion process, and ignore supply-side factors. In reality both demand- and supply-side factors must be taken into account (see Box 7.6).

BOX 7.6 Diffusion of robotics.

The first commercial industrial robots were developed in the 1960s, and in the 1980s many believed that robots would replace most forms of manual work. However, in 1995 the density of robots in use—the number of robots per 10 000 workers—was only 21 in the UK, 33 in the United States, 69 in Germany and 338 in Japan. This raises two questions: why has the diffusion of robots been so slow, and why are there such large differences in the rates of diffusion in different countries? Economists tend to argue that the level of investment in industrial robots, like all capital equipment, is a function of labour costs: the higher labour costs, the more likely firms are to substitute robots for labour. This is clearly part of the explanation, as rankings of labour costs are similar to those for robot density: Japan, Sweden, Germany, United States, France and the UK. However, more detailed studies reveal other factors affecting the diffusion of robots, such as industry structure and work organization.

The automobile industry has traditionally been the largest customer for robots. The most common applications in this sector are in spot welding, machine loading and surface treatment. The main requirement is high accuracy, or rather repeatability. Therefore those countries with the largest automobile sector electronics industry have begun to employ large numbers of robots in assembly, changing the rate and pattern of diffusion.

Work organization has also affected the number and type of robots used in different countries. Expensive, sophisticated robots are common in the UK and USA in firms characterized by low levels of training. Therefore robots have to be made 'idiot proof' in order to minimize operator involvement. In contrast, cheaper, less complex robots are more common in Japan where operators are trained to work with the robots and to perform routine programming and maintenance. Moreover, many firms which have poor control of the quality of materials and components have been forced to adopt sophisticated component feeding and sensor systems to allow for component variability, whereas firms which have made investments in quality management have been able to use cheaper, simpler equipment.

Thus the diffusion of industrial robots has not followed a simple logistics curve based on some cost function. Rather, patterns of adoption have varied as industrial robots and users' needs have co-evolved.[32] Robots were originally conceived as being direct replacements for workers, so-called 'steel collar' workers, or 'universal automation', but have become increasingly specialized such that there are now robots designed specifically for assembly, spraying or welding applications. At the same time users have grown sophisticated and their needs have fragmented, some demanding 'turnkey' integrated solutions, others preferring to build their own systems from various components. Therefore it is meaningless to think of the adoption of industrial robots as a process of simple diffusion.

Sociological models place greater emphasis on the relationship between demand- and supply-side factors.[30] The early appropriability models focus almost exclusively on the supply side, and assume that innovations of sufficient value will be adopted. This suggests that the most important issues are the relative advantage of an innovation. The subsequent dissemination model assumes that the availability of information and communication channels are the most critical issues in diffusion. The utilization model incorporates demand-side issues, in particular problems of adoption and application, both structural and perceptual. Finally, there are most recent communication models of diffusion, which are based on feedback between developers and potential adopters.

The communication perspective considers how individual psychological characteristics such as attitude and perception affect adoption. Individual motivations, perceptions, likes and dislikes determine what information is reacted to and how it is processed. Potential adopters will be guided and prejudiced by experience, and will have 'cognitive maps' which filter information and guide behaviour. Social context will also influence individual behaviour. Social structures and meaning systems are locally constructed, and therefore highly context-specific. These can distort the way in which information is interpreted and acted upon. Therefore the perceived value of an innovation, and therefore its subsequent adoption, is not some objective fact, but instead depends on individual psychology and social context. These factors are particularly important in the later stages of diffusion.

Initially, the needs of early adopters or innovators dominate, and therefore the characteristics of an innovation are most important. Innovations tend to evolve over time through improvements required by these early users, which may reduce the relative cost to later adopters. However, early adopters are almost by definition 'atypical', for example, they tend to have superior technical skills. As a result the preferences of early adopters can have a disproportionate impact on the subsequent development of an innovation, and result in the establishment of inferior technologies or abandonment of superior alternatives.

Bandwagons may occur where an innovation is adopted because of pressure caused by the sheer number of those who have already adopted an innovation, rather than by individual assessments of the benefits of an innovation. In general, as soon as the number of adopters has reached a certain threshold level, the greater the level of ambiguity of the innovations benefits, the greater the subsequent number of adopters. This process allows technically inefficient innovations to be widely adopted, or technically efficient innovations to be rejected. Examples include the QWERTY keyboard, originally designed to prevent professional typists from typing too fast and jamming typewriters; and the DOS operating system for personal computers, designed by and for computer enthusiasts.

Bandwagons occur due to a combination of competitive and institutional pressures. Where competitors adopt an innovation, a firm may adopt because of the threat of lost competitiveness, rather than as a result of any rational evaluation of benefits. For example, many firms adopted flexible manufacturing systems (FMS) in the 1980s in response to increased competition, but most failed to achieve significant benefits. The main institutional pressure is the threat of lost legitimacy, for example, being considered by peers or customers as being less progressive or competent. For example, in the early 1990s most leading firms established websites on the World Wide Web (WWW) because it was perceived to be progressive, rather than because of any immediate commercial benefits.

The critical difference between bandwagons and other types of diffusion is that they require only limited information to flow from early to later adopters. Indeed, the more ambiguous the benefits of an innovation, the more significant bandwagons are on rates of adoption.[31] Therefore the process of diffusion must be managed with as much care as the process of development. In short, better products do not necessarily result in more sales. Not everybody requires a better mousetrap.

Forecasting Patterns of Adoption

Forecasting can help to identify what might be required in the future, and to estimate how many are likely to be required in a given time period. However, in the case of innovative products forecasting is difficult, as the products and markets may not be well defined. For example, when Apple launched its first personal digital assistant (PDA), the Newton, it forecast first-year sales of 400 000, but in fact sold just 70 000. This was partly due to the poor performance of the software for recognizing handwriting, but also because Apple failed to position the product clearly between traditional paper organizers and sub-notebook computers.

The most appropriate choice of forecasting method will depend on:

- What we are trying to forecast
- Rate of technological and market change
- Availability and accuracy of information
- The company's planning horizon
- The resources available for forecasting

In practice there will be a trade-off between the cost and robustness of a forecast. The more common methods of forecasting such as trend extrapolation and time series are of limited use for new products, because of the lack of past data. However, regression analysis can be used to identify the main factors driving demand for a given product, and therefore provide some estimate of future demand, given data on the underlying drivers.

For example, a regression might express the likely demand for the next generation of digital mobile phones in terms of rate of economic growth, price relative to competing systems, rate of new business formation, and so on. Data are collected for each of the chosen variables and coefficients for each derived from the curve which best describes the past data. Thus the reliability of the forecast depends a great deal on selecting the right variables in the first place. The advantage of regression is that, unlike simple extrapolation or time series analysis, the forecast is based on cause and effect relations. Econometric models are simply bundles of regression equations, including their interrelationship. However, regression analysis is of little use where future values of an explanatory value are unknown, or where the relationship between the explanatory and forecast variables may change.

Leading indicators and analogues can improve the reliability of forecasts, and are useful guideposts to future trends in some sectors. In both cases there is a historical relationship between two trends. For example, new business start-ups might be a leading indicator of the demand for fax machines in six months' time. Similarly, business users of mobile telephones may be an analogue for subsequent patterns of domestic use.

Such 'normative' techniques are useful for estimating the future demand for existing products, or extensions of existing products, but are of limited utility in the case of radical new products. Exploratory forecasting, in contrast, attempts to explore the range of future possibilities. The most common methods are:

- Customer and market surveys
- Brainstorming
- Delphi or expert opinion
- Scenario development

Most companies conduct customer surveys of some sort. In consumer markets this can be problematic simply because customers are unable to articulate their future needs. For example, market research would not have been very helpful to Sony in the development of the first domestic video cassette recorder or personal stereo. In industrial markets, customers tend to be better equipped to communicate their future requirements. Consequently, in industrial markets innovations often originate from customers. Companies can also consult their direct sales force, but these may not always be the best guide to future customer requirements. Information is often filtered in terms of existing products and services, and biased in terms of current sales performance rather than long-term development potential.

Structured idea generation, or brainstorming, aims to solve specific problems or to identify new products or services. Typically, a small group of experts is gathered together and allowed to interact. A chairman records all suggestions without comment or criticism. The aim is to identify, but not evaluate, as many opportunities or solutions as possible. Finally, members of the group vote on the different suggestions. The best results are obtained when representatives from different functions are present, but this can be difficult to manage. Brainstorming does not produce a forecast as such, but can provide useful input to other types of forecasting.

The opinion of outside experts, or Delphi method, is useful where there is a great deal of uncertainty or for long time horizons. The relevant experts may include suppliers, dealers, customers, consultants and academics. The Delphi method begins with a postal survey of expert opinion on what the future key issues will be, and the likelihood of the developments. The response is then analysed, and the same sample of experts resurveyed with a new, more focused questionnaire. This procedure is repeated until some convergence of opinion is observed, or conversely if no consensus is reached. In Europe, governments and transnational agencies use Delphi studies to help formulate policy. In Japan, large companies and the government routinely survey expert opinion in order to reach some consensus in those areas with the greatest potential for long-term development. Used in this way, the Delphi method can to a large extent become a self-fulfilling prophecy.

Scenario development may involve many different forecasting techniques, including computer-based simulation. Typically, it begins with the identification of the critical indicators, which might include use of brainstorming and Delphi techniques. Next, the reasons for the behaviour of these indicators is examined, perhaps using regression techniques. The future events which are likely to affect these indicators are identified. These are used to construct the best, worst and most likely future scenarios. Finally, the company assesses the impact of each scenario on its business. The goal is to plan for the outcome with the greatest impact, or better still, retain sufficient flexibility to respond to several different scenarios. Scenario development is a key part of the long-term planning process in those sectors characterized by high capital investment, long lead times and significant environmental uncertainty, such as energy, aerospace and telecommunications.

7.7 Summary and Further Reading

In this chapter we have examined how the maturity of technologies and markets affects the process of marketing an innovation. Where both technologies and markets are relatively mature, the key issue is how to differentiate a product or service for competing offerings. In this case many of the standard marketing techniques can be applied, but other tools such as quality function deployment (QFD) are useful. Where existing technologies are applied to new markets, what we call architectural innovation, the key issue is the resegmentation of markets to identify potential new applications. Where new technologies are applied to existing markets, the key issue is to assess the advantage the technology may have over existing solutions in specific applications, and then identify target users based on behavioural characteristics. Finally, where both technologies and markets are complex, the key issue is the relationship between developers and potential users.

The diffusion of an innovation depends on the characteristics of the innovation, the nature of potential adopters, and the process of communication. The relative advantage, compatibility, complexity, trialability and observability of an innovation all affect the rate of diffusion. The skills, psychology, social context and infrastructure of adopters also affect adoption. Epidemic models assume that innovations spread by communication between adopters, but bandwagons do not require this. Instead, early adopters influence the development of an innovation, but subsequent adopters may be more influenced by competitive and peer pressures.

The standard marketing texts for management students are Phillip Kotler's *Principles of Marketing* (Prentice-Hall, 1992), which focuses on consumer products, and Frederick Webster's *Industrial Marketing Strategy* (Wiley, 1991), which covers industrial products. However, neither adequately deals with the particular case of innovative new products and services. A number of American texts cover the related but more narrow issue of marketing high-technology products, including William Davidow's *Marketing High Technology* (Free Press, 1986) and *Essentials of Marketing High Technology* by William Shanklin and John Ryans, Jr. (Lexington, 1987). The former is written by a practising engineer/marketing manager, and therefore is strong on practical advice, and the latter is written by two academics, and provides a more coherent framework for analysis. Vijay Jolly's *Commercializing New Technologies* (Harvard Business School Press, 1998) provides a process model based on the experiences of leading firms such as 3M and Sony, which consists of five subprocesses or stages, but the framework is biased towards mass consumer markets.

There are few texts which focus exclusively on the more generic problems of applying conventional marketing tools and techniques to innovative new products and processes, but the best attempts to date are the chapter on 'Securing the future' in Gary Hamel and C. K. Prahalad's *Competing for the Future* (Harvard Business School Press, 1994) and the chapter on 'Learning from the market' in Dorothy Leonard's *Wellsprings of Knowledge* (Harvard Business School Press, 1995). Dawn Iacobucci has edited an excellent compilation of current theory and practice of business-to-business and other relationship-based marketing in *Networks in Marketing* (Sage, London, 1996), much of which is relevant to the development and marketing of complex products and services. It also provides a sound introduction to the more general subject of networks, which will be discussed in the next chapter. We discuss the specific case of complex product systems in a special issue of *Research Policy*, **29**, 2000.

References

1   Dvir, D., S. Lipovetsky, A. Shenhar and A. Tishler (1998) 'In search of project classification: a non-universal approach to project success factors', *Research Policy*, **27**, 915–935.
2   Tidd, J. and K. Bodley (2001) 'Effect of novelty on new product development processes and tools', *R&D Management* (submitted).
3   Tidd, J. and C. Driver (2000) 'Technological and market competencies and financial performance', in Tidd, J. (ed.), *From Knowledge Management to Strategic Competence: Measuring technological, market and organizational innovation.* Imperial College Press, London, pp. 94–125.
4   Luchs, B. (1990) 'Quality as a strategic weapon', *European Business Journal*, **2** (4), 34–47.
5   Clayton, T. and G. Turner (2000) 'Brands, innovation and growth', in Tidd, J. (ed), *From Knowledge Management to Strategic Competence: Measuring technological, market and organizational innovation.* Imperial College Press, London, pp. 77–93.
6   Burn, G.R. (1990) 'Quality function deployment', in Dale, B. G. and Plunkett, J. J. (eds), *Managing Quality.* Philip Allan, London, pp. 66–88.
7   Dimancescu, D. and K. Dwenger (1995) *World-Class New Product Development.* American Management Association, New York.
8   Griffin, A. (1992) 'Evaluating QFD's use in US firms as a process for developing products', *Journal of Product Innovation Management,* **9**, 171–187.
9   Buzzell, P. D. and Gale, B. T. (1987) *The PIMS Principle.* Free Press, New York.
10 Moriarty, P. L. T. and D. J. Reibstein (1986) 'Benefit segmentation in industrial markets', *Journal of Business Research,* **14**, 463–486.
11 Lauglaug, A.S. (1993) 'Technical-market research—get customers to collaborate in developing products', *Long Range Planning,* **26** (2), 78–82.
12 Christensen, C.M. (2000) *The Innovator's Dilemma.* HarperCollins, New York.
13 Davidow, W.H. (1986) *Marketing High Technology.* Free Press, New York.
14 Millier, P. (1989) *The Marketing of High-Tech Products: Methods of analysis.* Editions d'Organisation, Paris (in French).
15 Weiss, A. M. and J. Heide (1993) 'The nature of organizational search in high technology markets', *Journal of Marketing Research,* **30**, 220–233.
16 Anselm, M., A. Bleakley and K. Watson (1999) *Intellectual Property and Media Law.* Blackstone Press, London.
17 Byrne, N. (1998) *Licensing Technology.* Jordan, Bristol.
18 Hobday, M., H. Rush and J. Tidd (2000) 'Complex product systems', *Research Policy,* **29**, 793–804.
19 Wilson, L. O., A. M. Weiss and G. John (1990) 'Unbundling of industrial systems', *Journal of Marketing,* **27**, 123–138.

20 Cooper, R. L. G. and E. J. Kleinschmidt (1993) 'Screening new products for potential winners', *Long Range Planning*, **26** (6), 74–81.
21 Hamel, G. and C. K. Prahalad, (1994) *Competing for the Future*. Harvard Business School Press, Boston.
22 More, P. L. A. (1986) 'Developer/adopter relationships in new industrial product situations', *Journal of Business Research*, **14**, 501–517.
23 Leonard-Barton, D. and D. K. Sinha (1993) 'Developer–user interaction and user satisfaction in internal technology transfer', *Academy of Management Journal*, **36** (5), 1125–1139.
24 Hakansson, H. (1995) 'The Swedish approach to Europe', in Ford, D. (ed.), *Understanding Business Markets*. The Dryden Press, London, pp. 232–261.
25 Webster, F. E. Jr (1991) *Industrial Marketing Strategy*, 3rd edn. John Wiley & Sons, New York.
26 Rogers, E. M. (1995) *Diffusion of Innovations*. Free Press, New York.
27 Leonard-Barton, D. and D. K. Sinha (1993) 'Developer–user interaction and user satisfaction in internal technology transfer', *Academy of Management Journal*, **36** (5), 1125–1139.
28 Leonard-Barton, D. (1990) 'Implementing new production technologies: exercises in corporate learning', in von Glinow, M.A. and Mohmian, S. A. (eds), *Managing Complexity in High Technology Organizations*. CUP, pp. 160–187.
29 Lissom, F. and J. S. Metcalfe (1994) 'Diffusion of innovation ancient and modem: a review of the main themes', in Dodgson, M. and Rothwell, P.L. (eds), *The Handbook of Industrial Innovation*. Edward Elgar, Cheltenham, pp. 106–141.
30 Williams, F. and D. V. Gibson (1990) *Technology Transfer: A communications perspective*. Sage, London.
31 Abrahamson, E. and L. Plosenkopf (1993) 'Institutional and competitive band-wagons: using mathematical modelling as a tool to explore innovation diffusion', *Academy of Management Journal*, **18** (3), 487–517.
32 Tidd, J. (1991) *Flexible Manufacturing Technologies and International Competitiveness*. Pinter, London.

Chapter 8

LEARNING THROUGH ALLIANCES

Almost all innovations demand some form of collaborative arrangement, for development or commercialization, but the failure rate of such alliances remains high. In this chapter we examine the role of collaboration in the development of new technologies, products and businesses. Specifically, we address the following issues:

- Why do firms collaborate?
- What types of collaboration are most appropriate in different circumstances?
- How do technological and market factors affect the structure of an alliance?
- What organizational and managerial factors affect the success of an alliance?
- How can a firm best exploit alliances for learning new technological and market competencies?

We begin with a discussion of the main theoretical arguments for collaboration, and review some of the more practical benefits. Next we link the rationale for collaboration with different forms and structures of alliances, focusing on the specific cases of supplier relations, strategic alliances and innovation networks. Next we identify recent trends and patterns in collaborative activity, and finally, we discuss how to better manage alliances, including the potential to acquire new market or technological knowledge.

8.1 Why Collaborate?

In Chapter 2 we examined the role of technological and market competencies in developing an innovation strategy. We discussed the advantages and disadvantages of a strategy of technological leadership, and examined the links between different strategies and the sources of innovation. In this chapter we review strategies for exploiting external sources of innovation. Firms collaborate for a number of reasons:

- To reduce the cost of technological development or market entry
- To reduce the risk of development or market entry
- To achieve scale economies in production
- To reduce the time taken to develop and commercialize new products

In any specific case, a firm is likely to have multiple motives for an alliance (see Box 8.1). However, for the sake of analysis it is useful to group the rationale for collaboration into technological, market and organizational motives (Figure 8.1). Technological reasons include the cost, time and complexity of development. In the current highly competitive business environment, the R&D function, like all other aspects of business, is forced to achieve greater financial efficiency, and to examine critically whether in-house development is the most efficient approach. In addition, there is an increasing recognition that one company's peripheral technologies are usually another's core activities, and that it often makes sense to source such technologies externally, rather than to incur the risks, costs and most importantly of all, timescale associated with in-house development. The rate of technological change, together with the increasingly complex nature of many technologies, means that few organizations can now afford to maintain in-house expertise in every potentially relevant technical area. Many products incorporate an increasing range of technologies as they evolve, for example, automobiles now include much computing hardware and software to monitor and control the engine, transmission, brakes and in some cases suspension. Therefore most R&D and product managers now recognize that no company, however large, can continue to survive as a technological island. For example, when developing the Jaguar XK8 Ford collaborated with Nippondenso in Japan to develop the engine management system and ZF in Germany to develop the transmission system and controls. In addition, there is a greater appreciation of the important role that external technology sources can play in providing a window on emerging or rapidly advancing areas of science. This is particularly true when developments arise from outside a company's traditional areas of business, or from overseas.

Two factors need to be taken into account when making the decision whether to 'make or buy' a technology: the transaction costs, and strategic implications.[1] Transaction cost analysis focuses on organizational efficiency, specifically where market transactions involve significant uncertainty. Risk can be estimated, and is defined in terms of a probability distribution, whereas uncertainty refers to an unknown outcome. Projects involving technological innovation will feature uncertainties associated with completion, performance and pre-emption by rivals. Projects involving market entry will feature uncertainties due to lack of geographical or product market knowledge. In such cases firms are often prepared to trade potentially high financial returns for a reduction in uncertainty.

However, sellers of technological or market know-how may engage in opportunistic behaviour. By opportunistic behaviour we mean high pricing or poor performance. Generally, the fewer potential sources of technology, the lower the bargaining power of the purchaser, and the higher the transaction costs. In addition, where the technology is complex it can be difficult to assess its performance.

FIGURE 8.1   A model for collaboration.

Therefore transaction costs are increased where a potential purchaser of technology has little knowledge of the technology. In this respect the acquisition of technology differs from subcontracting more routine tasks such as production or maintenance work, as it is difficult to specify contractually what must be delivered.[2]

As a result, the acquisition of technology tends to require a closer relationship between buyers and sellers than traditional market transactions, resulting in a range of possible acquisition strategies and mechanisms. The optimal technology acquisition strategy in any specific case will depend on the maturity of the technology, the firm's technological position relative to competitors and the strategic significance of the technology.[3] Some form of collaboration is normally necessary where the technology is novel, complex or scarce. Conversely, where the technology is mature, simple or widely available, market transactions such as subcontracting or licensing are more appropriate. However, the cumulative effect of outsourcing various technologies on the basis of comparative transaction costs may limit future technological options and reduce competitiveness in the long term.[4]

Therefore in practice, transaction costs are not the most significant factors affecting the decision to acquire external technology. Factors such as competitive advantage, market expansion and extending product portfolios are more important.[5] Adopting a more strategic perspective focuses attention on long-term organizational effectiveness, rather than short-term efficiency. The early normative strategy literature emphasized the need for technology development to support corporate and business strategies, and therefore technology acquisition decisions began with an evaluation of company strengths and weaknesses. The more recent resource-based approach emphasizes the process of resource accumulation or learning.[6] Competency development requires a firm to have an explicit policy or intent to use collaboration as an opportunity to learn rather than minimize costs. This suggests that the acquisition of external technology should be used to complement internal R&D, rather than being a substitute for it. In fact, a strategy of technology acquisition is associated with diversification into increasingly complex technologies.[7]

Thus neither transaction costs nor strategic behaviour fully explain actual behaviour, and to some extent the approaches are complementary. For example, a survey of top executives found that the two most significant issues considered when evaluating technological collaboration were the strategic importance of the technology and the potential for decreasing development risk.[8] Thus both strategic and transaction cost factors appear to be significant. Strategic considerations suggest *which* technologies should be developed internally, and transaction costs influence *how* the remaining technologies should be acquired. Firms attempt to reduce transaction costs when purchasing external technology by favouring existing trading partners to other sources of technology.[9] In short, for successful technology acquisition the choice of partner may be as important as the search for the best technology. For both partners, the transaction costs will be lower when dealing with a firm with which they are familiar: they are likely to have some degree of mutual trust, shared technical and business information and existing personal social links.

TABLE 8.1   Reasons for collaboration ($n = 106$).

	Mean score *(1 = low, 5 = high)*
In response to key customer needs	4.1
In response to a market need	4.1
In response to technology changes	3.8
To reduce risk of R&D	3.8
To broaden product range	3.7
To reduce R&D costs	3.7
To improve time to market	3.6
In response to competitors	3.5
In response to a management initiative	3.3
To be more innovative in product development	3.3

Source: From Littler, D. A. (1993). *Risks and Rewards of Collaboration*, UMIST.

There is also a growing realization that exposure to external sources of technology can bring about other important organizational benefits, such as providing an element of 'peer review' for the internal R&D function, reducing the 'not invented here' syndrome, and challenging in-house researchers with new ideas and different perspectives. In addition, many managers realize the tactical value of certain types of externally developed technology. Some of these are increasingly viewed as a means of gaining the goodwill of customers or governments, of

BOX 8.1 Philips and Sony.

The alliance between Philips and Sony to develop, produce and commercialize the compact disc (CD) is a good example of the multiple objectives of strategic alliances.

Philips had developed the prototype for the CD by 1978, after six years of development, but recognized that it would be difficult for the company to turn the concept into a world standard. Philips had previously experienced the commercial failure of its video laser disc system. Therefore in 1979 Philips approached Sony to form a strategic alliance. Sony was chosen because it had the requisite development and manufacturing capability, and provided access to the Japanese market. Also, like Philips, Sony had recently suffered commercial defeat with its Betamax video format.

Philips had developed the basic prototypes of the recording technologies, but the two firms jointly developed the commercial chips necessary for the modulation, control and correction of the digital signal. Sony also developed three integrated circuits which eliminated 500 components, making the CD player smaller, cheaper to produce and more reliable.

Philips and Sony quickly moved to establish their technology as the international standard, both by official and de facto means. Their format was adopted by the influential Electronic Association of Japan, which effectively blocked competing standards from Japanese manufacturers. Moreover, both firms used their in-house recording and pressing facilities to produce CD recordings, CBS/Sony in Japan and Philips/PolyGram in Germany, and thus ensure a supply of music titles. In 1982 the CD was launched in the Japanese market, and in Europe and the USA in 1983. Sales of CD players and recording exceeded all forecasts: 3 million players in 1985, 9 million in 1986; a cumulative total of 59 million CD recordings by 1985, and 136 million by 1986.

In short, the alliance between Philips and Sony had many motives, including access to complementary technologies, economies of scale in production, establishment of international standards and access to international markets. It was successful because in each case the motives of the respective partners were complementary, rather than competitive.

providing a united front for the promotion of uniform industry-wide standards, and to influence future legislation.

The UMIST survey of more than 100 UK-based alliances confirms the relative importance of market-induced motives for collaboration (Table 8.1). Specifically, the most common reasons for collaboration for product development are in response to changing customer or market needs. However, these data provide only the motives for collaboration, not the outcomes. The same survey found that although many firms formed alliances in an effort to reduce the time, cost or risk of R&D, they did not necessarily realize these benefits from the relationship. In fact, the study concluded that around half of the respondents believed that collaboration made development more complicated and costly. However, it is important to relate benefits to the objectives of collaboration. For example, firms that entered into alliances specifically to reduce the cost or time of development often achieved this, whereas firms that formed alliances for other reasons were more likely to complain that the cost and time of development increased. The study also identified a number of potential risks associated with collaboration:

- Leakage of information
- Loss of control or ownership
- Divergent aims and objectives, resulting in conflict

Around a third of respondents claimed to have experienced such problems. The problem of leakage is greatest when collaborating with potential competitors, as it is difficult to isolate the joint venture from the rest of the business and therefore it is inevitable that partners will gain access to additional knowledge and skills. This additional information may take the form of market intelligence, or more tacit skills or knowledge. Consequently a firm may lose control of the venture, resulting in conflict between partners.

8.2 Forms of Collaboration

No single form of collaboration is optimal in any generic sense. Some firms, such as Philips, favour joint ventures, whereas others, such as Asea Brown Boveri (ABB), favour acquisition. However, in practice technological and market characteristics will constrain options, and company culture and strategic considerations will determine what is possible and what is desirable. For

TABLE 8.2   Forms of collaboration.

Type of collaboration	Typical duration	Advantages (rationale)	Disadvantages (transaction costs)
Subcontract/ supplier relations	Short term	Cost and risk reduction Reduced lead time	Search costs, product performance and quality
Licensing	Fixed term	Technology acquisition	Contract cost and constraints
Consortia	Medium term	Expertise, standards, share funding	Knowledge leakage Subsequent differentiation
Strategic alliance	Flexible	Low commitment Market access	Potential lock-in Knowledge leakage
Joint venture	Long term	Complementary know-how Dedicated management	Strategic drift Cultural mismatch
Network	Long term	Dynamic, learning potential	Static inefficiencies

example, in the case of cross-border company acquisition, the potential for synergy and likelihood of success is greatest where there is some overlap in technologies, products or markets as this creates the potential for consolidation of R&D, production or marketing. In contrast, such overlaps are a major cause of failure of alliances because they create the potential for conflict and competition. Therefore firms should consider alliance partners with complementary technology, products or markets.[10]

Alliances can be characterized in a number of different ways. For example, whether they are horizontal or vertical. Horizontal relationships include cross-licensing, consortia and collaboration with potential competitors of sources of complementary technological or market know-how. Vertical relationships include subcontracting, and alliances with suppliers or customers. The primary motive of horizontal alliances tends to be access to complementary technological or market know-how, whereas the primary motive for vertical alliances is cost reduction. An alternative way of viewing alliances is in terms of their strategic significance or duration (Table 8.2). In these terms, contracting and licensing are tactical, whereas strategic alliances, formal joint ventures and innovation networks are strategic and more appropriate structures for learning. We discuss each of these in turn, focusing on the three most distinct cases of supplier relations, strategic alliances and innovation networks.

Supplier Relations and Subcontracting

The subcontracting or 'outsourcing' of non-core activities has become popular in recent times. Typically, arguments for subcontracting are framed in terms of strategic focus, or 'sticking to the knitting', but in practice most subcontracting or outsourcing arrangements are based on the potential to save costs: suppliers are likely to have lower overheads and variable costs, and may benefit from economies of scale if serving other firms.

Resource dependence and agency theory are more commonly used to explain vertical relationships, and are concerned with the need to control key technologies in the value chain. The seminal work of von Hippel[11] and subsequent work by others have encouraged firms to identify and form relationships with 'lead' users, and more recently perceptions of the practices of Japanese manufacturers have led many firms to form closer relationships with suppliers.[12] Indeed, closer links between firms, their suppliers and customers may help to reduce the cost of components, through specialization and sharing information on costs. However, factors such as the selection of suppliers and users, timing and mode of their involvement, and the novelty and complexity of the system being developed may reduce or negate the benefit of close supplier–user links.[13]

The quality of the relationship with suppliers and the timing of their involvement in development are critical factors. Traditionally such relationships have been short-term, contractual arm's-length agreements focusing on the issue of the cost, with little supplier input into design or engineering. In contrast the 'Japanese' or 'partnership' model is based on long-term relationships, and suppliers make a significant contribution to the development of new products. The latter approach increases the visibility of cost–performance trade-offs, reduces the time

FIGURE 8.2 How objectives and nature of supply market influence
supplier relationships.

to market and improves the integration of component technologies. In certain
sectors, particularly machine tools and scientific equipment, there is a long tradition of collaboration between manufacturers and lead users in the development
of new products. Figure 8.2 presents a range of potential relationships with suppliers. Note that in this diagram we are not suggesting any trend from left to
right, but rather that different types of relationship are appropriate in different
circumstances, in essence an argument for carefully segmenting supply needs
and suppliers, instead of the wholesale adoption of simplistic fashions such as
'partnerships' or business-to-business (so-called 'B2B') supply intranets.

On the vertical axis we have objectives ranging from cost reduction, quality
improvement, lead-time reduction through to product and process innovation.
On the horizontal axis we distinguish between three types of supply market:

- *Homogeneous*—all potential suppliers have very similar performance
- *Differentiated*—suppliers differ greatly and one clearly superior
- *Indeterminate*—suppliers differ greatly under different conditions

In the case of homogeneous supply conditions and a primary objective to reduce
costs, we would argue that a traditional market/contractual relationship is the
ideal arrangement. In its most recent form this might be achieved by means of a
business-to-business intranet exchange or club, whereby potential suppliers to a
specific customer or sector pool their price and other data, or bid for specific contracts. Examples include Covisint in the automobile industry, established by
Ford, General Motors and DaimlerChrysler, and MetalSite formed by a group of
the largest steel producers in the USA. Such developments are not confined to
manufacturing, and British Airways, American, United, Delta and Continental
have established an electronic procurement hub for routine supplies with an
annual turnover of $32bn. In the UK the retailers Kingfisher, Tesco and Marks &

Spencer have joined the Worldwide Retail Exchange (WWRX) in an effort to reduce the cost of purchases by up to 20%. Savings of 5–10% are more typical of such exchanges, but as with other applications of Internet technology the most significant savings are in transaction costs rather than the goods purchased. Estimates and efficiencies vary, but reports suggest transactions costs can be just 10% of conventional supply chains. Such developments attempt to exploit buyer power, and make supplier prices more transparent. They are the closest thing in the real world to the market of 'perfect information' found in economics textbooks. Nonetheless, there are still some concerns that these might evolve into cartels controlled by the existing dominant companies, and thereby restrict new entrants and potential competition. However, where the supply market is more differentiated, other types of relationship are likely be more appropriate. In this case some form of 'partnership' or 'lean' relationship is often advocated, based on the quality and development lead-time benefits experienced by Japanese manufacturers of consumer durables, specifically cars and electronics. Lamming identifies a number of defining characteristics of such partnership or 'lean' supply relations:[14]

- Fewer suppliers, longer-term relations
- Greater equity—real 'cost transparency'
- Focus on value flows—the relationship, not the contract
- Vendor assessment, plus development
- Two-way or third-party assessment
- Mutual learning—share experience, expertise, knowledge and investment

These principles are based on a distillation of the features of the best Japanese manufacturers in the automobile and electronics sectors, and more recent experiments in other contexts, such as aerospace in the UK and USA,[15] and as such may represent best practice under certain conditions. Nishiguchi compared supplier relations in Japan and the UK, and found that lean or partnership approaches had significant advantages over market relations, including more supportive customers and less erratic trade.[16] This resulted in measurable differences in operational performance, such as a reduction in inventory held by customers of 90%, and tool development time reduction by some 70%. However, trade-offs existed. In the lean relationships customers were rated by suppliers as being significantly more demanding than in the market relationships, and involved a much higher degree of monitoring by customers. Perhaps of greater strategic significance, in the lean relationships the suppliers' sales were dominated by a few key customers, and asset specificity, a measure of how much a suppliers' plant and equipment are dedicated to a particular customer, was much higher. These two factors make suppliers in lean relations very vulnerable to the fortunes of their key customers. For example, in the UK the retail chain Marks & Spencer is often presented as the model of supplier relations, but following its poor market and financial performance in the late 1990s, many of its long-term supply 'partners' have been abandoned or ordered to cut costs or be deselected. Nevertheless, 'partnership' models have fast become the norm in both the private and public sectors, irrespective of the supply market conditions or objectives of the relationship. For example, one study found that the main explanation for the adoption of lean supply practices was managerial choice, rather than any rationale based on external factors such as industry structure or supply needs.[17]

However, in the case of indeterminate supply markets a partnership or lean supply strategy may be suboptimal or even dysfunctional. We shall revisit the case of Japanese business groups later in this chapter, but in anticipation of that discussion there is evidence that such rigid supply structures may offer static efficiencies in terms of cost savings, quality improvement and reduction in development lead time, but may suffer dynamic inefficiencies when it comes to developing novel technologies, products and processes. On the one hand, the increase in the global sourcing of technology has reduced the chance that an existing 'partner' will be the most appropriate supplier, and on the other hand the tacit nature or 'stickiness' of technological knowledge suggests that a market transaction would be inadequate.[18] Therefore where innovation is the primary objective of the supply relationship, and the supply market is neither homogenous nor clearly differentiated, a temporary, ad hoc relationship with a supplier may be more appropriate. These have some features common to horizontal strategic alliances, in that they are clearly focused, project-based forms of collaboration. In such cases the relationship is neither market nor partnership, but a hybrid (see Box 8.2). Loose coupling is appropriate where multi-technology products are characterized by uneven rates of advance in the underlying technologies, and in such cases technology consultants or systems integrators act as a buffer between the suppliers and users of the technology.[19] For suppliers, technological competencies and problem-solving capabilities are associated with high gross margins and a larger share of overseas business.[20]

TABLE 8.3   Supplier relationship factors contributing to successful new product development.

Factor	Most successful	Least successful	Difference*
Strength of supplier's top management commitment	6.14	5.22	0.91
Direct cross-functional, inter-company communication	6.05	4.87	1.18
Strength of customer's top management commitment	5.70	4.95	0.75
Familiarity with supplier's capability prior to project	5.64	4.58	1.07
Customer requirements information sharing	5.12	4.22	0.90
Joint agreement on performance measures	5.07	4.20	0.88
Supplier membership/participation on customer's project team	5.02	3.73	1.29
Technology sharing	4.84	3.77	1.07
Strength of consensus that right supplier was selected	4.83	3.88	0.95
Formal trust development practices	4.14	3.07	1.07
Common and linked information systems	4.07	2.96	1.11
Shared education and training	3.44	2.29	1.15
Risk/reward sharing schemes	3.13	2.47	0.65
Co-location of customer/supplier personnel	2.95	1.84	1.11
Technology information sharing	2.44	1.62	0.82
Shared plant and equipment	2.44	1.62	0.82

* All differences statistically significant at 5% level.
1 = no use, 7 = significant/extensive. N = 83.
Source: Derived from Ragatz, G. L., R. B. Handfield and T. V. Scannell (1997) 'Success factors for integrating suppliers into new product development', *Journal of Product Innovation Management*, **14**, 190–202.

BOX 8.2 Globetronics: evolution of supply relationships.

Globetronics Bhd. was formed in 1990 by two Malaysians formerly employed by Intel. The Malaysian Technology Development Corporation (MTDC) provided 30% of the venture capital, and the company was subsequently floated in 1997 to raise additional capital for growth. The company's primary activites are similar to the majority of transnational semiconductor firms based in Malaysia, and involve post-fabrication manufacture of semiconductors, including assembly and packaging. Indeed, the company's main customers are American and Japanese trans-nationals. The significant difference is that domestic ownership and management have allowed Globetronics to more easily capture value-added activities such as development and marketing.

The company now has seven business divisions and a new plant in the Philippines. Two of the businesses are joint ventures with the Japanese firm Sumitomo. The relationship with Sumitomo began as a simple subcontracting agreement, but over the years a high level of trust has been achieved and two joint ventures have been established. The first, SGT, was created in 1994, and is 49% owned by Globetronics. It is the largest manufacturer in the world and the only company outside of Japan to produce ceramic substrate semiconductor packages. The second joint venture, SGTI, was created in 1996, and is 30% owned by Globetronics. In both cases the Japanese partner has maintained majority ownership, but it is clear that the Malaysian partner has made some progress in assimilating the technological and design capabilities. This provides a promising model for companies in developing countries, to escape dependent subcontracting relationships by using joint ventures to upgrade their technological and market competencies.

Source: Extract from Tidd, J. and M. Brocklehurst (1999) 'Routes to technological learning and development: an assessment of Malaysia's innovation policy and performance', *Technological Forecasting and Social Change*, **63** (2).

Table 8.3 lists some of the management practices found to contribute to a supplier relationship for successful new product development. This list suggests a number of good practices common to partnership or lean approaches, but un-bundles these practices from the need for long-term, stable co-dependent relationships. The low rating given to co-location and shared equipment suggests a more arm's-length relation, albeit highly integrated for the purposes of the project. Note the relatively high ranking of the need for consensus that the right supplier has been chosen.

Technology Licensing

The issue of intellectual property and the basis of licensing was discussed in the previous chapter. Licensing offers a firm the opportunity to exploit the intellectual property of another firm, normally in return for payment of a fee and royalty based on sales. Typically a technology licence will specify the applications and markets in which the technology may be used, and often will require the buyer to give the seller access to any subsequent improvements in the technology.

In theory, licensing-in a technology has a number of advantages over internal development, in particular lower development costs, less technological and market risk, and faster product development and market entry. Potential drawbacks to licensing-in include restrictive clauses imposed by the licenser, loss of control of operational issues such as pricing, production volume and product quality, and the potential transaction costs of search, negotiation and adaptation.

In practice, the relative costs and benefits of licensing-in will depend on the nature of the technologies and markets and strategy and capability of the firm. A survey of more than 200 firms in the chemical, engineering and pharmaceutical industries found that the most important reasons for licensing were related to the speed of access, rather than cost. Factors such as quickly acquiring knowledge required for product development, keeping pace with competitors and increasing sales were found to be most important, and factors such as the cost of development least important.[21] The study found that the most significant problems associated with licensing-in are entry costs such as the choice of suitable technology and licenser, and the loss of control of decision-making. Differences in emphasis exist across sectors; for example, pharmaceutical firms experience higher search costs than engineering firms, and engineering firms place greater emphasis on the potential for reducing the cost and improving the speed of market entry. For example, Eli Lilly licensed-in basic cephalosporin technology from the National Research and Development Corporation. Using its in-house skills, it was able to produce a wide range of these antibiotics, hence adding value to the licensed technology.

In some cases, however, there is a reluctance to license-in technology which may adversely affect the differentiation of end products, if customers became aware of the fact. Many firms express concerns regarding the constraints imposed by international licensing agreements, specifically the common requirement to 'grant-back' any improvements made to the technology. For example, ICI claims increasing globalization and concentration within the chemical industry as reducing the scope for licensing technology. For these reasons an increasing number of firms are careful to license only components of any process or product in order to allow scope for subsequent improvement and differentiation. For example, Mitsubishi Chemical licensed a well-established process technology from a US competitor, but chose not to license the catalyst or polymer design. This allowed the company to avoid having to grant-back its subsequent improvements to the catalyst and polymer design to the American competitor. Nippondenso adopted a similar strategy when licensing technology from potential competitors.

However, this approach to licensing is only viable where the technology can be easily 'unbundled'. For example, Kirin, the Japanese food and drink manufacturer, finds that in most cases it is able to negotiate and exploit simple licences for its brewery and food businesses, but not for its pharmaceutical products. The company prefers formal joint ventures to develop new pharmaceutical products because of the complex interrelated technologies, patents and skills required.

Research Consortia

Research consortia consist of a number of organizations working together on a relatively well-specified project. The rationale for joining a research consortium includes sharing the cost and risk of research, pooling scarce expertise and equipment, performing pre-competitive research and setting of standards. They may take many different forms, the most centralized being pooled investment in a common research facility or new venture, and the least centralized being co-ordinated research co-located in the various member firms. Typically, European firms have favoured the former, whereas American firms have tended to adopt the latter type. Japanese firms appear to favour a hybrid form in which shared research facilities are used in parallel to co-ordinated in-house research. These differences in structure are due to technical, competitive and legal reasons.

The original research consortia were the industry-based research associations formed in the UK during the First World War. The idea was to encourage small firms to fund research and the research associations were largely a response to the competitive threat of German manufacturers. They were funded by a combination of government funds and contributions from member firms. Many of the associations have survived and are now commercial contract research organizations. The concept of research associations transferred to Japan in the 1950s, and a number of research consortia were formed to support the development of the automobile component industry. In 1961 the Engineering Association Act was passed in Japan, allowing firms to form consortia without being prosecuted under anti-trust law, and also provided tax benefits for consortia. However, the goals and structure of the Japanese consortia are very different from those in the UK.

In Japan, the Technology Research Association system provides a structure to bring together firms from a wide range of different industries. Unlike their British counterparts, the Japanese associations tend to be temporary organizations, and are disbanded when the project is completed, whereas the British associations have tended to become permanent organizations. Members of the Japanese associations tend to be large firms with extensive in-house R&D capabilities, whereas members of British associations tend to be much smaller companies with little in-house R&D. Finally, the Japanese associations tend to be in high-technology areas, whereas the British associations originally concentrated on support for mature industries.

The USA was relatively late to adopt research consortia because of a strong belief in the efficiency of a free market economy resulting in severe anti-trust (anti-monopoly) legislation, which made it difficult to organize consortia. Also the early dominance of large firms in many of the leading sectors made it easier for firms to rely on their own resources to conduct research. However, the National Cooperative Research Act was passed in the USA in 1984 in an effort to emulate the apparent success of the Japanese consortia. As a result, the Microelectronic and Computer Technology Corporation (MCC) (see Box 8.3) and SEMATECH (semiconductor manufacturing technology initiative) were able to be established.[22]

There are significant differences between the Japanese and American research consortia.[23] Almost all members of the Japanese consortia conduct research in member firms, compared to less than a half of the American consortia members.

BOX 8.3 Microelectronic and Computer Technology Corporation (MCC).

MCC was formed by a number of US firms in 1982, including computer manufacturers Sperry, NCR, DEC, Honeywell, and producers of semiconductor devices such as AMD and Motorola. MCC was formed in response to the perceived loss of competitiveness of the US computing industry, and fear of the Japanese fifth-generation computer project. Indeed no foreign-owned firms were allowed to join the MCC. The formation of the MCC challenged the existing anti-trust (anti-monopoly) laws in the USA, and subsequently the National Cooperative Research Act came into effect in 1984 to allow firms to collaborate for basic research under certain circumstances. Since the Act more than 400 R&D consortia have been formed in the USA.

A state-of-the-art research facility was built in Austin, Texas, and in its first 10 years of operation was funded for more than $500m. by its member firms. Four broad areas were targeted for research: computer-aided design, packaging interconnect, software and advanced computer architecture. The success of MCC has been mixed. On the one hand it was awarded 117 US patents, licensed 182 technologies and published more than 2400 technical reports. However, there is little evidence of any commercial outputs or any significant technology transfer to its member firms. Thus in the 1990s the research emphasis of the MCC has shifted from strategic research for its corporate members, to lower-level and shorter-term projects, many funded by the US and foreign governments. Two modes of technology transfer were evaluated in the case of MCC. First, transfer to member firms. Second, the establishment of new technology spin-off firms. Every effort was made to promote technology transfer to member firms, and a formal standard technology package (STP) was introduced whereby technology release dates were announced and shareholders invited to MCC to receive the technology package. However, in a survey of member firms, only a fifth of managers believed that the MCC would create useful technology, but almost half predicted problems of transferring these technologies to the member firms. Researchers at the MCC shared these concerns:

'we were caught in the paradox that faces many R&D consortia sooner or later. Our success depended on how successfully our shareholders adopted MCC technology. Yet we had virtually no control once MCC technology was in the hands of the shareholders.'

'clearly the technology transfer problem must be viewed from both the re-searcher and customer viewpoints . . . most of the participants have been literally wasting their research investment in MCC by failing to put in place effective mechanisms and people for marketing, selling, developing, and supporting MCC technology once it reached the successful prototype stage.'

(quoted in Gibson and Rogers, 1994, 339–340)[22]

The US consortia favour separate joint facilities and research in universities. Therefore the Japanese and American consortia face different organizational problems. The biggest problem the Japanese must tackle is how to co-ordinate research in member firms, whereas the biggest problem for the Americans is how to manage technology transfer from the centre to the member firms. In addition, the Japanese consortia are more focused on applied product development and pilot production, whereas the American consortia tend to concentrate on idea generation and technical feasibility studies. Therefore the success of research consortia depends on their motives, structure and membership.

Consortia, defined as multi-firm collaborations, take two main forms, between competitors or between non-competing firms. Firms commonly collaborate with competitors in the development of pre-competitive technologies. This form of collaboration is particularly attractive when supported by government or EU funds, as in the case of the Framework programme for European research and technological development. For example, CRL, part of the Thorn group, participated some years ago in a government-funded consortium working on ferroelectric liquid crystal (FLC) technology, bringing its expertise in colour and grey scale to the collaboration. Since the end of this consortium, the company has continued to develop the technology itself, and recently launched a low-power, low-cost monochrome FLC display. In addition, CRL's printer shuttle arrays were developed with support from the EU-funded ESPRIT programme.

Collaboration between firms in different industries appears to raise much less concern about proprietary positions. In most cases, they are viewed as an attractive means of leveraging in-house skills by working with organizations possessing complementary technical capabilities. Intra-industry collaborations are more important in non-competitive areas, such as in the areas of health, safety and the environment, and in setting new standards or influencing legislation. For example, the 1990 US Clean Air Act placed the onus on automobile manufacturers and oil companies to provide the basic science which will act as a realistic foundation for future legislation. Competing oil companies and auto manufacturers set up the Auto-oil consortium to provide this science.

Nevertheless, even in consortia involving non-competing firms, it appears that vested interests can sometimes lead to difficulties. For example, in the collaboration between auto manufacturers and oil companies aimed at reducing toxic emissions from car exhausts, there exist serious differences of opinion between these two groups of firms about whether the main thrust of the research should be directed towards improved engine efficiencies, or towards better gasoline formulations.

Strategic Alliances and Joint Ventures

Strategic alliances, whether formal or informal, typically take the form of an agreement between two or more firms to co-develop a new technology or product. Whereas research consortia tend to focus on more basic research issues, strategic alliances involve near-market development projects. However, unlike more formal joint ventures, a strategic alliance typically has a specific end goal and timetable, and does not normally take the form of a separate company. There are two basic types of formal joint venture: a new company formed by two or more separate organizations, which typically allocate ownership based on shares of stock controlled; or a more simple contractual basis for collaboration. The critical distinction between the two types of joint venture is that an equity arrangement requires the formation of a separate legal entity. In such cases management is delegated to the joint venture, which is not the case for other forms of collaboration. A range of strategic alliances and joint ventures are discussed in detail in section 8.4.

Doz and Hamel identify a range of motives for strategic alliances and suggest strategies to exploit each:[24]

- To build critical mass through co-option
- To reach new markets by leveraging co-specialized resources
- To gain new competencies through organizational learning

In a co-option alliance critical mass is achieved through temporary alliances with competitors, customers or companies with complementary technology, products or services. Through co-option a company seeks to group together other relatively weak companies to challenge a dominant competitor. Co-option is common where scale or network size is important, such as mobile telephony and airlines. For example, Airbus (see Box 8.4) was originally created in response to the dominance of Boeing, and Symbian in response to Microsoft's dominance. Greater international reach is a common related motive for co-option alliances. Fujitsu initially used its alliance with ICL to develop a market presence in Europe, as did Honda with Rover. However, co-option alliances may be inherently unstable and transitory. Once the market position has been achieved, one partner may seek to take control through acquisition, as in the case of Fujitsu and ICL, or to go unilateral, as in the case of Honda and Rover.[25]

In a co-option alliance partners are normally drawn from the same industry, whereas in co-specialization partners are usually from different sectors. In a co-specialized alliance partners bring together unique competencies to create the opportunity to enter new markets, develop new products or build new businesses. Such co-specialization is common in systems or complex products and services. However, there is a risk associated with co-specialization. Partners are required to commit to partners' technology and standards. Where technologies are emerging and uncertain and standards are yet to be established, there is a high risk that a partner's technology may become redundant. This has a number of implications for co-specialization alliances. First, that at the early stages of an emerging market where the dominant technologies are still uncertain, flexible forms of collaboration such as alliances are preferable, and at later stages when market needs are clearer and the relevant technological configuration better defined, more formal joint ventures become appropriate.[26] Second, to restrict the use of alliances to instances where the technology is tacit, expensive and time-consuming to develop. If the technology is not tacit, a licence is likely to be cheaper and less risky, and if the technology is not expensive or time-consuming to develop, in-house development is preferable.[27] If resources and relationships allow, some form of network hedging strategy might be advisable, as suggested later in the section on innovation networks. We will discuss the acquisition of competencies through alliances in section 8.5.

BOX 8.4 Airbus Industrie.

Airbus Industrie was formed in France in 1969 as a joint venture between the German firm MBB (now DASA) and French firm Aérospatiale, to be joined by CASA of Spain in 1970 and British Aerospace (now BAe Systems) in 1979. Airbus is not a company, but a Groupment d'Intérêt Economique (GIE), which is a French legal entity which is not required to publish its own accounts. Instead, all costs and any profits or losses are absorbed by the member companies. The partners make components in proportion to their share of Airbus Industrie: Aérospatiale and DASA each have 37.9%, BAe 20% and CASA 4.2%.

At that time the international market for civil aircraft was dominated by the US firm Boeing, which in 1984 accounted for 40% of the airframe market in the non-communist world. The growing cost and commercial risk of airframe development had resulted in consolidation of the industry and a number of joint ventures. In addition, product life cycles had shortened due to more rapid improvements in engine technology. The partners identified an unfilled market niche for a high-capacity/short medium-range passenger aircraft, as more than 70% of the traffic was then on routes of less than 4600 km. Thus the Airbus A300 was conceived in 1969. The A300 was essentially the result of the French and German partners, the former insisting on final assembly in France, and the latter gaining access to French technology. The first A300 flew in 1974, followed by a series of successful derivatives such as the A310 and the A320. The British partner played a leading role in the subsequent projects, bringing both capital and technological expertise to the venture. Airbus has since proved to be highly innovative with the introduction of fly-by-wire technology, and common platforms and control systems for all its aircraft to reduce the cost of crew training and aircraft maintenance. In 2000 the group announced plans to develop a double-decker 'super' jumbo, the A3XX, with seats for 500–650 passengers and costing an estimated US$12bn to develop. This would challenge Boeing in the only market it continues to dominate.

In 1998 Airbus outsold Boeing for the first time in history. In 1999 Daimler-Chrysler (DASA), Aérospatiale and CASA merged to form the European Aeronautic Defence and Space Company (EADS), making BAe Systems, formerly British Aerospace, the only non-EADS member of Airbus. The group plans to move from the unwieldy GIE structure to become a company. This would allow streamlining of its manufacturing operations, which are currently geographically dispersed across the UK, France, Germany and Spain, and more importantly help create financial transparency to help identify and implement cost savings. Also, some customers have reported poor service and support as Airbus has to refer such work to the relevant member company.

Airbus demonstrates the complexity of joint ventures. The primary motive was to share the high cost and commercial risk of development. On the one hand, the French and German participation was underwritten by their respective governments. This fact has not escaped the attention of Boeing and the US government, which provides subsidies indirectly via defence contracts. On the other, all partners had to some extent captive markets in the form of national airlines, although almost three-quarters of all Airbus sales were ultimately outside the member countries. Finally, there were also technology motives for the joint venture. For example, BAe specializes in development of the wings, Aérospatiale the avionics, DASA the fuselages and CASA the tails. However, as suggested above, there are now strong financial, manufacturing and marketing reasons for combining the operations within a single company.

Innovation Networks

The concept of innovation networks has become popular in recent years, as it appears to offer many of the benefits of internal development, but with few of the drawbacks of collaboration. Networks have been claimed by some to be a new hybrid form of organization that has the potential to replace both firms (hierarchies) and markets, in essence the 'virtual corporation', whereas others believe them to be simply a transitory form of organization, positioned somewhere between internal hierarchies and external market mechanisms. Whatever the case, there is little agreement on what constitutes a network, and the term and alternatives such as 'web' and 'cluster' have been criticized for being too vague and all-inclusive.[28] Different authors adopt different meanings, levels of analysis and attribute networks with different characteristics. For example, academics on the Continent have focused on social, geographical and institutional aspects of networks, and the opportunities and constraints these present for innovation.[29] In contrast, Anglo-Saxon studies have tended to take a systems perspective, and have attempted to identify how best to design, manage and exploit networks for innovation.[30] Figure 8.3 presents a framework for the analysis of different network perspectives in innovation studies.

Whilst there is little consensus in aims or means, there appears to be some agreement that a network is more than an aggregation of bilateral relationships or dyads, and therefore the configuration, nature and content of a network impose additional constraints and present additional opportunities. A network can be thought of as consisting of a number of positions or nodes, occupied by individuals, firms, business units, universities, governments, customers or other actors, and links or interactions between these nodes. A network perspective is concerned with how these economic actors are influenced by the social context in which they are embedded and how actions can be influenced by the position of actors. A network can influence the actions of its members in two ways.[31] Firstly, through the flow and sharing of information within the network. Secondly, through differences in the position of actors in the network, which causes power and control imbalances. Therefore the position an organization occupies in a network is a matter of great strategic importance, and reflects its power and influence in that network. Sources of power include technology, expertise, trust, economic strength and legitimacy. Networks can be tight or loose, depending on the quantity (number), quality (intensity) and type (closeness to core activities) of the interactions or links. Such links are more than individual transactions, and require significant investment in resources over time.

	Focus on general innovativeness	Focus on discrete innovations
Social network focus	Regional and business groups; communities of scientists and engineers	Diffusion and commercialization of innovations
Actor network focus	Portfolios of strategic alliances	Networks mobilized for a specific innovation

FIGURE 8.3 Different network perspectives in innovation research. Source: Derived from Conway, S. and F. Steward (1998) 'Mapping innovation networks', *International Journal of Innovation Management*, **2** (2), 223–254.

Networks are appropriate where the benefits of co-specialization, sharing of joint infrastructure and standards and other network externalities outweigh the costs of network governance and maintenance. Where there are high transaction costs involved in purchasing technology, a network approach may be more appropriate than a market model, and where uncertainty exists a network may be superior to full integration or acquisition. Historically, networks have evolved from long-standing business relationships. Any firm will have a group of partners that it does regular business with—universities, suppliers, distributors, customers and competitors. Over time mutual knowledge and social bonds develop through repeated dealings, increasing trust and reducing transaction costs. Therefore a firm is more likely to buy or sell technology from members of its network.[32] Firms may be able to access the resources of a wide range of other organizations through direct and indirect relationships, involving different channels of communication and degrees of formalization. Typically, this begins with stronger relationship between a firm and a small number of primary suppliers, which share knowledge at the concept development stage. The role of the technology gatekeeper, or heavyweight project manager, is critical in this respect. In many cases organizational linkages can be traced to strong personal relationships between key individuals in each organization. These linkages may subsequently evolve into a full network of secondary and tertiary suppliers, each contributing to the development of a subsystem or component technology, but links with these organizations are weaker and filtered by the primary suppliers. However, links amongst the primary, secondary and tertiary supplier groups may be stronger to facilitate the exchange of information.

This process is path-dependent in the sense that past relationships between actors increase the likelihood of future relationships, which can lead to inertia and constrain innovation. Indeed much of the early research on networks concentrated on the constraints networks impose on members, for example preventing the introduction of 'superior' technologies or products by controlling supply and distribution networks. Organizational networks have two characteristics that affect the innovation process: activity cycles and instability.[33] The existence of activity cycles and transaction chains creates constraints within a network. Different activities are systematically related to each other and through repetition are combined to form transaction chains. This repetition of transactions is the basis of efficiency, but systemic interdependencies create constraints to change. For example, the Swiss watch industry was based on long-established networks of small firms with expertise in precision mechanical movements, but as a result was slow to respond to the threat of electronic watches from Japan.

Similarly, Japan has a long tradition of formal business groups, originally the family-based *zaibatsu*, and more recently the more loosely connected *keiretsu*. The best-known groups are the three ex-*zaibatsu*—Mitsui, Mitsubishi and Sumitomo, and the three newer groups based around commercial banks—Fuji, Sanwa and Dal Ichi Kangyo (DKB). There are two types of *keiretsu*, although the two overlap. The vertical type organizes suppliers and distribution outlets hierarchically beneath a large, industry-specific manufacturer, for example Toyota Motor. These manufacturers are in turn members of *keiretsu* which consist of a large bank, insurance company, trading company and representatives of all major industrial groups. These inter-industry *keiretsu* provide a significant internal market for intermediate products. In theory, benefits of membership of a *keiretsu* include access to low-cost, long-term capital, and access to the expertise of firms in related industries. This is particularly important for high-technology firms. In practice, research suggests that membership of *keiretsu* is associated with below-average profitability and growth,[34] and independent firms like Honda and Sony are often cited as being more innovative than established members of *keiretsu*. However, the *keiretsu* may not be the most appropriate unit of analysis, as many newer, less formal clusters of companies have emerged in modern Japan.

However, as the role of a network is different for all its members, there will always be reasons to change the network and possibilities to do so. A network can never be optimal in any generic sense, as there is no single reference point, but is inherently adaptable. This inherent instability and imperfection mean that networks can evolve over time. For example, Belussi and Arcangeli discuss the evolution of innovation networks in a range of traditional industries in Italy.[35]

More recent research has examined the opportunities networks might provide for innovation, and the potential to explicitly design or selectively participate in networks for the purpose of innovation, that is a path-creating rather than path-dependent process.[36] A study of 53 research networks found two distinct dynamics of formation and growth. The first type of network emerges and develops as a result of environmental interdependence, and through common interests—an emergent network. However, the other type of network requires some triggering entity to form and develop—an engineered network.[37] In an engineered network a nodal firm actively recruits other members to form a network, without the rationale of environmental interdependence or similar interests. Different types of

TABLE 8.4   Competitive dynamics in network industries.

	Type of network	
	Unconnected, closed	*Connected, open*
System attributes	Incompatible technologies	Compatible across vendors and products
	Custom components and interfaces	Standard components
Firm strategies	Control standards by protecting proprietary knowledge	Shape standards by sharing knowledge with rivals and complementary markets
Source of advantage	Economies of scale, customer lock-in	Economies of scope, multiple segments

Source: Adapted from Garud, R. and A. Kumaraswamy (1993) 'Changing competitive dynamics in network industries', *Strategic Management Journal*, **14**, 351–369.

network may present different opportunities for learning (Table 8.4). In a closed network a company seeks to develop proprietary standards through scale economies and other actions, and thereby lock customers and other related companies into its network.[38] Obvious examples include Microsoft in operating systems and Intel in microprocessors for PCs. In the case of open networks complex products, services and businesses have to interface with others and it is in everyone's interest to share information and to ensure compatibility (see Box 8.5). Virtual innovation networks are beginning to emerge, based on firms that are connected via intranet/extranet/Internet and exchange information within a business relationship to create value. To date such virtual networks are most common in supply chain and customer order automation, but recent examples include product development. For example, in supply chain management Herve Thermique, a French manufacturer of heating and air conditioners, uses an extranet to co-ordinate its 23 offices and 8000 suppliers, and General Electric has an extranet bidding and trading system to manage its 1400 spliers; Boeing has a Web-based order system for its 700 customers worldwide which features 410 000 spare parts; and in product development, Caterpillar's customers can amend designs during assembly, and Adaptec co-ordinates design and production of microchips in Hong Kong, Taiwan and Japan.[39]

8.3 Patterns of Collaboration

In this section we examine how technology and markets affect how firms collaborate. Research on collaborative activity has been plagued by differences in definition and methodology. Essentially there have been two approaches to studying collaboration. The approach favoured by economists and strategists is based on aggregate data and examines patterns within and across different sectors. This type of research provides useful insights into how technological and market characteristics affect the level, type and success of collaborative activities. The other

BOX 8.5 The development of Linux: a case of network innovation?

The computer operating system Linux has been largely developed by a network of voluntary programmers, often referred to as the 'Linux community'. This is probably one of the few true examples of a 'cyber' or virtual organization. Linus Torvalds first suggested the development of a free operating system to compete with the DOS/Windows monopoly in 1991, and quickly attracted the support of a group of volunteer programmers: 'having those 100 part-time users was really great for all the feedback I got. They found bugs that I hadn't because I hadn't been using it the way they were . . . after a while they started sending me fixes or improvements. . . this wasn't planned, it just happened.' Thus Linux grew from 10 000 lines of code in 1991 to 1.5 million lines by 1998. Its development coincided with and fully exploited the growth of Internet and later Web forms of collaborative working. The provision of the source code to all potential developers promotes continuous incremental innovation, and the close and sometimes indistinguishable developer and user groups promote concurrent development and debugging. The weaknesses are potential lack of support for users and new hardware, availability of compatible software and forking in development.

By 1998 there were estimated to be more than 7.5 million users and almost 300 user groups across 40 countries. Linux had achieved a 17% share of the market for server operating systems, although its share of the PC operating system market was much lower, and Apache, a Linux application Web server program, accounted for half the market. Although Linux is available free of charge, a number of businesses have been spawned by its development. These range from branding and distribution of Linux, development of complementary software and user support and consultancy services. For example, although Linux can be downloaded free of charge, RedHat Software provides an easier installation program and better documentation for around US$50, and in 1998 achieved annual revenues of more than US$10m.

type of research is based on structured case studies of specific alliances, usually within a specific sector, but sometimes across national boundaries, and provides richer insights into the problems and management of collaboration.

Industry structure and technological and market characteristics result in different opportunities for joint ventures across sectors, but other factors determine the strategy of specific firms within a given sector. At the industry level, high levels of R&D intensity are associated with high levels of technologically oriented joint ventures, probably as a result of increasing technological rivalry. This suggests that technologically oriented joint ventures are perceived to be a viable strategy in industries characterized by high barriers to entry, rapid market growth and large expenditures on R&D. However, within a specific sector, joint venture activity is not associated with differences in capital expenditure or R&D intensity. A study of joint ventures in the USA found that technologically oriented alliances tend to increase with the size of firm, capital expenditure and R&D intensity.[40] Similarly, the number of marketing and distribution-oriented joint ventures increases with firm size and capital expenditure, but is not affected by R&D intensity. At the level of the firm, different factors are more important. For example, there are significant differences in the motives of small and large firms. In general, large firms use joint ventures to acquire technology, whilst smaller firms place greater emphasis on the acquisition of market knowledge and financial support.

Joint venture activity is high in the chemical, mechanical and electrical machinery sectors, as firms seek to acquire external technological know-how in order to reduce the inherent technological uncertainty in those sectors. In contrast, joint ventures are much less common in consumer goods industries, where market position is the result of product differentiation, distribution and support. If obtaining complementary assets or resources are a primary motive for collaboration, we would expect alliances to be concentrated in those sectors in which mutual ignorance of the partner's technology or markets is likely to be high.[41] Similarly, joint ventures would occur more frequently between partners who are in industries relatively unrelated to one another, and that such alliances are likely to be short-lived as firms learn from each other. Surveys of alliances in so-called high-technology sectors such as software and automation appear to confirm that access to technology is the most common motive. Market access appears to be a more common motive for collaboration in the computer, microelectronics, consumer electronics and telecommunications sectors (Table 8.5).

TABLE 8.5   Technology strategic alliances by type and sector.

	Number	Technology (%)	Market (%)	Technology/ market ratio*	Primary motive
Aerospace	228	34	13	2.6	Technology
Automation	278	41	31	1.3	Technology
Automotive	205	27	52	0.5	Market
Chemicals	410	16	51	0.3	Market
Computers	198	28	51	0.6	Market
Consumer electronics	58	19	53	0.4	Market
Energy	141	31	23	1.4	Technology
Microelectronics	383	33	52	0.6	Market
Software	344	38	24	1.6	Technology
Telecommunications	366	28	35	0.8	Market

*Technology/market ratio >1 implies technology-intensive; <1 implies market-intensive.
Source: Data derived from Hagedoorn, J. (1993) 'Understanding the rationale of strategic technology partnering', *Strategic Management Journal*, **14**, 371–385.

However, these data need to be treated with some caution as in many cases partners exchange market access for technology access or vice versa. For example, Japanese firms rarely sell technology, but are often prepared to exchange technology for access to markets. Conversely, European firms commonly trade market access for technology.[42] In this way firms limit the potential for paying high price premiums for market or technologies because of their lack of knowledge.

A breakdown of alliances by region provides some further explanation. Patterns within and between triad regions are very different. Alliances between

US firms appear to be common in all fields. Alliances between European firms are concentrated in software development and telecommunications, but there is relatively little collaborative activity within the European automation, microelectronics and computing industries. Alliances between Japanese firms appear to be much less common than expected. This may reflect the weakness of the database, but is more likely to reflect the rationale for strategic alliances. The most common reason for international alliances is market access, whereas the most common reason for intraregional alliances is technology acquisition.

The patterns of collaboration between the different triad regions provide some support for this argument. The data do not provide any indication of the direction of technology transfer, but knowledge of national strengths and weaknesses allows some analysis. Alliances between American and European firms are significant in all fields. Alliances between American and Japanese firms are only significant in computers and microelectronics, presumably the former dominated by the US partners, and the latter by the Japanese. There appears to be relatively little collaboration between Japanese'and European companies, perhaps reflecting the weakness of the European electronics industry.

Given the problems of management and organization, potential for opportunistic behaviour and the limited success of alliances it might be expected that the popularity of alliances might decline as firms gain experience of such problems. However, according to the Co-operative Agreements and Technology Indicators (CATI) database the number of technology alliances increased from less than 300 in 1990 to more than 430 in 1993. It is possible to identify a number of significant trends in recent years (Figure 8.4).

Overall, the number of alliances has increased over time, and networks of collaboration appear to have become more stable, being based around a number of

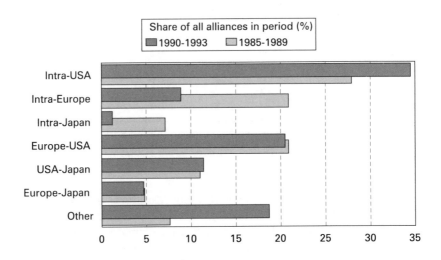

FIGURE 8.4 Trends in strategic technology alliances, 1985–93. Source: Derived from Hagedoorn, J. (1996) 'Trends and patterns in strategic technology partnering since the early seventies', *Review of Industrial Organization*, **11**, 612.

nodal firms in different sectors. These networks are not necessarily closed, but rather represent the dynamic partnering behaviour of large, leading firms in each of the sectors. The nodal firms are relatively stable, but their partners change over time. Contrary to the claims of globalization, the number of domestic alliances has increased faster than international ones. This trend is particularly strong in the USA. Distinct sectoral patterns exist. In the heavy electrical equipment and aerospace industries, most of the collaborative activity is confined within each of the triad regions: Europe, Japan and North America. In contrast, most of the activity in the chemical and automotive sectors is across the triad regions. This suggests that the primary motive for collaborating with domestic firms is access to technology, but market access is more important in the case of cross-border alliances. The most recent data from the MERIT-CATI database indicate that flexible forms of collaboration such as strategic alliances have become more popular than the more formal arrangements such as joint ventures. In 1970 more than 90% of the relationships were formal joint ventures, but this had fallen to 50% by the mid-1980s and is currently only 15%, the balance being strategic alliances of some type.[43] This trend has been most marked in high technology sectors where firms seek to retain the flexibility to switch technology.

8.4 Effect of Technology and Organization

Our study of how 23 UK and 15 Japanese firms acquired technology externally identified the conditions under which each particular method is favoured.[44] The relative importance of different external sources to each of the UK-based companies is summarized in Figure 8.5. Each of these sources is discussed in turn, and examples provided.

It is possible to identify two dimensions which affect companies' attitudes towards technology acquisition: the characteristics of the technology and the organization's 'inheritance' (Table 8.6). Together, the eight factors in Table 8.6 determine the knowledge acquisition strategy of a firm. The relevant characteristics of the technology include:

- Competitive significance of the technology
- Complexity of the technology
- Codifiability, or how easily the technology is encoded
- Credibility potential, or political profile of the technology

An organization's inheritance encompasses those characteristics which, at least in the short run, are fixed and therefore represent constraints within which the R&D function develops its strategies for acquiring technology. These include:

- Corporate strategy, for example, a leadership versus follower position
- Capabilities and existing technical know-how
- Culture of the firm, including receptivity to external knowledge
- 'Comfort' of management with a given technical area

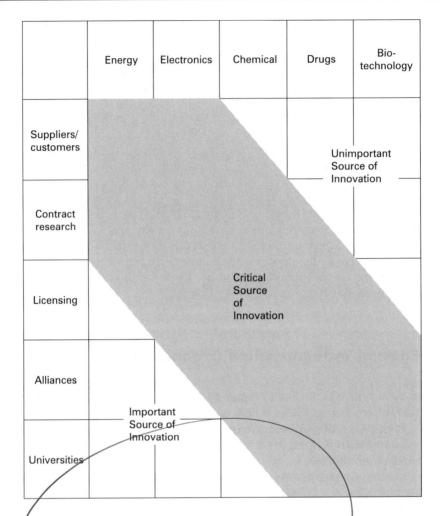

	Energy	Electronics	Chemical	Drugs	Bio-technology
Suppliers/customers					
Contract research					
Licensing					
Alliances					
Universities					

Unimportant Source of Innovation

Critical Source of Innovation

Important Source of Innovation

FIGURE 8.5   Relative importance to UK-based firms of external sources of technology.
Source: Adapted from Tidd, J. and M. Trewhella (1997) 'Organizational and technological antecedents for knowledge acquisition', *R&D Management*, **27** (4), 359–375.

Competitive Significance

Without doubt, the competitive significance of the technology is the single most important factor influencing companies' decisions about how best to acquire a given technology.

Strategies for acquiring pacing technologies, i.e. those with the potential to become tomorrow's key technologies, vary. For example, some organizations, such as AEA Technology, seek to develop and maintain at least some in-house expertise in many pacing technologies, so they will not be 'wrong-footed' if conditions change or unexpected advances occur. In the past, this policy enabled the company to recognize the importance of finite element analysis to its modelling core competence, and to acquire the necessary aspects of this technology before its competitors. Other firms, such as Kodak, also recognize the need to monitor developments in a number of pacing technologies, but see universities or joint ventures as the most efficient means of achieving this. The company sponsors a large amount of research in leading universities throughout the world, and has also set up a number of joint venture programmes with firms in complementary industries. Guinness, for example, identified genetic engineering as a pacing technology and seconded a member of staff to work at a leading university for three years. The outcome of this initiative was a new biological product, protected by a confidentiality agreement with the university. Although this genetically engineered species cannot yet be used in food and drink products, the company has successfully internalized the technology, understands its potential, and is well placed to evaluate new developments in the area, or to take advantage of any changes in legislation and public attitudes.

In the UK universities are a widely used external source of technology. These relationships range from support for Ph.D. candidates, extramural research awards for post-doctoral staff to carry out research in a specified area, to more formal contract research and collaborative schemes such as the LINK scheme jointly funded by the DTI and a number of companies to conduct precompetitive research in a specified area. Firms use university research for a number of reasons: to access specialist technical support; to extend in-house research; and to provide a window on emerging technologies.

Extensions to existing in-house research typically involve using universities to conduct either fundamental research, aimed at gaining a better understanding of an underlying area of science, or more speculative extensions to existing in-house programmes which cannot be justified internally because of their high risk, or because of limited in-house resources. For example, Zeneca has made extensive use of universities to undertake fundamental studies into the molecular biology of plants and the cloning of genes. Although not key technologies, access to state-of-the-art knowledge in these areas is vital to support a number of the organization's core agricultural activities. Similarly, CRL, the research organization of Thorn, utilized technology originally developed at Edinburgh and Cambridge universities in its spatial light modulators and ultra-low power consumption gas sensors, respectively.

University-funded research can also be used as windows on emerging or rapidly advancing fields of science and technology. Companies view access to such information as being critical in making good decisions about if or when to internalize a new technology. For example, Azko launched a series of university-funded research programmes in the USA during the late 1980s. During its first three years, these programmes yielded 40 patent applications.

Most companies look to acquire base technologies externally or, in the case of non-competitive technologies, by co-operative efforts. Companies recognize that their base technologies are often the core competencies of other firms. In such cases, the policy is to acquire specific pieces of base technology from these firms, who can almost always provide better technology, at less cost, than could have been obtained from in-house sources. Materials testing, routine analysis and computing services are common examples of technical services now acquired externally.

TABLE 8.6   Links between technology acquisition strategy, organizational factors and characteristics of technology.

Organizational and technological factors	Acquisition mechanism (most favoured/ alternative)	Rationale for decision

I. Characteristics of the organization

Corporate strategy:

Leadership	In-house R&D/equity acquisition	Differentiation, first-mover, proprietary technology
Follower	Licence/customers and suppliers/contract	Low-cost imitation

Fit with competencies:

Strong	In-house R&D	Options to leverage competencies
Weak	Contract/licence/consortia	Access to external technology

Company culture:

External focus	Various	Cost-effectiveness of source
Internal focus	In-house/joint venture	Learning experience

Comfort with new technology:

High	In-house corporate/university	High risk and potential high reward
Low	Licence/customers and suppliers/consortia	Lowest risk option

II. Characteristics of the technology

Competitive importance:

Base	Licence/contract/customers/ suppliers	Cost-effective/secure source
Key	In-house R&D/joint venture	Maximize competitive advantage
Pacing	In-house corporate/university	Future position/learning
Emerging	University/in-house corporate	Watching brief

Complexity:

High	Consortia/universities/suppliers	Specialization of know-how
Low	In-house R&D/contract/ suppliers	Division of labour

Codifiability:

High	Licence/contract/university	Cost-effectiveness of source
Low	In-house R&D/joint venture	Learning/tacit know-how

Credibility potential:

High	Consortia/customer/ government	High profile source
Low	University/contract/licence	Cost-effectiveness of source

Source: Adapted from Tidd, J. and M. Trewhella (1997) 'Organizational and technological antecedents for knowledge acquisition', *R&D Management,* **27** (4), 359–375.

Complexity of the Technology

The increasingly interdisciplinary nature of many of today's technologies and products means that, in many technical fields, it is not practical for any firm to maintain all necessary skills in-house. This increased complexity is leading many organizations to conclude that, in order to stay at the forefront of their key technologies, they must somehow leverage their in-house competencies with those available externally. For example, the need to acquire external technologies appears to increase as the number of component technologies increases. In extreme cases of complexity networks of specialist developers may emerge which serve companies which specialize in systems integration and customization for end-users.

Zeneca's core skills centre on genetic engineering/molecular biology (which allows new characteristics to be inserted into plants), cell biology (which enables the regeneration of plants) and rapid screening and testing techniques for plants and seeds. These key technologies have been developed, and are retained, internally. Such is their complexity, however, that the company seeks to leverage these proprietary skills with complementary technologies accessed from other sources. Examples include techniques based on genetic fingerprinting, to speed up plant breeding by enabling desirable characteristics to be identified without having to grow the plant to maturity; and the use of anti-sense technology to isolate and clone agronomically important genes.

In recent years, acquisition has again become a popular means of acquiring technology. Normally, the rationale is to establish a position quickly in a particular technical area. However, feelings about the effectiveness of this route are mixed; many acquisitions have suffered from the loss or demotivation of key staff, or have failed to realize their expected potential for other reasons. Nevertheless, a few companies claim spectacular successes amongst their acquisitions. The common factors here appear to be prior experience of the markets in which the new technology would be used, and a compatible culture between the two organizations. For example, Eli Lilly identified a small US company, Agouron Pharmaceuticals, working on an enzyme believed to be a catalyst in tumour growth. The company considered this technology sufficiently promising to invest $4.5m. to acquire an 8% stake in the company and first claim to any resulting drugs.

Codifiability of the Technology

The more that knowledge about a particular technology can be codified, i.e. described in terms of formulae, blueprints and rules, the easier it is to transfer, and the more speedily and extensively such technologies can be diffused. Knowledge that cannot easily be codified, often termed 'tacit' is, by contrast, much more difficult to acquire, since it can only be transferred effectively by experience and face-to-face interactions. All else being equal, it appears preferable to develop tacit technologies in-house. In the absence of strong intellectual property rights (IPR) or patent protection, tacit technologies provide a more durable source of competitive advantage than those which can easily be codified.

For example, Kodak maintains all of its strategic technologies in-house, even if these are considered mature, because of the large amount of tacit know-how embodied in even these technologies. The existence of difficult-to-codify tacit knowledge is one of the factors that has allowed it to maintain a competitive advantage in one particular core technology, even though the basic features of this technology have been in use for over 100 years. Similarly, the design skills of many Italian firms have allowed them to remain internationally competitive despite significant weaknesses in other dimensions. The difficulty of maintaining a competitive advantage when technology is easily codifiable is highlighted by Guinness, which developed a small plastic, gas-filled, device that gives canned beer the same creamy head as keg beer. This 'widget' initially provided the company with a source of competitive advantage and extra sales, but the innovation was soon copied widely throughout the industry, to the extent that widgets are now almost a requirement for any premium canned beer.

Credibility Potential

The credibility given to the company by a technology, or by the source of the technology, is a significant factor influencing the way companies decide to acquire a technology. Particular value is placed on gaining credibility or goodwill from governments, customers, market analysts, and even from the company's own top management, academic institutions and potential recruits. For example, Celltech's collaboration with a large US chemical firm appears to have enhanced the former's market credibility. Not only did the collaboration demonstrate the organization's ability to manage a multimillion dollar R&D project, but the numerous patents and academic publications that arose from it were also felt to have improved the company's scientific standing. Similarly, in Japan the mobile telecoms services provider Do Mo Co worked closely with the national telephone services provider NTT, although it had the depth and range of technologies required to develop telephony equipment and products. The rationale for the relationship was to influence future standards and to increase the credibility of its consumer telephone products in a market in which it was increasingly difficult to differentiate by means of product or service (see Box 8.6).

Corporate Strategy

One of the most important factors affecting the balance between in-house generated, and externally acquired, technology is the degree to which company strategy dictates that it should pursue a policy of technological differentiation or leadership (see Chapter 3). For example, Kodak distinguishes between two types of technical core competencies: strategic, i.e. those activities in which the company must be a world leader because they represent such an important source of competitive advantage, and enabling, i.e. skills required for success, but which do not have to be controlled internally. Although all strategic activities are retained in-house, the company is prepared to access enabling technologies externally, if the overall technology is sufficiently complex.

Some companies adopt a policy of intervention in the technology supply market, until the market becomes sufficiently competitive to ensure reliable sources of technology continue to be available at reasonable prices. For example, the extent to which BP is prepared to rely on external sources of technology depends, amongst other things, on the nature of the supply market. When only a few suppliers exist, BP will develop key items of technology itself, and pass these on to its suppliers in order to ensure their availability. However, once sufficient suppliers have entered the market to make it competitive, its policy is to conduct no further in-house development in that area. Indeed, one of the declared aims of BP's in-house R&D activities is to 'force the pace' at which the industry as a whole innovates.

Firm Competencies

An organization's internal technical capabilities are another factor influencing the way in which it decides to acquire a given technology. Where these are weak, a firm normally has little choice but to acquire from outside, at least in the short run, whereas strong in-house capabilities often favour the internal development of related technologies, because of the greater degree of control afforded by this route. In such cases, the main driving force behind the acquisition strategy is speed to market. For example, speed to market is a critical success factor for many firms in consumer markets. Such firms select the technology acquisition method that provides the fastest means of commercialization. When the required expertise is available in-house, this route is normally favoured because it allows greater control of the development process, and is therefore usually quicker. However, where suitable in-house capabilities are lacking, external sourcing is almost always faster than building the required skills internally. Gillette, for example,

---

BOX 8.6 Symbian.

Symbian is a joint venture between Psion, Nokia, Ericsson and Motorola which develops and licenses operating systems for wireless devices such as cell phones and electronic organizers. The members, all electronics manufacturers, formed Symbian in 1998 to help reduce the chance that they would become low-margin 'box-shifters', as has happened in the PC market. The venture was initially established to exploit the Epoc operating system developed by Psion, which owned 40% (now 28%) of Symbian. The two Scandinavian telecoms each invested £57.5m. for their 30% share. Motorola joined Symbian later. It is estimated that in 2000 Psion invested £8m. in Symbian, but accounted for as much as 90% of Psion's stock market value. Licensees are required to pay a royalty of US$5 per smart phone using Epoc, and $10 for other devices. If Epoc is used by just 15% of the billion wireless devices estimated to be sold in 2003, licence income would be US$900m. Symbian is currently developing what it hopes will become the standard for the next generation of wireless devices. However, two doubts remain. First, the competitive response of companies such as Microsoft, with Windows CE, and strategic conflicts between members of Symbian.

found that one of its new products required laser spot-welding competencies that the company lacked, and given the limited market window was forced to go outside to acquire this technology.

Company Culture

Every company has its own culture, that is 'the way we do things around here'. We will discuss culture in more detail in the next chapter, but here we are concerned with the underlying values and beliefs that play an important role in technology acquisition policies. A culture of 'we are the best' is likely to contribute towards to a rather myopic view of external technology developments, and limit the potential for learning from external partners. Some organizations, however, consistently reinforce the philosophy that important technical developments can occur almost anywhere in the world. Consequently, staff in these companies are encouraged to identify external developments, and to internalize potentially important technologies before the competition. However, in practice few firms have formal 'technology scouting' personnel or functions.

For example, Glaxo emphasizes that companies need to guard against becoming captives of their own in-house expertise, since this limits the scope of its activities to what can be achieved through internal resources. With this in mind, the company has expanded its research effort by placing many of its more specialized R&D activities overseas. This, it is claimed, allows its research to benefit from different cultural and scientific approaches, and from being brought into intimate contact with the many different markets it serves. Local perspectives are particularly important for product development, but international networks can also be used to acquire access to basic research.

Kodak's philosophy is that world-class organizations must access technology wherever it resides, and that a culture of 'not invented here' is a prescription for second-class citizenship in the global marketplace. Like Glaxo, this firm also has a number of foreign research laboratories. For example, Japan is now the centre of this organization's worldwide efforts in molecular beam epitaxy, a method of growing crystals for making gallium arsenide chips. A key role for overseas laboratories is to monitor technology developments in host countries. Local champions from around the world are closely networked so that technical advances made in one geographic location are rapidly disseminated around the organization as a whole. Such is this company's determination to maintain a 'window' on potential sources of technology that it has set up joint ventures with many large and small companies worldwide, including links with Matsushita, Canon, Nikon, Minolta, Fuji and Apple. In the past, the company has also worked with biotechnology companies such as Cetus on human diagnostics kits, and with Amersham International to develop immunoassay kits and biosensors.

Management Comfort

The degree of comfort management has with a given technology manifests itself at the level of the individual R&D manager or management team, rather than at the level of the organization as a whole. Management comfort is multifaceted. One aspect is related to a management team's familiarity with the technology. Another reflects the degree of confidence that the team can succeed in a new technical area, perhaps because of a research group's track record of success in related fields. Attitude to risk is also a factor.[45]

All else being equal, the more comfortable a company's managers feel with a given technology, the more likely that technology is to be developed in-house. For example, the current business of Zeneca Seeds was built on the basis of providing an outlet for the parent organization's in-house biotechnology expertise. This means that the concept of world-leading in-house technology sits very comfortably with the organization's top management, which is reflected by the fact that annual in-house R&D expenditure exceeds the firm's annual capital expenditure by a considerable margin. Similarly, AEA Technology's core technologies of plant life extension, environmental sciences, modelling and land remediation treatment all derive from its nuclear industry background. Top management's comfort with these technologies has led them to encourage staff to build on these skills, and to use these as a springboard for diversification into new scientific areas.

8.5 Managing Alliances for Learning

So far we have discussed collaboration as a means of accessing market or technological know-how, or acquiring assets. However, alliances can also be used as an opportunity to learn new market and technological competencies, in other words to internalize a partner's know-how. Seen in this light, the success of an alliance becomes difficult to measure.

Collaboration is an inherently risky activity, and less than half achieve their goals. A study of almost 900 joint ventures found that only 45% were mutually agreed to have been successful by all partners.[46] Other studies confirm that the success rate is less than 50%.[47, 48]

It is difficult to assess the success of a collaborative venture, and in particular termination of a partnership does not necessarily indicate failure if the objectives have been met. For example, around half of all alliances are terminated within seven years, but in some cases this is because the partners have subsequently merged. It is common for a collaborative arrangement to evolve over time, and objectives may change. For example, a licensing agreement may evolve into a joint venture. Finally, an apparent failure may result in knowledge or experience that may be of future benefit. An alliance is likely to have a number of different objectives, some explicit others implicit, and outcomes may be planned or unplanned. Therefore any measure of success must be multidimensional and dynamic in order to capture the different objectives as they evolve over time. Reasons for failure include strategic divergence, procedural problems and cultural mismatch. Table 8.7 presents the most common reasons for the failure of alliances, based on a meta-analysis of the 16 studies. The studies reviewed differ in their samples and methodologies, but 11 factors appear in a quarter of the studies, which provides some level of confidence.

TABLE 8.7 Common reasons for the failure of alliances based on a review of 16 studies.

Reason for failure	% studies reporting factor (n = 16)
Strategic/goal divergence	50
Partner problems	38
Strong–weak relation	38
Cultural mismatch	25
Insufficient trust	25
Operational/geographic overlap	25
Personnel clashes	25
Lack of commitment	25
Unrealistic expectations/time	25
Asymmetric incentives	13

Source: Derived from Duysters, G., G. Kok and M. Vaandrager (1999) 'Crafting successful strategic technology partnerships', *R&D Management*, **29** (4), 343–351.

Firms have different expectations of alliances and these affect their evaluation of success. Those firms which view product development collaboration as discrete events with specific aims and objectives are more likely to evaluate the success of the relationship in terms of the project cost and time and ultimate product performance. However, a small proportion of firms view collaboration as an opportunity to learn new skills and knowledge and to develop longer-term relationships. In such cases measures of success need to be broader. If learning is a major goal, it is necessary for partners to have complementary skills and capabilities, but an even balance of strength is also important. The more equal the partners, the more likely an alliance will be successful. Both partners must be strong financially and in the technological, product or market contribution they make to the venture. A study of 49 international alliances by management consultants McKinsey found that two-thirds of the alliances between equally matched partners were successful, but where there was a significant imbalance of power almost 60% of alliances failed.[49] Consequently in the case of a formal joint venture equal ownership is the most successful structure, 50–50 ownership being twice as likely to succeed as other ownership structures. This appears to be because such a structure demands continuous consultation and communication between partners, which helps anticipate and resolve potential conflicts, and problems of strategic divergence. Our own study of Anglo-Japanese joint ventures identified three sources of strategic conflict between parent firms: product strategy; market strategy; and pricing policy. These were primarily the result of coupling complementary resources with divergent strategies, what we refer to as the 'trap of complementarity'. In essence, parents with complementary resources almost inevitably have different long-term strategic objectives. Too many joint ventures are established to bridge gaps in short-term resources, rather than for long-term strategic fit.[50]

This suggests that firms must learn to design alliances with other firms, rather than pursue ad hoc relationships. By design we do not mean the legal and financial details of the agreement, but rather the need to select a partner which can contribute what is needed, and needs what is offered, of which there is sufficient prior knowledge or experience to encourage trust and communication, to allow areas of potential conflict such as overlapping products or markets to be designed out. Partners must specify mutual expectations of respective contributions and benefits. They should agree on a business plan, including contingencies for possible dissolution, but allow sufficient flexibility for the goals and structure of the alliance to evolve. It is important that partners communicate on a routine basis, so that any problems are shared. Without such explicit design, collaboration may make product development more costly, complex and difficult to control (Table 8.8). Thus whilst the *failure* of an alliance is most likely to be the result of strategic divergence, the *success* of an alliance depends to a large extent on what can be described as operational and people-related factors, rather than strategic factors such as technological, market or product fit (Table 8.9). The most important operational factors are agreement on clearly stated aims and responsibilities, and the most important people factors are high levels of commitment, communication and trust. A survey of 135 German firms gives us a better idea of the relative importance of these different factors.[51] The study found that firms take people-related, economic and technological factors into consideration, but that these three groups of variables are largely independent of each other. Factor analysis confirms that the people-related factors are more significant than either the economic or technological considerations, specifically creation of trust, informal networking and learning.

TABLE 8.8   The effect of collaboration on the product development process ($n = 106$).

	Agree/ strongly agree	Disagree/ strongly disagree
Makes product development more costly	51	22
Complicates product development	41	35
Makes development more difficult to control	41	38
Makes development more responsive to supplier needs	36	26
Allows development to adapt better to uncertainty	27	43
Accelerates product development	25	58
Makes development more responsive to customer needs	22	50
Allows development to respond better to market opportunities	15	63
Enhances competitive benefits arising through development	12	65
Facilitates the incorporation of new technology in development	7	70

Source: Adapted from Bruce *et al.* (1995, p. 542), with kind permission from Elsevier Science Ltd, The Boulevard, Langford Lane, Kidlington OX5 1GB, UK.[52]

Factors which contribute to the success of an alliance include:[52]

- The alliance is perceived as important by all partners
- A collaboration 'champion' exists
- A substantial degree of trust between partners exists

- Clear project planning and defined task milestones are established
- Frequent communication between partners, in particular between marketing and technical staff
- The collaborating parties contribute as expected
- Benefits are perceived to be equally distributed

Mutual trust is clearly a significant factor, when faced with the potential opportunistic behaviour of the partners, for example failure to perform or the leakage of information. Trust may exist at the personal and organizational levels, and researchers have attempted to distinguish different levels, qualities and sources of trust.[53] For example, the following bases of trust in alliances have been identified:

- Contractual—honouring the accepted or legal rules of exchange, but can also indicate the absence of other forms of trust
- Goodwill—mutual expectations of commitment beyond contractual requirements
- Institutional—trust based on formal structures
- Network—because of personal, family or ethnic/religious ties
- Competence—trust based on reputation for skills and know-how
- Commitment—mutual self-interest, committed to the same goals

These types of trust are not necessarily mutually exclusive, although over-reliance on contractual and institutional forms may indicate the absence of the types of trust. Goodwill is normally a second-order effect based on network, competence or commitment. In the case of innovation, problems may occur where trust is based on the network, rather than competence or commitment, as discussed earlier. Clearly, high levels of interpersonal trust are necessary to facilitate communication and learning in collaboration, but interorganizational trust is a more subtle issue. Organizational trust may be defined in terms of organizational routines, norms and values which are able to survive changes in individual personnel.[54] In this way organizational learning can take place, including new ways of doing things (operational or lower-level learning) and doing new things through diversification (strategic or higher-level learning). Organizational trust requires a longer time horizon to ensure that reciprocity can occur, as for any particular collaborative project one partner is likely to benefit disproportionately. In this way organizational trust may mitigate against opportunistic behaviour. However, in practice this may be difficult where partners have different motives for an alliance or differential rates of learning.

In Chapter 5 we examined the nature of core competencies. Conceiving of the firm as a bundle of competencies, rather than technology or products, suggests that the primary purpose of collaboration is the acquisition of new skills or competencies, rather than the acquisition of technology or products. Therefore a crucial distinction must be made between acquiring the skills of a partner, and simply gaining access to such skills. The latter is the focus of contracting, licensing and the like, whereas the internalization of a partner's skills demands closer and longer contact, such as formal joint ventures or strategic alliances.

TABLE 8.9   Factors affecting outcomes of collaborative product development (*n* = 106).

Factor	Respondents freely mentioning factor
Establishing ground rules	67
Clearly defined objectives agreed by all parties	41
Clearly defined responsibilities agreed by all parties	19
Realistic aims	10
Defined project milestones	11
People factors	54
Collaboration champion	22
Commitment at all levels	11
Top management commitment	10
Personal relationships	10
Staffing levels	3
Process factors	45
Frequent communication	20
Mutual trust/openness/honesty	17
Regular progress reviews	13
Deliver as promised	9
Flexibility	3
Ensuring equality	42
Mutual benefit	22
Equality in power/dependency	11
Equality of contribution	9
Choice of partner	39
Culture/mode of operation	13
Mutual understanding	12
Complementary strengths	12
Past collaboration experience	2

Source: Adapted from Bruce, M., F. Leverick and D. Littler (1995) 'A management framework for collaborative product development', in Bruce, M. and Biemans, W.G. (eds), *Product Development: Meeting the challenge of the design–marketing interface*, John Wiley & Sons, Chichester, p. 171.

It is possible to identify three factors that affect learning through alliances: intent, transparency and receptivity (Table 8.10). Intent refers to a firm's propensity to view collaboration as an opportunity to learn new skills, rather than to gain access to a partner's assets. Thus where there is intent, learning takes place by design rather than by default, which is much more significant than mere leakage of information. Transparency refers to the openness or 'knowability' of each partner, and therefore the potential for learning. Receptivity, or absorptiveness, refers to a partner's capacity to learn. Clearly, there is much a firm can do to maximize its own intent and receptivity, and minimize its transparency. Intent to learn will influence the choice of partner and form of collaboration. Transparency will depend on the penetrability of the social context, attitudes towards outsiders, i.e. clannishness, and the extent to which the skills are discrete and encodable. Explicit knowledge, such as designs and patents, are more easily encoded than tacit knowledge. This suggests that a harmonious alliance may not necessarily represent a win–win situation. On the contrary, where two partners attempt to extract value from their alliance in the same form, whether in terms of short-term economic benefits or longer-term skills acquisition, managers are likely to frequently engage in arguments over value sharing. Where partners have different goals, for example one partner seeks short-term benefits whereas the other seeks the acquisition of new skills, the relationship tends to be more harmonious, at least until one partner is no longer dependent on the other.

Therefore the preferred structure for an alliance will depend on the nature of the knowledge to be acquired, whereas the outcome will be determined largely by a partner's ability to learn, which is a function of skills and culture. Tactical alliances are most appropriate to obtain migratory or explicit knowledge, but more strategic relationships are necessary to acquire embedded or tacit knowledge.[55] Alliances for explicit knowledge focus on trades in designs, technologies or products, but by the very nature of such knowledge this provides only temporary advantages because of its ease of codification and movement. Alliances for embedded knowledge present a more subtle management challenge. This involves the transfer of skills and capabilities, rather than discrete packages of know-how. This requires personnel to have direct, intimate and extensive exposure to the staff, equipment, systems and culture of the partnering organization. However, the absorptive capacity of an organization is not a constant, and depends on the fit with the partner's knowledge base, organizational structures and processes, such as the degree of management formalization and centralization of decision-making and research.[56]

TABLE 8.10   Determinants of learning through alliances.

	Factors which promote learning
A. Intent to learn	
1. Competitive posture	Co-operate now, compete later
2. Strategic significance	High, to build competencies, rather than to fix a problem
3. Resource position	Scarcity
4. Relative power balance	Balance creates instability, rather than harmony
B. Transparency or potential for learning	
5. Social context	Language and cultural barriers
6. Attitude towards outsiders	Exclusivity, but absence of 'not invented here'
7. Nature of skills	Tacit and systemic, rather than explicit
C. Receptivity or absorptive capacity	
8. Confidence in abilities	Realistic, not too high or too low
9. Skills gap	Small, not too substantial
10. Institutionalization of learning	High, transfer of individual learning to organization

Source: Adapted from Hamel, G. (1991) 'Learning in international alliances', *Strategic Management Journal*, **12**, 91.

The conversion of tacit to explicit knowledge is a critical mechanism underlying the link between individual and organizational learning.[57] Through a process of dialogue, discussion, experience sharing and observation individual knowledge is amplified at the group and organizational levels. This creates an expanding community of interaction, or 'knowledge network', which crosses intra- and interorganizational levels and boundaries. These knowledge networks are a means to accumulate knowledge from outside the organization, share it widely within the organization, and store it for future use. Therefore the interaction of groups with different cultures, whether within or beyond the boundaries of the organization, is a potential source of learning and innovation.

Organizational structure and culture will determine absorptive capacity in interorganizational learning. Culture is a difficult concept to grasp and measure, but it helps to distinguish between national, organizational, functional and group cultures.[58] Differences in national culture have received a great deal of attention in studies of cross-border alliances and acquisitions, and the consensus is that national differences do exist and that these affect both the intent and ability to learn. In general, British and American firms focus more on the legal and financial aspects of alliances, but rarely have either the intent or ability to learn through alliances. In contrast, French, German and Japanese firms are more likely to exploit opportunities for learning.[59] The issue of national stereotypes aside, there may be structural reasons for these differences in the propensity to learn.

For example, Japanese firms have good historical reasons for exploiting alliances as opportunities for learning. Initially, Western firms typically entered Japan through alliances in which they provided technology in return for access to Japanese sales and distribution channels. This exchange of technology for market access appeared to offer value to both sides. However, while the Western partner often remained dependent on the Japanese partner for distribution and sales, the Japanese partner typically built up its technological skills and became less reliant on the Western partner. As a result, in the 1980s European and American partners began to lose technological leadership in many fields, and were forced to trade distribution and sales channels at home for access to the Japanese market. Therefore collaboration has shifted from relatively simple and well-defined licensing agreements or joint ventures, to more complex and informal relationships which are much more difficult to manage.

Most recently, firms from the USA and Europe have begun to use alliances for operational learning. Operational learning provides close exposure to what competitors are doing in Japan and how they are doing it. For example, to learn how Japanese partners manage their production facilities, supplier base or product development process. This is not possible from a distance, and requires close alliances with potential competitors. However, fewer firms in the West have exploited fully the potential of alliances for strategic learning, that is the acquisition of new technological and market competencies (see Box 8.7).

In contrast, many American and British firms find it difficult to learn through alliances. This appears to be because firms focus on financial control and short-term financial benefits, rather than the longer-term potential for learning. For example, firms will attempt to minimize the number and quality of people they contribute to a Japanese joint venture, and the time committed. As a result, little learning takes place and little or no corporate memory is built up.

At the lower level of analysis, different functional groups and project teams may have different cultures. For example, the differences between technical and marketing cultures are well documented, and are a major barrier to communication within an organization.[60] When such groups are required to communicate across organizations the potential for problems is even greater. There is some

BOX 8.7 Rover, Honda and BMW.

In Christmas 1978 BL, now Rover, signed a deal with Honda to build under licence the Ballade, as the new Triumph Acclaim. The project highlighted the vast quality and cost differentials between BL and Honda products, and exposed BL to Japanese engineering and work practices.

Since then Rover has relied on customizing Honda designs to develop its own derivatives: the Honda Civic and Rover 200/400, Honda Legend and Rover 800, and Honda Accord and Rover 600. The Rover 200/Honda Civic, launched in 1995, were the last product of the partnership. The alliance between Rover and Honda, and the subsequent acquisition of Rover by BMW, illustrates how alliances evolve, and how different firms choose to acquire technological, market and organizational competencies. Initially, Rover sought a relationship with Honda in order to introduce a new product, which it had neither the financial nor technological resources to develop itself. For Honda, this represented a low-cost and low-risk way of entering the European market and a means of developing local suppliers and dealers. Subsequently, Rover and Honda co-developed a number of cars, although Honda was clearly the dominant partner. As a result, Rover made some improvements to its work organization, product engineering and quality, and Honda shared components costs and learned a great deal about customizing its products for European markets, and how to manage British workers, suppliers and dealers. However, the learning was somewhat asymmetric, as Honda successfully established its own manufacturing facilities in the UK, whereas Rover failed to improve significantly its process capability or product quality. In 1994 some 16 years of collaboration ended when BMW purchased Rover for £920m. Honda was forced to terminate its relationship, and to sell its 20% share in Rover. The following year Rover attempted to recruit an additional 500 engineers, which is indicative of Honda's engineering support.

BMW had different motives for purchasing Rover. First and foremost, it hoped to gain access to the Land Rover division, with its strong brand, four-wheel-drive technology and profitable products. Second, it gained additional production capacity, with a relatively inexpensive workforce, which was a major consideration for a relatively small, independent car manufacturer. Finally, it completed its product portfolio: despite its previous aspirations to be a prestige car manufacturer, Rover's expertise is in small, front-wheel-drive cars, whereas BMW specializes in larger rear-wheel-drive cars. However, BMW significantly underestimated the problems at Rover, and its own ability to become a volume manufacturer. After five years of investment and substantial losses, in 2000 BMW disposed of almost all of Rover, selling it for a nominal £10 to a consortium optimistically called 'Phoenix', which was established by a group of ex-Rover managers. The future of Rover remains uncertain.

evidence that employees attempt to trade information based on the perceived economic interests of their firms, but that these perceptions differ. A study of 39 managers involved in alliances in the steel industry identified three clusters of behaviour regarding information trading: value-oriented, competition-oriented and complex decision-makers.[61] Value-oriented employees base their behaviour on the importance of the information to their own firm, independent of its potential value to the partner. Competition-oriented employees base their behaviour solely on the value of the information to competitors. The complex decision makers include both considerations, and also the potential for trading information.

8.6 Summary and Further Reading

In this chapter we have discussed the arguments for and against collaboration for the development of new technology, products and processes, and have identified the different forms and patterns of collaboration which exist. Essentially, firms collaborate to reduce the cost, time or risk of access to unfamiliar technologies or markets. Transaction costs analysis focuses on the static, short-term trade-offs between developing an innovation in-house versus external mechanisms, whereas a strategic learning framework focuses on the dynamic, longer-term potential for acquiring new technological, market or organizational competencies. The precise form of collaboration will be determined by the motives and preferences of the partners, but their choice will be constrained by the nature of the technologies and markets, specifically the degree of complexity and tacitness. The success of an alliance depends on a number of factors, but organizational issues dominate, such as the degree of mutual trust and level of communication. The transaction costs approach better explains the relationship between the reason for collaboration, and the preferred form and structure of an alliance. The strategic learning approach better explains the relationship between the management and organization of an alliance and the subsequent outcomes.

A good review of the theoretical issues is provided by a compilation of papers edited by Rod Coombs *et al.*, *Technological Collaboration* (Edward Elgar, 1996). The book includes a discussion of both economic and sociological analyses of collaboration, including transaction costs and evolutionary theories, as well as a review of the more recent network approaches. The literature on innovation networks is large and growing, but the following provide a good introduction: O. Jones, S. Conway and F. Steward, *Social Interaction and Organizational Change: Aston perspectives on innovation networks* (Imperial College Press, London, 2001); *International Journal of Innovation Management*, Special Issue on Networks, **2** (2) (1998); R. Gulati, 'Alliances and networks', *Strategic Management Journal*, **19**, 293–317 (1998); and F. Belussi and F. Arcangeli, 'A typology of networks' in *Research Policy*, **27**, 415–428 (1998).

For a less academic treatment of alliances, Bleeke and Ernst provide a practical guide, albeit a little dated, for managers of collaborative projects in *Collaborating to Compete* (Wiley, 1993), written by two management consultants at McKinsey & Co, and based on a survey of international alliances and acquisitions. In *Alliance Advantage* (Harvard Business School Press, 1998) Yves Doz and Gary Hamel develop a framework to help understand and better manage alliances, drawing on their earlier work on learning through alliances. On the more specific subject of customer–supplier alliances, Jordan Lewis provides a practical guide based on studies of a number of American and British present and past exemplars such as

Motorola and Marks & Spencer in *The Connected Corporation* (Free Press, 1995). The example of Marks & Spencer is now even more interesting as it demonstrates some of the limitations of supplier partnerships. More academic and rigorous treatments of customer–supplier alliances are provided by Richard Lamming in *Beyond Partnership* (Prentice-Hall, 1993) and Toshihiro Nishiguchi in *Strategic Industrial Sourcing: The Japanese advantage* (Oxford University Press, 1994), both based mainly on the experience of the automobile industry.

References

1 McGee, J. E. and M. J. Dowling (1994) 'Using R&D cooperative arrangements to leverage managerial experience', *Journal of Business Venturing*, **9**, 33–48.
2 Hauschildt, J. (1992) 'External acquisition of knowledge for innovations—a research agenda', *R&D Management*, **22** (2), 105–110.
3 Welch, J. A. and P. R. Nayak (1992) 'Strategic sourcing: a progressive approach to the make or buy decision', *Academy of Management Executive*, **6** (1), 23–31.
4 Bettis, R. A., S. P. Bradley and G. Hamel (1992) 'Outsourcing and industrial decline', *Academy of Management Executive*, **6** (1), 7–21.
5 Atuaheme-Gima, K. and P. Patterson (1993) 'Managerial perceptions of technology licensing as an alternative to internal R&D in new product development: an empirical investigation', *R&D Management*, **23** (4), 327–336.
6 Robins, J. and M. I. Wiersema (1995) 'A resource-based approach to the multibusiness firm', *Strategic Management Journal*, 16 (4), 277–300.
7 Granstrand, O., E. Bohlin, S. Oskarsson and N. Sjoberg (1992) 'External technology acquisition in large multi-technology corporation', *R&D Management*, **22** (2), 111–133.
8 Tyler, B. B. and H. K. Steensma (1995) 'Evaluating technological collaborative opportunities: a cognitive modeling perspective', *Strategic Management Journal*, **16**, 43–70.
9 Bidault, F. and T. Cummings (1994) 'Innovating through alliances: expectations and limitations', *R&D Management*, **24** (2), 33–45.
10 Bleeke, J. and D. Ernst (1993) *Collaborating to Compete*. John Wiley & Sons, New York.
11 Von Hippel, E. (1988) *The Sources of Innovation*. Oxford University Press, Oxford.
12 Nishiguchi, T. (1994) *Strategic Industrial Sourcing: The Japanese advantage*. Oxford University Press, Oxford.
13 Leonard-Barton, D. and D. Sinha (1993) 'Developer–user interaction and user satisfaction in internal technology transfer', *Academy of Management Journal*, **36** (5), 1125–1139.
14 Lamming, R. (2000) 'Assessing supplier performance', in Tidd, J. (ed.), *From Knowledge Management to Strategic Competence*. Imperial College Press, London, pp. 229–253.
15 Bozdogan, K., J. Deyst, D. Hoult and M. Lucas (1998) 'Architectural innovation in product development through early supplier integration', *R&D Management*, **28** (3), 163–173.
16 Nishiguchi, T. (1994) *Strategic Industrial Sourcing: The Japanese advantage*. Oxford University Press, Oxford.
17 Bidault, F., C. Despres and C. Butler (1998) 'The drivers of cooperation between buyers and suppliers for product innovation', *Research Policy*, **26**, 719–732; Ragatz, G. L., R. B. Handfield and T. V. Scannell (1997) 'Success factors for integrating suppliers into new product development', *Journal of Product Innovation Management*, **14**, 190–202.
18 Andersen, P. H. (1999) 'Organizing international technological collaboration in subcontractor relationships', *Research Policy*, **28**, 625–642.
19 Brusconi, S., A. Prencipe and K. Pavitt (2000) 'Knowledge specialisation and the boundaries of the firm', SPRU Electronic Working Paper Series, No. 46. SPRU, Brighton. www.sussex.ac.uk/spru
20 Kaufman, A., C. H. Wood and G. Theyel (2000) 'Collaboration and technology linkages: a strategic supplier typology', *Strategic Management Journal*, **21**, 649–663.
21 Atuahene-Gima, K. and P. Patterson (1993) 'Managerial perceptions of technology licensing as an alternative to internal R&D in new product development: an empirical investigation', *R&D Management*, **23** (4), 327–336.

22 Gibson, D. V. and E. M. Rogers (1994) *R&D Collaboration on Trial.* Harvard Business School Press, Boston.

23 Aldrich, H. E. and T. Sasaki (1995) 'R&D consortia in the US and Japan', *Research* Policy, **24** (2), 301–316.

24 Doz, Y. L. and G. Hamel (1998) *Alliance Advantage: The art of creating value through partnering.* Harvard Business School Press, Boston.

25 Carr, C. (1999) 'Globalisation, strategic alliances, acquisitions and technology transfer. Lessons from ICL/Fujitsu and Rover/Honda and BMW', *R&D Management*, **29** (4), 405–421.

26 Mauri, A. J. and G. S. McMillan (1999) 'The influence of technology on strategic alliances', *International Journal of Innovation Management*, **3** (4), 367–378.

27 Jay Lambe, C. and R. E. Spekman (1997) 'Alliances, external technology acquisition, and discontinuous technological change', *Journal of Product Innovation Management*, **14**, 102–116.

28 DeBresson, C. and F. Amesse (1991) 'Networks of innovators: a review and introduction to the issues', *Research Policy*, **20**, 363–379.

29 Camagni, R. (1991) *Innovation Networks: Spatial perspectives.* Belhaven Press, London.

30 Nohria, N. and R. G. Eccles (1991) *Networks and Organizations.* Harvard Business School Press, Boston.

31 Gulati, R. (1998) 'Alliances and networks', *Strategic Management Journal*, **19**, 293–317.

32 Bidault, F. and W. A. Fischer (1994) 'Technology transactions: networks over markets', *R&D Management*, **24** (4), 373–386.

33 Hakansson, H. (1995) 'Product development in networks', in Ford, D. (ed.), *Understanding Business Markets: Interaction, relationships and networks.* The Dryden Press, New York, pp. 487–507.

34 Nakateni, I. (1984) 'The economic role of financial corporate groupings', in Masahiko Aoki (ed.), *The Economic Analysis of the Japanese Firm.* North-Holland, Amsterdam, pp. 227–258.

35 Belussi, F. and F. Arcangeli (1998) 'A typology of networks: flexible and evolutionary firms', *Research Policy*, **27**, 415–428.

36 Galaskiewicz, J. (1996) 'The "new network analysis" and its application to organizational theory and behaviour', and Aranjo, L. and G. Easton, 'Networks in socioeconomic systems' in Iacobucci, D. (ed.), *Networks in Marketing.* Sage, London, pp. 19–31.

37 Doz, Y. L., P. M. Olk and P. S. Ring (2000) 'Formation processes of R&D consortia: Which path to take? Where does it lead?', *Strategic Management Journal*, **21**, 239–266.

38 Tidd, J. (1997) 'Complexity, networks & learning: integrative themes for research on innovation management', *International Journal of Innovation Management*, **1** (1), 1–22.

39 Passiante, G. and P. Andriani (2000) 'Modelling the learning environment of virtual knowledge networks', *International Journal of Innovation Management*, **4** (1), 1–31.

40 Berg, S., J. Duncan and P. Friedman (1982) *Joint Venture Strategies and Corporate Innovation.* Gunn and Ham, Cambridge, Mass.

41 Balakrishnan, S. and M. P. Koza (1995) 'An information theory of joint ventures', in Gomez-Mejia, L. R. and Lawless, M. W (eds), *Advances in Global High Technology Management: Strategic alliances in high technology.* JAI Press, Greenwich, Conn., Vol. 5, Part B, pp. 59–72.

42 Krubasik, E. and H. Lautenschlager (1993) 'Forming successful strategic alliances in high-tech businesses', in Bleeke, J. and Ernst, D. (eds), *Collaborating to Compete.* John Wiley & Sons, New York, pp. 55–65.

43 Duysters, G., G. Kok and M. Vaandrager (1999) 'Crafting successful strategic technology partnerships', *R&D Management*, **29** (4), 343–351.

44 Tidd, J. and M. Trewhella (1997) 'Organizational and technological antecedents for knowledge acquisition and learning', *R&D Management*, **27** (4), 359–375.

45 Tyler, B. B. and P. R. Nayak (1995) 'Evaluating technological collaborative opportunities: a cognitive modeling perspective', *Strategic Management Journal*, **16**, 43–70.

46 Harrigan, K. R. (1986) *Managing for Joint Venture Success.* Lexington Books, Lexington, Mass.

47 Dacin, M. T., M. A. Hitt and E. Levitas (1997) 'Selecting partners for successful international alliances', *Journal of World Business*, **32** (1), 321–345.

48 Spekmen, R. E., A. I. Lynn, T. C. MacAvoy and I. Forbes (1996) 'Creating strategic alliances which endure', *Long Range Planning*, **29** (3), 122–147.

49 Bleeke, J. and D. Ernst (1993) *Collaborating to Compete.* John Wiley & Sons, New York.

50 Tidd, J. and Y. Izumimoto (2001) 'Knowledge exchange and learning through international joint ventures: an Anglo-Japanese experience', *Technovation*, **21** (2).

51 Brockhoff, K. and T. Teichert (1995) 'Cooperative R&D partners' measures of success', *International Journal of Technology Management*, **10** (1), 111–123.

52 Bruce, M., F. Leverick and D. Littler (1995) 'Complexities of collaborative product development', *Technovation*, **15** (9), 535–552.

53 Hoecht, A. and P. Trott (1999) 'Trust, risk and control in the management of collaborative technology development', *International Journal of Innovation Management*, **3** (3), 257–270.

54 Dodgson, M. (1993) 'Learning, trust, and technological collaboration', *Human Relations*, **46** (1), 77–95.

55 Badaracco, J. I. (1991) *The Knowledge Link: How firms compete through strategic alliances.* Harvard Business School Press, Boston, Mass.

56 Lane, P. J. and M. Lubatkin (1998) 'Relative absorptive capacity and inter-organizational learning', *Strategic Management Journal*, **19**, 461–477.

57 Nonaka, I. and H. Takeuchi (1995) *The Knowledge-Creating Company.* Oxford University Press, Oxford.

58 Levinson, N. S. and M. Asahi (1995) 'Cross-national alliances and interorganizational learning', *Organizational Dynamics*, Autumn, 50–63.

59 Hamel, G. (1991) 'Competition for competence and inter-partner learning within international strategic alliances', *Strategic Management Journal*, **12**, 83–103; Jones, K. K. and W. E. Shill (1993) 'Japan: allying for advantage', in Bleeke, J. and Ernst, D. (eds), *Collaborating to Compete.* John Wiley & Sons, New York, pp. 115–144; Sasaki, T. (1993) 'What the Japanese have learned from strategic alliances', *Long Range Planning*, **26** (6), 41–53.

60 Biemans, W. G. (1995) 'Internal and external networks in product development', in Bruce, M. and Biemans, W. G. (eds), *Product Development: Meeting the challenge of the design-marketing interface.* John Wiley & Sons, Chichester, pp. 137–159.

61 Schrader, S. (1995) 'Informal alliances: information trading between firms', in Gomez-Mejia, L. R. and Lawless, M. W. (eds), *Advances in Global High-Technology Management: Strategic alliances in high technology.* JAI Press, Greenwich, Conn. Vol. 5, Part B, pp. 31–55.

Part IV

BUILDING EFFECTIVE IMPLEMENTATION MECHANISMS

So far we have been looking at how an organization identifies and positions itself strategically, and how it establishes effective linkages with its marketplace and with other organizations. We now move to look in more detail at how it mobilizes and organizes the internal and external processes which enable innovation to happen.

Innovation success depends not only on clear strategic direction and effective external positioning, but also on being able to manage projects from initial idea or opportunity to a successful commercial product or service, or an effective new internal process. This involves a sequence of problem-solving activities and needs a staged framework for decision-making about whether or not to continue with development, allocation of resources and so on. And this in turn requires skills in managing projects, linking different functional resources together, knowledge sharing, managing both technical and market development, managing the change process itself, and ensuring that learning is captured from the experience of the project. Chapter 9 explores these themes.

Implementation also raises the question of whether the innovation can be managed within the existing organizational framework, or whether new arrangements are needed. One option for more radical innovations—where either the technologies or markets are unfamiliar—is to establish an internal corporate venture. The aim is to encourage entrepreneurial activity and experimentation, but at the same time to draw on the resources of the parent organization. Therefore internal ventures can be a means to leverage existing competencies in new markets or to acquire new competencies, perhaps in response to disruptive innovation. Chapter 10 looks in detail at this.

Chapter 9

MANAGING THE INTERNAL PROCESSES

Up till now we have been looking at the innovation process in terms of phases in time, moving from scanning and selecting strategic options, resourcing and implementation. Implicit in this is the presence of routines which help enable management of activities through these phases. For example:

- Scanning the environment for relevant signals and processing these
- Selecting projects which have a good strategic fit
- Monitoring and managing projects through the various stages of development
- Deciding where and when to stop projects, and where and when to accelerate them
- Reviewing and capturing learning from completed projects

For many enterprises these activities are often carried out on an ad hoc basis, and not in systematic fashion. But research evidence suggests that a degree of structure and discipline is an important component of success.

This chapter looks in more detail at *how* organizations manage these elements within the innovation process, and reports on some of the routines which appear to have been associated with effective performance at each of the stages. Innovation management is essentially about building and embedding such routines within the organization—but it is also about reviewing, improving and on occasions replacing them with new and more appropriate ones to cope with what is a constantly changing environment. In other words, it is about building dynamic capability.

9.1 Enabling Scanning

Table 9.1 gives some examples of key enabling routines which are associated with picking up and processing signals about possible inputs to the innovation process.

TABLE 9.1   Examples of scanning routines.

Market-related signals	*Technology-related signals*
• *Defining the boundaries of the marketplace.* Essentially this involves asking the deceptively simple question 'what business are we in?' This kind of question prompts discussion of current and potential markets and assists in looking for new opportunities. Sometimes innovation can take the form of repositioning—offering the same basic product or service but addressed in a new way to different markets. For example, Amazon.com is seen as an online retailer but is trying to broaden its business by positioning itself also as a software developer and supplier[1] • *Understanding market dynamics.* Closely linked to the above is understanding where potential markets may arise as a consequence of various kinds of change. For example, the cellular phone business has moved from a specialist, high-price business market into the general marketplace as a result of both technological and cultural change. Similarly low cholesterol and other healthy foods are increasingly becoming relevant to a large segment of the population as a result of changing social attitudes and education. Building up such understanding of the changing marketplace requires various forms of communication and interaction, from monitoring through to customer panels and surveys[4] Knowledge of this kind is a powerful input to planning both product and process innovation—for example, the shift to wide-spread use of cellular phones is a powerful trigger for process innovation around increasing capacity and flexibility within the factory. Benetton have a sophisticated IT system installed in each of their shops such that they can quickly identify which lines are selling well on a daily basis—and tailor production to this. The same information also guides the development of their systems—process innovation • *Market forecasting.* A wide range of techniques are available for trying to understand the likely dynamics of new markets, running from simple extrapolation of current trends through to complex techniques for handling discontinuous change, such as Delphi panels and scenario writing.[11] Such forecasting needs to move beyond sales-related information to include other features which will influence the potential market—for example, demographic, technological, political and environmental	• *Technological forecasting.* Opportunities arise in part from the continuing advances in knowledge which make new products, services and processes possible. Various techniques exist for exploring technological futures, ranging from simple extrapolation of performance parameters and rates of development to complex, non-linear techniques. Some, like Delphi panels and scenarios, are similar to market forecasting techniques, whilst others are more closely aligned to technological development models[2, 3] • *Developing extensive links.* Research has consistently shown that those organizations which adopt an active as opposed to a parochial approach to seeking out links with possible suppliers of technology or information are more successful innovators.[5, 6] Possible sources with which links can be made include suppliers, universities, research/technology institutions, other users and producers, trade associations, international bodies (e.g. for standards), etc. The principle behind this is to multiply the range of channels along which technological intelligence can flow; this principle also suggests that different kinds of inputs are important, for example scanning journals, visiting exhibitions, attending conferences.[7] There is also research to suggest that encouraging the development of an 'invisible college' of contacts between technologists outside the firm is an important source of ideas[8–10] Chapter 8 explores some of these themes in greater detail • A recent but powerful variation on this theme has been the growth of *benchmarking*.[12] In this process enterprises make structured comparisons with others to try and identify new ways of carrying out particular processes or to explore new product concepts. The learning triggered by benchmarking may arise from comparing between similar organizations (same firm, same sector, etc.), or it may come from looking outside the sector but at similar products or processes. For example,

issues.[12] For example, the present concern for environmentally friendly 'green' products is likely to increase and will be shaped by a variety of these factors. From this information come valuable clues about the type of performance which the market expects from a particular manufacturer or service provider—and hence the targets for process innovation.

- *Working with users.* An important routine is to involve customers in providing information about the kinds of products and services which they require. This can be done through regular surveys, through customer panels and other forms of involvement. There is a growing trend towards joint cost-reducing process innovation, where customers and suppliers work together to reduce prices or increase quality or some other performance parameter.[15, 16] The advantages and limitations of customer involvement were discussed in Chapter 7

- *Continuing interaction.* Successful innovation depends on maintaining a strong user perspective over time: this argues for mechanisms which emphasize continuing interaction rather than a one-off information-gathering exercise. Mechanisms for doing so include involvement of users in the project team and two-way visiting between sites[17]

- *Communicating user perspectives into the rest of the organization.* An important set of routines is concerned with making sure that the user perspective is communicated to all those different functions and disciplines within the organization and not simply retained as marketing information. Amongst recipes for achieving this are to rotate staff so that they spend some time out working with and listening to customers, and the introduction of the concept that 'everybody is someone's customer'. (Of course, this assumes that the firm is in the right market with the right set of customers to begin with—the risk of getting it wrong strategically will be compounded if the wrong kinds of messages are being communicated)

- *'Voice of the customer' techniques.* An increasing number of tools and structured frameworks are now available for trying to identify, clarify, articulate and communicate 'the voice of the customer' throughout the organization. Based on the principles of quality function deployment (QFD) these tools usually take as their starting point the customer needs as expressed in the customer's own words or images and gradually and systematically decompose them into tasks for the various elements within the organization[18, 19]

Southwest Airlines became the most successful carrier in the USA by dramatically reducing the turnaround times at airports—an innovation which it learned from studying pit stop techniques in the Formula 1 Grand Prix events. Similarly the Karolinska hospital in Stockholm made significant improvements to its cost and time performance through studying inventory management techniques in advanced factories[13, 14]

- Other search techniques include looking at 'best practice' *demonstration projects* and *'reverse engineering'*. This theme is discussed more fully in Chapter 4.

9.2 Enabling Strategy-making

Scanning the environment identifies a wide range of potential targets for innovation and effectively answers the question 'what *could* we do?' But even the best-resourced firm will need to balance this with some difficult choices about which options it will explore—and which it will leave aside. This process should not simply be about responding to what competitors do or customers ask for in the marketplace. Nor should it simply be a case of following the latest technological fashion. Successful innovation strategy requires understanding the key parameters of the competitive game (markets, competitors, external forces, etc.) and also the role which technological knowledge can play as a resource in this game. How can it be accumulated and shared, how can it be deployed in new products/services and processes, how can complementary knowledge be acquired or brought to bear, etc. Such questions—as we saw in Chapter 3—are as much about the management of the learning process within the firm as about investments or acquisitions—and building effective routines for supporting this process is critical to success.

Strategy-making essentially involves a combination of analysis (of possible innovation options), choice (selection of which of these to commit resources to) and planning (deciding how to make the innovation happen). Some routines associated with enabling these activities are given in Table 9.2.

TABLE 9.2   Examples of enabling routines to support strategy-making.

Routines to help enable . . .	Examples
Articulating/defining strategic framework for innovation Exploring fit with business strategy	Research has repeatedly shown that firms that simply innovate on impulse are poor performers. Equally, those which understand the overall business, including their technological competence their marketing competence and their desired development trajectory are more likely to succeed.[20] A number of structured methodologies are available which try to support the exploration of the 'fit' between proposed product innovations and the existing competence base—for example, the SWORD approach.[21] Similar frameworks are available for process innovation—for example the 'Making it fit' programme developed by the UK Department of Trade and Industry to help smaller firms with this issue[22–25]
Developing a strategic concept	The purpose of this is to move an outline idea to something with clearer shape and form, on which decisions about resource commitments can be made. This concept can also be tested in the marketplace, explored within design, development and manufacturing and considered in terms of its strategic implications and fit. It can be used to provide the vision for the development team; the clearer the vision,

the more focused the development process can be. In the case of process innovation the concept can be tested on the 'internal market'—those users who will be affected by the change and whose 'buy-in' is needed. Tools for helping here include simulation and prototyping—for example, in introducing new production management software a common practice is to 'walk through' the operation of core processes using computer and organizational simulation

Testing the concept

Much of the concept definition/product specification stage is about information and one important routine involves pilot testing of the concept in the marketplace and amongst those with technological knowledge. Such investment (what Cooper calls 'buying a look') is usually justified in terms of avoiding problems at a later stage, and in helping refine the specification[27]

Several techniques are available to support this process—for example, 'product mapping' and 'focus groups'—and concept testing can be applied to various aspects of the overall product.[26] One area of current concern, for example, is the 'greening' of existing product ranges, and many firms are actively involved in exploring alternative and complementary concepts which stress an environmentally friendly dimension

Again similar routines can be applied to process innovation. Pilot plant trials are often used in developing and scaling up processes whilst there is increasing use of advanced simulation technology to explore various dimensions with key users. Process mapping is a widely used technique in ensuring effective design, especially of cross-functional processes where the workflow is not always clearly understood[28]

Integrating different perspectives

Many of the problems in product innovation arise from the multifunctional nature of development and the lack of a shared perspective on the product being developed and/or the marketplace into which it will be introduced. A common problem is that 'X wasn't consulted, otherwise they would have told you you can't do that . . .'. This places a premium on involving all groups at the earliest possible, i.e. the concept definition/product specification, stage. Several structured approaches now exist for managing this, including quality function deployment and functional mapping.[29] For example, reviewing the possibilities for modular design, for using parts common to other products in a range, for value engineering of key components and for using different assembly techniques offer powerful ways of cutting costs and avoiding delays and problems in development. The availability of simulation technology, especially computer-aided design, has helped facilitate this kind of early discussion and refinement of the concept

In process innovation the early involvement of key users and the incorporation of their perspectives are strongly associated with improved overall performance and also with acceptability of the process in operation. This methodology has had a strong influence on, for example, the implementation of major integrated computer systems which by definition cut across functional boundaries[30, 31]

Early involvement of key suppliers

Extending this idea of early involvement in concept development, an increasingly important routine is to *bring suppliers of components and subsystems into the discussion.* Their specialist expertise can often provide unexpected ways of saving costs and time in the subsequent development and production process. Increasingly, product development is being treated as a co-operative activity in which networks of players, each with a particular knowledge set, are co-ordinated towards a shared objective. Examples include automotive components, aerospace and electronic capital equipment, all of who make growing use of formal supplier involvement programmes[32-34]

Working with users

An important variation on the theme of involving customers in concept development is the idea of *working with lead users.* In industries like semiconductors and instrumentation research suggests that the richest understanding of needed new products is held by only a few organizations, who are ahead of the majority of firms in the sector.[16] Equally, finding the most demanding customer in a particular sector is a valuable approach; stretching the concept to meet their needs will ensure that most other potential users come within the envelope[35]

In process innovation this has also proved to be an important routine—both in order to secure acceptance (where early involvement of users is now seen as critical) and also in obtaining improved quality process design[36]

Screening and sifting

Screening techniques are another important internal selection mechanism. In many firms the choice is not necessarily of going for only one product concept but of selecting out likely runners for further exploration and development. Techniques for screening range from simple judgemental methods to complex mathematic.[37] However it is important to recognize that even advanced and powerful screening tools will only work if the corporate will is present to implement the recommended decisions; for example, Cooper and Kleinschmidt found that the majority of firms studied (885) performed poorly at this stage, and often failed to kill off weak concepts[20]

Interaction with other outsiders

Interaction with outsiders also needs to take account of external regulatory frameworks—for example in product standards, environmental controls, safety legislation. Concept testing (Box 9.2) can be helped by close involvement with and participation in organizations which have responsibilities in these areas

---

BOX 9.1 Strategic concept—the case of the Honda Accord.

A good example here is the case of the Honda Accord, described in refs 16 and 26, of a car but with the basic concept 'man maximum, machine minimum'. This captured the feel which they wanted to give customers; in the 1990 redesign, a different concept—'an adult sense of reliability' was used. This led to images—such as 'a rugby player in a business suit' to characterize the kind of person who would drive the car and the kinds of expectations—physically rugged, sporty but with gentlemanly behaviour—which design features would have to include. Other phrases, e.g. 'tough spirit' were also used; the result was a set of messages with which the design team could work. For example, the stress-free reliable component led to many modifications in noise reduction and engine control.

BOX 9.2 Concept testing of the Powerbook.

An example of concept testing in the marketplace is the development of the Apple Powerbook, widely acknowledged to be one of the most successful and attractive designs in a highly competitive marketplace (estimates suggest there are nearly 400 different machines to choose from). Apple was a comparative latecomer to the market and its first portable computer was a notable flop; the Powerbook was originated in 1990 and launched in late 1991. Its success was partly due to using a product-mapping approach, which focuses less on the product than on how people interact with it. Studies compared the Powerbook with major competitors along 159 dimensions, from opening the box to using it on a tight aeroplane seat. Amongst ideas which emerged from this mapping were the positioning of the trackball in the centre (to suit left- and right-handed users), the design of the hinge to permit different viewing angles, retractable feet to enable a sloping working position on a desk, positioning of the disk drive so that aeroplane seats would not restrict access and strengthened ribs to prevent scuffing and damage. The concept was further tested by a panel of 68 users in six different studies (*Business Week*, 20/4/1992, pp. 112–113, cited in Gupta[26]).

9.3 Enabling Effective Resource Provision

The resource phase involves combining new and existing knowledge (available within and outside the organization) to offer a solution to the problem of innovation. It involves both generation of technological knowledge (via R&D carried out within and outside the organization) and technology transfer (between internal sources or from external sources).

The challenge in effective R&D is not simply one of putting resources into the system; it is how those resources are used. Effective management of R&D requires a number of organizational routines, including clear strategic direction, effective communication and 'buy-in' to that direction, and integration of effort across different groups. Part II of this book discusses such R&D management challenges in some detail.

But not all firms can afford to invest in R&D; for many smaller firms the challenge is to find ways of using technology generated by others or to complement internally generated core technologies with a wider set drawn from outside (see Chapter 8). This places emphasis on the strategy system discussed above—the need to know which to carry out where and the need for a framework to guide policy in this area. Firms can survive even with no in-house capability to generate technology—but to do so they need to have a well-developed network of external sources which can supply it, and the ability to put that externally acquired technology to effective use.

It also requires abilities in finding, selecting and transferring technology in from outside the firm. This is rarely a simple shopping transaction although it is often treated as such; it involves abilities like those listed in Table 9.3.

TABLE 9.3   Key abilities in technology transfer.

Ability	Why?
Building and maintaining a network of technology sources	To ensure a wide range of choice and availability, rather than being forced to take inappropriate solutions
Selecting	To ensure a good fit between internal needs and external offer
Negotiating	To ensure that what is transferred includes the knowledge and experience surrounding the technology and not simply the hardware or licence
Implementing	To ensure the process of transfer is effectively managed
Learning	To ensure that once transferred the development and internalization of the technology takes place

There are many cautionary tales of technology transfer in which there is a failure of one or more of these abilities leading to ineffective transfer. For example, there is the problem of dependency familiar to many small firms and to those in developing countries with less strong technological traditions. Here what is transferred is the basic product or process technology, but the surrounding package of knowledge about how to use and develop it, and how to internalize it, is missing, so that the firm continues to depend upon the supplier.[38] Negotiation of full technology transfer, including this intangible element, is becoming an important feature of many licensing deals.[39–41]

Another common problem with technology transfer is the lack of selection; inexperienced buyers may take on technology which is not suited to their particular needs. For example, a firm needing to improve its manufacturing flexibility may have heard of the concept of a flexible manufacturing system (a combination of computers, machine tools and other equipment). Such systems may offer flexibility under certain conditions—but there are many other alternatives. The ability to make informed choices across a range of technological possibilities and in the face of strong sales pressure is important if the firm is to avoid acquiring what is effectively 'technological jewellery'—a glamorous, high-tech fashion accessory which does not have any value beyond the cosmetic.

The rapid pace of technological change means that firms are increasingly being forced to look at some combination of internal generation and external acquisition. Whether it is product or process technology, the emphasis is increasingly on collaboration and on working with outside sources, whether in universities, research institutes or other firms. As Dodgson points out, these are not always successful and firms are being forced to learn new skills to ensure effective collaboration.[42]

The picture is thus becoming one in which it is not necessary to have all the technological resources in-house but rather one in which the firm knows how, where and when to obtain them from external and complementary sources. This model of the 'extended firm' can be seen in a number of industries where there is close collaboration between suppliers and users of technology—for example in the automobile or aerospace sectors.[43, 44] The capability to manage such networks can itself be a source of competitive advantage; if the firm can build up a successful network of external resources complementary to its own this may be just as effective as having all the resources in-house.[45] However, a key part of this capability is knowing which elements to outsource and which to retain in-house; the concept of the 'virtual' organization appears to involve considerable risk (see Part II).

Figure 9.1 draws on work by Arnold *et al.* (1993) which indicates that firms differ widely in their knowledge base and in their ability to access and make effective use of technological knowledge—what is sometimes called 'absorptive capacity'. Selection of the right approach to technology transfer depends on where firms are on this staircase. An important element in innovation support policy in many countries and regions has been the recognition of this problem amongst smaller firms and the development of various kinds of consulting assistance to help firms move up in their capability.

Technological knowledge can come from a variety of sources, as Table 9.4 shows. Each carries with it both strengths and weaknesses; the key management task is to ensure an appropriate match between the sources selected and the context of the firm in terms of its resources and its absorptive capacity. Box 9.3 gives some examples of this process at work.

There are also important implications here for those organizations concerned with supplying technology. Successful transfer of technology will only take place if these factors are taken into account—simply offering technology is not likely to

TABLE 9.4   Different mechanisms for acquisition of technology.

Mechanism	Strengths	Weaknesses
Mobilizing tacit knowledge	Internal, highly specific knowledge Hard to copy	Hard to mobilize Needs processes to articulate and capture[46, 47]
In-house formal R&D	Strategically directed Under full control Learning by doing Knowledge remains inside the firm	High cost and commitment Risks—no guarantee of success
In-house R&D and network links outside	As above but with less control over knowledge unless there is a clear contract on intellectual property rights	Costs and risks
Reverse engineering	Lower costs Offers insight into competitors' processes and products Knowledge can be inferred, but needs a level of skill to do so	Depends on ability to infer knowledge Knowledge may be protected anyway, e.g. in patent or copyright
Covert acquisition (industrial espionage!) plus internal R&D	Fast access to knowledge and relevance of that knowledge can be managed through internal capability	Illegal Costs of internal R&D
Covert acquisition	Fast access to knowledge	Illegal Risk of not being able to translate external knowledge to internal needs
Technology transfer and absorption	Easier access to knowledge—someone else has developed and packaged it	Costs Risk of not understanding or being able to make full use of technology May be prohibited from further exploration and learning by terms of licence, etc.
Contract R&D	Speed and focus	Costs Lack of control Lack of learning effect—someone else is carrying out the experimentation and learning process
Strategic R&D partnership	Links complementary knowledge sets Enables complex problems to be addressed	Costs Risks in partnership not working Lack of learning since technology development is carried out by other parties
Licensing	Fast access to knowledge	Costs Restricted learning—may also be prohibited by terms of licence
Purchasing	Fast access	Costs Lack of learning
Joint venture	Links complementary knowledge sets Enables complex problems to be addressed	Costs Risks in partnership not working Lack of learning since technology development is carried out by other parties
Acquisition of a company with the knowledge	Fast access to knowledge Control over knowledge	Costs May not be able to absorb knowledge

BOX 9.3 Learning from external sources of technology.

Taking this approach can often reveal new ways of dealing with an old and apparently intractable problem. For example, the Cosworth company are a well-known producer of high-performance engines for motor racing and performance car applications. They were seeking a source of aluminium castings which were cheap enough for volume use but of high enough precision and quality for their product; having searched throughout the world they were unable to find anyone suitable. Either they took the low-price route and used some form of die-casting which often lacked the precision and accuracy, or they went along the investment casting route which added significantly to the cost. Eventually they decided to go right back to basics and design their own manufacturing process; they set up a small pilot facility and employed a team of metallurgists and engineers with the brief to come up with an alternative approach that could meet their needs. After three years' work and a very wide and systematic exploration of the problem the team came up with a process which combined conventional casting approaches with new materials (especially a high grade of sand) and other improvements. The breakthrough was, however, the use of an electromagnetic pump which forced molten metal into a shell in such a way as to eliminate the air which normally led to problems of porosity in the final product. This innovation came from well outside the foundry industry, from the nuclear power field where it had been used to circulate the liquid sodium coolant used in the fast breeder reactor programme! The results were impressive; not only did Cosworth meet their own needs, they were also able to offer the service to other users of castings and to license the process to major manufacturers such as Ford and Daimler-Benz.

In another example, the small textile company J & J Cash were experiencing severe problems as a result of the inflexibility of their production equipment and design processes in the early 1980s. As narrow fabric weavers producing name tapes, labels and other woven goods, they represented too small a segment of the textile industry to attract the attentions of the main equipment suppliers. The result was that although sophisticated electronically controlled equipment was available for broadcloth weavers, nothing suitable was available for Cash's to adopt. Instead they were forced to generate their own; over a decade they built up a mixture of internal competence (acquired through a lengthy and not always successful process of learning by doing and experimenting) and external linkages such that by the end of the period they had managed to develop and implement their own microelectronics controls for a wide range of looms and a sophisticated computer-aided design and manufacturing system. The benefits this brought were significant; from a position in which their basic product took at least six weeks to produce they can now process orders on the day they are received. They have opened up new markets and expanded the business through the new opportunities which greater technological capability has brought; they have also become suppliers of technological know-how to other small firms in a similar position.[48]

Company types

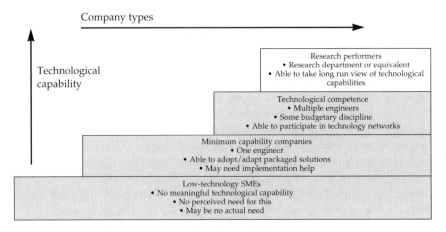

FIGURE   9.1

Source: Derived from Arnold, E. and B. Thuriaux (1998) 'Developing firms technological capabilities'. Working paper, Technopolis, Brighton.

guarantee successful take-up. Instead suppliers are increasingly recognizing the need to offer a package of support which may range from user education (for those with low capability or absorptive capacity) through to various kinds of transfer support to help configure solutions to particular needs.

9.4 Enabling Implementation

The task of making innovation happen—moving from idea through to successful products, services or processes—is essentially one of managing what Wheelwright and Clark call 'the development funnel'. That is, a gradual process of

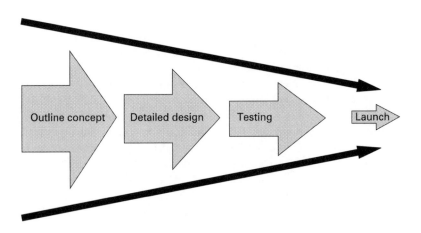

FIGURE 9.2   The new product development funnel.

reducing uncertainty through a series of problem-solving stages, moving through the phases of scanning and selecting and into implementation—linking market and technology-related streams along the way (Figure 9.2). The model is equally applicable in thinking about product or process change—the 'market' in process innovation may be one consisting of internal users but they also need to make decisions about whether or not to 'buy in' to the project.

At the outset anything is possible, but increasing commitment of resources during the life of the project makes it increasingly difficult to change direction. Managing innovation is a fine balancing act, between the costs of continuing with projects which may not eventually succeed (and which represent opportunity costs in terms of other possibilities) and the danger of closing down too soon and eliminating potentially fruitful options. Taking these decisions can be done on an ad hoc basis but experience suggests some form of structured development sysem with clear decision points and agreed rules on which to base go/no-go decisions, is a more effective approach.[49]

In the case of product innovation attention has been placed in practice on reconfiguring internal mechanisms for integrating and optimizing the process such as concurrent engineering, cross-functional working, advanced tools, early involvement, etc.[50] With shorter life cycles and demand for greater product variety, pressure is also placed upon new product development (NPD) systems to work with a wider portfolio of new product opportunities and to manage the risks associated with progressing these through development to launch. To deal with this, attention has focused on systematic screening, monitoring and progression frameworks such as Cooper's 'stage/gate' approach.[45, 51]

Most of these ideas are not in themselves new—for example, Lawrence and Lorsch drew attention to cross-functional teamworking and co-ordination mechanisms back in the 1960s, whilst Cooper reports on NASA's 'Phased Review Process' as a stage/gate model dating back to the same period.[52] But it can be argued that there is now growing consensus about their integration into a new model of 'good practice' in NPD.

These ideas developed around the creation and development of new physical products, but with the rise in the service economy attention has moved to their application in service innovation. Sectors like financial services or retailing are increasingly concerned with offering variations on their existing range and also totally new service concepts—and with this has come a realization that managing these innovations requires a systematic process. Whilst the applications may differ significantly, the relevance of many of the core principles—and the enabling routines—from physical product innovation is high.[53, 54]

Much of what has been learned about effective product development also has relevance for process change. Here success depends not only on good process design—does it do the job better than that which it will replace—but also on user acceptance—will it actually be used? This depends not only on securing the buy-in of users but also on themes like user involvement (to bring their experience and tacit knowledge to bear), user needs analysis (to ensure the new process takes account of concerns) and user education. These have direct analogues to good practice in product innovation.

Given their generic nature it will be useful to explore some of the enabling routines for successful implementation in a little more detail.

Early Involvement and Concurrent Working

Estimates suggest that up to 70% of a product's cost is determined at the design stage, and thus it would seem important to concentrate attention on hammering out any likely problems in manufacturing at this stage. (This represents what some writers are now calling 'learning before doing' and is a powerful source of innovation.[55]) Yet most firms spend less than 5% of their product budget on design and push instead for manufacture as soon as possible. Whilst this may reduce the time to market, it can also have a major effect upon costs. A variety of studies have consistently shown that attention to product simplification and design for manufacture can make substantial savings at later stages. For example, in a study of the IBM Lexington plant for computer printer manufacture, simplification of design led to a reduction of 3 : 1 in part numbers and this in turn meant a cut of 9 : 1 in adjustments.

The idea of interplay between designers, makers, sellers and users is not new. Indeed, it provides the basis for the product improvement process which operates today in which marketing, in touch with end-users, reports back to the design function information about problems, suggested improvements, etc. Von Hippel and others have drawn attention to this as an important source of innovation. Similarly the experience of making the product on the shop floor eventually finds its way back into the drawing office and leads to suggestions for improvements.[15, 56, 57]

But this is often a slow and reactive process which, it can be argued, is not very efficient as a mechanism for improving design performance in an era of shortening product life cycles, and increased competition on the basis of non-price factors. By contrast an integrated approach, like that suggested above, is essentially a proactive one in which the design is refined and developed on the basis of 'real-time' interaction so that it is constantly evolving and improving.

Considerable interest is now being shown in the idea of 'simultaneous engineering' as a means to ensure more rapid time to market for new product developments. Estimates suggest that being first into the market means a firm obtains a 50% market share for that product or service, and other benefits include reduced costs (of work hours and inventories) and improved customer relationships because of better, more rapid service. Examples of firms which have made dramatic cuts in their time to market include Honda (which cut its five-year new car development cycle by 50%), ATT (which also reduced by 50% the time taken to introduce its new cordless telephone), Hewlett-Packard (which reduced the time to develop its printers from 4.5 years to 22 months) and Xerox Corporation which made dramatic reductions in development times, cutting them from six to around three years on a range of office products. 'Cycle compression' is another phrase which is beginning to emerge, especially in the context of long development cycle products like military equipment and aircraft.[58]

The main advantage in such an approach comes from the early identification and resolution of conflicts—it stops the problems being thrown over the fence and demands a co-operative solution. Better information flow also brings in new inputs to design at a stage where they can be used to improve the design—as distinct from the traditional practice of apportioning blame to different areas because they failed to pass on information which could have helped avoid costly design faults.

Pisano has shown that similar patterns operate in process innovation, where such 'learning before doing' is essential in reducing development time and increasing the chances of a successful outcome.[55] Box 9.4 gives an illustration of the value of early and cross-functional involvement.

BOX 9.4 Integrated design in the motor industry.

Lamming provides an interesting illustration of this alternative approach in the motor industry. UK companies involved in joint ventures with Japanese partners have sometimes complained about the lack of detail on drawings sent from Japan—assuming that correct product quality can only be achieved through precise (often pedantic) specification at the design and draughting stages prior to 'release' to production. The Japanese method of early (and therefore quick) release from design to production, followed by continuous development of the product by production departments, has show three major areas of benefit, however, which have gradually been realized by the UK partners. First, modification of the product in production ensures continuous improvement in process efficiency (and thus reduction in costs, improvements in quality, etc.). Second, design improvements suggested by production have a natural path for communication, and may be incorporated with a minimum of difficulty. Third, early release of the product enables the designers to concentrate on the replacement model, thus reducing development periods by eliminating 'afterthought'. The apparent 'sloppiness' of some Japanese engineering information (e.g. drawings) is in fact the sign of a more open design authority which is shared for mutual benefit (between departments) rather than jealously guarded for individual 'professional' security. The technique is sometimes referred to by Japanese as using the factory as the laboratory of the designer.[59]

This kind of approach, which emphasizes teamwork and co-operation, needs to be set against the traditional structure of design which often sees it as a distant function, pursuing goals very different from those of the rest of the organization. Successful teams stress mutual learning—indeed, some companies prefer to make continuing use of such teams since the investment in group development is so valuable. They need a clear goal towards which they can all work—and the leadership needs full authority to challenge what has traditionally been done. For example, in a report on the development of Nissan's Maxima car the project engineer was able to preserve his design team authority over the heads of board-level management. Such an approach avoids costly last-minute changes to placate senior management—a major difference from US counterparts where senior management often had extensive influence on the process. The benefits of this approach soon became clear: the Maxima was developed within 30 months and also won the industry's top quality award soon after its introduction.[60] Such approaches have since become widespread in the car and other complex product industries.

As with all of these concepts, the important management skill is in knowing where and when they are appropriate. For example, 'cycle compression' approaches may not be a good idea in high-risk projects like construction, whilst (as Chapter 5 discusses) new approaches like that employed successfully in the Maxima case can sometimes be pushed too far and become 'core rigidities' which inhibit effectiveness.

Stage/Gate Decision Process

As Cooper suggests, successful innovators tend to operate some form of structured, staging process.[61] As products or new processes move through the development funnel there is a need to assess performance characteristics and to ensure that progress forward is linked to successful achievement of these goals. Cooper proposes a series of stage gates (Figure 9.3) and many variations (e.g. 'fuzzy gates') on this approach exist; the important point is to ensure that there is a structure in place which reviews both technical and marketing data at each stage.

Teamworking

One of the most powerful resources for enabling rapid development is the use of cross-functional teams which contain representatives of all the disciplines involved in the innovation and which has the autonomy to progress the project. Teams of this kind are not formed simply by grouping people together; successful practice involves extensive investments in team-building, providing them with the necessary training to solve problems, to manage conflict, to interact with other parts of the organization and with outside stakeholders, etc.[62] Chapter 11 discusses teamworking in greater detail and Box 9.5 gives an example of the value of developing this resource.

Shared Project Vision

Empowering teams and providing them with autonomy and resources will only work if they have a clear sense of direction. One important way of providing this is to involve them in the process of vision-building, evolving the product concept in the context of a clear understanding of the underlying business drivers and competitive realities. An example of the need for clear project vision has been reported.[63] When Digital Equipment Corporation began to challenge the dominance of Sun Microsystems in the workstation market, part of the vision was the clear need to base operations on the Unix language rather than DEC's proprietary VMS software. This forced a recognition of the need for substantial change in all aspects of the project, from design thinking through to software and hardware design and construction. Ultimately the efforts paid off, because the particular product (the 3100) paved the way for several others in the same series, whilst at the same time creating a new capability in the way in which new products are developed.

Sometimes the vision is critical to carrying the company forward into new territory. When Intel was facing strong competition from Far Eastern producers

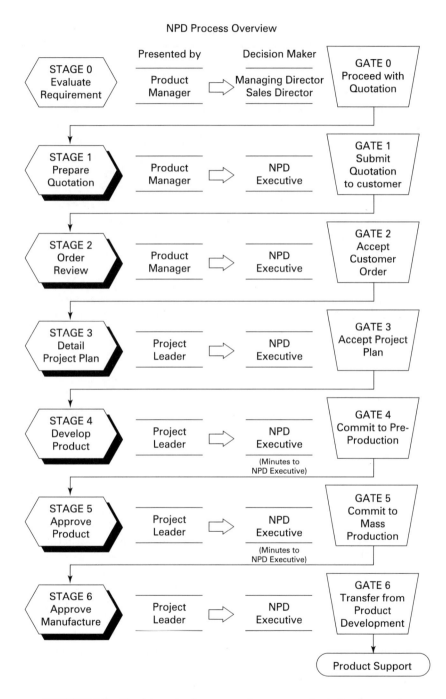

FIGURE 9.3   The 'stage/gate process for new product development.

BOX 9.5 The Team Taurus project.

The 'Team Taurus' project at Ford illustrates the potential of this approach. At the time of its development Taurus was a new concept car, which represented a departure both in terms of product and the organization involved in its development. It was a demanding project, requiring more than 4000 newly designed components and completely new transmission, engine and suspension systems. The core team worked hard to break down the walls which had traditionally separated their activities, and where necessary the team expanded to incorporate other perspectives and ideas—for example, extensively consulting the manufacturing workforce regarding the difficulties in manufacturing the new 'soft shapes' in body components. Whilst computer tools were extensively used, the underlying team integration was critical in resolving the many design changes and challenges. A core value of incorporating the best ideas, rather than the familiar, was developed and this placed stress on open-ended problem-solving rather than using old routines. Team roles were explicitly explored and developed; in particular the team leader became much more of a team captain/facilitator than a member of supervisory management.[63]

Significantly, firms need to take care to capture the learning about team organization and management. Whilst the early experiences of developing the Taurus were positive, Walton reports a very different outcome for later generations and one which highlights a lack of effective teamworking.[64]

---

in the memory chip market Groves and Noyce reported on the need to 'think the unthinkable', i.e. get out of memory production (the business on which Intel had grown up) and to contemplate moving into other product niches. They trace their subsequent success to the point where they found themselves 'entering the void' and creating a new vision for the business.[65]

Appropriate Project Structures

Closely linked with the concept of teamworking is the need to get a good match between the demands of a development and the operating structure which enables it. In a 10-year study of 2899 projects, 46% of the projects were successful but project management structure was an important determinant.[66] Traditionally the choice is between functional teams, cross-functional project teams or some form of matrix between the two. However, in recent studies other models emerge which appear correlated with success.[29] Four main types can be identified:

1. Functional structure—a traditional hierarchical structure where communication between functional areas is largely handled by function managers and according to standard and codified procedures.
2. Lightweight product manager structure—again a traditional hierarchical structure but where a project manager provides an overarching co-ordinating structure to the interfunctional work.

3. Heavyweight product manager structure—essentially a matrix structure led by a product (project) manager with extensive influence over the functional personnel involved but also in strategic directions of the contributing areas critical to the project. By its nature this structure carries considerable organizational authority.

4. Project execution teams—a full-time project team where functional staff leave their areas to work on the project, under project leader direction.

Project management structure does appear to be strongly correlated with success, and of the available options functional structures are probably weakest.

Associated with these different structures are different roles for team members and particularly for project managers. For example, the 'heavyweight project manager' has to play several different roles, which include extensive interpreting and communication between functions and players. Similarly, team members have multiple responsibilities.

This implies the need for considerable efforts at team-building and development—for example, to equip the team with the skills to explore problems, to resolve the inevitable conflicts which will emerge during the project, to manage relationships inside and outside the project. Chapter 11 discusses this theme in greater detail.

The choice of which to use depends on the kinds of task being undertaken—for example, heavyweight teams are used when projects involve diverse and uncertain customer needs, whereas projects involving well-understood needs and technology can rely on more traditional approaches. Wheelwright and Clark classify projects into a number of different types, including:

- Derivative projects—involving small changes to existing products or systems
- Breakthrough projects—those which create new markets or products and require significant resources and a strategic view
- Platform projects—projects which involve significant incremental improvements but are still linked to same basic platform
- R&D projects—future-oriented, speculative but exploring where the company might be in five years or more
- Alliances—cross-company projects, designed to share costs and risks, but also posing problems of co-operation and co-ordination

Each of these is likely to require different combinations of project structure and team; once again, effective innovation management is strongly linked to understanding the requirements of particular situations and configuring the project accordingly.

Advanced Support Tools

1. Computer-based tools—particularly computer-aided design and manufacturing (CAD/CAM)—permit extensive simulation and shared exploration of concepts, and also accelerate the actual development process by automating key tasks. In addition communicating information in electronic form between

design and manufacturing functions significantly reduces the time required in development. Recent developments have extended the concept of computer-supported co-operative work (CSCW) to develop systems which enable communication and interaction between CAD users working at different locations but on the same project.

2. Rapid prototyping technologies and approaches are another powerful technological resource in product development. These approaches rely on a variety of techniques, but typically aim to produce a physical model of a concept quickly so that it can be evaluated and explored earlier in the development cycle. For example, the use of polymer resins and computer-controlled shaping equipment can quickly move from a CAD concept to a physical replica of the idea.

3. Quality function deployment (QFD) represents a powerful structured methodology for exploring and steering the interaction between different contributors in the product development process.[18, 19] The power of QFD is less in the data representation than in its role as a common structure over which discussion and debate between different functions can take place. It provides a common language and a systematic mechanism for exploring and resolving many of the typical issues.

4. Design rules treat one of the common problems in product development which is that design ideas which make sense at one stage pose problems for others further down the chain. For example, positioning a screw in a particular place may look fine on the drawing board or CAD screen, but may pose a major problem in the manufacturing stage, because of difficulties of access, or complexity of operation. This type of difficulty has led to a series of design methodologies governed by various rules to ensure consideration of downstream operations; these are often grouped under the heading of 'design for manufacture'.[67] Amongst considerations are design for ease of assembly, design for speed, design for simplification, design for minimum adjustment, etc. Closely related are rules which aim to reduce cost and simplify component count; these are usually classed under the label 'value engineering' or 'value analysis'.

Tidd and Bodley report on a review of the range of formal tools and techniques available to support the new product development process, and examine the use and usefulness of these by means of a survey of 50 projects in 25 firms. They adopted a four-stage model to examine the process of new product development: idea generation; screening and selection; development; commercialization and review, and identified the effect of project novelty on the frequency of use and perceived usefulness of a range of tools and methods. In terms of usefulness, focus groups, partnering customers and lead users and prototyping were all considered to be more effective for high-novelty projects, and segmentation least useful. Cross-functional development teams were commonplace for all types of project, but were significantly more effective for the high-novelty cases. In addition, many tools rated as useful were not commonly used, and conversely some tools in common use were considered to have low levels of usefulness.[68]

Market Development Routines

In parallel with technological development is the process of identifying, exploring and preparing the market for launch of a new product or service (see also Chapter 7). Enabling routines here include:

1. *Customer testing*—essentially taking out prototypes of the product to users (or bringing the users in to test them out). This is particularly important in ensuring that the original concept still holds; for example, the Ford Edsel was one of the best-researched product concepts in the company's history. The final product failed disastrously—mainly because the market had moved on in terms of customer tastes in the time it took to develop the production model. Such tests can also be used to explore customer preferences which provide important information about pricing policy, advertising strategy, etc. For more complex products it may be necessary to allow the user an extended period of use to permit learning and familiarization with the product and how to make the best use of it.
2. *Test marketing*—the next step in the process of market development, this involves various kinds of trying out of the marketing strategy. For example, in pre-test marketing potential customers are exposed to the product concept and undertake what is essentially a shopping simulation, using coupons instead of real money. This helped refine marketing plans and predictions, for example about likely shares. Full test marketing involves a trial sale of the new product to a controlled group of customers; effectively it is a pilot of the full marketing launch. Such testing can reveal actual as opposed to simulated data on acceptance, concerns, adoption rates and speeds, etc. It also offers the opportunity to test different launch strategies—for example, two different regions could be used, each employing a different launch strategy. There is general acceptance of the point that test marketing is worthwhile; although it involves costs in terms of trial production, test administration and data processing it effectively 'buys a look' before the company commits itself fully to launching a new product. It is an approach which works well with products which can be cheaply developed and modified in response to test data.
3. One approach to test marketing is the concept of *alpha, beta and gamma testing*, in which different releases of the product under development are issued to controlled groups of users. This strategy allows feedback of positive and negative responses which can be built into the final version; it is simultaneously a good way of enhancing product quality and user need fit whilst also pre-advertising/'warming up' the marketplace. This approach is extensively used in the area of computer software, where user feedback is an important source of product improvement and final development.
4. *Development of a marketing strategy* for the new product. This is essentially similar to other strategic development, involving a mixture of analysis of the target market and the relevant strengths, weaknesses, threats and opportunities. Typically such an analysis will specify in some detail the particular segments being targeted, the pattern of buyer behaviour which shapes that market, the nature and strength of competition and the overall dynamics of the marketplace. Developing the strategy will also require more detailed projections of market

shares and sales, leading to a detailed financial budget. Other aspects include positioning the product against competing offerings and planning the entry, in terms of target pricing, advertising plans, etc. Essentially this involves developing the 'marketing mix'—considering product, promotion, pricing and distribution—which will form the backbone of the marketing effort.[11, 37]

5. *Develop a marketing plan*—this is essentially a formal documented plan covering objectives, strategies and programmes to underpin the product launch. Once again the key theme of early involvement is relevant here; marketing planning should begin in parallel with product planning once the concept is established. The objectives should be clearly rather than vaguely defined—for example '. . . to obtain a 20% share of the industrial drill lubricant market in two years' time . . .'—so that it becomes possible to measure progress and see whether the marketing is on course.

6. *Develop a support organization*—innovation not only involves extensive interaction and integration with internal functions, it also needs linking with external channels of distribution and promotion. Whether these are owned by the firm or external, the principle of early involvement is still critical. A number of new product launches have failed because levels of service or support have been lacking; this argues for careful selection and involvement of these.[69]

9.5 Applying the Approach to Process Innovation

Similar patterns relate to process innovation, that is, changes in the way in which the organization produces its outputs or carries out its tasks. The importance of ensuring a good strategic fit between the strengths and weaknesses of the current processes and the proposed changes, the need to scan for opportunities, the need for capabilities in generating or acquiring suitable technology, etc. are all relevant preconditions for success. Within the process careful project planning and monitoring and the ability to manage what may often be extended projects crossing many departmental boundaries and disrupting 'normal' work for long periods will be critical skills.

In addition there is a need for continuity in process innovation; even more than product innovation, success here depends not on occasional giant leaps and dramatic radical innovation but on a steady stream of change resulting from regular review and fine tuning of the organization's processes. For example, Jaikumar's analysis of the implementation of flexible manufacturing systems in the USA and Japan concluded that the superior performance of the latter was strongly related to the continuing and interactive nature of the innovation process.[47, 70] There may be occasional major steps, such as the installation of a new generation of equipment, or the computerization of the organization's information system, but long-term success depends upon a continuing pattern of change. Without such an approach it is likely that processes will drift out of alignment and become inappropriate; the 1990s fashion for radical 'business process re-engineering' was less about bringing new ideas into the organization than about conducting a belated review of the drift away from effective processes which had resulted from inattention and lack of continuous review in the past.[71]

At the searching and scanning phase one of the key points is to ensure a thorough exploration of *internal* strengths and weaknesses—where the processes and activities within the organization help and where they hinder it reaching its strategic goals. Also critical at this stage is to explore opportunities arising not only in *embodied* technology (in the form of machines and equipment) but also in organizational and system changes. In some cases reconfiguration of the existing operations without the introduction of new elements is sufficient to contribute advantage.[72]

The importance of strategically managing process innovation is highlighted when we examine cases where it is absent. Whilst process innovation is commonplace, progress can be erratic; improvements across a broad front or occurring randomly may not be sufficient to enable a firm to remain competitive. Simply improving things—or adopting improvements developed elsewhere—is no guarantee that they will develop technological competence or help achieve overall business objectives. In order to contribute, process innovation must be focused and managed towards clear strategic ends.

Examples abound of firms which have adopted expensive and complex innovations to upgrade their processes but which have failed to obtain competitive advantage from process innovation.[73–75]

A number of writers offer useful methodological frameworks and tools to guide development and implementation of process innovation. In auditing and developing process innovation options, an important distinction should be made between what Hayes *et al.* call 'structural' and 'infrastructural' elements.[76] Structural elements include the basic building blocks—for example, in manufacturing they would include the number, location, size, quality of facilities, the type and capacity of equipment, the basic choice of manufacturing process, the range and extent of support services (power, water, drainage, etc.) and the nature and range of the external supply and distribution networks. Infrastructural elements are, on the other hand, less tangible but by no means less important; they include things like the *systems* for controlling production, for managing quality, for introducing new products, for maintaining plant and equipment and the overall information flow management system in the factory. They also include the human resource dimensions—the quality, age, experience, flexibility, etc. of the workforce, the way in which work is organized, the ways in which the contribution of different functions is co-ordinated, the communication patterns within the factory and the overall command and control infrastructure. Finally, the underlying culture—the set of shared beliefs and values which shape the behaviour of people working in the factory—represents a key element in the infrastructure. Similar distinctions can be drawn in service operations, for example between equipment like computer networks and organizational arrangements and systems.

Process innovation involves auditing the relative strengths or weaknesses in each of these areas and then exploring and deciding upon options for their development. A number of model frameworks are available—for example refs 23, 77, 78—which help to structure this, but most are based on the steps detailed under the headings below.

Identify Targets for Competing (Where Do We Want to Get to?)

The beginning of the process is the development of an understanding of the basis of competitiveness with regard to the chosen product or market. In a multi-product or multi-market company it will be necessary to explore the over-all portfolio of products and markets and to group these into separate businesses or product families.

Having separated out the different product/market families it is necessary to explore systematically what the determinants of competitiveness are in that segment of the market. Hill makes a useful distinction between what he terms 'order qualifying' and 'order winning' factors; the former refer to those factors which must be offered just to be able to participate in a particular market. It is important not to equate this kind of 'benchmarking' to simply catching up with competitors; the same analysis can be applied to explore the deployment of process capabilities which are ahead of competitors, for example in speed or responsiveness.

Audit Current Performance (Where Are We Now?)

The next stage is to assess the contribution of current processes—structure and infrastructure—to achieving this. Such an internal audit requires a careful examination of the ways in which different aspects help or hinder competitive performance and an indication of the priorities for change.

Exploring and assessing internal capability, especially in the infrastructural areas, is an activity which can provide valuable opportunities for learning and development. There is a danger that process innovation becomes synonymous with the replacement of equipment and facilities; this is to ignore the many intangible elements in the system and the considerable levels of tacit and accumulated know-how which are present in the infrastructure.

Explore Options for Innovation

This next stage involves an extensive search process, trying to find appropriate mechanisms for developing capability by enhancing areas of strength and improving areas of weakness. Success here is associated with wide-ranging exploration of opportunities; although the tendency is often to view process inno-vation in terms of investment in new plant and equipment, much can be achieved through reorganization and through sustained incremental innovation.

Wide search also includes looking at alternative options for reaching the same goal; for example, in manufacturing flexibility is a key strategic objective and can be achieved through investments in various forms of advanced technology, such as flexible manufacturing systems. However, flexibility can also be achieved through reorganization, changes in work organization, redeployment of machin-ery and people, etc. and such innovations may represent less expensive and more organizationally acceptable solutions. By the same token, change need not always be radical; although rapid improvements in key performance areas are impor-tant, the potential of sustained incremental improvement in areas like quality and flexibility should not be underestimated.[79, 80]

Change Management

Within process innovation the question of implementation takes on particular significance. Not only must the project be managed along what may be a complex development funnel (as with product innovation) but the market into which it will be launched is an internal one, often involving the same people. This raises the questions of project and of change management.

As Voss points out, implementation is often neglected in innovation studies yet it is often the site of the most serious difficulties.[81] Part of the implementation problem arises from a lack of attention at the strategic planning stage to dimensions of the proposed change—for example, ensuring suitable development of both infrastructure and structural elements. Since many process innovations represent major changes in 'the way we do things round here' the question of managing cultural change and overcoming resistance to innovation needs to be addressed, and planning for such organizational development is an important element in manufacturing strategy formulation. To some extent implementation difficulties can be reduced through involving those likely to be affected by the change in some of the strategy formulation and debate.

One way of looking at implementation is to see it involving continuing cycles of mutual adaptation of both technology and organization; this has important implications for reviewing the way in which such change is managed.[82] Trying to introduce changes in the ways in which products are made or services delivered is a co-operative effort which requires inputs of knowledge and expertise from across the organization. Extensive work on successful implementation of IT systems—probably the most widely used class of process innovations over the past 40 years—repeatedly stresses the need to involve users in order to get better designed systems and to get commitment to making them work.[83–85]

Managing organizational change is problematic largely because human beings are programmed to resist or at least be cautious about change. Change is often perceived as threatening, painful, disruptive and sometimes dangerous; resistance has both cognitive and emotional components. Some of this resistance can be dealt with in formal ways—by training, communicating information, etc.—but emotional responses—anxieties about loss of status, power, influence, fear of risk-taking, etc.—cannot be directly. Instead it is necessary to create a climate in which these concerns can be surfaced, issues and conflicts can be addressed and in which individuals can find reassurance.

Organizational development (OD) is a generic term to describe the set of practices and methodologies which have evolved around introducing planned organizational change.[86] OD involved diagnosis and intervention; this is often effected through internal or external change agents who act as catalysts or facilitators of change. There is also a wide variety of tools and techniques for dealing with particular problems—for example, conflict resolution, training in creativity, participation and building commitment. One of the challenges for innovation management in the future is likely to be making more widespread and effective use of OD approaches to manage the continuing development and adaptation of organizations.

Amongst routines associated with effective change management are:

1. *Establish a clear change management strategy at top level* (a process which will itself involve considerable challenge and conflict in order to get real agreement and commitment to a common set of goals). Once this has been done, the next stage is to communicate this shared vision to the rest of the organization—essentially this will involve a cascade process down through the organization during which opportunities are set up for others to challenge and take 'ownership' of the same shared vision.

2. *Communication*—probably the single most effective key to successful implementation but requires a major effort if it is to succeed. It must be active, not passive, open (rather than allowing information to flow on a 'need-to-know' basis), timely (in advance of change—the informal communication network will disseminate this information anyway and a slow formal system will undermine credibility), and above all, two-way in operation. Unless there are channels through which people can express their responses and ideas and voice their concerns then no amount of top-down communication will succeed in generating commitment. Other features in communication which contribute to success are the use of multiple media—videos, presentations, face-to-face sessions—in addition to traditional memos and notice boards, and the holding of communication meetings on company time—itself a clear expression of commitment to the project.

3. *Early involvement*—managers often resist the idea of participation since it appears to add considerably to the time taken to reach a decision or to get something done. But there are two important benefits to allowing participation and allowing it to take place as early as possible in the change process. The first is that without it—even if attempts have been made to consult or to inform—people will not develop a sense of 'ownership' of the project or commitment to it—and may express their lack of involvement later in various forms of resistance. And the second is that involvement and encouragement of participation can make significant improvements in the overall project design.

4. *Create an open climate*, in which individual anxieties and concerns can be expressed and the ideas and knowledge held within the organization can be used to positive effect. Once again, this involves generating a sense of 'ownership' of the project and commitment to the shared goals of the whole organization—rather than an 'us and them' climate.

5. *Set clear targets*—with major change programmes it is especially important to set clear targets for which people can aim. People need feedback about their performance and the establishment of clear milestones and goals is an important way of providing this. In addition, one of the key features in successful organizational development is to create a climate of continuous improvement in which the achievement of one goal is rewarded but is also accompanied by the setting of the next.

   In their work on implementation strategies for advanced manufacturing technology (AMT), Smith and Tranfield identify two discrete phases of target setting—the 'sprint' and the 'performance ratchet'. In the former all the efforts of the organization are focused on achieving a major target—for example, reducing defects by 50% or increasing output by 30%—and everything is directed towards achieving that clear goal. Such a sprint has enormous power in harnessing a widely differing staff to a single goal and brings about the development of a new working culture. But the momentum of such a sprint cannot be maintained for ever and a second mechanism is needed to ensure that the gains made are consolidated.[87]

6. *Invest in training*. Traditionally training is seen as a necessary evil, a cost which must be borne in order that people will be able to push the correct buttons to work a particular new piece of equipment. Successful organizational change depends on viewing training far more as an *investment* in developing not only specific skills but also in creating an alternative type of organization—one which understands why changes are happening and one which is capable of managing some of the behavioural processes involved in change. This requires a substantial increase in the resources devoted to training, extending them to cover broader kinds of input, much of this devoted to individual development.

9.6 Enabling Learning

The final stage in any innovation process should be one of review of the completed project and an attempt to capture learning from the experience. This is an optional stage and many organizations fail to carry out any kind of review, simply moving on to the next project and running the risk of repeating mistakes made in previous projects. Others do operate some form of structured review or post-project audit; however, this does not of itself guarantee learning since emphasis may be more on avoiding blame and trying to cover up mistakes.

Effective learning, both in terms of accumulating technological knowledge and knowledge about how to manage the innovation process, requires a commitment to open and informed review. Developing such learning abilities is now seen as a critical role for strategic management.[76, 88, 89] We discuss some of the mechanisms which facilitate building a 'learning organization' in Chapter 11.

As we saw in Chapter 3, firms which exhibit competitive advantage—the ability to win and to do so continuously—demonstrate 'timely responsiveness and rapid product innovation, coupled with the management capability to effectively co-ordinate and redeploy internal and external competencies'.[90] They possess 'dynamic capability' and developing processes within the organization to enable this is the key. The lack of such capability can explain many failures, even amongst large and well-established organizations. For example, the:

- Failure to recognize or capitalize on new ideas which conflict with an established knowledge set—the 'not invented here' problem[91]
- Problem of being too close to existing customers and meeting their needs too well—and not being able to move into new technological fields early enough[92]
- Problem of adopting new technology—following technological fashions—without an underlying strategic rationale[71]
- Problem of lack of codification of tacit knowledge[46]

The costs of not managing learning—of lacking the dynamic capability—are high. So we need to look hard at the ways in which organizations can learn—and learn to learn in conscious and strategic fashion. This is why routines play such an important role in managing innovation—they represent the firm-specific patterns of behaviours which enable a firm to solve particular problems.[93] In other words, they embody what an organization (and the individuals within it) has learned about how to learn.

We should also recognize the problem of unlearning. Not only is learning to learn a matter of acquiring and reinforcing new patterns of behaviour—it is often about forgetting old ones. Letting go in this way is by no means easy, and there is a strong tendency to return to the status quo or equilibrium position—which helps account for the well-known 'not invented here' problem in innovation.

All of this argues strongly that firms should undertake some form of review of innovation projects in order to help them develop both technological and managerial capability. One way of representing the learning process which can take place in organizations is to use a simple model of a learning cycle. Here learning is seen as requiring:

1. Structured and challenging reflection on the process—what happened, what worked well, what went wrong, etc.
2. Conceptualizing—capturing and codifying the lessons learned into frameworks and eventually procedures to build on lessons learned.
3. Experimentation—the willingness to try and manage things differently next time, to see if the lessons learned are valid.
4. Honest capture of experience (even if this has been a costly failure) so we have raw material on which to reflect.

Effective learning from and about technology management depends on establishing a learning cycle around these themes. To help with the process there is a variety of tools and mechanisms, and Table 9.5 gives some examples.

TABLE 9.5   Examples of tools to support learning in innovation projects.

Enabling routine	Characteristics
Post-project reviews	On the positive side, PPRs work well when there is a structured framework against which to examine the project, exploring the degree to which objectives were met, the things which went well and those which could be improved, the specific learning points raised and the ways in which they can be captured and codified into procedures which will move the organization forward in terms of managing technology in future. But such reviews depend on establishing a climate in which people can honestly and objectively explore issues which the project raises. For example, if things have gone badly the natural tendency is to cover up mistakes or try and pass the blame around. Meetings can often degenerate into critical sessions with little being captured or codified for use in future projects. The other weakness of PPRs is that they are not so useful for the smaller-scale, regular incremental change which make up a part of technology management. They are best suited to distinct projects—for example developing a new product or service or implementing a new process. A checklist for successful PPRs would include:

- Ensure involvement of all perspectives
- Collect relevant facts and work with these, not opinions
- Ensure objective, non-judgemental/blame-free environment
- Employ a facilitator to manage the process of the review
- Ensure some capture of knowledge for next time—what actions could we take and how can we systematically ensure they take place?
- Define measures to detect and monitor progress

Policies and procedures

Devising procedures is a powerful way of capturing knowledge and formalizing it—moving it from 'rules of thumb' and personal heuristics to something which can be shared and communicated to others.

They can be simple—for example, in many Japanese plants working on 'total productive maintenance' programmes, operators are encouraged to document the operating sequence for their machinery. This is usually a step-by-step guide, often illustrated with photographs and containing information about 'know-why' as well as 'know-how'. This information is usually contained on a single sheet of paper and displayed next to the machine. It is constantly being revised as a result of continuous improvement activities, but it represents the formalization of all the little tricks and ideas which the operators have come up with to make that particular step in the process more effective.

On a larger scale, capturing knowledge into procedures also provides a structured framework within which to operate more effectively. Increasingly organizations are being required by outside agencies and customers to document their processes and how they are managed, controlled and improved—for example, in the quality area under ISO 9000, in the environmental area under ISO 14000 and in an increasing number of customer/supplier initiatives such as Ford's QS9000.

Once again there are strengths and weaknesses in using procedures as a way of capturing learning. On the plus side there is much value in systematically trying to reflect on and capture knowledge derived from experience—it is the essence of the learning cycle. But it only works if there is commitment to learning and a belief in the value of the procedures and their subsequent use. Otherwise the organization simply creates procedures which people know about but do not always observe or use. There is also the risk that, having established procedures, the organization then becomes resistant to changing them—in other words, it blocks out further learning opportunities

Benchmarking

Benchmarking is the general name given to a range of techniques which involve comparisons between two examples of the same process so as to provide opportunities for learning. Benchmarking can, for example, be used to compare how different companies manage the product development processes; where one is faster than the other there are learning opportunities in trying to understand how they achieve this. Benchmarking works in two ways to facilitate learning. First, it provides a powerful motivator since comparison often highlights gaps which—if they are not closed—might well lead to problems in competitiveness later. And second, it provides a structured way of looking at new concepts and ideas. It can take several forms:

- Between similar activities within the same organization
- Between similar activities in different divisions of a large organization
- Between similar activities in different firms within a sector
- Between similar activities in different firms and sectors

The last group is often the most challenging since it brings completely new perspectives. By looking at, for example, how a supermarket manages its supply chain a manufacturer can gain new insights into logistics. By looking at how an engineering shop can rapidly set up and change over between different products can help a hospital use its expensive operating theatres more effectively.

Benchmarking offers a structured methodology for learning. It is increasingly being used by external agencies who see it as a lever with which to motivate particularly smaller enterprises to learn and change. Examples here include the PROBE approach and the National Benchmarking Index, both being used in the UK and supported by the Department of Trade and Industry.

The potential of benchmarking is both in the early stages of the technology management process—as part of the scanning for signals for change—and also at the end, as a way of assessing whether the process could be managed better

Auditing

Related to benchmarking, auditing offers another structured way of reflecting on the process of technological change and how it has been/is being managed. The analogy can be drawn with financial auditing where the health of the company and its various operations can be seen through auditing its books. The principle is simple; using what we know about successful and unsuccessful innovation and the conditions which bring it about, we can construct a checklist of questions to ask of the organization. We can then score its performance against some model of 'best practice' and identify where things could be improved. We can also use real examples and factual data to support the scores we allocate. (An example of a simple innovation audit is given in Chapter 13.)

Learning with others

One approach to capturing learning in structured fashion is to work with other organizations or individuals, sharing perspectives and challenging complacent views and ideas. Shared learning works on all stages of the learning cycle and provides an extra source of traction in moving around it successfully. For example, it brings together different backgrounds and consequently different concepts and theories which may offer fresh insights. It offers the chance for shared or multiple experiments—'let's try something different this time . . .'—and it provides a supportive but challenging focus for reflection. It is harder to avoid confronting difficult but important issues if there is a group of peers pushing and challenging for answers.

One of the main attributes of learning networks is that they help maintain the learning cycle by inputs at all its key stages—challenging reflection, introduction of new concepts, shared experimentation and exchange of different experiences.

Learning networks of this kind can take many forms. Sometimes they are informal groupings of managers who get together to share experiences and discuss possible solutions on a regular basis. Increasingly such networks are taking on a more structured form, aimed at helping capture and share learning around particular themes or amongst particular groups[94, 95]

Further Reading

Some of the basic approaches to scanning the competitive environment can be found in marketing texts such as Kotler,[11] whilst Whiston provides a comprehensive guide to technological forecasting.[2] Some of the tools of forecasting are described well in ref. 3 and the theme of future scanning is picked up in books by Schwartz and de Geus.[96, 97] There are a number of prescriptive methodologies for product and process innovation management, including Cooper's work on product innovation,[98] and Robert[99] and Brown[100] provide a similar perspective on process innovation. Terry Hill's description of change in a fictitious organization in *The Strategy Quest* provides a good feel for the implementation process,[77] this echoes the popular work *The Goal* by Goldratt and Cox in describing change in a manufacturing enterprise.[101]

A good overview of the implementation issues can be found in Rhodes and Wield *Implementing New Technologies*[102] and specific examples of implementation of different technologies—e.g. Internet and IT systems[103–105]—and in different contexts—for example, in social services.[106] Project management texts include a number of standard reference works and handbooks[107, 108] whilst the management of specific types of projects—e.g. software development or large-scale complex projects—are covered in refs 87, 109 and 110. Project teams and the people issues are dealt with in Demarco's book and in a number of other sources.[111, 112] Change management is a broad field with many prescriptive texts; Burnes provides a good overview of the key themes whilst Smith and Tranfield offer some case study-based examples.[87, 113] A number of books offer perspectives drawn from a long research tradition in organizational development,[114–118] two recent practical guides being Senge's *The Dance of Change* and Sharke's *The Change Management Toolkit*. Finally, there are some popular books which attempt to extract lessons from companies which have undergone major transformations.[119]

References

1   'Amazon, the software company', in *The Economist*, 14 October 2000, p. 92.

2   Whiston, T. (1979) *The Uses and Abuses of Forecasting*. Macmillan, London.

3   Millett, S. and E. Honton (1991) *A Manager's Guide to Technology Forecasting and Strategy Analysis Methods*. Battelle Press, Columbus, Ohio.

4   Guiltinan, J. and G. Paul (1991) *Marketing Management; Strategies and programs*, 4th edn. McGraw-Hill, New York.

5   Carter, C. and B. Williams (1957) *Industry and Technical Progress*. Oxford University Press, Oxford:.

6   Rothwell, R. (1992) 'Successful industrial innovation: critical success factors for the 1990s'. *R&D Management*, **22** (3), 221–239.

7   Bessant, J. (1999) 'The rise and fall of "Supernet": A case study of technology transfer policy for smaller firms', *Research Policy*, **28** (6), 601–614.

8   Urban, G., J. Hauser and N. Dholakia (1987) *Essentials of New Product Management*. Prentice-Hall, Englewood Cliffs, NJ.

9   Allen, T. (1987) *Managing the Flow of Technology*. MIT Press, Cambridge, Mass.

10 Bessant, H. and D. Francis (1999) 'Implementing learning networks', *Technovation*, **19** (6/7), 373–383.

11 Kotler, P. (1976) *Marketing Management, Analysis, Planning and Control*, 3rd edn. Prentice-Hall, Englewood Cliffs, NJ.

12 Miles, I. *et al.* (1988) *Information Horizons*. Edward Elgar, London.

13 Camp, R. (1989) *Benchmarking—the Search for Industry Best Practices That Lead to Superior Performance*. Quality Press, Milwaukee, Wis.

14 Kaplinsky, R., F. den Hertog and B. Coriat (1995) *Europe's Next Step*. Frank Cass, London.

15 Von Hippel, E. (1988) *The Sources of Innovation*. MIT Press, Cambridge, Mass.

16 Herstatt, C. and E. von Hippel (1992) 'Developing new product concepts via the lead user method', *Journal of Product Innovation Management*, **9** (3), 213–221.

17 Treacy, M. and F. Wiersema (1995) *The Discipline of Market Leaders*. Addison-Wesley, Reading, Mass.

18 Shillito, M. (1994) *Advanced QFD: Linking technology to market and company needs.* John Wiley, New York.

19 Hauser, J. and D. Clausing (1988) 'The house of quality', *Harvard Business Review,* May–June, 63–73.

20 Cooper, R. and E. Kleinschmidt (1990) *New Products: The key factors in success.* American Marketing Association, Chicago.

21 Carson, J. (1989) *Innovation: A battleplan for the 1990s.* Gower, Aldershot.

22 Hill, T. (1993), *Manufacturing Strategy,* 2nd edn. Macmillan, London, 230 pp.

23 Gregory, M. and K. Platts (1988), *Competitive Manufacturing,* IFS Publications, Kempston, on behalf of the Department of Trade and Industry, London.

24 Bessant, J. (1997) 'Developing technology capability through manufacturing strategy'. *International Journal of Technology Management,* **14** (2/3/4), 177–195.

25 DTI (1998) *Making It Fit: Guide to developing strategic manufacturing.* UK Department of Trade and Industry, London.

26 Gupta, A. (1994) 'Developing powerful technology and product concepts', in Souder, W. and Sherman, J. (eds), *Managing new technology development.* McGraw-Hill, New York.

27 Cooper, R. (1999) 'The invisible success factors in product innovation', *Journal of Product Innovation Management,* **16** (2).

28 Davenport, T. (1992) *Process innovation: Re-engineering work through information technology.* Harvard University Press, Boston, Mass., 326 pp.

29 Wheelwright, S. and K. Clark (1992) *Revolutionising Product Development.* Free Press, New York.

30 Mumford, E. (1979) *Designing Human Systems.* Manchester Business School Press, Manchester.

31 Bessant, J. and J. Buckingham (1993) 'Organizational learning for effective use of CAPM', *British Journal of Management,* **4** (4), 219–234.

32 Bessant, J. *et al.* (1999) *Using Supply Chains to Transfer Best Practice—Case Studies and Final Report.* Report to Department of Trade and Industry, London.

33 Hines, P. *et al.* (1999) *Value Stream Management: The development of lean supply chains.* Financial Times Management, London.

34 Rich, N. and P. Hines (1997) 'Supply chain management and time-based competition: the role of the supplier association', *International Journal of Physical Distribution and Logistics Management,* **27** (3/4), 210–225.

35 Rothwell, R. and P. Gardiner (1983) 'Tough customers, good design', *Design Studies,* **4** (3), 161–169.

36 Legge, K. *et al.* (eds) (1991) *Case Studies in Information Technology, People and Organizations.* Blackwell, Oxford.

37 Crawford, C. and C. Di Bennedeto (1999) *New Products Management.* Irwin, Homewood, Ill.

38 UNIDO (1995) *Technology Transfer Management.* United Nations Industrial Development Organization, Vienna.

39 Saad, M. (1996) 'Development of learning capabilities via the transfer of advanced manufacturing technology: the case of two Algerian firms', *Science, Technology and Development,* **14** (1), 21–35.

40 Burrows, A. (1987) *The Development of CNC Machine Tools in South Korea.* Ph.D. thesis, University of Edinburgh.

41 Menon, M. *et al.* (1984) *Technological Change: Enhancing the benefits.* Commonwealth Secretariat, London.

42 Dodgson, M. (1993) *Technological Collaboration in Industry.* Routledge, London.

43 Lamming, R. (1993) *Beyond Partnership.* Prentice-Hall, London.

44 Kaplinsky, R., J. Bessant and R. Lamming (1999) *Using Supply Chains to Diffuse 'Best Practice'.* Centre for Research in Innovation Management, Brighton.

45 Teece, D., G. Pisano *et al.* (1992) *Dynamic Capabilities and Strategic Management.* University of Berkeley, Calif.

46 Nonaka, I. (1991) 'The knowledge creating company', *Harvard Business Review,* Nov.–Dec., 96–104.

47   Bohn, R. (1994) 'Measuring and managing technological knowledge', *Sloan Management Review,* Fall, 61–73.

48   Bessant, J. (1985) 'Microelectronics in textile machinery', in Bhalla, A. and James, D. (eds), *Blending of New and Traditional Technologies.* Tycooly International, Dublin.

49   Cooper, R. (1994) 'Third-generation new product processes', *Journal of Product Innovation Management,* **11** (1), 3–14.

50   Thomas, R. (1993) *New Product Development: Managing and forecasting for strategic success.* John Wiley, New York.

51   Bessant, J. and D. Francis (1997) 'Implementing the new product development process', *Technovation,* **17** (4), 189–197.

52   Lawrence, P. and J. Lorsch (1967) *Organization and Environment.* Harvard University Press, Cambridge, Mass.

53   Cooper, R. *et al.* (1994) 'What distinguishes the top performing new products in financial services?', *Journal of Product Innovation Management,* **11** (4), 281–300.

54   Edgett, S. and S. Jones (1991) 'New product development in the financial service industry', *Journal of Marketing Management,* **7**, 271–284.

55   Pisano, G. (1996) The Development Factory: Unlocking the potential of process innovation. Harvard Business School Press, Boston, Mass.

56   Foxall, G. (1987) 'Strategic implications of user-initiated innovation', in Rothwell, R. and Bessant, J. (eds), *Innovation, Adaptation and Growth,* Elsevier, Amsterdam.

57   De Benedetto, C. (1994) 'Defining markets and users for new technologies', in Souder, W. and Sherman, J. (eds), *Managing New Technology Development.* McGraw-Hill, New York.

58   Stalk, G. and T. Hout (1990) *Competing against Time: How time-based competition is reshaping global markets.* Free Press, New York.

59   Bessant, J. and R. Lamming (1988) 'Design for efficient manufacturing', in Wild, R. (ed.), *International Handbook of Operations Management.* Cassell, London.

60   'Firm thrives as Japanese know-how brings startling results', in *Financial Times,* April 7, 1990, London, p. 6.

61   Cooper, R. (1988) 'The new product process: a decision guide for management', *Journal of Marketing Management,* **3** (3), 238–255.

62   Kessler, E. and A. Chakrabart (1996) 'Innovation speed: a conceptual model of context, antecdents and outcomes', *Academy of Management Journal,* **21** (4), 1143–1191.

63   Jelinek, M. and J. Litterer (1994) 'Organizing for technology and innovation', in Souder, W. and Sherman, J. (eds), *Managing New Technology Development.* McGraw-Hill, New York.

64   Walton, M. (1997) *Car: A drama of the American workplace.* Norton, New York.

65   Groves, A. (1996) *Only the Paranoid Survive.* Bantam Books, New York.

66   Souder, W. and J. Sherman (eds) (1994) *Managing New Technology Development.* McGraw-Hill, New York.

67   Whitney, J. (1988) 'Manufacturing by design', *Harvard Business Review,* July–Aug., 83–91.

68   Tidd, J. and K. Bodley (2001) 'The effects of project novelty on the new product development process', *R&D Management* (submitted).

69   Calantone, R. and M. Monoya (1994) 'Product launch and follow-on', in Souder, W. and Sherman, J. (eds), *Managing New Technology Development.* McGraw-Hill, New York.

70   Jaikumar, R. (1985) 'Post-industrial manufacturing', *Harvard Business Review,* Aug.–Sept.

71   Bessant, J. (1991) *Managing Advanced Manufacturing Technology: The challenge of the fifth wave.* NCC-Blackwell, Oxford/Manchester.

72   Schonberger, R. (1992) *Japanese Manufacturing Techniques: Nine hidden lessons in simplicity.* Free Press, New York.

73   Ettlie, J. (1988) *Taking Charge of Manufacturing.* Jossey-Bass, San Francisco.

74   Kearney, A. T. (1989) *Computer-integrated Manufacturing—Competitive Advantage or Technological Dead-end?,* A. T. Kearney Consultants, London.

75   Kearney, A. T. (1992) 'Total quality—time to take off the rose-tinted spectacles', *TQM Magazine.*

76 Hayes, R., S. Wheelwright and K. Clark (1998) *Dynamic Manufacturing: Creating the learning organization*. Free Press, New York.

77 Hill, T. (1995) *The Strategy Quest*. Pitman, London.

78 Brown, S. (2000) *Manufacturing the Future*. Prentice-Hall, London.

79 Schroeder, D. and A. Robinson (1991) 'America's most successful export to Japan—continuous improvement programmes', *Sloan Management Review*, **32** (3), 67–81.

80 Boer, H. *et al.* (1999) *CI Changes: From suggestion box to the learning organization*. Ashgate, Aldershot.

81 Voss, C. (1986) 'Implementation of advanced manufacturing technology', in Voss, C. (ed.), *Managing Advanced Manufacturing Technology*. IFS Publications, Kempston.

82 Leonard-Barton, D. (1988) 'Implementation as mutual adaptation of technology and organization', *Research Policy*, **17**, 251–267.

83 Majchrzak, A. (1988) *The Human Side of Factory Automation*. Jossey-Bass, San Francisco.

84 McLoughlin, I. and J. Clark (1994) *Technological Change at Work*, 2nd edn. Open University Press, Milton Keynes.

85 Clark, J. (1995) *Managing Innovation and Change: People, technology and strategy*. Sage, London.

86 French, W. and C. Bell (1995) *Organizational Development; Behavioural science interventions for organization improvement*, 4th edn. Prentice-Hall, Englewood Cliffs, NJ.

87 Smith, S. and D. Tranfield (1990) *Managing Change*. IFS Publications, Kempston.

88 Leonard-Barton, D. (1992) 'The organization as learning laboratory'. *Sloan Management Review*, **34** (1), 23–38.

89 Gann, D. and A. Salter (1998) 'Learning and innovation management in project-based, service enhanced firms', *International Journal of Innovation Management*, **2** (4), 431–454.

90 Teece, D. and G. Pisano (1994) 'The dynamic capabilities of firms: an introduction', *Industrial and Corporate Change*, **3** (3), 537–555.

91 Utterback, J. (1994) *Mastering the Dynamics of Innovation*. Harvard Business School Press, Boston, Mass., 256 pp.

92 Christenson, C. (1997) *The innovator's dilemma*. Harvard Business School Press, Cambridge, Mass.

93 Nelson, R. and S. Winter (1982) *An Evolutionary Theory of Economic Change*. Harvard University Press, Cambridge, Mass.

94 Holti, R. and S. Whittle (1998) *Guide to Developing Effective Learning Networks in Construction*. CIRIA/Tavistock Institute of Human Relations, London.

95 Bessant, J. and G. Tsekouras (2000) 'Developing learning networks', *A.I. and Society*, **15** (2), 82–98.

96 De Geus, A. (1996) *The Living Company*. Harvard Business School Press, Boston, Mass.

97 Schwartz, P. (1996) *The Art of the Long View: Planning for the future in an uncertain world*. Doubleday, New York.

98 Cooper, R. (1993) *Winning at New Products*. Kogan Page, London.

99 Robert, M. (1995) *Product Innovation Strategy—pure and simple*. McGraw-Hill, New York.

100 Brown, S., *et al.* (2000) *Strategic Operations Management*. Butterworth Heinemann, Oxford.

101 Goldratt, E. and J. Cox (1993) *The goal*. Gower Publishing, Aldershot.

102 Rhodes, E. and D. Wield (1994) *Implementing New Technologies*. Basil Blackwell, Oxford.

103 Clements, R. (1999) *IS Manager's Guide to Implementing and Managing Internet Technology*. Prentice-Hall, Englewood Cliffs, NJ.

104 Goetsch, D. and S. Davis (1995) *Implementing Total Quality*. Prentice-Hall, Englewood Cliffs, NJ.

105 Grover, V. and S. Jeong (1995) 'The implementation of business process re-engineering', *Journal of Management Information Systems*, **12** (1), 109–144.

106 Schoech, D. (1999) *Human Services Technology: Understanding, designing and implementing computer and internet application in social services*. Haworth, New York.

107 Lock, D. (1997) *Project Management*. Prentice-Hall, Englewood Cliffs, NJ.

108 Dinsmore, P. (ed.) (1993) *The AMA Handbook of Project Management*. AMACOM, New York.

109 Rea, K. and B. Lientz (1998) *Breakthrough Technology Project Management*. Academic Press, New York.

110 Rush, H., T. Brady and M. Hobday (1997) *Learning between Projects in Complex Systems*. Centre for the Study of Complex Systems, CENTRIM, University of Brighton.

111 DeMarco, T. and T. Lister (1999) *Peopleware: Productive projects and teams*. Dorset House, New York.

112 Kharbanda, O. and M. Stallworthy (1990) *Project Teams*. NCC-Blackwell, Manchester.

113 Burnes, B. (1992) *Managing Change*. Pitman, London.

114 Bennis, W. (2000) *Managing the Dream: Reflections on leadership and change*. Perseus Books, New York.

115 Senge, P. (1999) *The Dance of Change: Mastering the twelve challenges to change in a learning organization*. Doubleday, New York.

116 Sharke, G. (1999) *The Change Management Toolkit*. WinHope Press, New York.

117 Pritchard, W. and R. Beckhard (eds) (1992) *Changing the Essence: The art of creating and leading fundamental change in organizations*. Jossey Bass, San Francisco.

118 Hesselbein, F., M. Goldsmith and R. Beckhard (eds) (1997) *Organization of the Future*, Jossey-Bass/The Drucker Foundation, San Francisco.

119 Tichy, N. and S. Sherman (1999) *Control your Destiny or Someone Else Will; Lessons in mastering change*. Harper Business, New York

Chapter 10

LEARNING THROUGH CORPORATE VENTURES

In Chapter 9 we examined the processes necessary to develop new products and processes within the existing corporate environment, based on core competencies identified in Chapter 6. In this chapter we explore how firms develop technologies, products and processes outside their existing core competencies. Specifically, we will discuss the role of corporate ventures in the development of new technologies, products and businesses. The key questions are:

- What is the purpose of the corporate venture?
- What is the best way to structure, manage and grow a corporate venture?
- What is the profile of a typical corporate entrepreneur?
- How do technologies and markets affect the opportunities for entrepreneurship?

10.1 What is a Corporate Venture?

An organization that seeks to apply its competencies to a new market or business, or needs to acquire new competencies to respond to potentially disruptive innovation has three options:[1]

1. Attempt to change the competencies and culture within the existing organizational structure and processes.
2. Acquire an organization that has the necessary competencies.
3. Develop a separate organization within itself, with different structures, processes and cultures.

The first option, the objective of change management, is time-consuming and the outcomes uncertain. Some approaches to change management were discussed in

Chapter 9. The second option requires a suitable acquisition to exist, is expensive and the outcomes variable. In most cases the organization acquired takes time to become integrated, and in many cases key personnel are lost in the process.[2] The third option is usually called corporate venturing or internal corporate venturing to distinguish it from venturing which takes the form of investments in smaller companies. If managed effectively, a corporate venture has the resources of a large organization and the entrepreneurial benefits of a small one.

A corporate venture differs from conventional R&D and product development activities in its objectives and organization (see Box 10.1). The former seek to exploit existing technological and market competencies, whereas the primary function of a new venture is to learn new competencies. In practice the distinction may be less clear. For example, technical staff at 3M are expected to use 15% of their time exploring ideas outside their existing projects, and at the corporate level this translates into a target of at least 25% of sales from products less than five years old. In Chapter 6 we reviewed the arguments for different structures for, and location of, R&D activities. The most effective organization and management of a new venture will depend on two dimensions: the strategic importance of the venture for corporate development, and its proximity to the core technologies and business.[3]

Typically, top management has risen through the ranks of the organization, and therefore will be familiar with the evaluation of proposals related to the existing lines of business. However, by definition, new venture proposals are likely to require assessment of new technologies and/or markets. The following checklist can be used to assess the strategic importance of a new venture:

- Would the venture maintain our capacity to compete in new areas?
- Would it help create new defensible niches?
- Would it help identify where not to go?
- To what extent could it put the firm at risk?
- How and when could the firm exit from the venture?

Assessment of the second dimension, the proximity to existing skills and capabilities, is more difficult. On the one hand, a new venture may be driven by newly developed skills and capabilities, but on the other a new venture may drive the development of new skills and capabilities. The former is consistent with an 'incremental' strategy in which diversification is a consequence of evolution, the latter with a 'rational' strategy which begins with the identification of new market opportunity. The relative merits and implications of these contrasting approaches were discussed in detail in Chapter 3.

Whatever the primary motive for establishing a new venture, the proposal should identify potential opportunities for positive synergies across existing technologies, products or markets. A checklist for assessing the proximity of the venture proposal to existing skills and capabilities would include:

- What are the key capabilities required for the venture?
- Where, how and when is the firm going to acquire the capabilities, and at what cost?
- How will these new capabilities affect current capabilities?

BOX 10.1 Matsushita Research Institute Tokyo (MRIT).

Matsushita Research Institute Tokyo (MRIT) blurs the distinction between central research laboratory, venture group and joint venture organization. Matsushita is one of the largest manufacturers of consumer electronics in the world, and ranked in the global top 10 investors in R&D: $3.2bn in 1994. Trade names include Panasonic and Technics.

Matsushita has a more conventional central research facility at its headquarters in Osaka, which employs 230 researchers working on basic research, and a dedicated corporate product development division that employs 3000 researchers. However, MRIT has a different role. MRIT is organized as a separate limited company, wholly owned by Matsushita, which is an unusual structure for a Japanese research organization. It is located in Tokyo and employs almost 250 scientists and engineers. About three-quarters of its funding is from its parent company, and the remainder from research contracts and government projects. It was established to support diversification through the creation and incubation of new technologies and markets. To this end, MRIT has developed a number of new technologies and identified new applications for existing technologies, partly through its own efforts, partly via government programmes, and partly through collaboration with academic and business partners in Japan, Europe and the USA.

MRIT has worked on advanced materials and surface science with Imperial College and Cambridge University in the UK, and on optical computing and neural networks with MIT and the University of California in the USA. MRIT is also a leading participant in the Japanese government's national research programme on micro-machines. None of these programmes has immediate relevance to existing businesses within Matsushita, but MRIT seeks to develop fundamental expertise in such emerging technologies in order to identify and grow future new business opportunities.

- Where else could they be exploited?
- Who else might be able to do this, perhaps better?

Assessment of a new venture along these two dimensions will help determine the organization and management of the venture. In particular, the strategic importance will determine the degree of administrative control required, and the proximity to existing skills and capabilities will determine the degree of operational integration that is desirable. In general, the greater the strategic importance, the stronger the administrative linkages between the corporation and venture. Similarly, the closer the skills and capabilities are to the core activities, the greater the degree of operational integration necessary for reasons of efficiency. Putting the two dimensions together creates a number of different options for the organization and management of a new venture (Figure 10. 1). In this chapter we explore the design and management of internal corporate ventures. Chapter 8 examined the role and management of joint ventures and alliances.

Technology

	Base	Related	Unrelated
Base	Internal Development		Joint Venture
Related		Corporate Venture	
Unrelated	Joint Venture		Acquisition

Market

FIGURE 10.1   Role of corporate venturing. Source: Adapted from Burgleman (1984, p. 544).[3]

10.2 Reasons for Corporate Venturing

The management structures and processes necessary for routine operations are very different from those required to manage innovation. The pressures of corporate long-range strategic planning on the one hand, and the short-term financial control on the other, combine to produce a corporate environment that favours carefully planned and stable growth based on incremental developments of products and processes:

- Budgeting systems favour short-term returns on incremental improvements
- Production favours efficiency rather than innovation
- Sales and marketing are organized and rewarded on the basis of existing products and services

Such an environment is unlikely to be conducive to radical innovation. An internal corporate venture attempts to exploit the resources of the large corporation, but provide an environment more conducive to radical innovation. A corporate venture is likely to be necessary when a firm attempts to enter a new market or to develop a new technology. The key factors that distinguish a potential new venture from the core business are risk, uncertainty, newness and significance. A corporate venture is a separate organization or system designed to be consistent with the needs of new, high-risk, but potentially high-growth businesses. The term 'intrapreneurship' is sometimes used to describe such entrepreneurial activity within a corporate setting. However, it is not sufficient to promote entrepreneurial behaviour within a large organization. Entrepreneurial behaviour is not an end in itself, but must be directed and translated into desired business outcomes. Entrepreneurial behaviour is not associated with superior organizational performance, unless it is combined with an appropriate strategy in a heterogeneous or uncertain environment.[4] This suggests the need for clear strategic objectives for corporate venturing and appropriate organizational structures and processes to achieve those objectives.

There are a wide range of motives for establishing corporate ventures:[5]

- Exploit underutilized resources
- Introduce pressure on internal suppliers
- Divest non-core activities
- Satisfy managers' ambitions
- Spread the risk and cost of product development
- Combat cyclical demands of mainstream activities
- Grow the business
- Diversify the business
- Develop new technological or market competencies

We will discuss each of these motives in turn, and provide examples. The first three are primarily operational, the remainder primarily strategic.

To Exploit Underutilized Resources in New Ways

This includes both technological and human resources. Typically, a company has two choices where existing resources are underutilized—either to divest and out-source the process or to generate additional contribution from external clients. However, if the company wants to retain direct and in-house control of the tech-nology or personnel it can form an internal venture team to offer the service to external clients. For example, at Cadbury Schweppes the Information Technology Division was extracted from Group Management Services forming a separate business unit to supply the internal needs of the group—Cadbury Limited and Coca-Cola and Schweppes Beverages Limited. With the mechanisms in place for operation as a trading entity ITnet Limited began to seek and develop external clients, who now provide a significant proportion of its revenues.

To Introduce Competitive Pressure on to Internal Suppliers

This is a common motive, given the current fashion for outsourcing and market testing internal services. When a business activity is separated to introduce competitive pressure a choice has to be made—whether the business is to be subjected to the reality of commercial competition, or just to learn from it. If the corporate clients are able to go so far as to withdraw a contract, which is not con-ducive to learning, the business should be sold to allow it to compete for other work. For example, General Motors exposed its dominant supplier Delco to such competitive pressure by requiring it to earn a certain proportion of its sales from external sales.

To Divest Non-core Activities

Much has been written of the benefits of strategic focus, 'getting back to basics', and creating the 'lean' organization–rationalization which prompts the divestment of those activities which can be outsourced. However, this process can threaten the skill diversity required for an ever-changing competitive environment. New ventures can provide a mechanism to release peripheral business activities, but to retain some management control and financial interest.

To Satisfy Managers' Ambitions

As a business activity passes through its life cycle it will require different management styles to bring out the maximum gain. This may mean that the management team responsible for a business area will need to change, whether between conception to growth, growth to maturity or maturity to decline phases. A paradoxical situation often arises because of the changing requirements of a business area: top managers in place who are ambitious and want to see growth and managing businesses which are reaching the limits of that growth. To retain the commitment of such managers the corporation will have to create new opportunities for change or expansion. These managers are not only potential facilitators for venture opportunities, but potential creators of venture opportunities. For example, Intel has long had a venture capital programme that invests in related external new ventures, but in 1998 it established the New Business Initiative to bootstrap new businesses developed by its staff: 'they saw that we were putting a lot of investment into external companies and said that we should be investing in our own ideas . . . our employees kept telling us they wanted to be more entrepreneurial'. The initiative invests only in ventures unrelated to the core microprocessor business, and in 1999 attracted more than 400 proposals, 24 of which are being funded.

To Spread the Risk and Cost of Product Development

Two situations are possible in this case: (1) where the technology or expertise needs to be developed further before it can be applied to the mainstream business or sold to current external markets, or (2) where the volume sales on a product awaiting development must sell to a target greater than the existing customer groups to be financially justified. In both cases the challenge is to understand how to venture outside current served markets. Too often, when the existing customer base is not ready for a product, the research unit will just continue their development and refinement process. If intermediary markets were exploited these could contribute to the financial costs of development, and to the maturing of the final product.

To Combat Cyclical Demands of Mainstream Activities

In response to the problem of cyclical demand Boeing set up two groups, Boeing Technology Services (BTS) and Boeing Associated Products (BAP), specifically with the function of keeping engineering and laboratory resources more fully employed when its own requirements waned between major development programmes. The remit for BTS was 'to sell off excess engineering laboratory capacity without a detrimental impact on schedules or commitments to major Boeing product-line activities'; it has stuck carefully to this charter, and been careful to turn off such activity when the mainstream business requires the expertise. BAP was created to commercially exploit Boeing inventions that are usable beyond their application to products manufactured by Boeing. About 600 invention disclosures are submitted by employees each year, and these are reviewed in terms of their marketability and patentability. Licensing agreements are used to exploit these inventions, 259 agreements are currently active. Beyond the financial benefits to the company and to the employees of this programme it is seen to foster the innovation spirit within the organization.

To Learn About the Process of Venturing

Venturing is a high-risk activity because of the level of uncertainty attached, and one cannot expect to understand the management process as one does for the mainstream business. If a learning exercise is to be undertaken, and a particular activity is to be chosen for this process, it is critical that goals and objectives are set, including a review schedule. This is important not just for the maximum benefit to be extracted but for the individuals who will pioneer that venture. For example, NEES Energy, a subsidiary of New England Electric Systems Inc., was set up to bring financial benefits, but was also expected to provide a laboratory to help the parent company learn about starting new ventures.[6]

Many companies develop hobby-size business activities to provide this 'learning by doing', but seldom is a time limit set on this learning stage, and as a consequence, no decision is formally made for the venture activities to be considered 'proper businesses'. The implications of this practice are to drain the enterprising managers of their enthusiasm and erode the value of potential opportunities.

To Diversify the Business

Whilst the discussion so far has implied that business development would be on a relatively small scale, this need not be the case. Corporate ventures are often formed in an effort to create new businesses in a corporate context, and therefore represent an attempt to grow via diversification. Therefore a decline in the popularity of internal ventures is associated with an emphasis on greater corporate focus and greater efficiency. For example, the identification and re-engineering of *existing* business processes became fashionable in the mid-1990s, but as firms have begun to exhaust the benefits of this approach they are now exploring options for creating *new* businesses. Such diversification may be vertical, that is downstream or upstream of the current process in order to capture a greater proportion of the value added; or horizontal, that is by exploiting existing competencies across additional product markets.

For example, the fossil fuel energy sector has been facing for a long time the threat of extinction—coal, gas, oil reserves being exhausted. The cloud that has hung on the horizon is the collapse of its core business, and the temptation is therefore to diversify into other business areas that will ensure the continued existence of the firm. BP, Elf, Shell, Standard Oil and Total all set up corporate venturing initiatives when oil companies were first experiencing declining margins and an unfavourable world economic climate with diversification as their main objective. These initiatives were primarily exercised through investment in external opportunities, although some have pursued venture opportunities based on internal technologies and expertise.

To Grow the Business

This underlies many of the other motives. As a separate issue to be considered here, there is the drive to achieve growth in a corporate whose primary markets are maturing. For example, the UK water companies have a fully mature customer base, the regions are insular in their operation and the only opportunity for growth is beyond this mainstream and local activity, a situation which is driving their diversification into related and unrelated areas. Two water companies were recently reported to have shown interest in Tarmac's divestment of Econowaste, which could fetch up to £100m. In seeking to grow the business, or make better commercial use of existing expertise, one has to challenge the more normal small scale of response to such initiatives.

Often the push is to analyse new or adapted products, processes or techniques, and relatively little emphasis is put on the expansion of the business considered as a whole. Severn Trent International, in contrast, has been set up with the task of taking Severn Trent Water's core business capabilities in water and waste water management to new international markets. This direct transfer of skills must surely imply less uncertainty than venturing into both new technologies and new markets.

To Develop New Competencies

Growth and diversification are generally based on the exploitation of existing competencies in new product markets, but a corporate venture can also be used as an opportunity for learning new competencies. Organizational learning has four components:[7]

- Knowledge acquisition
- Information interpretation
- Information distribution
- Organizational memory

An organization can acquire knowledge by experimentation, which is a central feature of formal R&D and market research activities. However, different functions and divisions within a firm will develop particular frames of reference and filters based on their experience and responsibilities, and these will affect how they interpret information. Greater organizational learning occurs when more varied interpretations are made, and a corporate venture can better perform this function as it is not confined to the needs of existing technologies or markets.

Similarly, a corporate venture can act as a broker or clearing house for the distribution of information within the firm. In practice, large organizations often do not know what they know. Many firms now have databases and groupware to help store, retrieve and share information, but such systems are often confined to 'hard' data. As a result, functional groups or business units with potentially synergistic information may not be aware of where such information could be applied. Organizational learning occurs when more of an organization's components obtain new knowledge and recognize it as of potential use.

Organizational memory is the process by which knowledge is stored for future use. Such information is stored either in the memories of members of an organization, or in the operating procedures and routines of the organization. The former suffers from all of the shortcomings of human memory, with the additional organizational problem of personnel loss or turnover. Organizational procedures and routines may provide a more robust memory, but difficulty in anticipating future needs means that much non-routine information is never stored in this way. Over time these routines create and are reinforced by artefacts such as organizational structures, procedures and policies which suit existing technologies and markets, but make it difficult to store and retrieve non-routine information. A corporate venture can act as a repository for such knowledge.

Organizational learning is more difficult in conventional product development activities because of the cost and time pressures. For example, there will be a trade-off between reducing the time and cost of development of a specific product, and documenting what has been learnt for future development projects.

In practice, the primary motives for establishing a corporate venture are strategic: to meet strategic goals and long-term growth in the face of maturity in existing markets (Table 10.1). However, personnel issues are also important. Sectorial and national differences exist. In the USA, new ventures are also used to stimulate and develop entrepreneurial management, and in Japan they help provide employment opportunities for managers and staff relocated from the core businesses (Table 10.2). Nonetheless, the primary objectives are strategic and long term, and therefore warrant significant management effort and investment.

10.3 Managing Corporate Ventures

A corporate venture is rarely the result of a spontaneous act or serendipity. Corporate venturing is a process that has to be managed. The management challenge is to create an environment that encourages and supports entrepreneurship, and to identify and support potential entrepreneurs (see Box 10.2). In essence, the venturing process is simple, and consists of identifying an opportunity for a new venture, evaluating that opportunity and subsequently providing

TABLE 10.1   Objectives of corporate venturing in the UK.

Objective	Mean rank*
1. Long-term growth	4.58
2. Diversification	3.50
3. Promote entrepreneurial behaviour	2.68
4. Exploit in-house R&D	2.23
5. Short-term financial returns	2.08
6. Reduce/spread cost of R&D	1.81
7. Survival	1.76

(n = 90). * Scale: 1 = minimum, 5 = maximum importance.
Source: From Withers (1997) *Window on Technology: Corporate venturing in practice.* Withers, London.

TABLE 10.2   Comparison of motives for internal corporate venturing in the USA and Japan.

	US firms (n = 43)	Japanese firms (n = 149)
To meet strategic goals	76	73
Maturity of the base business	70	57
To provide challenges to managers*	46	15
To survive	35	28
To develop future managers*	30	17
To provide employment*	3	24

* Denotes statistically significant difference. Reprinted by permission of Harvard Business School Press. From *Corporate Venturing: Creating new businesses within the firm* by Block, Z. and MacMillan, I. C., NIA, Boston, 1993. Copyright ©1993 by the President and Fellows of Harvard College: all rights reserved.

adequate resources to support the new venture. There are six distinct stages, divided between definition and development.[8]

Definition Stages

1. Establish an environment that encourages the generation of new ideas and the identification of new opportunities, and establish a process for managing entrepreneurial activity.
1. Select and evaluate opportunities for new ventures, and select managers to implement the venturing programme.
3. Develop a business plan for the new venture, decide the best location and organization of the venture and begin operations.

Development Stages

4. Monitor the development of the venture and venturing process.
5. Champion the new venture as it grows and becomes institutionalized within the corporation.
6. Learn from experience in order to improve the overall venturing process.

BOX 10.2 Corporate venturing at Nortel Networks.

Nortel Networks is a leader in a high-growth, high-technology sector, and around a quarter of all its staff are in R&D, but it recognizes that it is extremely difficult to initiate new businesses outside the existing divisions. Therefore in December 1996 it created the Business Ventures Programme (BVP) to help to overcome some of the structural shortcomings of the existing organization, and identify and nurture new business ventures outside the established lines of business: 'the basic deal we're offering employees is an extremely exciting one. What we're saying is "come up with a good business proposal and we'll fund and support it. If we believe your business proposal is viable, we'll provide you with the wherewithal to realize your dreams".' The BVP provides:

- Guidance in developing a business proposal
- Assistance in obtaining approval from the Board
- An incubation environment for start-ups
- Transition support for longer-term development

The BVP selects the most promising venture proposals which are then presented jointly by the BVP and employee(s) to the Advisory Board. The Advisory Board applies business and financial criteria in its decision whether to accept, reject or seek further development, and if accepted the most appropriate executive sponsor, structure and level of funding. The BVP then helps to incubate the new venture, including staff and resources, objectives and critical milestones. If successful, the BVP then assists the venture to migrate into an existing business division, if appropriate, or creates a new line or business or spin-off company: 'the programme is designed to be flexible. Among the factors determining whether or not a venture will become a separate company are the availability of key resources within Nortel, and the suitability of Nortel's existing distribution channels . . . Nortel is not in this programme to retain 100% control of all ventures. The key motivators are to grow equity by maximizing return on investment, to pursue business opportunities that would otherwise be missed, and to increase employee satisfaction.'

In 1997 the BVP attracted 112 business proposals, and given the staff and financial resources available aimed to fund up to five new ventures. The main problems experienced have been the reaction of managers in established lines of business to proposals outside their own line of: 'At the executive council level, which represents all lines of business, there is a lot of support . . . where it breaks down in terms of support is more in the political infrastructure, the middle to low management executive level where they feel threatened by it . . . the first stage of our marketing plan is just titled "overcoming internal barriers". That is the single biggest thing we've had to break through.' Initially, there was also a problem capturing the experience of ventures that failed to be commercialized: 'failures were typically swept under the rock, nobody really talked about them . . . that is changing now and the focus is on celebrating our failures as well as our successes, knowing that we have learned a lot more from failure than we do from success. Start-up venture experience is in high demand. Generally, it's the projects that fail, not the people.'

Identification of Corporate Ventures

Creating an environment which is conducive to entrepreneurial activity is the most important, but most difficult stage. Superficial approaches to creating an entrepreneurial culture can be counterproductive. Instead, venturing should be the responsibility of the entire corporation, and top management should demonstrate long-term commitment to venturing by making available sufficient resources and implementing the appropriate processes.

The conceptualization stage consists of the generation of new ideas and identification of opportunities that might form the basis of a new business venture. The interface between R&D and marketing is critical during the conceptualization stage, but the scope of new venture conceptualization is much broader than the conventional activities of the R&D or marketing functions, which understandably are constrained by the needs of existing businesses. At this stage three basic options exist:

1. Rely on R&D personnel to identify new business opportunities based on their technological developments, that is, essentially a 'technology-push' approach.
2. Rely on marketing managers to identify opportunities, and direct the R&D staff into the appropriate development work, essentially a 'market-pull' approach.
3. Encourage marketing and R&D personnel to work together to identify opportunities.

The technology-push approach has been described as being 'first generation R&D', the 'market-pull' strategy as 'second generation' and the close coupling[9] 'third generation', the implication being that firms should progress to close coupling. The issue of strategic positioning was discussed in detail in Chapter 6. In theory, the third option is most desirable as it should encourage the coupling of technological possibilities and market opportunities at the concept stage, before substantial resources are committed to evaluation and development. However, in practice technology push appears to be the dominant strategy. This is because at the conceptualization stage highly specialized technical knowledge is required about what is feasible and what is not, and therefore what the characteristics of the final product are likely to be. Nevertheless, R&D personnel may become locked into a specific technical solution or address the needs of atypical users. Therefore management must ensure that R&D personnel are sufficiently flexible to modify or drop their proposals should technical issues or market requirements dictate.

Drucker identifies a number of sources of ideas and opportunities, and argues that the search process should be systematic rather than relying on serendipity.[10] He suggests seven common sources of opportunities which should be monitored on a routine basis:

- Demographic changes
- New knowledge
- Incongruities (i.e. gaps between expectations and reality)
- Changes in industry or market structure

- Unexpected successes or failures
- Process needs
- Changes in perception

Other sources of ideas include trade shows and exhibitions and trade journals. In the specific case of new business ventures there are four primary sources of ideas:

- The 'bright idea'
- Customers requesting a new product or service
- Internal analysis of a company's competencies and business processes
- Scanning of external opportunities in related technologies, markets or services

Contrary to popular perceptions, the 'bright idea' is the least common and most risky source of new business ventures, because the other sources are more directly stimulated by a market need, technological expertise or both together. These can be the initiative of either someone at operational or managerial level; the former may have difficulties finding an effective champion, whereas the latter may be too powerful, having the influence to force through an idea before it is exhaustively tested. A balance needs to be achieved between screening and championing the proposal. In contrast, a business venture based on a customer request has the highest chance of success as a potential market is to some extent predetermined. However, such ventures are typically based on an adaptation or extension of an existing product or service, and therefore less likely to spawn radical new businesses. These tend to be bottom-up initiatives, and the most difficult problem is to decide how the potential new business relates to the existing business or division. By far the two most promising corporate ventures are the result of systematic scanning of the internal and external environments, a process we advocated in Chapter 2.

Scanning the internal environment   The systematic scanning of the organization involves the search and evaluation of shelved concepts, novel combinations of existing technologies and new applications for existing competencies. This type of activity is sometimes referred to as 'knowledge management', and is based on the notion that large organizations typically do not know what they know, and fail to exploit existing knowledge. For example, Boisot developed the concept of C-space (culture space) to analyse the flow of knowledge within and between organizations.[11] It consists of two dimensions: *codification*, the extent to which information can be easily expressed, and *diffusion*, the extent to which information is shared by a given population. Using this framework he proposes a social learning cycle which involves four stages: scanning, problem-solving, diffusion and adsorption (Figure 10.2).

Knowledge management has now become a staple of the consultancy industry. It is possible to identify two distinct approaches to knowledge management. The first is based on investments in IT, usually based on intranet technology. The second approach is more people and process-based, and attempts to encourage staff to identify, store, share and use information throughout the organization. Research suggests that as in previous cases of process innovation, the benefits of the technology are not fully realized unless the organizational aspects are first

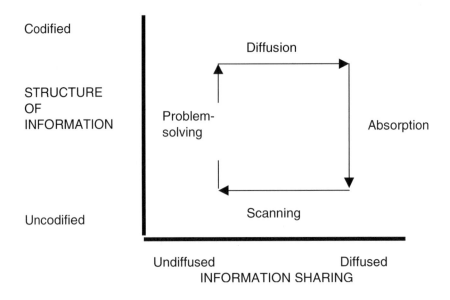

FIGURE 10.2   The social learning curve in culture space.

Source: Griffiths, D. and M. Boisot (2000) 'Are there any competencies out there? Identifying and using technical competencies', in Tidd, J. (ed.), *From Knowledge Management to Strategic Competence*. Imperial College Press, London, pp. 199–228.

dealt with. A wide range of knowledge management strategies are possible (Table 10.3). No single approach will be appropriate in all circumstances, and the optimum strategy will depend on the existing organizational structure, processes and culture, as well as the availability of resources and urgency of action. In an R&D context, Coombs identifies 'knowledge management practices' which include mapping knowledge relationships, managing intellectual property, information management and human resource management.[12] Another approach advocates the use of formally appointed 'knowledge brokers' to systematically scavenge the organization for old or unused ideas, to pass these around the organization and imagine their application in different contexts.[13] For example, Hewlett-Packard created a SpaM group to help identify and share good practice among its 150 business divisions. Before the new group was formed, divisions were unlikely to share information because they often competed for resources and were measured against each other. Similarly, Skandia, a Swedish insurance company active in overseas markets, attempts to identify, encourage and measure its intellectual capital, and has appointed a 'knowledge manager' who is responsible for this. The company has developed a set of indicators that it uses both to manage knowledge internally, and for external financial reporting. However, improved communication is not an end in itself. It is desirable to distinguish between more general experiments to improve the work environment or to make it more democratic, from those practices proven to improve performance. For instance, simply creating a participative climate at work will not generate new

TABLE 10.3   Knowledge management strategies.

Strategy	Characteristics	Requirements	Risks
Ripple	Bottom-up, continuous improvement, e.g. quality management	Process tools, sustained motivation	Isolation from technical excellence
Integration	Integration of functional knowledge within processes, e.g. product development	Improved interfaces, early involvement, overlapping phases	Conformity, co-ordination burden
Embedding	Coupling of systems, products and services, e.g. enterprise resource planning (ERP)	Common information systems and technology, motivation and rewards	Loss of autonomy, system complexity
Bridge	New knowledge by novel combination of existing competencies, e.g. architectural innovations	Common language and objectives	High control needs, technical feasibility, market failure
Transfer	Exploiting existing knowledge in a new context, e.g. related diversification	New market knowledge	Inappropriate technology, customer support and service

Source: Adapted from Friso den Hertog, J. and E. Huizenga (2000) *The Knowledge Enterprise.* Imperial College Press, London.

business ventures, whereas improved internal communications combined with management support and a critical assessment of new business proposals will help create new businesses.[14]

Scanning the external environment   Scanning the external environment consists of searching, filtering and evaluating potential opportunities from outside the organization, including related and emerging technologies, new market and services, which can be exploited by applying or combining with existing competencies. A study of corporate entrepeneurship in 169 companies concluded that 'opportunity recognition, which is a precursor to entrepreneurial behaviour, is often associated with a flash of genius, but in reality is probably more often the end result of a laborious process of environmental scanning'.[15] External scanning can be conducted at various levels. It can be an operational initiative with market- or technology-focused managers becoming more conscious of new developments within their own environments, or a top-driven initiative where venture managers or professional capital firms are used to monitor and invest in potential opportunities. For example, the TRIZ system developed by Genrich Altshuller identifies standard solutions to common technical problems distilled from an analysis of 1.5 million patents, and applies these in different contexts. Many leading companies use the system, including 3M, Rolls-Royce and Motorola.[16] Venture capital firms can help firms to monitor the external environment without distraction, and to take equity stakes in potential partners fairly anonymously. This practice is common in the pharmaceutical industry, where firms use a range of strategies to tap into the knowledge of biotechnology firms, including direct investment, licensing deals and indirect investment through professionally managed venture funds. Direct investments are favoured for technologies of high strategic importance, licensing for process and product developments, and indirect investments for windows on emerging technologies.[17]

Development of Corporate Ventures

Having identified the potential for a new venture, a product champion must convince higher management that the business opportunity is both technically feasible and commercially attractive and therefore justifies development and investment. Potential corporate entrepreneurs face significant political barriers:

- They must establish their legitimacy within the firm by convincing others of the importance and viability of the venture
- They are likely to be short of resources, but will have to compete internally against established and powerful departments and managers
- As advocates of change and innovation, they are likely to face at best organizational indifference, and at worst hostile attacks

To overcome these barriers a potential venture manager must have political and social skills, in addition to a viable business plan. In addition, the product champion must be able to work effectively in a non-programmed and unpredictable environment. This contrasts with much of the R&D conducted in the operating divisions which is likely to be much more sequential and systematic. Therefore a product champion requires dedication, flexibility and luck to manage the transition from product concept to corporate venture, in addition to sound technical and market knowledge. The product champion is likely to require a complementary organizational champion, who is able to relate the potential venture to the strategy and structure of the corporation. A number of key roles must be filled when a new venture is established:[18]

- The technical innovator, who was responsible for the main technological development
- The business innovator or venture manager, who is responsible for the overall progress of the venture
- The product champion, who promotes the venture through the early critical stages
- The executive champion or organizational champion, who acts as a protector and buffer between the corporation and venture
- A high-level executive responsible for evaluating, monitoring and authorizing resources for the venture, but not the operation of specific ventures

A new venture requires two types of skill: the technical knowledge necessary to develop the product, process or knowledge base; and the management expertise necessary to communicate and sell to the markets and parent organization (Table 10.4). The dilemma that has to be resolved in each case is whether to allow and develop technical experts to play a role in selling the product or managing the business, or to place managers above their heads to take the baton on.

To take project managers to venture manager status is often dangerous. Whilst these individuals understand the product fully, they may have difficulties in maximizing the cost/price differential, perhaps not always realizing the commercial value of the product and being less experienced in the negotiation process. It can be equally difficult to identify a manager who can communicate the product characteristics to customers with real needs, relay those needs to the product development team, and communicate and justify venture management needs to the corporate centre.

Assessing the Venture

The most appropriate filter to apply to a potential venture will depend on the motive for venturing. Roberts illustrates the point:

> The best time to detect if a CEO has a strategy or not is to observe the management team at work when trying to evaluate opportunities, especially those somewhat remote from the current business. On these occasions, we noticed that when faced with unfamiliar opportunities, management would put them through a hierarchy of different filters. The ultimate filter was always a fit between the products, customers and markets that the opportunity brought and one key element, or driving force, of the business. This is a clear signal that management had a sound filter for its decision.[19]

TABLE 10.4   Systematic differences between R&D and marketing personnel.

	R&D personnel	Marketing personnel
Work environment		
Structure	Well defined	Ill defined
Methods	Scientific and codified	Ad hoc and intuitive
Data	Systematic and objective	Unsystematic and subjective
Pressures	Internal: How long will it take?	External: How long do we have?
Professional orientation		
Assumptions	Serendipity	Planning
Goals	New ideas: Can it be improved?	Big ideas: Does it work?
Performance criteria	Technical quality	Commercial value
Education and experience	Deep and focused	Broad

Without the type of strategic filters discussed in Chapter 6, managers are forced to rely on narrow financial methods of evaluation, such as potential sales growth, margins or net present value. The seduction to new opportunities is highest when a company is cash rich. For example, as illustrated in Chapter 4, Daimler Benz in the mid-1980s began an acquisition trail of many unrelated businesses, which have subsequently been disposed of. This distraction to top management may also be a contributing factor for Mercedes Benz losing its hold in its home market to BMW. Similarly, Sony and Matsushita have made questionable decisions to diversify into US film production, respectively Columbia and MCA.

In assessing any venture it is essential to specify the purpose and the criteria for success in the new market, business or technology. Ultimately the style of assessment adopted will depend on the size of the potential venture, the abilities of the people who currently understand the product and whether new partners or managers are expected to be introduced following assessment. A plan needs to be written by the managers involved in the venture, in part to test whether they understand the business as well as the technology. It is essential for in-house managers to be fully involved in the market research. The use of market research consultants should be limited to providing a first pass of potential markets. No one can know the product better, especially if it is new, and has niche applications, than the people who have worked on its development, and whose future careers may depend on it.

The purpose and nature of a business plan for a new venture differ from that for established businesses. The main purpose of the venture plan is to establish if and how to conduct the new business, and to attract key personnel and resources. The purpose of a plan for an existing business is to monitor and control performance. The technical and commercial aspects of a new venture plan will have much greater uncertainty than that for existing businesses. There are 10 essential elements of a new venture plan (Table 10.5).

TABLE 10.5   Components of a typical business plan for a new venture.

1. Description of the proposed business, including its objectives and characteristics

2. Strategic relationship between the new business and the parent firm

3. The target markets, including size, trends, reasons for purchase and specific target customers

4. Assessment of the present and anticipated competition

5. Human, physical and financial resources required

6. Financial projections, including assumptions and sensitivity analysis

7. Well-defined milestones and go/no-go conditions

8. Principal risks and how they will be managed

9. Definition of failure, and conditions under which the venture should be terminated

10. Description of the venture's management and compensation required

Every new venture is an industrial experiment, and therefore the experiment must be designed to allow the assumptions and risks to be evaluated. The plan will be based on assumptions concerning the technology, product, market, economy, competition and the business environment, and given the inherent uncertainty of a new venture it is essential that testing of these assumptions is included in the go/no-go criteria. Similarly, contingency plans should be included to minimize any technological, market, management or financial risk.

The main criteria for assessing the business plan for a corporate venture are strategic fit and potential to enhance competitive position. But beyond such basic requirements, there appear to be significant differences between the criteria applied by American and Japanese firms (Table 10.6). American firms typically expect a high return on investment from corporate ventures, and therefore favour technologies that have high potential for premium pricing or rapid growth. Japanese firms appear to favour ventures that use related technologies to create

TABLE 10.6   Criteria for selecting corporate ventures.

	USA (n = 39)	Japan (n = 126)
Strategic fit	4.1	3.9
Competitive advantage	4.0	3.8
Potential return on investment*	3.9	3.6
Existence of market*	3.9	4.4
Potential sales	3.9	3.9
Risk/reward ratio	3.8	3.6
Presence of product champion	3.6	4.0
Synergy	3.5	3.7
Opportunity to create new market*	3.1	3.8
Closeness to present technology*	2.9	3.5
Patentability*	2.3	2.9

new markets. This suggests that American firms view such ventures as opportunities to generate cash for the core business, whereas the Japanese see them as an opportunity to create new businesses. There is relatively little research on corporate venturing in Europe, but the experience of corporate ventures in the UK suggests a pattern closer to that of the American experience.

Following development of an initial plan for the project, milestones for progress assessment should be developed and agreed upon by those responsible for monitoring and managing the venture. Milestones will ideally be a mix of financial and strategic. Strategic milestones can focus managers more on the long-term business direction rather than the (often) short-term financial criteria. Examples of milestones for the initial stages of a venture include: achievement of product development within time stated; product having been demonstrated on at least three sites; a sale to an important customer has been finalized.

10.4 Structures for Corporate Ventures

The choice of location and structure for a new venture will depend on a number of factors, the most fundamental being how close the activities are to the core business. How close a venture's focal activity is to the parent firm's technology, products and markets will determine the learning challenges the venture will face and the most appropriate linkages with the parent. In practice, there is likely to be some trade-off between the desire to optimize learning and the desire to optimize the use of existing resources. The venture will need to acquire resources, know-how and information from the corporate parent, get sufficient attention and commitment, but at the same time be protected politically and allowed optimal access to the target market. Consideration of these sometimes conflicting requirements will determine the best location and structure for the venture.

The classic study by Burgelman and Sayles of six internal ventures within a large American corporation demonstrated the managerial and administrative difficulties of establishing and managing internal ventures.[20] The study confirmed that no single organizational solution is optimal, and that different structures and processes are required in different circumstances. The choice of structure will depend on the level and urgency of the venturing activity, the nature and number of ventures to be established, and the corporate culture and experience. More fundamentally, it will depend on the balance between the desire to learn new competencies and the need to leverage existing competencies (Figure 10.3). For example, in e-business established firms are faced with the decision whether to develop separate businesses to exploit the opportunities, or to fully integrate e-business with the existing business. Neither strategy nor structure appears to be inherently superior, and depends on a consideration of the relatedness of the assets, operations, management and brand.[21] Design options for corporate ventures include:

- Direct integration with existing business
- Integrated business teams
- A dedicated staff function to support efforts company wide
- A separate corporate venturing unit, department or division
- Divestment and spin-off

Each structure will demand different methods of monitoring and management, that is, procedures, reporting mechanisms and accountability. These choices are illustrated by our own study of corporate venturing in the UK, as described in the following sections.

FIGURE 10.3   The structure of a corporate venture depends on the balance between the desire to learn and leverage competencies.

Source: Adapted from Tidd, J. and S. Taurins (1999) 'Learn or leverage? Strategic diversification and organizational learning through corporate ventures', *Creativity and Innovation Management*, 8 (2), 122–129.

Direct Integration

Direct integration as an additional business activity is the preferred choice where radical changes in product or process design are likely to impact immediately on the mainstream operations and if the people involved in that activity are inextricably involved in day-to-day operations. For example, many engineering-based companies have introduced consultancy to their business portfolio, and in other technical organizations with large laboratory facilities these too have been sold out for analysis of samples, testing of materials, etc. In such cases it is not possible to outsource such activities because the same personnel and equipment are required for the core business.

The Natural History Museum (NHM) provides a good example. In the late 1980s funding was withdrawn from the museum, and it had to continue to reduce its costs and to find new sources of revenue. A principal aim was to generate sufficient revenue streams to avoid a massive reduction in research capacity, and avoid further redundancies. The NHM's resource of some 300 scientists has been developed in a commercial capacity from ground level up. The transformation from research to consultancy work required a complete cultural change. Heads of department ('keepers') were made responsible for identifying and developing the consultant activity, in addition to their normal operational management duties. Given the pervasive nature of the scientific expertise scattered throughout the organization and across departments, an integrated approach to venturing was the only realistic option. Science consultancy is now earning in excess of £1m. per annum, and the museum has been able to buy new capital equipment to support its work.

Integrated Business Teams

Integrated business teams are most appropriate where the expertise will have been nurtured within the mainstream operations, and may support or require support from those operations for development. Strategically, the product is sufficiently related to the mainstream business's key technologies or expertise that the centre wishes to retain some control. This control may either be to protect the knowledge that is intrinsic in the activity or to ensure a flow-back of future development knowledge. A business team of secondees is established to co-ordinate sourcing of both internal and external clients, and is usually treated as a separate accounting entity in order to ease any subsequent transition to a special business unit.

An example of this type of venture is provided by the development of an expert system within Welsh Water. The original system for planning water distribution and supply was devised by Cardiff University, but the system was co-developed and prototyped by a new business team working with the mainstream divisions. The new business team was created and supervised by the Enterprise Division, although it worked closely with the other divisions at operational level. The development team consisted of secondees released from other divisions for a duration of either 6 or 12 months. When the product was fully developed, it was passed to the Enterprise Division for sale externally.

New Ventures Department

A new ventures department is a group separate from normal line management that facilitates external trading. It is most suitable when projects are likely to emerge from the operational business on a fairly frequent basis and when the proposed activities may be beyond current markets or the type of product package sold is different. This is the most natural way for the trading of existing expertise to be developed when it lies fragmented through the organization, and each source is likely to attract a different type of customer. The group has responsibility for marketing, contracting and negotiation, but technical negotiation and supply of services take place at operational level.

Imperial College of Science, Technology and Medicine is a good example. Two separate venture organizations exist. One, IMPEL, is responsible for patenting and licensing technologies and products that emerge, and the other, ICON, for contracting out expertise or processes. ICON combs the organization for potential leading-edge process-oriented technologies, which are supported by available and willing expertise, and attempts to match these with market opportunities. ICON also offers solutions to problems identified by potential clients. For example, ICON manages external access to the ion implantation facility at Imperial, which has been applied to completely new market applications.

Techniques here are built very much on internal competencies that could not be separated from the mainstream activities and could not really be spun out or licensed to another company. In fact, development cycles are so short that it would not be realistic to spin off an individually developed technique. There are important additional benefits to the college through this activity: companies that initially commission a consultancy project may subsequently fund a related research project; also, researchers are brought far closer to the needs of technology users.

New Venture Division

A new venture division provides a safe haven where a number of projects emerge throughout the organization, and allows separate administrative supervision. Strategically, top management can retain a certain level of control until greater clarity on each venture's strategic importance is understood, but the efficiency of the mainstream business needs to be maintained without distraction, so some autonomy is required. Operational links are loose enough to allow information and know-how to be exchanged with the corporate environment. The origins of such a division vary:

- An effort to bring existing technologies and expertise throughout the company together for adaptation to new or existing markets
- To combine research from different fields or locations, to accelerate the development of new products
- To purchase or acquire expertise currently outside of the business for application to internal operations, or to assist new developments

- To examine new market areas as potential targets for existing or adapted products within the current portfolio

Where a critical mass of projects exist, a separate new venture division allows greater focus on the external environment, and the distance from the core corporation facilitates a global and cross-divisional view to be taken. Unfortunately, the division can often become a kind of dustbin for every new opportunity, and therefore it is critical to define the limits of its operation and its mission, in particular the criteria for termination or continued support of specific projects.

For example, British Gas established a division to exploit internal and external technologies. The division took technology that existed within the company and sought to exploit it commercially, in terms of a licence, new application or market. By means of a venture capital fund, the division also identified external technologies that might enhance the company's mainstream technical knowledge.

Similarly, Rolls-Royce Business Ventures Limited was set up to exploit Rolls-Royce technology in new product areas. Its mission was to lay the foundations for new businesses which had a good fit with the technology and skills available to the parent company, but which were outside the mandate of the parent company's existing business groups. The company, which was given its own site, has now been wound up. Nevertheless, it established two spin-off companies during its short life: Stresswave Technology Limited and Reflex Manufacturing Systems Limited.

Special Business Units

Special dedicated new business units are wholly owned by the corporation. High strategic relevance requires strong administrative control. Businesses like this tend to come about because the activity is felt to have enough potential to stand alone as a profit centre, and can thus be assessed and operated as a separate business entity. The requirement is that key people can be identified and extracted from their mainstream operational role.

For the business to succeed under the total ownership and control of a large corporate it must be capable of producing significant revenue streams in the medium term. On average, the critical mass appears to be around 12% of total corporate turnover, in a £2bn business perhaps £20m., but in some cases the threshold for a separate unit is much higher. A potential new business must not only be judged on its relative size or profitability, but more importantly, by its ability to sustain its own development costs. For example, a profitable subsidiary may never achieve the status of a separate new business if it cannot support its own product development.

However, physically separating a business activity does not ensure autonomy. The greatest impediment to such a unit competing effectively in the market is a cosy corporate mentality. If managers of a new business are under the impression that the corporate parent will always assist, provide business and second its expertise and services at non-market rates, that business may never be able to survive commercial pressures. Conversely, if the parent plans to retain total ownership, the parent cannot realistically treat that unit independently. For example, a company which had been set up as a special business unit was undermined when the parent placed an order from an alternative supplier: the venture lost a large proportion of annual revenues, but more importantly that business lost all credibility in the eyes of its other customers. In 2000 Unilever established a ventures unit to invest in Internet businesses, established by staff or external start-ups in related businesses, and for the first time has allowed staff to take a financial interest in the new ventures.

Independent Business Units

Differing degrees of ownership will determine the administrative control over independent business units, ranging from subsidiary to minority interest. Control would only be exercised through a board presence if that were held. There are two reasons for establishing an independent business as opposed to divisionalizing an activity: to focus on the core business by removing the managerial and technical burden of activities unrelated to the mainstream business; or to facilitate learning from external sources in the case of enabling technologies or activities. This structure has benefits for both parent and venture:

- Defrayed risk for parent, greater freedom for venture
- Less supervisory requirement for parent, less interference for venture
- Reduced management distraction for parent, and greater focus for venture
- Continued share of financial returns for parent, greater commitment from managers of the venture
- Potential for flow-back or process improvements or product developments for parent, and learning for the venture

Whilst the mainstream corporation may not be short of cash for investment, bringing in external funding provides additional advantages, such as sharing of risk with other parties and insulating the venture from changes in corporate investment policy. When release of ownership is allowed, venture capital firms can provide valuable help. For example, CharterRail, the spin-off from GICN, was provided with new sources of capital, and assisted in developing its management team and board by the venture capital investors.

By releasing some ownership, executives of the new business can hold a share of the business, indeed this could be a requirement of their involvement. Securing a capital commitment from these key people ensures their personal commitment to its commercial success. In spin-offs that have emerged from Thorn EMI, GICN and ICI, an equity interest has been maintained in each, but a board presence in only two. Part ownership does not have to involve the centre managerially, but when control is reduced the centre must perceive the holding more as an investment than a subsidiary.

The assignment of technical personnel is one of the most difficult problems when establishing an independent business unit. If the individuals necessary to co-ordinate future product development are unwilling to leave the relative security and comfort of a large corporate facility, which is understandable, the new business may be stopped in its tracks. It is critical to identify the most desirable individuals for such an operation, assessed in terms of their technical ability and personal characteristics. It is also important to assess the effect of these individuals leaving the mainstream development operations, as the capability of the parent's operations could be easily damaged.

Nurtured Divestment

Nurtured divestment is appropriate where an activity is not critical to the mainstream business. The product or service has most likely evolved from the mainstream, and whilst supporting these operations it is not essential for strategic control. The design option provides a way for the corporate to release responsibility for a particular business area. External markets may be built up prior to separation, giving time to identify which employees should be retained by the corporate and providing a period of acclimatization for the venture. The parent may or may not retain some ownership.

Siemens has been very successful at developing nurtured divestments. It made a 25% stake in Tele-Processing Systems GmbH, which was started in 1986 by three Siemens employees who had developed products for the remote operation of computers, network auditing and in-house private branch exchanges (PBXs). Similarly, Siemens took a 15% stake in Micro Quartz GmbH which was set up in 1988 in order to take a technology using fused silicon tubes for the chromatography of gas to the manufacturing level, and 38% of ECT GmbH, a spin-off based on electron beam manufacturing equipment developed in-house.

Instead of a formal equity stake, a parent may support a spin-off by contracted or seconded technologies or expertise. Manpower may be seconded and technologies or know-how may be sold through some legal agreement, whether licence or sale with a confidentiality tie. For example, British Gas developed a real time expert system by forming a club of 35 companies. Once the prototype was ready, a new company was formed with the backing of a small number of the original club companies to market the product. British Gas provided the chairman and technical director of the new company. People who had been seconded from British Gas subsequently joined the new venture.

Complete Spin-off

No ownership is retained by the parent corporation in the case of a complete spin-off. This is essentially a divest option, where the corporation wants to pass over total responsibility for activity, commercially and administratively. This may be due to strategic unrelatedness or strategic redundancy, as a consequence of changing corporate strategic focus. A complete spin-off allows the parent to realize the hidden value of the venture, and allows senior management of the parent to focus on their main business.

For example, in 1991 Quaker Oats Co. spun off Fisher Price Inc. Quaker management saw this as allowing the company to concentrate its efforts and resources on its core grocery business and to give shareholders more choice as to the industry segments in which they invest. The toy operations were separated from the divisional structure to become a separate entity. Once rationalized as a separate business, shares were issued to Quaker Oats shareholders on a one-for-five basis, and existing shareholders were effectively used as buyers, with no need for formal divestment. In this way Fisher Price stock was separately floated and market capitalizations were enhanced beyond the previous sum of the whole.

10.5 Learning Through Internal Ventures

The success of corporate venturing varies enormously between firms, but on average around half of all new ventures survive to become operating divisions, which suggests that venturing may be a less risky strategy for diversification than acquisition or merger. Typically, a venture will achieve profitability within two to three years, and almost half are profitable within six years. However, the profitability of the overall corporate venturing process may be lower due to the effect of a few large failures. Four factors appear to characterize firms that are consistently successful at corporate venturing:[8]

1. Distinguish between bad decisions and bad luck when assessing failed ventures.
1. Measure a venture's progress against agreed milestones, and if necessary redirect.
3. Terminate a venture when necessary, rather than make further investments.
4. View venturing as a learning process, and learn from failures as well as successes.

There are two main causes of failure of internal ventures: strategic reversal and the emergence trap.[22] Strategic reversal occurs because of a conflict between the timescales of the new venture and the parent organization. An internal venture may be set up for a number of reasons: to support a strategy of diversification, because of a risk-taking top management, an excess of corporate cash or a decline in the firm's main line of business. Whatever the reasons, the internal or external environment is unlikely to remain stable for the life of the new venture. A change of climate can result in the premature termination of a venture. Even normal business cycles may affect the fortunes of a new venture. For example, there appears to be a strong correlation between changes in corporate profits and the number of new ventures set up.[23]

The other, more subtle cause of venture failure is the emergence trap. As a venture expands it may lead to internal territorial infringements, and success leads to jealousy and may result in attempts to undermine the venture. Differences between the culture and style of managers in the parent firm and new venture are likely to amplify these problems (Table 10.7). In particular, new venture divisions are highly visible and represent a concentration of expenditure, and are therefore more vulnerable to changes in corporate performance or management sentiment.

In practice there is a trade-off between rapid growth and learning. A new venture will not have an indefinite period in which to prove itself, and in most cases corporate management will set high targets for growth and financial return in order to offset the risk and uncertainty inherent in a new venture. If successful, the venture will quickly achieve a track record and therefore attract further support from corporate management, resulting in a virtuous spiral of growth and investment. Conversely, if the venture fails to deliver early growth in sales or returns, it may be starved of further support, thus increasing the likelihood of subsequent failure, a vicious spiral of low investment and decline. There are a number of ways to help avoid these problems:[22]

- Make corporate and divisional managers aware of the long-term benefits of venture operations
- Clearly specify the functions, procedures, boundaries and rewards of venture management
- Establish a limited number of ventures with independent budgets
- Establish and maintain multiple sources of sponsorship for ventures.

TABLE 10.7   Potential sources of conflict between corporate and new venture management.

Corporate management	New venture management
Modest uncertainty	Major technical and market uncertainties
Emphasis on detailed planning	Emphasis on opportunistic risk-taking
Negotiation and compromise	Autonomous behaviour
Corporate interests and rules	Individualistic and ad hoc
Homogeneous culture and experience	Heterogeneous backgrounds

Therefore it is critical to define the purpose of a new venture, in order to apply the most appropriate financial and organizational structures. Firms may organize and manage new ventures in order to maximize exploitation of existing know-how, or to optimize learning, but not both. Therefore it is critical to define clearly scope and focal activity of a new venture, so that the appropriate linkages to other functions can be established (see Box 10.3). Where the primary motive is learning, systems and structures to support the new business must be established, rather than simply capitalizing on rapid sales growth. The precise structure and linkages with the parent firm will depend on the relatedness of product and process technologies and product markets (Table 10.8).

The failure of the parent company to define and articulate the role of the venture is the proximate cause of most difficulties experienced with corporate ventures. Such conflicts can be minimized by ensuring that the primary motive for the venture is made explicit, and communicated to both corporate and venture management. In this way the most appropriate structure and management processes can be developed. Table 10.9 suggests the most appropriate links between the motives, structure and management of internal corporate ventures.

TABLE 10.8 New venture relatedness, focus and linkages with parent.

Venture type	Relatedness of:			Focal activity of venture	Linkages with parent firm
	Product technology	Process technology	Product market		
Product development	Low	Low	High	Development and production	Marketing
Technological innovation	Low	High	High	R&D	Research, marketing and production
Market diversification	High	High	Low	Branding and marketing	Development and production
Technology commercialization	High	Low	Low	Marketing and production	Development
Blue-sky	Low	Low	Low	Development, production and marketing	Finance

TABLE 10.9 Motives, structure and management of corporate ventures.

Primary motive	Preferred structure	Key management task
Satisfy managers' ambition	Integrated business team	Motivation and reward
Spread cost and risk of development	Integrated business team	Resource allocation
Exploit economies of scope	Micro-venture department	Reintegration of venture
Learn about venturing	New venture division	Develop new skills
Diversify the business	Special business unit	Develop new assets
Divest non-core activities	Independent business unit	Management of intellectual property rights

Source: Adapted from Tidd, J. and S. Taurins (1999) 'Learn or leverage? Strategic diversification and organisational learning through corporate ventures', *Creativity and Innovation Management*, **8** (2), 122–129.

BOX 10.3 Oxford University Press's (OUP) entry into multimedia.[24]

The Oxford University Press (OUP) is the largest university press in the world with a total in 1995 of just under 3000 employees and over 3000 titles published. It is not a company in the normal sense and has no shareholders, being legally a department of the University of Oxford, owned by the 'Chancellor, Masters, and Scholars of the University of Oxford'.

An electronic publishing department was created in 1986, which then consisted of an R&D manager and a secretary. A separate department was established because of the specialist skills required for the development and marketing of electronic products. Initially, the department had been subsidized from the Press's other activities. It started as a service centre for the publishing departments, but soon became an independent publishing unit, which has been a source of some tension with established departments. The performance of the existing book departments is assessed on turnover, so there is little financial reward for handing over material to electronic publishing, which is only required to pay a royalty to the originating department.

The aim was to exploit the skills of existing book staff and assets of the Press to differentiate the electronic products, but at the same time to develop new skills in electronic publishing. The background of the present staff is varied and includes book publishing, magazine publishing, software publishing, programming and television programming. The markets and distribution channels are also different from those for book products, so the electronic publishing department recruited its own dedicated marketing and sales staff for direct sales.

Electronic publishing differs from book publishing in a number of ways. Overall, there are many more activities and a much greater degree of involvement is required during software development. Another difference from books is that the changing technologies and markets lead to a need to bring out products much more quickly than is the norm with books. For example, planning has to be 10 years in advance for some books, such as the *Oxford English Dictionary*, whereas the aim is to publish most electronic titles within two years. Multimedia products also need after-sales support, unlike books. The complexity of the development process, the fast changing technology and markets and the lack of experience with similar products make forecasting sales extremely difficult and the current financial reporting systems inappropriate. Finally, electronic publishing also costs a lot more money. Microsoft's Encarta was reputed to have cost $5m. and OUP was reputed to be spending more than £1m. on its *Children's Encyclopaedia*.

Although the Press has published electronic titles for a number of years, these have been mainly text based and did not include video and animation. Early titles included the *Oxford English Dictionary*, the Bodleian pre-1920 catalogue, a series of medical databases, scientific and econometric software. Most have been derived from existing book products although a few have been developed independently. OUP's first true multimedia project was *The Oxford Children's Encyclopaedia*, launched in 1997. One of the main aims of the project was to establish a presence in the multimedia market. OUP recognizes that it cannot compete with companies like Microsoft in the number of software products being developed and the investment in each, but wants a presence in the market. It was a four-year project with about 150 different authors, about 60 subject specialists and 6 major consultants. One of the main learning outcomes was the development process required, including video and animation production.

The long-term aim is gradually to transfer responsibility to the book people, but this was seen as being too early given the stage of development of the market and the technology. The first stage was learning about the market and developing the necessary skills. The second stage is the dissemination of that learning to the other divisions. The third and final stage of complete transfer of responsibility to individual divisions was not envisaged to occur until well into the twenty-first century.

10.6 Summary and Further Reading

In this chapter we have explored the rationale, characteristics and management of internal corporate venturing. A firm may establish a corporate venture for a number of reasons, primarily to maintain or improve its competitiveness by exploiting existing processes or exploring more attractive product markets. However, a new venture also represents an opportunity to grow new businesses based on new technologies, products or markets. In such cases more strategic measures of success are needed.

Like any new business, a corporate venture requires a clear business plan and strong champion or intrapreneur who must identify the opportunity for a new venture, raise the finance and manage the development and growth of the business. Like any entrepreneur, the intrapreneur must be highly motivated and will demand a high level of autonomy. However, unlike his counterpart, the corporate intrapreneur requires a high degree of political and social skill. This is because the corporate entrepreneur has the advantage of the financial, technical and marketing resources of the parent firm, but must deal with internal politics and bureaucracy.

There are many books and journal articles on the more general subject of entrepreneurship, but relatively little has been produced on the more specific subject of intrapreneurship or corporate venturing. On the subject of internal corporate venturing Burgelman and Sayles's *Inside Corporate Innovation* (Macmillan, London, 1986) remains the best combination of theory and case studies, but the more recent book by Block and MacMillan, *Corporate Venturing: Creating new businesses within the firm* (Harvard Business School Press, Boston, 1993), provides a better review of research on internal corporate ventures. Given the renewed industry and academic interest in corporate ventures we would anticipate further research and publications in the next few years.

References

1 Christensen, C. M. (2000) *The Innovator's Dilemma*, 2 edn. HarperCollins, New York.
2 Ernst, H. and J. Vitt (2000) 'The influence of corporate acquisitions on the behaviour of key inventors', *R&D Management*, **30** (2), 105–119.
3 Burgelman, R. A. (1984) 'Managing the internal corporate venturing process', *Sloan Management Review*, **25** (2), Winter, 33–48.
4 Dess, G. G., G. T. Lumpkin and J. G. Covin (1997) 'Entrepreneurial strategy making and firm performance', *Strategic Management Journal*, **18** (9), 677–695.
5 Tidd, J. and S. Taurins (1999) 'Learn or leverage? Strategic diversification and organisational learning through corporate ventures', *Creativity and Innovation Management*, **8** (2), 122–129.
6 Kanter, R. M. (1985) 'Supporting innovation and venture development in established companies', *Journal of Business Venturing*, **1**, 47–60.
7 Huber, G. P. (1996) 'Organizational learning: the contributing processes and the literatures', in Cohen, M. D. and Sproull, L. S. (eds), *Organizational Learning*. Sage, London, pp. 124–162.
8 Block, Z. and I. C. MacMillan (1993) *Corporate Venturing: Creating new businesses within the firm*. Harvard Business School Press, Boston, Mass.
9 Roussel, P. A., K. N. Saad and T. J. Erickson (1991) *Third Generation R&D: Managing the link to corporate strategy*. Harvard Business School Press, Boston, Mass.

10 Drucker, P .F. (1985) *Innovation and Entrepreneurship*. Harper & Row, New York.

11 Griffiths, D. and M. Biosot (2000) 'Are there any competencies out there?', in Tidd, J. (ed.), *From Knowledge Management to Strategic Competence*. Imperial College Press, London, pp. 199–228.

12 Coombs, R. and R. Hull (1998) 'Knowledge management practices and path-dependency in innovation', *Research Policy*, **27**, 237–253.

13 Hargadon, A. and R. I. Sutton (2000) 'Building an innovation factory', *Harvard Business Review*, May–June, 157–166.

14 Kivimaki, M., H. Lansisalmi, M. Elovainio, A. Heikkila, K. Lindstrom, R. Harisalo, K. Sipila and L. Puolimatka (2000) 'Communication as a determinant of organizational innovation', *R&D Management*, **30** (1), 33–42.

15 Barringer, B. R. and A. C. Bluedorn (1999) 'The relationship between corporate entrepreneurship and strategic management', *Strategic Management Journal*, **20**, 421–444.

16 Altshuller, G. (1996) *And Suddenly the Inventor Appeared: TRIZ, the theory of inventive problem solving*. Blackwell, Oxford.

17 Tidd, J. and S. Barnes, (1999) 'Spin-in or spin-out? Corporate venturing in life sciences', *International Journal of Entrepreneurship and Innovation*, **1** (2), 109–116.

18 Maidique, M. A. (1980) 'Entrepreneurs, champions and technological innovation', *Sloan Management Review*, **21** (2), Winter, 59–76.

19 Roberts, M. (1992) 'The do's and don'ts of strategic alliances', *Journal of Business Strategy*, March/April, 50–53.

20 Burgelman, K. A. and L. R. Sayles (1986) *Inside Corporate Innovation*. Macmillan, London.

21 Gulati, R. and J. Garino (2000) 'Get the right mix of bricks and clicks', *Harvard Business Review*, May-June, 107–166.

22 Martin, M. J. C. (1994) *Managing Innovation and Entrepreneurship in Technology*. Wiley, New York.

23 Fast, N. (1979) 'A visit to a new venture graveyard', *Research Management*, **22** (2), 18–22.

24 Chen, S. (1997) 'Core capabilities and core rigidities in the multi-media industry', unpublished Ph.D. thesis, The Management School, Imperial College, University of London.

Part V

CREATING THE INNOVATIVE ORGANIZATION

Innovations—as we have seen—do not emerge in a vacuum, and one important influence on success and failure is the organizational context in which they are created and implemented. Organizations differ widely, but we have learned over time about some of the factors which make for a more or less supporting context. These include the structure of the organization, the roles played by key individuals, the training and development of staff, the way in which work is organized (teamwork, projects, etc.), the extent to which people are involved in innovation, and how the organization itself goes about learning and sharing knowledge. Chapter 11 reviews the various themes which contribute to creating an innovative organization.

Chapter 12 looks at the special case of creating a new organization, specifically small innovative enterprises. Much is expected of such innovative firms as a source of employment and growth, and as sources of additional revenue for universities and other so-called incubator organizations. However, experience suggests that the failure rate amongst this group is very high, and we identify the key management issues that must be addressed at each stage of the development of such enterprises.

Chapter 11

BUILDING THE INNOVATIVE ORGANIZATION

'People are our greatest asset.' This phrase—or variations on it—has become one of the clichés of management presentations, mission statements and annual reports throughout the world. Along with concepts like 'empowerment' and 'teamworking' it expresses a view of people being at the creative heart of the enterprise. But very often the reader of such words—and particularly those 'people' about whom they are written—may have a more cynical view, seeing organizations still operating as if people were part of the problem rather than the key to its solution.

In the field of innovation this theme is of central importance. It is clear from a wealth of psychological research that every human being comes with the capability to find and solve complex problems, and where such creative behaviour can be harnessed amongst a group of people with differing skills and perspectives extraordinary things can be achieved. We can easily think of examples. At the individual level innovation has always been about exceptional characters who combine energy, enthusiasm and creative insight to invent and carry forward new concepts. James Dyson with his alternative approaches to domestic appliance design, Spence Silver, the 3M chemist who discovered the non-sticky adhesive behind 'Post-it' notes and Shawn Fanning, the young programmer who wrote the Napster software and almost single-handedly shook the foundations of the music industry are good illustrations of this.

Innovation is increasingly about teamwork and the creative combination of different disciplines and perspectives. Whether it is in designing a new car in half the time usually taken, bringing a new computer concept to market, establishing new ways of delivering old services like banking, insurance or travel services, or in putting men and women routinely into space, success comes from people working together in high-performance teams.

This effect, when multiplied across the organization, can yield surprising results. In his work on US companies Pfeffer notes the strong correlation between

TABLE 11.1   Components of the innovative organization.

Component	Key features	Example references
Shared vision, leadership and the will to innovate	Clearly articulated and shared sense of purpose Stretching strategic intent 'Top management commitment'	4–8
Appropriate structure	Organization design which enables creativity, learning and interaction. Not always a loose 'skunk works' model; key issue is finding appropriate balance between 'organic and mechanistic' options for particular contingencies	1, 9–15
Key individuals	Promoters, champions, gatekeepers and other roles which energize or facilitate innovation	16–21
Effective teamworking	Appropriate use of teams (at local, cross-functional and interorganizational level) to solve problems. Requires investment in team selection and building	22–26
Continuing and stretching individual development	Long-term commitment to education and training to ensure high levels of competence and the skills to learn effectively	27–29
Extensive communication	Within and between the organization and outside. Internally in three directions—upwards, downwards and laterally	16, 25, 30, 31
High involvement in innovation	Participation in organization-wide continuous improvement activity	32–35
External focus	Internal and external customer orientation. Total quality culture	17, 36, 37
Creative climate	Positive approach to creative ideas, supported by relevant reward systems—a 'winners culture'	5, 38–41
Learning organization	High levels of involvement within and outside the firm in proactive experimentation, finding and solving problems, communication and sharing of experiences and knowledge capture and dissemination	27, 42–47

proactive people management practices and the performance of firms in a variety of sectors.[1] Such 'competitive advantage through people' is also to be found elsewhere; in a UK study of 70 high-performing firms a similar pattern of 'competitiveness through partnerships with people' was clear,[2] whilst similar studies confirm the pattern in German firms.[3] In a knowledge economy where creativity is at a premium, people really are the most important assets which a firm possesses. The management challenge is how to go about building the kind of organizations in which such innovative behaviour can flourish.

This chapter deals with the creation and maintenance of an innovative organizational context, one whose structure and underlying culture—pattern of values and beliefs—support innovation. It is easy to find prescriptions for innovative organizations which highlight the need to eliminate stifling bureaucracy, unhelpful structures, brick walls blocking communication and other factors stopping good ideas getting through. But we must be careful not to fall into the chaos trap—not all innovation works in organic, loose, informal environments or 'skunk works'—and these types of organization can sometimes act against the interests of successful innovation. We need to determine *appropriate* organization—that is, the most suitable organization given the operating contingencies. Too little order and structure may be as bad as too much.

Equally, 'innovative organization' implies more than a structure; it is an integrated set of components which work together to create and reinforce the kind of environment which enables innovation to flourish. Studies of innovative organizations have been extensive, although many can be criticized for taking a narrow view, or for placing too much emphasis on a single prescription like 'teamworking' or 'loose structures'. Nevertheless it is possible to draw out from these a set of components which appear linked with success; these are outlined in Table 11.1, and explored in the subsequent discussion.

11.1 Shared Vision, Leadership and the Will to Innovate

Innovation is essentially about learning and change and is often disruptive, risky and costly. So, as Box 11.1 shows, it is not surprising that individuals and organizations develop many different cognitive, behavioural and structural ways of reinforcing the status quo. Innovation requires energy to overcome this inertia, and the determination to change the order of things. We see this in the case of individual inventors who champion their ideas through, in entrepreneurs who build businesses through risk-taking behaviour and in organizations which manage to challenge the accepted rules of the game.

BOX 11.1

On 10 March 1875 Alexander Graham Bell called to his assistant 'Mr Watson, come here, I want you'—the surprising thing about the exchange being that it was the world's first telephone conversation. Excited by their discovery, they demonstrated their idea to senior executives at Western Union. Their written reply, a few days later, suggested that 'after careful consideration of your invention, which is a very interesting novelty, we have come to the conclusion that it has no commercial possibilities . . . we see no future for an electrical toy . . .'. Within four years of the invention there were 50 000 telephones in the USA and within 20 years there were 5 million. In the same time the company which Bell formed, American Telephone and Telegraph (ATT) over the next 20 years grew to become the largest corporation in the USA, with stock worth $1000/share. The original patent (number 174455) became the single most valuable patent in history.[48]

The converse is also true—the 'not invented here' problem, in which an organization fails to see the potential in a new idea, or decides that it does not fit with their current pattern of business. In other cases the need for change is perceived, but the strength or saliency of the threat is underestimated. We saw in Chapter 6 the difficulties which IBM experienced in the early 1990s in responding to the emerging 'client-server' and network shift in computing away from mainframes, and this is a good example of a firm which believed it had seen and assessed the threat but which nearly drove the company out of business. Similarly, General Motors found it difficult to appreciate and interpret the information about Japanese competition, preferring to believe that their access in US markets was due to unfair trade policies rather than recognizing the fundamental need for process innovation which the 'lean manufacturing' approach pioneered in Japan was bringing to the car industry.[49] Christensen provides powerful evidence to show the difficulties established firms have in interpreting the signals associated with a new and potentially disruptive technology.[50]

This is also where the concept of 'core rigidities', introduced in Chapter 5, becomes important.[43] We have become used to seeing core competencies as a source of strength within the organization, but the downside is that the mind-set which being highly competent in doing certain things can also block the organization from changing its mind. Thus ideas which challenge the status quo face an uphill struggle to gain acceptance; innovation requires considerable energy and enthusiasm to overcome barriers of this kind. One of the concerns in successful innovative organizations is finding ways to ensure that individuals with good ideas are able to progress them without having to leave the organization to do so.[51] Chapter 10 discusses this theme (of 'intrapreneurship') in more detail.

Changing mind-set and refocusing organizational energies requires the articulation of a new vision, and there are many cases where this kind of leadership is credited with starting or turning round organizations. Examples include Jack Welch of GE, Bill Gates (Microsoft), Steve Jobs (Pixar/Apple), Andy Groves (Intel) and Richard Branson (Virgin).[52, 53] Whilst we must be careful of vacuous expressions of 'mission' and 'vision', it is also clear that in cases like these there has been a clear sense of, and commitment to, shared organizational purpose arising from such leadership.

'Top management commitment' is a common prescription associated with successful innovation; the challenge is to translate the concept into reality by finding mechanisms which demonstrate and reinforce the sense of management involvement, commitment, enthusiasm and support. In particular, there needs to be long-term commitment to major projects, as opposed to seeking short-term returns. Since much of innovation is about uncertainty, it follows that returns may not emerge quickly and that there will be a need for 'patient money'. This may not always be easy to provide, especially when demands for shorter-term gains by shareholders have to be reconciled with long-term technology development plans. One way of dealing with this problem is to focus not only on returns on investment but on other considerations like future market penetration and growth or the strategic benefits which might accrue to having a more flexible or responsive production system (Chapter 6 discusses this theme in more detail). Box 11.2 gives an example of such leadership.

Part of this pattern is also top management acceptance of risk. Innovation is inherently uncertain and will inevitably involve failures as well as successes. Successful technology management thus requires that the organization be prepared to take risks and to accept failure as an opportunity for learning and development. This is not to say that unnecessary risks should be taken—rather, as Robert Cooper suggests, the inherent uncertainty in innovation should be reduced where possible through the use of information collection and research.[54]

One last point—we should not confuse leadership and commitment with always being the active change agent. In many cases innovation happens in spite of the senior management within an organization, and success emerges as a result of guerrilla tactics rather than a frontal assault on the problem. Much has been made of the dramatic turnaround in IBM's fortunes under the leadership of Lou Gerstner who took the ailing giant firm from a crisis position to one of leadership in the IT services field and an acknowledged pioneer of e-business. But closer analysis reveals that the entry into e-business was the result of a bottom-up team initiative led by a programmer called Dave Grossman. It was his frustration with the lack of response from his line managers that eventually led to the establishment of a broad coalition of people within the company who were able to bring the idea into practice and establish IBM as a major e-business leader. The message for senior management is as much about leading through creating space and support within the organization as it is about direct involvement.

BOX 11.2 The vision thing—how leadership contributes to transformational change.

In Chapter 7 we discussed how Nokia transformed itself from a conglomerate to the market leader in mobile telephones. Similarly, with roots in the nineteenth century Siemens grew to be one of the great names in electrical engineering and a major force in the German economy. But recent years have seen concerns about the company, criticism of it for a lack of focus and for being slow and unresponsive. Faced with this developing picture the company appointed a new board member in 1998—Edward Krubasik—who came from outside the firm. Restructuring under his leadership has led to the divestment of nearly £10bn of old businesses and to the repositioning of Siemens as a major IT and software player. In 1999 profits surged and the sales price tripled and 60% of the business is concerned with software. Perhaps most significant as an indicator of this new vision is the fact the Siemens employed 27 000 software engineers in 2000—more even than Microsoft!

11.2 Appropriate Organization Structure

No matter how well developed the systems are for defining and developing innovative products and processes they are unlikely to succeed unless the surrounding organizational context is favourable. Achieving this is not easy; it

involves creating the organizational structures and processes which enable technological change to thrive. For example, rigid hierarchical organizations in which
there is little integration between functions and where communication tends to
be top-down and one-way in character are unlikely to be very supportive of the
smooth information flows and cross-functional co-operation recognized as being
important success factors.

Much of the literature recognizes that organizational structures are influenced
by the nature of tasks to be performed within the organization. In essence the less
programmed and more uncertain the tasks, the greater the need for flexibility
around the structuring of relationships.[10] For example, activities like production,
order processing, purchasing, etc. are characterized by decision-making which is
subject to little variation. (Indeed in some cases these decisions can be automated
through employing particular decision rules embodied in computer systems, etc.)
But others require judgement and insight and vary considerably from day to
day—and these include those decisions associated with innovation. Activities of
this kind are unlikely to lend themselves to routine, structured and formalized
relationships, but instead require flexibility and extensive interaction. Several
writers have noted this difference between what have been termed 'programmed' and 'non-programmed' decisions and argued that the greater the level
of non-programmed decision-making, the more the organization needs a loose
and flexible structure.[14]

Considerable work was done on this problem in the late 1950s by researchers
Tom Burns and George Stalker who outlined the characteristics of what they
termed 'organic' and 'mechanistic' organizations.[12] The former are essentially environments suited to conditions of rapid change whilst the latter are more suited
to stable conditions; although these represent poles on an ideal spectrum they do
provide useful design guidelines about organizations for effective innovation.
Other studies include those of Rosabeth Moss-Kanter,[5] and Hesselbein et al.[15]

We should be careful, however, in assuming that innovation is simply confined
to R&D laboratories (where versions of this form of organization have often been
present). Increasingly, innovation is becoming a corporate-wide task, involving
production, marketing, administration, purchasing and many other functions;
this provides strong pressure for widespread organizational change towards
more organic models.

The relevance of Burns and Stalker's model can be seen in an increasing number of cases where organizations have restructured to become less mechanistic.
For example, General Electric in the USA underwent a painful but ultimately successful transformation, moving away from a rigid and mechanistic structure to a
looser and decentralized form.[53] ABB, the Swiss–Swedish engineering group,
have developed a particular approach to their global business based on operating
as a federation of small businesses, each of which retains much of the organic
character of small firms (Barnevik).[8] Other examples of radical changes in structure include the Brazilian white goods firm Semco and the Danish hearing aid
company Oticon.[55, 56]

Related to this work has been another strand which looks at the relationship
between different environments and organizational form. Once again the
evidence suggests that the higher the uncertainty and complexity in the
environment, the greater the need for flexible structures and processes to deal

with it.[57, 58] This partly explains why some fast-growing sectors, for example electronics or biotechnology, are often associated with more organic organizational forms, whereas mature industries often involve more mechanistic arrangements.

One important study in this connection was that originally carried out by Lawrence and Lorsch looking at product innovation. Their work showed that innovation success in mature industries like food packaging and growing sectors like plastics depended on having structures which were sufficiently differentiated (in terms of internal specialist groups) to meet the needs of a diverse marketplace. But success also depended on having the ability to link these specialist groups together effectively so as to respond quickly to market signals; they reviewed several variants on co-ordination mechanisms, some of which were more or less effective than others. Better co-ordination was associated with more flexible structures capable of rapid response.[59]

We can see clear application of this principle in the current efforts to reduce 'time to market' in a range of businesses.[60] Rapid product innovation and improved customer responsiveness are being achieved through extensive organizational change programmes involving parallel working, early involvement of different functional specialists, closer market links and user involvement, and through the development of teamworking and other organizational aids to co-ordination.

Another strand of work which has had a strong influence on the way we think about organizational design was that originated by Joan Woodward associated with the nature of the industrial processes being carried out.[9] Her studies suggested that structures varied between industries with a relatively high degree of discretion (such as small batch manufacturing) through to those involving mass production where more hierarchical and heavily structured forms prevailed. Significantly, the process industries, although also capital intensive, allowed a higher level of discretion.

Other variables and combinations which have been studied for their influence on structure include size, age and company strategy.[61, 62] The extensive debate on organization structure began to resolve itself into a 'contingency' model in the 1970s. In essence this view argues that there is no single 'best' structure, but that successful organizations tend to be those which develop the most suitable 'fit' between structure and operating contingencies. For example, it makes sense to structure an operation like McDonald's in a mechanistic and highly controlled form, in order to be able to replicate this model across the world and be able to deliver similar standards of product and service. But trying to develop a new computer operating system or genetically engineer a new drug would not be possible in such a structure.

Similarly, structures which enable a large international firm to carry out R&D simultaneously in several countries and to integrate their efforts through a series of procedures would be largely irrelevant and excessively bureaucratic for a small, high-tech start-up firm.

The Canadian writer Henry Mintzberg drew much of the work on structure together and proposed a series of archetypes which provide templates for the basic structural configurations into which firms are likely to fall.[13] These categories—and their implications for innovation management—are summarized in Table 11.2.

TABLE 11.2 Mintzberg's structural archetypes.

Organization archetype	Key features	Innovation implications
Simple structure	Centralized organic type—centrally controlled but can respond quickly to changes in the environment. Usually small and often directly controlled by one person. Designed and controlled in the mind of the individual with whom decision-making authority rests. Strengths are speed of response and clarity of purpose. Weaknesses are the vulnerability to individual misjudgement or prejudice and resource limits on growth	Small start-ups in high technology—'garage businesses' are often simple structures. Strengths are in energy, enthusiasm and entrepreneurial flair—simple structure innovating firms are often highly creative. Weaknesses are in long-term stability and growth, and over-dependence on key people who may not always be moving in the right business direction
Machine bureaucracy	Centralized mechanistic organization, controlled centrally by systems. A structure designed like a complex machine with people seen as cogs in the machine. Design stresses the function of the whole and specialization of the parts to the point where they are easily and quickly interchangeable. Their success comes from developing effective systems which simplify tasks and routinize behaviour. Strengths of such systems are the ability to handle complex integrated processes like vehicle assembly. Weaknesses are the potential for alienation of individuals and the build-up of rigidities in inflexible systems	Machine bureaucracies depend on specialists for innovation, and this is channelled into the overall design of the system. Examples include fast food (McDonald's), mass production (Ford) and large-scale retailing (Sainsbury's), in each of which there is considerable innovation, but concentrated on specialists and impacting at the system level. Strengths of machine bureaucracies are their stability and their focus of technical skills on designing the systems for complex tasks. Weaknesses are their rigidities and inflexibility in the face of rapid change, and the limits on innovation arising from non-specialists
Divisionalized form	Decentralized organic form designed to adapt to local environmental challenges. Typically associated with larger organizations, this model involves specialization into semi-independent units. Examples would be strategic business units or operating divisions. Strengths of such a form are the ability to attack particular niches (regional, market, product, etc.) whilst drawing on central support. Weaknesses are the internal frictions between divisions and the centre	Innovation here often follows a 'core and periphery' model in which R&D of interest to the whole organization, or of a generic nature is carried out in central facilities whilst more applied and specific work is carried out within the divisions. Strengths of this model include the ability to concentrate on developing competency in specific niches and to mobilize and share knowledge gained across the rest of the organization. Weaknesses include the 'centrifugal pull' away from central R&D towards applied local efforts and the friction and competition between divisions which inhibits sharing of knowledge

Professional bureaucracy	Decentralized mechanistic form, with power located with individuals but co-ordination via standards. This kind of organization is characterized by relatively high levels of professional skills, and is typified by specialist teams in consultancies, hospitals or legal firms. Control is largely achieved through consensus on standards ('professionalism') and individuals possess a high degree of autonomy. Strengths of such an organization include high levels of professional skill and the ability to bring teams together	This kind of structure typifies design and innovation consulting activity within and outside organizations. The formal R&D, IT or engineering groups would be good examples of this, where technical and specialist excellence is valued. Strengths of this model are in technical ability and professional standards. Weaknesses include difficulty of managing individuals with high autonomy and knowledge power
Adhocracy	Project type of organization designed to deal with instability and complexity. Adhocracies are not always long-lived, but offer a high degree of flexibility. Team-based, with high levels of individual skill but also ability to work together. Internal rules and structure are minimal and subordinate to getting the job done. Strengths of the model are its ability to cope with high levels of uncertainly and its creativity. Weaknesses include the inability to work together effectively due to unresolved conflicts, and a lack of control due to lack of formal structures or standards	This is the form most commonly associated with innovative project teams—for example, in new product development or major process change. The NASA project organization was one of the most effective adhocracies in the programme to land a man on the moon; significantly the organization changed its structure almost once a year during the 10-year programme, to ensure it was able to respond to the changing and uncertain nature of the project. Strengths of adhocracies are the high levels of creativity and flexibility—the 'skunk works' model advocated in the literature. Weaknesses include lack of control and over-commitment to the project at the expense of the wider organization
Mission-oriented	Emergent model associated with shared common values. This kind of organization is held together by members sharing a common and often altruistic purpose—for example in voluntary and charity organizations. Strengths are high commitment and the ability of individuals to take initiatives without reference to others because of shared views about the overall goal. Weaknesses include lack of control and formal sanctions	Mission-driven innovation can be highly successful, but requires energy and a clearly articulated sense of purpose. Aspects of total quality management and other value-driven organizational principles are associated with such organizations, with a quest for continuous improvement driven from within rather than in response to external stimulus. Strengths lie in the clear sense of common purpose and the empowerment of individuals to take initiatives in that direction. Weaknesses lie in over-dependence on key visionaries to provide clear purpose, and lack of 'buy-in' to the corporate mission

Box 11.3 gives an example of the importance of organizational structure and the need to find appropriate models.

The increasing importance of innovation and the consequent experience of high levels of change across the organization, have begun to pose a challenge for organizational structures normally configured for stability. Thus traditional machine bureaucracies—typified by the car assembly factory—are becoming more hybrid in nature, tending towards what might be termed a 'machine adhocracy' with creativity and flexibility (within limits) being actively encouraged. The case of 'lean production' with its emphasis on teamworking, participation in problem-solving, flexible cells and flattening of hierarchies is a good example, where there is significant loosening of the original model to enhance innovativeness.[63]

The key challenge here for managing innovation remains one of fit—of getting the most appropriate structural form for the particular circumstances. Another view of structure is that it is an artefact of what people believe and how they behave; if there is good fit, structure will enable and reinforce innovative behaviour. If it is contradictory to these beliefs—for example, restricting communication, stressing hierarchy—then it is likely to act as a brake on creativity and innovation.

The Emergence of Networks

All of the above discussion presumes that the organization in question is a single entity, a group of people organized in a particular fashion towards some form of collective purpose. But increasingly we are seeing the individual enterprise becoming linked with others in some form of collective—a supply chain, an industrial cluster, a co-operative learning club or a product development consortium. Such networks form for a variety of purposes, but increasingly a strong motive is to enhance innovative performance in some way. Consider some examples:

1. Studies of 'collective efficiency' have explored the phenomenon of clustering in a number of different contexts.[64–67] From this work it is clear that the model is not just confined to parts of Italy, Spain and Germany, but diffused around the world—and under certain conditions, extremely effective. For example, one town (Sialkot) in Pakistan plays a dominant role in the world market for specialist surgical instruments made of stainless steel. From a core group of 300 small firms, supported by 1500 even smaller suppliers, 90% of production (1996) was exported and took a 20% share of the world market, second only to Germany. In another case the Sinos valley in Brazil contains around 500 small-firm manufacturers of specialist high quality leather shoes. Between 1970 and 1990 their share of the world market rose from 0.3 to 12.5% and they now export some 70% of total production. In each case the gains are seen as resulting from close interdependence in a co-operative network.
2. Similarly, there has been much discussion about the merits of technological collaboration, especially in the context of complex product systems development.[68–70] Innovation networks of this kind offer significant advantages in

BOX 11.3 The emergence of mass production.

Perhaps the most significant area in which there is a change of perspective is in the role of human resources. Early models of organization were strongly influenced by the work of Frederick Taylor and his principles of 'scientific management'. These ideas—used extensively in the development of mass production industries like automobile manufacture—essentially saw the organization problem as one which required the use of analytical methods to arrive at the 'best' way of carrying out the organization's tasks. This led to an essentially mechanistic model in which people were often seen as cogs in a bigger machine, with clearly defined limits to what they should and should not do. The image presented by Charlie Chaplin in *Modern Times* was only slightly exaggerated; in the car industry the average task cycle for most workers was less than two minutes.

The advantages of this system for the mass production of a small range of goods were clear; productivity increases often ran into three figures with the adoption of this approach. For example, Ford's first assembly line, installed in 1913 for fly-wheel assembly, saw the assembly time fall from 20 man-minutes to 5, and by 1914 three lines were being used in the chassis department to reduce assembly time from around 12 hours to less than 2. But its limitations lay in the ability of the system to change, and in the capacity for innovation. By effectively restricting innovation to a few specialists, an important source of creative problem-solving, in terms of product and process development, was effectively cut off.

The experience of Ford and others highlights the point that there is no single 'best' kind of organization; the key is to ensure congruence between underlying values and beliefs and the organization which enables innovative routines to flourish. For example, whilst the 'skunk works' model may be appropriate to US product development organizations, it may be inappropriate in Japan where a more disciplined and structured form is needed. Equally, some successful innovative organizations are based on teamworking, whereas others are built around key individuals—in both cases reflecting underlying beliefs about how innovation works in those particular organizations. Similarly, successful innovation can take place within strongly bureaucratic organizations just as well as in those which there is a much looser structure—providing that there is underlying congruence between these structures and the innovative behavioural routines.

terms of assembling different knowledge sets and reducing the time and costs of development—but are again often difficult to implement.[71, 72]

3. Such networks can be used to foster technological learning across a group of firms or a sector. The case of CITER in Italy is a good example here. The predominantly small scale of firm operations in the fashion textile sector meant that none could afford the design technology or undertake research into process development in areas like dyeing. A co-operative research centre— CITER—was established and funded by members of the *consorzia* and chartered with work on technological problems related to the direct needs of the members. Over time this has evolved into a world-class research institute, but its roots are still in the local network of textile firms. It has become a powerful

mechanism for innovation and technology transfer and has helped to upgrade the overall knowledge base of this sector.[73]

4. Much has been written on the importance of developing co-operative rather than adversarial supply chain relationships.[74, 75] But it is becoming increasingly clear that the kind of 'collective efficiency' described above can operate in this context and contribute not only to improved process efficiency (higher quality, faster speed of response, etc.) but also to shared product development. The case of Toyota is significant here where the firm has continued to stay ahead despite increasing catch-up efforts on the part of Western firms and the consolidation of the industry. Much of this competitive edge can be attributed to its ability to create and maintain a high performance knowledge-sharing network.

Networking represents a powerful solution to the resource problem—no longer is it necessary to have all the resources for innovation (particularly those involving specialized knowledge) under one roof provided you know where to obtain them and how to link up with them. The emergence of powerful information and communications technologies have further facilitated the move towards networks and 'virtual organizations' are increasingly a feature of the business landscape.[76]

But obtaining the benefits of networking is not an automatic process—it requires considerable efforts in the area of co-ordination. Effective networks have what systems theorists call 'emergent properties'—that is, the whole is greater than the sum of the parts. But the risk is high that simply throwing together a group of enterprises will lead to suboptimal performance with the whole being considerably less than the sum of the parts due to friction, poor communications, persistent conflicts over resources or objectives, etc.

Research on interorganizational networking (ION) suggests that eight core processes need managing in a network, effectively treating it as if it were a particular form of organization.[77] (See Table 11.3.) The basic ION model asserts that networks will be more or less effective in the ways in which they handle these processes. For example, a network with no clear routes for resolving conflicts is likely to be less effective than one which has a clear and accepted set of norms—a 'network culture'—which can handle the inevitable conflicts which emerge.

Building and operating networks can be facilitated by a variety of enabling inputs—for example, the use of advanced information and communications technologies may have a marked impact on the effectiveness with which information processing takes place. Independent facilitation appears to have a strong influence on many of the behavioural dimensions.

Networking is increasingly offered as a way forward for industrial development. National and regional governments are trying to emulate the cluster effect which has proved so successful amongst small firms in Italy and Spain. Large firms are trying to develop their supply chains towards greater efficiency through supply chain learning and development programmes. Complex product systems are increasingly the subject of shared development projects amongst consortia of technology providers. But experience and research suggest that without careful management of these—and the availability of a shared commitment to deal with them—the chances are that such networks will fail to perform effectively.

TABLE 11.3   Core processes in interorganizational networking.

Process	Underlying questions
Network creation	How the membership of the network is defined and maintained
Decision-making	How (where, when, who, etc.) decisions get taken
Conflict resolution	How (and if) conflicts are resolved
Information processing	How information flows and is managed
Knowledge capture	How knowledge is articulated and captured to be available for the whole network
Motivation/commitment	How members are motivated to join/remain in the network—e.g. through active facilitation, shared concerns for development
Risk/benefit sharing	How the risks and benefits are shared
Integration	How relationships are built and maintained between individual representatives in the network

Source: Bessant and Tsekouras (2001).[77]

11.3 Key Individuals

Another important element is the presence of key enabling figures. The uncertainty and complexity involved in innovation mean that many promising inventions die before they make it to the outside world. One way round this problem is if there is a key individual (or sometimes a group of people) who is prepared to champion its cause and to provide some energy and enthusiasm to help it through the organizational system. Such key figures or project champions have been associated with many famous innovations—for example, the development of Pilkington's float glass process or Edwin Land and the Polaroid photographic process.[7, 21, 78–80] Box 11.4 gives an example.

There are, in fact, several roles which key figures can play which have a bearing on the outcome of a project. First, there is the source of critical technical knowledge—often the inventor **or** team leader responsible for an invention. He/she will have the breadth of understanding of the technology behind the innovation and the ability to solve the many development problems likely to emerge in the long haul from laboratory or drawing board to full scale. The contribution here is not only of technical knowledge; it also involves inspiration when particular technological problems appear insoluble, and it involves motivation and commitment.

Influential though such technical champions might be, they may not be able to help an innovation progress unaided through the organization. Not all problems are technical in nature; other issues such as procuring resources or convincing sceptical or hostile critics elsewhere in the organization may need to be dealt with. Here our second key role emerges—that of organizational sponsor.

BOX 11.4 Bags of ideas—the case of James Dyson.

In October 2000 the air inside Court 58 of the Royal Courts of Justice rang with terms like 'bagless dust collection', 'cyclone technology', 'Triple Vortex' and ' Dual Cyclone' as one of the most bitter of patent battles in recent years was brought to a conclusion. On one side was Hoover, a multinational firm with the eponymous vacuum suction sweeper at the heart of a consumer appliance empire. On the other a lone inventor—James Dyson—who had pioneered a new approach to the humble task of house cleaning and then seen his efforts threatened by an apparent imitation by Hoover. Eventually the court ruled in Dyson's favour.

This represented the culmination of a long and difficult journey which Dyson travelled in bringing his ideas to a wary marketplace. It began in 1979 when Dyson was using, ironically, a Hoover Junior vacuum cleaner to dust the house. He was struck by the inefficiency of a system which effectively reduced its capability to suck the more it was used since the bag became clogged with dust. He tried various improvements such as a finer mesh filter bag but the results were not promising. The breakthrough came with the idea of using industrial cyclone technology applied in a new way—to the problem of domestic cleaners.

Dyson was already an inventor with some track record and one of his products was a wheelbarrow which used a ball instead of a front wheel. In order to spray the black dust paint in a powder-coating plant they had installed a cyclone—a well-established engineering solution to the problem of dust extraction. Essentially, a mini-tornado is created within a shell and the air in the vortex moves so fast that particles of dust are forced to the edge where they can be collected whilst clean air moves to the centre. Dyson began to ask why the principle could not be applied in vacuum cleaners—and soon found out why. His early experiments—with the Hoover—were not entirely successful, but eventually he applied for a patent in 1980 for a vacuum cleaning appliance using cyclone technology.

It took another four years and 5127 prototypes and even then he could not patent the application of a single cyclone since that would only represent an improvement on an existing and proven technology. He had to develop a dual cyclone system which used the first to separate out large items of domestic refuse—cigarette ends, dog hairs, cornflakes, etc.—and the second to pick up the finer dust particles. But having proved the technology he found a distinct cold shoulder on the part of the existing vacuum cleaner industry represented by firms like Hoover, Philips and Electrolux. In typical examples of the 'not invented here' effect they remained committed to the idea of vacuum cleaners using bags and were unhappy with bagless technology. (This is not entirely surprising since suppliers such as Electrolux make a significant income on selling the replacement bags for their vacuum cleaners.)

Eventually Dyson began the hard work of raising the funds to start his own business—and it gradually paid off. Launched in 1993—14 years after the initial idea—Dyson now employs 1800 staff producing around 10 000 cleaners every day in their factory in Malmesbury in Wiltshire. The Dyson empire is worth around £530m. and has a number of product variants in its vacuum cleaner range; other products under development aim to re-examine domestic appliances like washing machines and dishwashers to try and bring similar new ideas into play. The basic

Dual Cyclone cleaner was one of the products identified by the UK Design Council as one of its 'millennium products'.

Perhaps the greatest accolade though is the fact that the vacuum cleaner giants like Hoover eventually saw the potential and began developing their own versions. Although Hoover lost the case they are planning to appeal, arguing that their version used a different technology developed for the oil and gas industry by the UK research consultancy BHR.

Whoever wins, Dyson has once again shown the role of the individual champion in innovation—and that success depends on more than just a good idea. Edison's famous comment that it is '1% inspiration and 99% perspiration' seems an apt motto here!

Typically this person has power and influence and is able to pull the various strings of the organization (often from a seat on the board); in this way many of the obstacles to an innovation's progress can be removed or the path at least smoothed. Such sponsors do not necessarily need to have a detailed technical knowledge of the innovation (although this is clearly an asset), but they do need to believe in its potential.

Recent exploration of the product development process has highlighted the important role which is played by the team members and in particular the project team leader. There are close parallels to the champion model; influential roles range from what Clark and Fujimoto call 'heavyweight' project managers who are deeply involved and have the organizational power to make sure things come together, through to the 'lightweight' project manager whose involvement is more distant. Research on Japanese product development highlights the importance of the *shusha* or team leader; in some companies (such as Honda) the *shusha* is empowered to override even the decisions and views of the chief executive! [78] The important message here is to match the choice of project manager type to the requirements of the situation—and not to use the 'sledgehammer' of a heavyweight manager for a simple task.

Key roles are not just on the technical and project management side; Studies of innovation (going right back to Project SAPPHO and its replications) also highlighted the importance of the 'business innovator', someone who could represent and bring to bear the broader market or user perspective.[17]

Although innovation history is full of examples where such key individuals—acting alone or in tandem—have had a marked influence on success, we should not forget that there is a downside as well. Negative champions—project assassins—can also be identified, whose influence on the outcome of an innovation project is also significant but in the direction of killing it off. For example, there may be internal political reasons why some parts of an organization do not wish for a particular innovation to progress—and through placing someone on the project team or through lobbying at board level or in other ways a number of obstacles can be placed in its way. Equally, our technical champion may not always be prepared to let go of his/her pet idea, even if the rest of the organization has decided that it is not a sensible direction in which to progress. Their ability to mobilize support and enthusiasm and to surmount obstacles within the organization can sometimes lead to wrong directions being pursued, or the continued chasing up what many in the organization see as a blind alley.

One other type of key individual is worth mentioning, that of the 'technological gatekeeper'. Innovation is about information and, as we saw above, success is strongly associated with good information flow and communication. Research has shown that such networking is often enabled by key individuals within the organization's informal structure who act as 'gatekeepers'—collecting information from various sources and passing it on to the relevant people who will be best able or most interested to use it. Thomas Allen, working at MIT, made a detailed study of the behaviour of engineers during the large-scale technological developments surrounding the Apollo rocket programme. His studies highlighted the importance of informal communications in successful innovation, and drew particular attention to gatekeepers—who were not always in formal information management positions but who were well connected in the informal social structure of the organization—as key players in the process.[16]

This role is becoming of increasing importance in the field of knowledge management where there is growing recognition that enabling effective sharing and communication of valuable knowledge resources is not simply something which can be accomplished by advanced IT and clever software—there is a strong interpersonal element.[81, 82]

11.4 Stretching Training and Development

A core characteristic associated with high-performance organizations is the extent to which they commit to training and development. Studies at national, sector and individual company level repeatedly stress the relationship between investment of this kind and innovation capability.[28, 29, 83] The argument here is that the ability of an organization to make the best use of new equipment or to produce products and services with novelty in design, quality or performance depends to a large extent on the knowledge and skills of those involved in producing such innovations.

Equipping people with the skills they need to understand and operate new equipment, procedures or concepts is an important step, but training and development can take a broader role. It has considerable potential, for example, as a motivator—people value the experience of acquiring new skills and abilities, and also feel valued as part of the organization. For example, a recent survey of continuous improvement in the UK (essentially concerned with increasing levels of participation in innovation) found that the opportunity for personal development was ranked higher than financial motivators as a reward mechanism.[84]

Training and development are also essential complements to enabling people to take on more responsibility and demonstrate more initiative—so-called 'empowerment' exercises. Harnessing creativity and encouraging experiment depend on people having the necessary skills and confidence to deploy them—and this places considerable emphasis on long-term training and development strategy.[3, 83]

Training is also valuable as part of a wider change programme. When major innovations are introduced people often resist the change for a variety of reasons, not all of which are rational or clearly articulated.[85, 86] A major component of this is often the sense that the innovation will require abilities or skills which the individual does not possess, or pose challenges which are not fully understood. Training—not only in the narrow sense of 'know-how' but also a component of education around the strategic rationale for the change (the 'know-why')—can provide a powerful lubricant for oiling the wheels of such innovation programmes.[87] For example, in studies of the introduction of computer-aided enterprise management systems (ERP), the presence, or absence, of such extensive training (beyond the minimum usually offered by suppliers of computer-aided production management (CAPM) systems) was a major determinant of successful implementation.[88]

One other aspect of training and development concerns its use to develop the habit of learning. A core element in any 'learning organization' will be the continual discovery and sharing of new knowledge—in other words, a continuing and shared learning process.[42] But to put this in place requires that employees understand *how* to learn; an increasing number of organizations have recognized that this is not an automatic process and have begun implementing training programmes designed less to equip employees with skills than to engender the habit of learning. So, for example, some firms offer access to courses in foreign languages, hobby skills and other activities unrelated to work but with the twin aims of motivating staff and getting them back into the habit of learning.

11.5 High Involvement in Innovation

Whereas innovation is often seen as the province of technical specialists in R&D, engineering or design, the underlying creative skills and problem-solving abilities are possessed by everyone. If mechanisms can be found to focus such abilities on a regular basis across the entire company, the resulting innovative potential is enormous. Although each individual may only be able to develop limited, incremental innovations, the sum of these efforts can have far-reaching impacts.[89]

For example, it is now widely accepted that the 'quality miracle' worked by Japanese manufacturing industry in the post-war years, owes much to what they term *kaizen*—continuous improvement. Firms like Toyota and Matsushita receive millions of suggestions for improvements every year from their employees—and the vast majority of these are implemented.[90, 91] Figures indicate that Western firms have begun to close this gap although they still have a long way to go to catch up. For example, the chief executive of Leyland Trucks (a firm with 738 employees) reported (1998) that 'Our operating costs are reducing year on year due to improved efficiencies. We have seen a 35% reduction in costs within two and a half years by improving quality. There are an average of 21 ideas per employee today compared to nil in 1990. Our people have accomplished this.'[92] Box 11.5 gives an example.

Underpinning such continuous incremental innovation is the organizational culture to support and encourage over the long term. This simple point has been recognized in a number of different fields, all of which converge around the view that higher levels of participation in innovation represents a competitive advantage. For example:

BOX 11.5 High involvement in innovation.

At first sight XYZ systems does not appear to be anyone's idea of a 'world class' manufacturing outfit. Set in a small town in the Midlands with a predominately agricultural industry, XYZ employs around 30 people producing gauges and other measuring devices for the forecourts of filling stations. Their products are used to monitor and measure levels and other parameters in the big fuel tanks underneath the stations, and on the tankers which deliver to them. Despite their small size (although they are part of a larger but decentralized group) XYZ have managed to command around 80% of the European market. Their processes are competitive against even large manufacturers, their delivery and service level the envy of the industry. They have a fistful of awards for their quality and yet manage to do this across a wide range of products some dating back 30 years, which still need service and repair. They use technologies from complex electronics and remote sensing right down to basics—they still make a wooden measuring stick, for example.

Their success can be gauged from profitability figures, but also from the many awards which they receive and continue to receive as one of the best factories in the UK.

Yet if you go through the doors of XYZ you would have to look hard for the physical evidence of how they achieved this enviable position. This is not a highly automated business—it would not be appropriate. Nor is it laid out in modern facilities; instead they have clearly made much of their existing environment and organized it and themselves to best effect.

Where does the difference lie? Fundamentally in the approach taken with the workforce. This is an organization where training matters—investment is well above the average and everyone receives x hours per year, not only in their own particular skills area but also across a wide range of tasks and skills. One consequence of this is that the workforce are very flexible; having been trained to carry out most of the operations they can quickly move to where they are most needed. The payment system encourages such co-operation and teamworking, with its simple structure and emphasis on payment for skill, quality and teamworking. The strategic targets are clear and simple, and are discussed with everyone before being broken down into a series of small manageable improvement projects in a process of policy deployment. All around the works there are copies of the 'bowling chart' which sets out simply—like a tenpin bowling scoresheet—the tasks to be worked on as improvement projects and how they could contribute to the overall strategic aims of the business. And if they achieve or exceed those strategic targets—then everyone gains through a profit-sharing and employee ownership scheme.

Being a small firm there is little in the way of hierarchy, but the sense of teamworking is heightened by active leadership and encouragement to discuss and explore issues together—and it does not hurt that the operations director practises a form of MBWA—management by walking about!

Perhaps the real secret lies in the way in which people feel enabled to find and solve problems, often experimenting with different solutions and frequently failing—but at least learning and sharing that information for others to build on. Walking round the factory it is clear that this place is not standing still—whilst major investment in new machines is not an everyday thing, little improvement projects—*kaizens* as they call them—are everywhere. More significant is the fact that the operations director is often surprised by what he finds people doing—it is clear that he has not got a detailed idea of which projects people are working on and what they are doing. But if you ask him if this worries him the answer is clear—and challenging. 'No, it doesn't bother me that I don't know in detail what's going on. They all know the strategy, they all have a clear idea of what we have to do [via the 'bowling charts']. They've all been trained, they know how to run improvement projects and they work as a team. And I trust them. . . .'

1. In the field of quality management it has become clear that major advantages accrue from better and more consistent quality in products and services. Crosby's work on quality costs suggested the scale of the potential savings (typically 20–40% of total sales revenue), and the experience of many Japanese manufacturers during the post-war period provide convincing arguments in favour of this approach.[93–96] But the underlying recipe for achieving 'total quality' is an old one, originally articulated in the early part of the twentieth century and making extensive play on the contribution which participation in the process of finding and solving quality problems could make.

2. The concept of 'lean manufacturing' has diffused widely during the past 10 years and is now applied in manufacturing and services as diverse as chemicals production, hospital management and supermarket retailing.[97] Lean thinking as a concept emerged from detailed studies of assembly plants in the car industry.[49] This work highlighted significant differences between the best and the average plants along a range of dimensions, including productivity, quality, and time. Efforts to identify the source of these significant advantages revealed that the major differences lay not in higher levels of capital investment or more modern equipment, but in the ways in which production was organized and managed.

    . . . our findings were eye-opening. The Japanese plants require one-half the effort of the American luxury-car plants, half the effort of the best European plant, a quarter of the effort of the average European plant, and one-sixth the effort of the worst European luxury car producer. At the same time, the Japanese plant greatly exceeds the quality level of all plants except one in Europe—and this European plant required four times the effort of the Japanese plant to assemble a comparable product . . ..

    Central to this alternative model was an emphasis on teamworking and participation in innovation.

3. Lean manufacturing brought a sense of urgency and focus to a discussion which had been going on for at least the previous decade surrounding what were loosely called 'Japanese manufacturing techniques'.[98] This bundle of approaches (which included umbrella ideas like 'just-in-time' and specific techniques like poke yoke) were credited with having helped Japanese manufacturers gain significant competitive edge in sectors as diverse as electronics,

motor vehicles and steel making.[99–101] Underpinning these techniques was a philosophy which stressed high levels of employee involvement in the innovation process, particularly through sustained incremental problem-solving—*kaizen*.[102, 103]

4. The transferability of such ideas between locations and into different application areas has also been extensively researched. It is clear from these studies that the principles of 'lean' manufacturing can be extended into supply and distribution chains, into product development and R&D and into service activities and operations.[74, 104, 105] Nor is there any particular barrier in terms of national culture; high-involvement approaches to innovation have been successfully transplanted to a number of different locations.[55, 106, 107]

5. Studies of high-performance organizations, especially those which achieve significant productivity improvements through their workforces, place considerable emphasis on involvement in innovation. Characteristic of such cases is a blurring of the lines of responsibility for the innovation process, moving away from specialists and towards higher levels of participation by others in incremental innovation as a complement to specialist activity.[108]

6. Work on the successful implementation of advanced technologies in manufacturing and services also points towards the value of high levels of involvement. It has become apparent through a range of studies that success depends on securing commitment through participative design, and on extensive problem-solving activity around reconfiguring both technology and the organizational context.[109–111]

7. Surveys of award-winning companies which have been recognized (by their peers' votes, by external performance measures, by independent auditing, etc.) to have achieved a high-class competitive edge increasingly converge in the importance attached to employee involvement and participation in continuous improvement (CI). For example, winners of the European Quality Award (Yellow Pages, Xerox, Ericsson) lay particular emphasis on the importance of CI in achieving these goals.

So there is a considerable weight of experience now available to support the view that enhanced performance can and does result from increasing involvement in innovation through CI. But there is also a secondary effect which should not be underestimated; the more people are involved in change, the more receptive they become to change itself. Since the turbulent nature of most organizational environments is such that increasing levels of change are becoming the norm, involvement of employees in CI programmes may provide a powerful aid to effective management of change.

Since much of such employee involvement in innovation focuses on incremental change it is tempting to see its effects as marginal. Studies show, however, that when taken over an extended period it is a significant factor in the strategic development of the organization. Perhaps more important is the fact that it conditions the organization to accept change as the norm rather than the exception; given that many problems in successful innovation are concerned with organizational adaptation, CI may offer a way of smoothing the process.

A key issue here is what is sometimes called 'policy deployment'—essentially a process of connecting the high-level strategic goals of the business with specific tasks and targets with which individuals and groups can engage. This requires two key enablers—the creation of a clear and coherent strategy for the business and the deployment of it through a cascade process which builds understanding and ownership of the goals and sub-goals.[35]

This is a characteristic feature of many Japanese *kaizen* systems and may help explain why there is such a strong 'track record' of strategic gains through continuous improvement. In such plants overall business strategy is broken down into focused three-year mid-term plans (MTPs); typically the plan is given a slogan or motto to help identify it. This forms the basis of banners and other illustrations, but its real effect is to provide a backdrop against which efforts over the next three years can be focused. The MTP is specified not just in vague terms but with specific and measurable objectives—often described as pillars. These are, in turn, decomposed into manageable projects which have clear targets and measurable achievement milestones, and it is to these that CI is systematically applied.

Policy deployment of this kind requires suitable tools and techniques and examples include *hoshin* (participative) planning, how–why charts, 'bowling charts' and briefing groups.[112]

In the end the task is one of building a shared set of values which bind people in the organization together and enable them to participate in its development. As one manager put it in a UK study, '. . . we never use the word empowerment! You can't empower people—you can only create the climate and structure in which they will take responsibility. . . .'[92] Box 11.6 provides another example.

BOX 11.6

Dutton Engineering does not, at first sight, seem a likely candidate for world class. A small firm with 28 employees, specializing in steel cases for electronic equipment, it ought to be amongst the ranks of hand-to-mouth metal bashers of the kind which you can find all round the world. Yet Dutton has been doubling its turnover, sales per employee have doubled in an eight-year period, rejects are down from 10 to 0.7% and over 99% of deliveries are made within 24 hours—compared to only 60% being achieved within one week a few years ago. This transformation has not come overnight—the process started in 1989—but it has clearly been successful and Dutton are now held up as an example to others of how typical small engineering firms can change.

At the heart of the transformation which Ken Lewis, the original founder and architect of the change, has set in train is a commitment to improvements through people. The workforce are organized into four teams who manage themselves, setting work schedules, dealing with their own customers, costing their own orders and even setting their pay! The company has moved from traditional weekly pay to a system of 'annualized hours' where they contract to work for 1770 hours in a year—and tailor this flexibly to the needs of the business with its peaks and troughs of activity. There is a high level of contribution to problem-solving, encouraged by a simple reward system which pays £5–£15 for bright ideas, and by a bonus scheme whereby 20% of profits are shared.[113]

11.6 Effective Teamworking

BOX 11.7

It takes five years to develop a new car in this country. Heck, we won World War 2 in four years. . . .' Ross Perot's critical comment on the state of the US car industry in the late 1980s captured some of the frustration with existing ways of designing and building cars. In the years that followed significant strides were made in reducing the development cycle, with Ford and Chrysler succeeding in dramatically reducing time and improving quality. Much of the advantage was gained through extensive teamworking; as Lew Varaldi, project manager of Ford's Team Taurus project put it, '. . . it's amazing the dedication and commitment you get from people . . . we will never go back to the old ways because we know so much about what they can bring to the party . . .'[11]

Innovation is primarily about combining different perspectives in solving problems, and there is thus—as Box 11.7 shows—much potential value in teamworking. Experiments indicate that groups have more to offer than individuals in terms of both fluency of idea generation and in flexibility of solutions developed. Focusing this potential on innovation tasks is the prime driver for the trend towards high levels of teamworking—in project teams, in cross-functional and interorganizational problem-solving groups and in cells and work groups where the focus is on incremental, adaptive innovation.

Considerable work has been done on the characteristics of high-performance project teams for innovative tasks, and the main findings are that such teams rarely happen by accident.[114] They result from a combination of selection and investment in team-building, allied to clear guidance on their roles and tasks, and a concentration on managing group process as well as task aspects. A variety of studies have been carried out involving different US companies, aimed at identifying key drivers and barriers to effective performance, and they share the conclusion that effective team-building is a critical determinant of project success.[26, 114] Bixby et al. drew similar conclusions in their work with organizations associated with the Ashridge Management College teamworking programme; their model for 'superteams' includes components of building and managing the internal team and also its interfaces with the rest of the organization.[23] Key elements include:

- Clearly defined tasks and objectives
- Effective team leadership
- Good balance of team roles and match to individual behavioural style
- Effective conflict resolution mechanisms within the group
- Continuing liaison with external organization

Teams typically go through four stages of development, popularly known as 'forming, storming, norming and performing'.[115] That is, they are put together and then go through a phase of resolving internal differences and conflicts around leadership, objectives, etc. Emerging from this process is a commitment to shared values and norms governing the way the team will work, and it is only after this stage that teams can move on to effective performance of their task.

Central to team performance is the make-up of the team itself, with good matching between the role requirements of the group and the behavioural preferences of the individuals involved. Belbin's work has been influential here in providing an approach to team role matching. He classifies people into a number of preferred role types—for example, 'the plant' (someone who is a source of new ideas), 'the resource investigator', 'the shaper' and the 'completer/finisher'. Research has shown that the most effective teams are those with diversity in background, ability and behavioural style. In one noted experiment highly talented but similar people in 'Apollo' teams consistently performed less well than mixed, average groups.[89]

Team-building is not the only aspect affecting performance. Other influential factors include:

- Team size
- Team structure
- Team process—the way in which meetings are organized and decisions taken
- Team leadership
- Team environment/organizational context

Holti and Neumann provide a useful summary of the key factors involved in developing teamworking.[116] Although there is considerable current emphasis on teamworking, we should remember that teams are not always the answer. In particular, there are dangers in putting nominal teams together where unresolved conflicts, personality clashes, lack of effective group processes and other factors can diminish their effectiveness. Tranfield *et. al.* look at the issue of teamworking in a number of different contexts and highlight the importance of selecting and building the appropriate team for the task and the context.[117]

Teams are increasingly being seen as a mechanism for bridging boundaries within the organization—and indeed, in dealing with interorganizational issues. Cross-functional teams can bring together the different knowledge sets needed for tasks like product development or process improvement—but they also represent a forum where often deep-rooted differences in perspectives can be resolved.[118] Lawrence and Lorsch in their pioneering study of differentiation and integration within organizations found that interdepartmental clashes were a major source of friction and contributed much to delays and difficulties in operations. Successful organizations were those which invested in multiple methods for integrating across groups—and the cross-functional team was one of the most valuable resources.[59] But, as we indicated above, building such teams is a major strategic task—they will not happen by accident, and they will require additional efforts to ensure that the implicit conflicts of values and beliefs are resolved effectively.

Teams also provide a powerful enabling mechanism for achieving the kind of decentralized and agile operating structure which many organizations aspire to. As a substitute for hierarchical control, self-managed teams working within a defined area of autonomy can be very effective. For example, Honeywell's defence avionics factory reports a dramatic improvement in on-time delivery—from below 40% in the 1980s to 99% in 1996—to the implementation of self-managing teams.[119] In the Netherlands one of the most successful bus companies is Vancom Zuid-Limburg which has improved both price and non-price perform-ance and has high customer satisfaction ratings. Again they attribute this to the use of self-managing teams and to the reduction in overhead costs which results. In their system one manager supervises over 40 drivers where the average for the sector is a ratio of 1 : 8. Drivers are also encouraged to participate in problem-finding and solving in areas like maintenance, customer service and planning.[120]

11.7 Creative Climate

'Microsoft's only factory asset is the human imagination'

(Bill Gates)

Many great inventions came about as the result of lucky accidental discoveries—for example, Velcro fasteners, the adhesive behind 'Post-it' notes or the principle of float glass manufacturing. But as Louis Pasteur observed, 'chance favours the prepared mind' and we can usefully deploy our understanding of the creative process to help set up the conditions within which such 'accidents' can take place.

Two important features of creativity are relevant in doing this. The first is to recognize that creativity is an attribute which everyone possesses—but their pre-ferred *style* of expressing it varies widely.[121] Some people are comfortable with ideas which challenge the whole way in which the universe works, whilst others prefer smaller increments of change—ideas about how to improve the jobs they do or their working environment in small incremental steps. (This explains in part why so many 'creative' people—artists, composers, mad scientists—are also seen as 'difficult' or living outside the conventions of acceptable behaviour.) This has major implications for how we manage creativity within the organization; innovation, as we have seen, involves bringing something new into widespread use, not just inventing it. Whilst the initial flash may require a significant creative leap, much of the rest of the process will involve hundreds of small problem-finding and solving exercises—each of which needs creative input. And though the former may need the skills or inspiration of a particular individual the latter require the input of many different people over a sustained period of time. Developing the light bulb or the Post-it note or any successful innovation is actually the story of the combined creative endeavour of many individuals.

Organizational structures are the visible artefacts of what can be termed an innovative culture—one in which innovation can thrive. Culture is a complex concept, but it basically equates to the pattern of shared values, beliefs and agreed norms which shape behaviour—in other words, it is 'the way we do things round here' in any organization. Schein suggests that culture can be understood in terms of three linked levels, with the deepest and most inaccessible being what each individual believes about the world—the 'taken for granted' assumptions. These shape individual actions and the collective and socially nego-tiated version of these behaviours defines the dominant set of norms and values for the group. Finally, behaviour in line with these norms creates a set of arte-facts—structures, processes, symbols, etc.—which reinforce the pattern.[122]

Given this model it is clear that management cannot directly change culture—but it can intervene at the level of artefacts—by changing structures or pro-cesses—and by providing models and reinforcing preferred styles of behaviour. Such 'culture change' actions are now widely tried in the context of change pro-grammes towards total quality management and other models of organization which require more participative culture.

Kanter[5] provides a list of environmental factors which contribute to stifling innovation; these include:

- Dominance of restrictive vertical relationships
- Poor lateral communications
- Limited tools and resources
- Top-down dictates
- Formal, restricted vehicles for change
- Reinforcing a culture of inferiority (i.e. innovation always has to come from outside to be any good)
- Uunfocused innovative activity
- Unsupporting accounting practices

The effect of these is to create and reinforce the behavioural norms which inhibit creativity and lead to a culture lacking in innovation. It follows from this that developing an innovative climate is not a simple matter since it consists of a com-plex web of behaviours and artefacts. And changing this culture is not likely to happen quickly or as a result of single initiatives (such as restructuring or mass training in a new technique).

Instead, building a creative climate involves systematic development of organizational structures, communication policies and procedures, reward and recognition systems, training policy, accounting and measurement systems and deployment of strategy. Mechanisms for doing so in various different kinds of organizations and in different national cultures are described by a number of authors including Rickards, Ekvall, Cook, Leonard and Swap.[38-41]

Of particular relevance in this area is the design of effective reward systems. Many organizations have reward systems which reflect the performance of repeated tasks, rather than encourage the development of new ideas. Progress is associated with 'doing things by the book' rather than challenging and changing things. By contrast, innovative organizations look for ways to reward creative behaviour, and to encourage its emergence. Examples of reward systems include the establishment of a 'dual ladder' which enables technologically innovative staff to progress within the organization without needing to move across to management posts.[123]

One aspect of this worth highlighting concerns the emerging idea of 'intrapre-neurship'—internal entrepreneurship.[51] In an organization with a supportive and innovative culture, individuals with bright ideas can progress them with support and encouragement from the system. For example, in 3M the culture encourages individuals to follow up interesting ideas and allows them up to 15% of their time for such activity. If things look promising, there are internal venture funds to enable a more thorough exploration—and if the individual thinks he/she can build a business out of the idea, 3M will back it and give them the responsibility to run it. In this way the company has grown through organic, 'intrapreneurial' means. Chapter 10 explores this theme in more detail.

11.8 External Focus

Characteristic of successful innovating organizations is an orientation which is essentially open to new stimuli from outside. Whether the signals are of threats or opportunities, these organizations have approaches which pick them up and communicate them through the organization. Developing a sense of external orientation—towards key customers or major technological developments—and ensuring that this pervades organizational thinking at all levels are of considerable importance in building an innovative organization.

One of the consistent themes in the literature on innovation success and failure concerns the need to understand user needs. Developing this sense of customer requirements is essential in dealing with the external marketplace as we saw in Chapter 7, but it is also a principle which can be usefully extended within the organization. By developing a widespread awareness of customers—both internal and external—quality and innovation can be significantly improved. This approach—which forms one of the cornerstones of 'total quality management' thinking—contrasts sharply with the traditional model in which problems were passed on between sequential elements in the innovation process, and where there was no provision for feedback or mutual adjustment.[36]

Of course, not all industries have the same degree of customer involvement—and in many the dominant focus is more on technology. This does not mean that customer focus is an irrelevant concept; the issue here is one of building relationships which enable clear and regular communication, providing inputs for problem-solving and shared innovation.[124]

Mechanisms for enabling a broader awareness of internal and external customers vary but examples include:

- Voice of the customer techniques (such as quality function deployment)[125]
- Visits to customers and suppliers by different groups of employees[126, 127]
- Internal customer training
- Involvement with customers/secondment to customers[113]

11.9 Extensive Communication

Closely linked to the customer focus point in the previous section is the requirement for extensive communication. By this we mean communication which is multidirectional (up, down and laterally) and which makes use of multiple channels and media. Many problems occur in the innovation process through failures in communication, particularly between different functional elements in the process. Developing mechanisms for resolving conflicts and improving clarity and frequency of communication across such interfaces are critical to innovation success, particularly since so much problem-solving depends on combining different knowledge sets which may be widely distributed across the organization.

Whilst some organizations may benefit from 'gatekeeper' figures which can channel and focus communication, most require more structured approaches. Mechanisms for enhancing communication include:

- Job rotation and secondment
- Cross-functional teams and projects
- Policy-deployment and review sessions
- Team briefings
- Multiple media—video, notice boards, electronic mail, etc.

This latter theme is becoming highly relevant as organizations recognize the need to think actively about knowledge management. Innovation is increasingly seen as requiring the creating, combination, sharing and deployment of knowledge—and this places strong emphasis on the channels and mechanisms which are used for communication. New technologies such as 'groupware' and intranets are being widely used to facilitate this, but attention is also being paid to the social organization of knowledge networks.[46, 82]

11.10 The Learning Organization

Much recent discussion has focused on the concept of 'learning organizations', seeing knowledge as the basis for competition in the twenty-first century. Mobilizing and managing knowledge becomes a primary task and many of the recipes offered for achieving this depend upon mobilizing a much higher level of participation in innovative problem-solving and on building such routines into the fabric of organizational life.[42, 43, 45]

Innovation can be represented as a learning cycle, involving a process of experiment, experience, reflection and consolidation. Managing the process is primarily a function of the creation of conditions under which learning opportunities emerge and are exploited. A key determinant or relative success or failure is the ability to manage this learning cycle in explicit form—for example, in the development of new products or the implementation of new process technology.[128-130]

Crucially, what is learned and developed with each cycle of innovation is not only technological knowledge to add to the firm-specific knowledge base (in formal and tacit form), but also knowledge about how to manage the process itself. To take an analogy, human beings not only acquire new content of knowledge as they grow, but they also learn to learn; some develop more effective learning strategies than others, whilst for others it is a case of 'some people never learn'. Over time, successful innovators review and build upon particular courses of action and internalize particular routines for managing the innovation challenge—for example, ways of getting close to users, ways of managing projects, ways of harnessing and sharing information, ways of exciting and supporting intrapreneurship, etc.

There is, of course, no guarantee that the cycle will be completed; evidence suggests many organizations repeat mistakes and fail to learn from earlier problems in innovation. This has prompted much discussion about the process of post-innovation auditing and consolidation—and the need to move beyond blame accounting or simple financial or cost–benefit auditing to more comprehensive reviews. There is also the question of 'unlearning'—of eliminating those routines which do not contribute to success. Part of learning new tricks is the ability to forget old ones—and the reason old dogs are difficult to teach is that the old patterns are very deeply embedded.[50, 88, 131]

This discussion implies the presence not only of a learning loop around the acquisition and absorption of technological knowledge but a second, double, loop concerned with learning and improving the innovation process itself.[44] Organizations do not learn, it is the people within them who do; routines are thus directed at creating the stage on which they act and the scripts they work to. In particular we are interested in the routines which the organization develops to enable the learning process, and in particular in the ways in which individual and shared learning can be mobilized. For example, Garvin[42] suggests the following mechanisms as important:

- Training and development of staff
- Development of a formal learning process based on a problem-solving cycle
- Monitoring and measurement
- Documentation
- Experiment
- Display
- Challenge existing practices
- Use of different perspectives
- Reflection—learning from the past

11.11 Organizational Innovation

The preceding section has explored some of the major features of innovative organizations, and indicated a wide range of characteristics which have been found to be important. What this highlights is the danger of simplistic prescriptions for organization design; whilst loose and organic forms may be appropriate under some conditions they are by no means always so. And innovation is not simply influenced by structure—many other dimensions of organizational process (such as leadership, teamworking and participation) are also important.

It is worth concluding this chapter with a brief look at the concept of organizational innovation—that is, obtaining competitive advantage through reconfiguring organizations. A good example is 'total quality management' (TQM) which aims to create new organizational behaviour around improved quality and continuous innovation. Components of TQM include:

- Underlying values and beliefs about the nature of quality, the limits to quality (perfection versus acceptable levels of defects), whose responsibility quality is, etc.
- Processes for assuring quality, moving from inspection to underlying process management (using various tools for monitoring, measuring and improving)

- Structures covering how quality is managed, with a shift from specialized inspectors and quality correction to overall prevention and control at the point at which problems emerge
- Strategic framework, in which quality is seen as a major objective and deployed within local and individual objectives

Not surprisingly, given the extent of change implied, many TQM programmes fail and others have been extensively re-engineered and relaunched. Frameworks have been developed (such as that for the European Quality Award or the Baldrige Award in the USA which provide a structure for developing and assessing progress on TQM, and these have been used to enable 'benchmarking' between organizations seeking to learn about organizational innovation. There is growing evidence that a long-term commitment to TQM can yield significant competitive advantage, and this is reflected by the business performance of those enterprises which have won TQM awards such as the Deming Prize, Baldrige Award or the European Quality Award.[132]

Its implementation is often accompanied by the recognition that without concomitant organizational change many investments in new technologies are unlikely to yield their full potential benefits. Good examples of this kind of change include work on business process re-engineering (BPR) in sectors like banking and insurance.[133–135]

Business process re-engineering came to prominence following work by Hammer and others with major service sector organizations such as banks and insurance companies which had invested heavily in IT as a way of raising productivity. The absence of significant gains despite this investment led to the recognition that 'computerizing chaos' would simply compound the problem and that what was needed was a fundamental rethink about the overall design of organization and processes within these enterprises. Process re-engineering effectively takes a blank sheet of paper and asks 'how could we best perform this process to achieve customer satisfaction?'—and then compares the resulting model with what actually happens. Typically, it identifies unnecessary activities which fail to add value and which introduce delays and redundancy into the system; not surprisingly BPR also highlights areas where there is overmanning and has thus been a catalyst for many 'downsizing' programmes.

Although some of the tools used (which draw heavily on systems theory) are sometimes new, the underlying concept of BPR is essentially familiar in industrial engineering and traditional organization and methods (O&M) practice. Its popularity during the 1990s—and the significant benefits reported through BPR projects—is an indication of the extent to which organizational innovation had been neglected over the previous two decades.

It is also important to recognize that organizational innovation is not confined within the firm but is increasingly being applied to inter-enterprise relationships. In theoretical terms, uncertain and turbulent environmental conditions are forcing fims into relationships in which coupling shifts from stable 'pooled' arrangements in which each unit is largely independent of others and towards 'reciprocal' modes which require much higher levels of interdependence. The consequence is that interorganizational co-ordination arrangements shift from traditional links governed by procedure and rules—to more fluid and co-operative arrangements which stress longer-term partnerships and mutual development. This in turn represents a major challenge, as Lamming points out, to the basic type of adversarial relationship which has existed in many industries.[74] Thus we are seeing an increased incidence of networking as a mode of operation, bringing together many different organizations in mutually beneficial arrangements for complex product development, rapid and high-quality supply, fast time to market, etc.

Developing effective networks is not simply a matter of identifying groups of firms with a common purpose. Just as effective teams do not happen by accident, so high-performance networks require attention to internal processes and to their overall management—or governance, as many commentators have started to term it.[136] Core processes of network operation such as decision-making and conflict resolution depend on active leadership/management and on facilitation.[77]

TQM, BPR and networking are typical examples of organizational innovations, but many others can be identified—such as 'mass customization', cellular manufacturing, 'virtual firms' and the development of the 'lean enterprise'. The danger with all of these programmes is that they are seen as one-off radical changes rather than as part of a continuing programme of organizational adaptation and development. Just as technological changes progress mainly through incremental improvements punctuated by dramatic and visible radical shifts, so organizational innovation needs to be managed as a similar combination. Without this perspective there is a real risk that—as has, perhaps, been the fate of TQM and BPR in recent years—these changes are seen simply as fashions which come and go, leaving the underlying organization unchanged.

Once again the main conclusion to emerge for effective innovation management is that informed choices must be made (requiring a good understanding of the process) and appropriate options selected (to suit particular circumstances).

Further Reading

The field of organizational behaviour is widely discussed and there are some good basic texts, including Morgan,[137] Buchanan and Huczynski[138] and Mintzberg[13]. Specific issues surrounding the development of innovative organizations are well treated by Hesselbein,[15] Leifer,[139] Kanter[140] and Clark,[141] whilst the core text by Burns and Stalker is still valuable reading.[12] Peters is typical of the new 'chaos' school of thought which opposes bureaucratic forms[11, 131] but other studies suggest that this needs tempering with some elements of structure.

Many books and articles look at specific aspects—for example, the development of creative climates,[38, 40, 41, 142] teamworking,[24, 116, 118, 143] or continuous improvement.[32, 33, 91] Increasingly, the theme of organizational learning is being seen as central, and a number of good descriptive and prescriptive texts are available.[47, 144–147] Case studies of innovative organizations focus on many of the issues highlighted in this chapter; good examples include refs 76, 139, 148–152. In particular, a number of books discuss the relationship between management and shop floor and the potential for more participative forms.[86, 140, 153–155]

References

1 Pfeffer, J. (1994) *Competitive Advantage through People*. Harvard Business School Press, Boston, Mass.

2 Francis, D. (1997) *Competitiveness through Partnerships with People*. Department of Trade and Industry, London.

3 Huselid, M. (1995) 'The impact of human resource management practices on turnover, productivity and corporate financial performance', *Academy of Management Journal*, **38**, 647.

4 Kay, J. (1993) *Foundations of Corporate Success: How business strategies add value*. Oxford University Press, Oxford, 416 pp.

5 Kanter, R. (1984) *The Change Masters*. Unwin, London.

6 Hamel, G. (2000) *Leading the Revolution*. Harvard Business School Press, Boston, Mass.

7 Nayak, P. and J. Ketteringham (1986) *Breakthroughs: How leadership and drive create commercial innovations that sweep the world*. Mercury, London.

8 Champy, J. and N. Nohria (eds) (1996) *Fast Forward*. Harvard Business School Press, Cambridge, Mass.

9 Woodward, J. (1965) *Industrial Organization: Theory and practice*. Oxford University Press, Oxford.

10 Thompson, J. (1967) *Organizations in Action*. McGraw-Hill, New York.

11 Peters, T. (1988) *Thriving on Chaos*. Free Press, New York.

12 Burns, T. and G. Stalker (1961) *The Management of Innovation*. Tavistock, London.

13 Mintzberg, H. (1979) *The Structuring of Organizations*. Prentice-Hall, Englewood Cliffs, NJ.

14 Perrow, C. (1967) 'A framework for the comparative analysis of organizations', *American Sociological Review*, **32**, 194–208.

15 Hesselbein, F., M. Goldsmith and R. Beckhard (eds) (1997) *Organization of the Future*. Jossey-Bass/The Drucker Foundation, San Francisco.

16 Allen, T. (1977) *Managing the Flow of Technology*. MIT Press, Cambridge, Mass.

17 Rothwell, R. (1992) 'Successful industrial innovation: critical success factors for the 1990s', *R&D Management*, **22** (3), 221–239.

18 Rubenstein, A. (1994) 'Ideation and entrepreneurship', in Souder, W. and Sherman, J. (eds), *Managing New Technology Development*. McGraw-Hill, New York.

19 Bess, J. (1995) *Creative R&D leadership: Insights from Japan*. Quorum Books, Westport, Conn.

20 Tichy, N. and M. Devanna (1986) *The Transformational Leader*. Wiley, New York.

21 Dyson, J. (1997) *Against the Odds*. Orion, London.

22 Kharbanda, O. and M. Stallworthy (1990) *Project Teams*. NCC-Blackwell, Manchester.

23 Bixby, K. (1987) *Superteams*. Fontana, London.

24 Katzenbach, J. and D. Smith (1992) *The Wisdom of Teams*. Harvard Business School Press, Boston, Mass.

25 Francis, D. and D. Young (1988) *Top Team Building*. Gower, Aldershot.

26 Thamhain, H. and D. Wilemon (1987) 'Building high performing engineering project teams', *IEEE Transactions on Engineering Management*, **EM-34** (3), 130–137.

27 Pedler, M., T. Boydell and J. Burgoyne (1991) *The Learning Company: A strategy for sustainable development*. McGraw-Hill, Maidenhead.

28 Jarvis, V. and S. Prais (1995) *The Quality of Manufactured Products in Britain and Germany*. National Institute of Economic and Social Research, London.

29 Prais, S. (1995) *Productivity, Education and Training*. Cambridge University Press, Cambridge.

30 Spence, W. (1994) *Innovation; The communication of change in ideas, practices and products*. Chapman and Hall, London.

31 De Meyer, A. (1985) 'The flow of technological innovation in an R&D department', *Research Policy*, **4**, 315–328.

32 Imai, M. (1997) *Gemba Kaizen*. McGraw-Hill, New York.

33 Boer, H. *et al.* (1999) *CI Changes: From suggestion box to the learning organization*. Ashgate, Aldershot.

34 Robinson, A. (1991) *Continuous Improvement in Operations*. Productivity Press, Cambridge, Mass.

35 Bessant, J. and D. Francis (1999) 'Developing strategic continuous improvement capability', *International Journal of Operations and Production Management*, **19** (11).

36 Oakland, J. (1989) *Total Quality Management*. Pitman, London

37 Brown, S. *et al.* (2000) *Strategic Operations Management*. Butterworth Heinemann, Oxford.

38 Leonard, D. and W. Swap (1999) *When Sparks Fly: Igniting creativity in groups*. Harvard Business School Press, Boston, Mass.

39 Ekvall, G. (1990) 'The organizational culture of idea management', in Henry, J. and Walker, D. (eds), *Managing innovation*. Sage, London, pp. 73–80.

40 Cook, P. (1999) *Best Practice Creativity*. Gower, Aldershot.

41 Rickards, T. (1997) *Creativity and Problem Solving at Work*. Gower, Aldershot.

42 Garvin, D. (1993) 'Building a learning organization', *Harvard Business Review*, July/Aug., 78–91.

43 Leonard-Barton, D. (1995) *Wellsprings of Knowledge: Building and sustaining the sources of innovation*. Harvard Business School Press, Boston, Mass., 335 pp.

44 Argyris, C. and D. Schon (1970) *Organizational Learning*. Addison-Wesley, Reading, Mass.

45 Senge, P. (1990) *The Fifth Discipline*. Doubleday, New York.

46 Nonaka, I. (1991) 'The knowledge creating company', *Harvard Business Review*, Nov.–Dec., 96–104.

47 Starkey, K. (1996) *How Organizations Learn*. International Thomson Business Press, London.

48 Womack, J. (1990) in *American Heritage*, Sept./Oct., p. 58.

49 Womack, J., D. Jones, and D. Roos (1991) *The Machine that Changed the World*. Rawson Associates, New York.

50 Christenson, C. (1997) *The Innovator's Dilemma*. Harvard Business School Press, Cambridge, Mass.

51 Pinchot, G. (1985) *Intrapreneuring—Why You Don't Have to Leave a Corporation to Become an Entrepreneur*. Harper and Row, New York.

52 'Patience of Jobs pays off', *Financial Times* (1995) London, June 13, p. 7.

53 Moody, F. (1995) *I Sing the Body Electronic*. Hodder and Stoughton, London.

54 Cooper, R. (1994) 'Third-generation new product processes', *Journal of Product Innovation Management*, **11** (1), 3–14.

55 Kaplinsky, R., F. den Hertog and B. Coriat (1995) *Europe's Next Step*. Frank Cass, London.

56 Semler, R. (1993) *Maverick*. Century Books, London.

57 Miles, R. and C. Snow (1978) *Organizational Strategy, Structure and Process*. McGraw-Hill, New York.

58 Lawrence, P. and P. Dyer (1983) *Renewing American Industry*. Free Press, New York.

59 Lawrence, P. and J. Lorsch (1967) *Organization and Environment*. Harvard University Press, Cambridge, Mass.

60 Stalk, G. and T. Hout (1990) *Competing against Time: How time-based competition is reshaping global markets*. Free Press, New York.

61 Child, J. (1980) *Organizations*. Harper and Row, London.

62 Greiner, L. (1972) 'Evolution and revolution as organizations grow', *Harvard Business Review*, July/Aug., 37–46.

63 Adler, P. (1992) 'The learning bureaucracy: NUMMI', in Staw, B. and Cummings, L. (eds), *Research in Organizational Behaviour*. JAI Press, Greenwich, Conn.

64 Piore, M. and C. Sabel (1982) *The Second Industrial Divide*. Basic Books, New York.

65 Porter, M. (1997) 'Location, knowledge creation and competitiveness', in *Knowledge Capitalism: Competitiveness re-evaluated*. Academy of Management, Boston, Mass.

66 Nadvi, K. (1997) *The Cutting Edge: Collective efficiency and international competitiveness in Pakistan*. Institute of Development Studies, University of Sussex.

67 Humphrey, J. and H. Schmitz (1996) 'The triple C approach to local industrial policy', *World Development*, **24** (12), 1859–1877.

68 Dodgson, M. (1991) *Technological Collaboration and Organizational Learning*. Science Policy Research Unit, University of Sussex.

69 Hobday, M. (1994) *Complex Product Systems*. Science Policy Research Unit, University of Sussex.

70 Marceau, J. (1994) 'Clusters, chains and complexes: three approaches to innovation with a public policy perspective', in Rothwell, R. and Dodgson, M. (eds), *The Handbook of Industrial Innovation*. Edward Elgar, Aldershot.

71 Tidd, J. (1997) 'Complexity, networks and learning: integrative themes for research on innovation management', *International Journal of Innovation Management*, **1** (1), 1–22.

72 Oliver, N. and M. Blakeborough (1998) 'Innovation networks: the view from the inside', in Grieve Smith J. and Michie, J. (eds), *Innovation, Co-operation and Growth*. Oxford University Press, Oxford.

73 Rush, H. *et al.* (1996) *Technology Institutes: Strategies for best practice*. International Thomson Business Press, London.

74 Lamming, R. (1993) *Beyond Partnership*. Prentice-Hall, London.

75 Hines, P. *et al.* (1999) *Value Stream Management: The Development of Lean Supply Chains*. Financial Times Management, London.

76 Dell, M. (1999) *Direct from Dell*. HarperCollins, New York.

77 Bessant, J. and G. Tsekouras (2001) 'Developing learning networks'. *A.I. and Society*, **15** (2), 82–98.

78 Clark, K. and T. Fujimoto (1992) *Product Development Performance*. Harvard Business School Press, Boston, Mass.

79 Henry, J. and D. Walker (1990) *Managing Innovation*. Sage, London.

80 Kidder, T. (1981) *The Soul of a New Machine*. Penguin, Harmondsworth.

81 Blackler, F. (1995) 'Knowledge, knowledge work and organizations', *Organization Studies*, **16** (6), 1021–1046.

82 Sapsed, J. *et al.* (2000) 'Wealth from knowledge—innovation in R&D management', *R&D Management Conference 2000*.

83 IPD (1995) *People Make the Difference*. Institute of Personnel and Development, London.

84 Bessant, J. and S. Caffyn (1997) 'High involvement innovation', *International Journal of Technology Management*, **14** (1), 7–28.

85 Smith, S. and D. Tranfield (1990) *Managing Change*. IFS Publications, Kempston.

86 Burnes, B. (1992) *Managing Change*. Pitman, London.

87 Walton, R. E. (1986) *Human Resource Practices for Implementing AMT: Report of the Committee on Effective Implementation of AMT*. National Research Council, Washington, DC.

88 Bessant, J. and J. Buckingham (1993) 'Organizational learning for effective use of CAPM', *British Journal of Management*, **4** (4), 219–234.

89 Bessant, J. (1999) 'Developing continuous improvement capability', *International Journal of Innovation Management*, **2** (4), 409–429.

90 Kaplinsky, R. (1994) *The Challenge of Easternisation*. Frank Cass, London.

91 Schroeder, D. and A. Robinson (1991) 'America's most successful export to Japan—continuous improvement programmes', *Sloan Management Review*, **32** (3), 67–81.

92 DTI (1997) *Competitiveness through Partnerships with People*. Department of Trade and Industry, London.

93 Deming, W. E. (1986) *Out of the Crisis*. MIT Press, Cambridge, Mass.

94 Crosby, P. (1997) *Quality is Free*. McGraw-Hill, New York.

95 Dertouzos, M., R. Lester and L. Thurow (1989) *Made in America: Regaining the productive edge*. MIT Press, Cambridge, Mass.

96 Garvin, D. (1988) *Managing Quality*. Free Press, New York.

97 Womack, J. and D. Jones (1997) *Lean Thinking*. Simon and Schuster, New York.

98 Schonberger, R. (1982) *Japanese Manufacturing Techniques: Nine hidden lessons in simplicity*. Free Press, New York.

99 Bessant, J. (1991) *Managing Advanced Manufacturing Technology: The challenge of the fifth wave*. NCC/Blackwell, Oxford/Manchester.

100 Shingo, S. (1983) *A Revolution in Manufacturing: The SMED system*. Productivity Press, Cambridge, Mass.

101 Suzaki, K. (1988) *The New Manufacturing Challenge*. Free Press, New York.

102 Imai, K. (1987) *Kaizen*. Random House, New York.

103 Lillrank, P. and N. Kano (1990) *Continuous Improvement; Quality control circles in Japanese industry*. University of Michigan Press, Ann Arbor.

104 Wheelwright, S. and K. Clark (1992) *Revolutionizing Product Development*. Free Press, New York.

105 Leonard-Barton, D. and W. Smith (1994) 'Transforming R&D and manufacturing capabilities', in Souder, W. and Sherman, J. (eds), *Managing New Technology Development*. McGraw-Hill, New York.

106 Ishikure, K. (1988) 'Achieving Japanese productivity and quality levels at a US plant', *Long Range Planning*, **21** (5), 10–17.

107 Wickens, P. (1987) *The Road to Nissan: Flexibility, quality, teamwork*. Macmillan, London.

108 Pfeffer, J. and J. Veiga (1999) 'Putting people first for organizational success', *Academy of Management Executive*, **13** (2), 37–48.

109 Ettlie, J. (1988) *Taking Charge of Manufacturing*. Jossey-Bass, San Francisco.

110 Jaikumar, R. (1985) 'Post-industrial manufacturing', *Harvard Business Review*, Aug./Sept.

111 Majchrzak, A. (1988) *The Human Side of Factory Automation*. Jossey-Bass, San Francisco.

112 Shiba, S., A. Graham and D. Walden (1993) *A New American TQM: Four practical revolutions in management*. Productivity Press, Portland, Oregon, 565 pp.

113 Lewis, K. (1994) *How to Transform Your Company*. Management Books 2000, London.

114 Forrester, R. and A. Drexler (1999) 'A model for team-based organization performance', *Academy of Management Executive*, **13** (3), 36–49.

115 Tuckman, B. and N. Jensen (1977) 'Stages of small group development revisited', *Group and Organizational Studies*, **2**, 419–427.

116 Holti, R., J. Neumann and H. Standing (1995) *Change Everything at Once: The Tavistock Institute's guide to developing teamwork in manufacturing*. Management Books 2000, London.

117 Tranfield, D. *et al.* (2000) 'Strategies for managing the teamworking agenda: developing a methodology for team-based organization', *International Journal of Production Economics*, **65**, 33–42.

118 Jassawalla, A. and H. Sashittal (1999) 'Building collaborative cross-functional new product teams', *Academy of Management Executive*, **13** (3), 50–53.

119 DTI (1996) UK *Software Purchasing Survey*. Department of Trade and Industry, London.

120 Van Beasekom, M. (1996) *Participation Pays! Cases of successful companies with employee participation*. Netherlands Participation Institute, The Hague.

121 Kirton, M. (1980) 'Adaptors and innovators', *Human Relations*, **3**, 213–224.

122 Schein, E. (1992) *Organizational Culture and Leadership*. Jossey-Bass, San Francisco.

123 Badawy, M. (1997) *Developing Managerial Skills in Engineers and Scientists*. Wiley, New York.

124 Schonberger, R. (1990) *Building a Chain of Customers*. Free Press, New York.

125 Hauser, J. and D. Clausing (1988) 'The house of quality', *Harvard Business Review*, May-June, 63–73.

126 Sirkin, H. and G. Stalk (1990) 'Fix the process, not the problem', *Harvard Business Review*, July/Aug., 26–33.

127 Leonard-Barton, D. (1992) 'The organization as learning laboratory', *Sloan Management Review*, **34** (1), 23–38.

128 Bowen, H. *et al.* (1994) 'Regaining the lead in manufacturing', *Harvard Business Review*, Sept./Oct., 108–144.

129 Hayes, R., S. Wheelwright and K. Clark (1988) *Dynamic Manufacturing: Creating the learning organization*. Free Press, New York.

130 Maidique, M. and B. Zirger (1985) 'The new product learning cycle', *Research Policy*, **14** (6), 299–309.

131 Peters, T. (1997) *The Circle of Innovation*. Coronet, London.

132 Garvin, D. (1991) 'How the Baldrige Award really works', *Harvard Business Review*, Nov./Dec., 80–93.

133 Hammer, M. and J. Champy (1993) *Re-engineering the Corporation*. Nicholas Brearley, New York.

134 Harrington, H. (1991) *Business Process Improvement; The breakthrough strategy for total quality, productivity and competitiveness*. McGraw-Hill, New York.

135 Davenport, T. (1992) *Process Innovation: Re-engineering work through information technology*. Harvard University Press, Boston, Mass., 326 pp.

136 Gereffi, G. (1994) 'The organization of buyer-driven global commodity chains: how U.S. retailers shape overseas production networks', in Gereffi, G. and Korzeniewicz, P. (eds), *Commodity Chains and Global Capitalism*. Praeger, London.

137 Morgan, G. (1986) *Images of Organization*. Sage, London.

138 Buchana, D. and A. Huczynski (1997) *Organizational Behaviour: An introductory text*. Prentice-Hall, London.

139 Leifer, R. *et al.* (2000) *Radical innovation*. Harvard Business School Press, Boston, Mass.

140 Kanter, R. (1996) *World Class*. Simon and Schuster, New York.

141 Clark, P. and N. Staunton (1989) *Innovation and Technology in Organisations*. Routledge, London.

142 McCloughlin, I. (1998) 'Creative technological change', in Preece, D and Bessant, J. (eds), *The Management of Technology and Innovation*. Routledge, London.

143 Tranfield, D. *et al.* (1998) 'Teamworked organisational engineering: Getting the most out of teamworking', *Management Decision*, **36** (6).

144 De Geus, A. (1996) *The Living Company*. Harvard Business School Press, Boston, Mass.

145 Pisano, G. (1994) 'Knowledge, integration and the locus of learning: An empirical analysis of process development', *Strategic Management Journal*, **15**, 85.

146 Prokesch, S. (1997) 'Unleashing the power of learning', *Harvard Business Review*, Sept./Oct., 147–168.

147 Saad, M. (1996) 'Development of learning capabilities via the transfer of advanced manufacturing technology: the case of two Algerian firms', *Science, Technology and Development*, **14** (1), 21–35.

148 Gundling, E. (2000) *The 3M way to Innovation: Balancing people and profit*. Kodansha International, New York.

149 Kanter, R. (ed.) (1997) *Innovation: Breakthrough thinking at 3M, DuPont, GE, Pfizer and Rubbermaid*. Harper Business, New York.

150 Baden-Fuller, C. and M. Pitt (1996) *Strategic Innovation*. Routledge, London.

151 Japan, Management, and Association (1987) *Canon Production System: Creative involvement of the total workforce*. Productivity Press, Cambridge, Mass.

152 Legge, K. *et al.* (eds) (1991) *Case Studies in Information Technology, People and Organizations*. Blackwell, Oxford.

153 Preece, D. (1995) 'Organizations and technical change', in Bessant, J. and Preece, D. (eds), Routledge Series *Management of Technology*. Routledge/International Thompson, London.

154 Dawson, P. (1996) 'Technology and quality: change in the workplace', in Bessant, J. and Preece, D. (eds), *Management of Technology and Innovation*, International Thomson Business Press, London.

155 Clark, J. (1995) *Managing Innovation and Change: People, technology and strategy*. Sage, London.

Chapter 12

CREATING INNOVATIVE NEW FIRMS

Much of what we have discussed so far has been directed to the issue of managing innovation in large, complex organizations. Most of the management structures and processes we have identified are equally applicable to smaller organizations, but other factors are unique to smaller firms, such as funding and growth. Contrary to popular belief, the majority of small firms are not particularly innovative, so here we examine the nature of innovative small firms and the issues particular to their creation, management and growth.

12.1 Sources of New Technology-based Firms

In Chapter 5 we identified four categories of small firms, including specialist suppliers, supplier dominated, superstars and NTBFs. There is a wealth of research on small and medium-sized enterprises (SMEs), and in particular their role in innovation and economic growth. However, we are concerned here with a subset of SMEs which are based on new technologies. Such firms differ from other SMEs because typically they are established by highly qualified personnel, require large amounts of capital and are characterized by greater technical and market risk.

Much of what we know about new technology-based firms (NTBFs) is based on the experience of firms in the USA, in particular, the growth of biotechnology, semiconductor and software firms. Many of these originated from a parent or 'incubator' organization, typically either an academic institution or large well-established firm. Examples of university incubators include Stanford which spawned much of Silicon Valley, the Massachusetts Institute of Technology (MIT) which spawned Route 128 in Boston, and Imperial and Cambridge in the UK. MIT in particular has become the archetype academic incubator, and in addition to the creation of Route 128, its alumni have established some 200 NTBFs in northern California, and account for more than a fifth of employment in Silicon

Valley.[1] The so-called MIT model has been adopted worldwide, so far with limited success. For example, in 1999 Cambridge University in the UK formed a UK government-sponsored joint venture with MIT to help develop spin-offs in the UK. However, to put such initiatives into perspective, Hermann Hauser, a venture capitalist, notes 'Stanford alumni have produced companies worth a trillion dollars. MIT half a trillion dollars. If Cambridge is getting to $20bn we will be lucky.' One reason is the differences in scale. Mike Lynch, founder of the software company Autonomy, observes 'Silicon Valley is 60 miles long and in the last few months there will have been 70 to 80 money raisings in the $50 million to $200 million range. In Cambridge we might think of one, perhaps.'

Examples of large incubator firms include the Xerox PARC and Bell Laboratories in the USA which spawned Fairchild Semiconductor which in turn led to numerous spin-offs including Intel, Advanced Memory Systems, Teledyne and Advanced Micro-Devices. Similarly, Engineering Research Associates (ERA) led to more than 40 new firms, including Cray, Control Data Systems, Sperry and Univac. In many cases, incubator firms provide the technical entrepreneurs, and the associated academic institutions provide the additional qualified manpower.

NTBF spin-offs tend to cluster around their respective incubator organizations, forming regional networks of expertise. The firms tend to remain close to their parents for a number of technical and personal reasons. Most NTBFs retain contacts with their parent organizations to gain financial and technical support, and are often reluctant to disrupt their social and family lives whilst establishing a new venture. Perhaps surprisingly, the mortality rate of NTBFs is lower than that of most types of new firm, around 20–30% in 10 years compared to more than 80% for other types of new business.[2] One explanation for the higher survival rate of NTBFs is that the barriers to entry are higher than for many other businesses, in terms of expertise and capital. Therefore those NTBFs which are able to overcome such barriers are more likely to survive. The concentration of start-ups in region can create positive feedback, through demonstration effects and by increasing the demand for, and experience of, supporting institutions, such as venture capitalists, legal services and contract research and production, thereby improving the environment and probability of success of subsequent start-ups. Failures are an inherent part of such a system, and providing a steady stream of new venture proposals exists and venture capitalists maintain diverse investment portfolios and are ruthless with failed ventures, the system continues to learn from both good and bad investments.

However, the unique circumstances of the US environment in the 1970s and 1980s question the generalizability of the lessons of Silicon Valley and Route 128. Specifically, the role of the defence industry investment, liberal tax regimes and sources of venture capital were unique. In addition, it is important to distinguish the evolutionary growth of such regional clusters of NTBFs, from more recent attempts to establish science parks based around universities. For example, success of science parks in Europe and Asia in the 1990s, and other attempts to emulate the early US experiences, has been limited.[3] A survey comparing high-technology firms located on and off university science parks concluded that there were no statistically significant differences between their technological inputs, such as expenditure on R&D, and outputs, such as new products and patents.[4]

12.2 University Incubators

The creation and sharing of intellectual property is a core role of a university, but managing it for commercial gain is a different challenge. Most universities with significant commercial research contracts understand how to license, and the roles of all parties—the academics, the university and the commercial organization—are relatively clear. In particular, the academic will normally continue with the research whilst possibly having a consultancy arrangement with the commercial company. However, forming an independent company is a different matter. Here both the university and the scientist must agree that spin-out is the most viable option for technology commercialization and must negotiate a spin-out deal. This may include questions of, for example, equity split, royalties, academic and university investment in the new venture, academic secondment, identification and transfer of intellectual property and use of university resources in the start-up phase. In short, it is complicated. As Chris Evans, founder of Chiroscience and Merlin Ventures notes: 'Academics and universities . . . have no management, no muscle, no vision, no business plan and that is 90% of the task of exploiting science and taking it to the market place. There is a tendency for universities to think, "we invented the thing so we are already 50% there". The fact is they are 50% to nowhere' (*Times Higher*, 27 March 1998). A characteristically provocative statement, but it does highlight the gulf between research and successful commercialization.

Since the mid-1980s the role of universities in the commercialization of technology has increased significantly. For example, the number of patents granted to US universities doubled between 1984 and 1989, and doubled again between 1989 and 1997. In 1979 the number of patents granted to US universities was only 264, compared to 2436 in 1997. There are a number of explanations for this significant increase in patent activity. Changes in government funding and intellectual property law played a role, but detailed analysis indicates that the most significant reason was technological opportunity. For example, changes in funding and law in the 1980s clearly encouraged many more universities to establish licensing and technology transfer departments, but the impact of these has been relatively small. For example, there is strong evidence that the scientific and commercial quality of patents has fallen since the mid-1980s as a result of these policy changes, and that the distribution of activity has a very long tail. Measured in terms of the number of patents held or exploited, or by income from patent and software licences, commercialization of technology is highly concentrated in a small number of elite universities which were highly active prior to changes to funding policy and law: the top 20 US universities account for 70% of the patent activity.[5] Moreover, at each of these elite universities a very small number of key patents account for most of the licensing income, the five most successful patents typically account for 70–90% of total income.[6] This suggests that a (rare) combination of research excellence and critical mass is required to succeed in the commercialization of technology. Nonetheless, technological opportunity has reduced some of the barriers to commercialization. Specifically, the growing importance of developments in the biosciences and software present new opportunities for universities to benefit from the commercialization of technology.

University spin-outs are an alternative to exploitation of technology through licensing, and involve the creation of an entirely new venture based upon intellectual property developed within the university. They may arise for a number of possible reasons:

- No existing company is ready or able to take on the project on a licensing basis
- The invention consists of a portfolio of products or is an 'enabling technology' capable of application in a number of fields
- The inventors have a strong preference for forming a company and are prepared to invest their time, effort and money in a start-up

As such they involve the 'academic entrepreneur' more fully in the detail of creating and managing a market entry strategy than is the case for other forms of commercialization. They also require major career decisions for the participants. Consequently, they highlight most clearly the dilemmas faced as the scientist tries to manage the interface between academe and industry. The extent to which an individual is motivated to attempt the launch of a venture depends upon three related factors—antecedent influences, the incubator organization and environmental factors:

- *Antecedent influences*, often called the 'characteristics' of the entrepreneur, include genetic factors, family influences, educational choices, and previous career experiences all contribute to the entrepreneur's decision to start a venture
- *Individual incubator experiences* immediately prior to start-up include the nature of the physical location, the type of skills and knowledge acquired, contact with possible fellow founders, the type of new venture or small business experience gained
- *Environmental factors* include economic conditions, availability of venture capital, entrepreneurial role models, availability of support services

There are relatively few data on the characteristics of the academic entrepreneur, partly due to the low numbers involved, but also because the traditional context within which they have operated, particularly as they apply to IPR and equity sharing, has meant that many have been unwilling to be researched. It is also probable that this is compounded by inadequate university data capture systems. Nevertheless, it is clear that in the USA, scientists and engineers working in universities have long become disposed towards the commercialization of research. A study of American universities in 1990 observed: 'Over the last eight years we have seen increasing legitimising of university–industry research interactions.'[7] A study of 237 scientists working in three large national laboratories in the USA found clear differences between the levels of education in inventors in national laboratories and those in a study of technical entrepreneurs from MIT.[8] The study found significant differences between entrepreneurs and non-entrepreneurs in terms of situational variables such as the level of involvement in business activities outside the laboratory or the receipt of royalties from past inventions. A study of scientists in four research institutes in the UK identified a relationship between attitudes to industry, number of industry links and commercial activity.[9] This begs the question: what is the direction of causation? Do entrepreneurial researchers seek more links outside the organization, or do more links encourage entrepreneurial behaviour?

Entrepreneurs, academic or otherwise, require a supportive environment. Surveys indicate that two-thirds of university scientists and engineers now support the need to commercialize their research, and half the need for start-up assistance.[10] There are two levels of analysis of the university environment, the formal institutional rules, policies and structures, and the 'local norms' within the individual department. There are a number of institutional variables which might affect academic entrepreneurship:

1. Formal policy and support for entrepreneurial activity from management.
2. Perceived seriousness of constraints to entrepreneurship, e.g. IPR issues.
3. Incidence of successful commercialization, which demonstrate feasibility and provide role models.

A survey of 778 life scientists working in 40 US universities concluded that developing formal policies may send a signal, but the effect on individual behaviour depends very much on whether these policies are reinforced by behavioural expectations.[11] They found that individual characteristics and local norms appear to be equally effective predictors of entrepreneurial activity, but only provided 'weak and unsystematic predictions of the forms of entrepreneurship'. Where successful, this can create a virtuous circle, the demonstration effect of a successful spin-out encouraging others to try. This leads to clusters of spin-outs in space and time, resulting in entrepreneurial departments or universities, rather than isolated entrepreneurial academics. Local norms or culture at the departmental level will influence the effectiveness of formal policies by providing a strong mediating effect between the institutional context and individual perceptions. Local norms evolve through self-selection during recruitment, resulting in staff with similar personal values and behaviour, and reinforced by peer pressure or behavioural socialization resulting in a convergence of personal values and behaviour. However, there is a potential conflict between the pursuit of knowledge and its commercial exploitation, and a real danger of lowering research standards exists. Therefore it is essential to have explicit guidelines for the conduct of business in a university environment:[12]

1. Specific guidelines on the use of university facilities, staff and students and intellectual property rights.
2. Specific guidelines for, and periodic reviews of, the dual employment of scientist-entrepreneurs, including permanent part-time positions.
3. Mechanisms to resolve issues of financial ownership and the allocation of research contracts between the university and the venture.

12.3 Profile of a Technical Entrepreneur

This section draws on the research by Roberts,[1] who studied 156 NTBFs which were spin-offs from MIT in the USA (herein referred to as 'The US study'), and

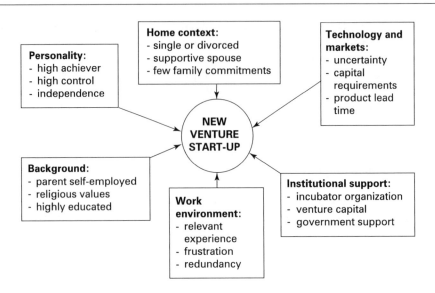

FIGURE 12.1   Factors affecting the decision to establish an NTBF.

Oakey,[13] who examined 131 NTBFs in the UK, and more general research on NTBFs (herein referred to as 'The UK study').

The creation of an NTBF is the interaction of individual skills and disposition and the technological and market characteristics. The US study emphasizes the role of personal characteristics, such as family background, goal orientation, personality and motivation, whereas the UK study stresses the role of technological and market factors. The decision to start an NTBF typically begins with a desire to gain independence and to escape the bureaucracy of a large organization, whether it be in the public or private sector. Thus the background, psychological profile and work and technical experience of a technical entrepreneur all contribute to the decision to form an NTBF (Figure 12.1).

Much of the American research on NTBFs, and more general studies of entrepreneurs, tends to emphasize the background and characteristics of a typical entrepreneur. Factors found to affect the likelihood of establishing a venture include:

- Family background
- Religion
- Formal education and early work experience
- Psychological profile

A number of studies confirm that both family background and religion affect an individual's propensity to establish a new venture. A significant majority of technical entrepreneurs have a self-employed or professional parent. Studies indicate that between 50 and 80% have at least one self-employed parent. For example, the US study found that four times as many technical entrepreneurs have a parent who is a professional, compared with other groups of scientists and engineers. The most common explanation for this observed bias is that the parent acts as a role model and may provide support for self-employment.

The effect of religious background is more controversial, but it is clear that certain religions are over-represented in the population of technical entrepreneurs. For example, in the USA and Europe Jews are more likely to establish an NTBF, and Chinese are more likely to in Asia. Whether this observed bias is the result of specific cultural or religious norms, or the result of minority status, is the subject of much controversy but little research. The US study suggests that dominant cultural values are more important than minority status, but even this work indicates that the effect of family background is more significant than religion. In any case, and perhaps more importantly, there appears to be no significant relationship between family and religious background and the subsequent probability of success of an NTBF.

Education and training are major factors that distinguish the founders of NTBFs from other entrepreneurs. The median level of education of technical entrepreneurs in the US study was a master's degree, and with the important exception of biotechnology based NTBFs, a doctorate was superfluous. Significantly, the levels of education of technical entrepreneurs do not differentiate them from other scientists and engineers. However, potential technical entrepreneurs tend to have higher levels of productivity than their technical work colleagues, measured in terms of papers published or patents granted: 6.35 versus 2.2 papers on average; and 1.6 patents versus 0.05. This suggests that potential entrepreneurs may be more driven than their corporate counterparts.

In addition to a master's-level education, on average, a technical entrepreneur will have around 13 years of work experience before establishing an NTBF. In the case of Route 128, the entrepreneurs' work experience is typically with a single incubator organization, whereas technical entrepreneurs in Silicon Valley tend to have gained their experience from a larger number of firms before establishing their own NTBF. This suggests that there is no ideal pattern of previous work experience. However, experience of development work appears to be more important than work in basic research. As a result of the formal education and experience required, a typical technical entrepreneur will be aged between 30 and 40 years when establishing his or her first NTBF. This is relatively late in life compared to other types of venture, and is due to a combination of ability and opportunity. On the one hand, it typically takes between 10 and 15 years for a potential entrepreneur to attain the necessary technical and business experience. On the other hand, many people begin to have greater financial and family responsibilities at this time. Thus there appears to be a window of opportunity to start an NTBF some time in the mid-thirties. Moreover, different fields of technology have different entry and growth potential. Therefore the choice of a potential entrepreneur will be constrained by the dynamics of the technology and markets. The capital requirements, product lead times and potential for growth are likely to vary significantly between sectors.

Much of the research on the psychology of entrepreneurs is based on the experience of small firms in the USA, so the generalizability of the findings must be questioned. However, in the specific case of technical entrepreneurs there appears to be some consensus regarding the necessary personal characteristics.

The two critical requirements appear to be an internal locus of control and a high need for achievement. The former characteristic is common in scientists and engineers, but the need for high levels of achievement is less common. Entrepreneurs are typically motivated by a high need for achievement (so-called 'n-Ach'), rather than a general desire to succeed. This behaviour is associated with moderate risk-taking, but not gambling or irrational risk-taking. A person with a high n-Ach:

- Likes situations where it is possible to take personal responsibility for finding solutions to problems
- Has a tendency to set challenging but realistic personal goals and to take calculated risks
- Needs concrete feedback on personal performance

However, the US study of almost 130 technical entrepreneurs and almost 300 scientists and engineers found that not all entrepreneurs have high n-Ach, only some do. Technical entrepreneurs had only moderate n-Ach, but low need for affiliation (n-Aff). This suggests that the need for independence, rather than success, is the most significant motivator for technical entrepreneurs. Technical entrepreneurs also tend to have an internal locus of control. In other words, technical entrepreneurs believe that they have personal control over outcomes, whereas someone with an external locus of control believes that outcomes are the result of chance, powerful institutions or others. More sophisticated psychometric techniques such as the Myers–Briggs type indicators (MBTI) confirm the differences between technical entrepreneurs and other scientists and engineers.

(a)

(b)

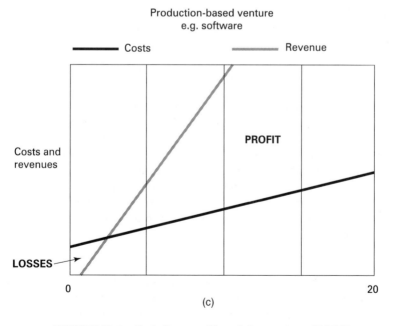

(c)

FIGURE 12.2   Cash flow profiles of three types of NTBF.

Numerous surveys indicate that around three-quarters of technical entre-preneurs claim to have been frustrated in their previous job. This frustration appears to result from the interaction of the psychological predisposition of the potential entrepreneur and poor selection, training and development by the parent organization. Specific events may also trigger the desire or need to establish an NTBF, such as a major reorganization or downsizing of the parent organization.

12.4 The Business Plan

The primary reason for developing a formal business plan for a new venture is to attract external funding. However, it serves an important secondary function. A business plan can provide a formal agreement between founders regarding the basis and future development of the venture. A business plan can help reduce self-delusion on the part of the founders, and avoid subsequent arguments con-cerning responsibilities and rewards.

No standard business plan exists, but in many cases venture capitalists will provide a pro forma for the business plan. Typically a business plan should be relatively concise, say no more than 10 sides, begin with an executive summary, and include sections on the product, markets, technology, development, produc-tion, marketing, human resources, financial estimates with contingency plans, and the timetable and funding requirements. Most business plans submitted to venture capitalists are strong on the technical considerations, often placing too much emphasis on the technology relative to other issues. As Roberts notes, 'entrepreneurs propose that they can do *it* better than anyone else, but may for-get to demonstrate that anyone wants *it*'.[1] He identifies a number of common problems with business plans submitted to venture capitalists: marketing plan, management team, technology plan and financial plan.

There were found to be serious inadequacies in all four of these areas, but the worst were in marketing and finance. Less than half of the plans examined pro-vided a detailed marketing strategy, and just half included any sales plan. Three-quarters of the plans failed to identify or analyse any potential competitors. As a result most business plans contain only basic financial forecasts, and just 10% conducted any sensitivity analysis on the forecasts. The lack of attention to marketing and competitor analysis is particularly problematic as research indi-cates that both factors are associated with subsequent success.

For example, the UK study found that in the early stages NTBFs rely too much on a few major customers for sales, and are therefore vulnerable. In the extreme case, half of NTBFs rely on a single customer for more than half of their first-year sales. This over-dependence on a small number of customers has three major drawbacks:

1. Vulnerability to changes in the strategy and health of the dominant customer.
2. A loss of negotiating power, which may reduce profit margins.
3. Little incentive to develop marketing and sales functions, which may limit future growth.

BOX 12.1 Johnson and Johnson Development Corporation.

Johnson and Johnson Development Corporation (JJDC) is an independent venture capital firm within the Johnson and Johnson group of companies, and aims to identify and fund new technologies and businesses in the pharmaceutical and health-care sector. JJDC was established in the USA 25 years ago and has since invested in more than 300 start-up businesses worldwide. In 1997 it created a dedicated European division, Johnson and Johnson Development Capital. Both companies exploit the scientific and market know-how of Johnson and Johnson and typically invest alongside professional venture capital firms in ventures in the start-up and early growth stages phases.

Funding

NTBFs are different from other new ventures in that there is often no marketable product available before or shortly after formation. Therefore, initial funding of the venture cannot normally be based on cash flow derived from early sales. The precise cash flow profile will be determined by a number of factors, including development time and cost, and the volume and profit margin of sales. Different development and sales strategies exist, but to some extent these factors are determined by the nature of the technology and markets (Figure 12.2(a)–(c)).

For example, biotechnology ventures typically require more start-up capital than electronics or software-based ventures, and have longer product development lead times. Therefore, from the perspective of a potential entrepreneur, the ideal strategy would be to conduct as much development work as possible within the incubator organization before starting the new venture. However, there are practical problems with this strategy, in particular ownership of the intellectual property on which the venture is to be based.

Given their strong desire for independence, most entrepreneurs seek to avoid external funding for their ventures. However, in practice this is not always possible, particularly in the latter growth stages. The initial funding required to form an NTBF includes the purchase of accommodation, equipment and other start-up costs, plus the day-to-day running costs such as salaries, heating, light and so on. Research in the USA and UK suggests that most NTBFs begin life as part-time ventures, and are funded by personal savings, loans from friends and relatives, and bank loans, in that order. Around half also receive some funding from government sources, but in contrast receive next to nothing from venture capitalists. Venture capital is typically only made available at later stages to fund growth on the basis of a proven development and sales record.

Research in the USA suggests that the initial capital needed to start an NTBF is relatively modest, typically less than $50 000 and in almost half of the cases less than $10 000 (1990 US dollars). However, the extent of the need for external funding will depend on the nature of the technology and the strategy of the NTBF. For example, an electronics or software-based venture will also demand high initial funding if a strategy of aggressive growth is to be achieved. The UK study shows that both the amount and source of initial funding for the formation of an NTBF vary considerably. For example, as software-based ventures typically require less start-up capital than either electronics or biotechnology ventures, it is more common for such firms to rely solely on personal funding. Biotechnology firms tend to have the highest R&D costs, typically in excess of £50 000, and consequently most require some external funding. In contrast, software firms typically require little R&D investment, and are less likely to seek external funds. The UK study found that almost three-quarters of the software firms were funded by profits after three years, whereas only a third of the biotechnology firms had achieved this.

The initial funding to establish an NTBF is rarely a major problem. However, Drucker suggests an NTBF requires financial restructuring every three years.[14] Other studies identify stages of development, each having different financial requirements:

1. Initial financing for launch.
2. Second-round financing for initial development and growth.
3. Third-round financing for consolidation and growth.
4. Maturity or exit.

In general, professional financial bodies are not interested in initial funding because of the high risk and low sums of money involved. It is simply not worth their time and effort to evaluate and monitor such ventures. However, as the sums involved are relatively small, typically of the order of tens of thousands of pounds, personal savings, remortgages and loans from friends and relatives are often sufficient. In contrast, third-round finance for consolidation is relatively easy to obtain, because by that time the venture has a proven track record on which to base the business plan, and the venture capitalist can see an exit route.

Venture capitalists are keen to provide funding for a venture with a proven track record and strong business plan, but in return will often require some equity or management involvement. Moreover, most venture capitalists are looking for a means to make capital gains after about five years. However, almost by definition technical entrepreneurs seek independence and control, and there is evidence that some will sacrifice growth to maintain control of their ventures. For the same reason, few entrepreneurs are prepared to 'go public' to fund further growth. Thus many entrepreneurs will choose to sell the business and found another NTBF. In fact, the typical technical entrepreneur establishes an average of three NTBFs. Therefore the biggest funding problem for an NTBF is likely to be for the second-round financing to fund development and growth. This can be a time-consuming and frustrating process to convince venture capitalists to provide finance. The formal proposal is critical at this stage. Professional investors will assess the attractiveness of the venture in terms of the strengths and personalities of the founders, the formal business plan and the commercial and technical merits of the product, probably in that order.

A survey of corporate funding of NTBFs in the UK found that around 15% of large companies had made investments in external new ventures, mainly in their own sector.[15] The typical investment (in 1997) was in excess of £500 000, and the investing companies preferred ventures requiring additional capital for expansion, rather than funds for start-up or early development. The most common problems encountered were agreement of the rate of return and details of corporate representation in the venture. The average period of investment was five to seven years, and corporate investors typically demanded a rate of return of 20–30%, which compares favourably with professional venture capitalists required returns of around 75%. Regarding professional venture capitalists, Figure 12.3 highlights two important issues. First, that the availability of venture capital varies worldwide, as we discussed in Chapter 4, and such disparities tend to be self-reinforcing as potential new ventures relocate to seek funding. The second point to note is the strong bias for finance for expansion, rather than start-ups, which is most significant in the UK. This creates a potential venture funding gap, between the initial, usually self-financed stage, and the first involvement of professional venture capital. In the UK this gap is in the region of £200 000–£750 000.[16]

Corporate investment in new ventures is increasingly popular in high-technology sectors, where large firms do not have access to all technologies in-house, and where emerging technologies remain unproven.[17] Investments in small biotechnology companies by pharmaceutical companies can be direct, or indirect investment through specialist venture funds (see Box 12.1). Direct investment is preferred where there is a high probability of technological success which is likely to impact the product pipeline in the near term. Indirect investments are concerned more with gaining windows on a range of early stage technologies with the *potential* to impact the future direction of the product pipeline.[18] There has been a marked increase in the number of pharmaceutical companies investing through specialist venture funds, recent examples being Novartis (Novartis Ventures) and Bayer (Bayer Innovation). At the same time, pharmaceutical companies and their venture funds appear to be investing increasingly in independent seed capital funds focused on early stage biotechnology, such as UK Medical Ventures (UK), New Medical Technologies (Switzerland) and Medical Technology Partners (USA). The precise objectives of such funds vary, but all share a common emphasis on strategic issues rather than purely financial. A principal investment criterion is 'no fit, no deal', the decision to invest being largely strategic, to 'scout for "out there" science'. The alternative mode of indirect venturing is participation in independent seed capital funds targeted at early stage investments. This included direct investment in seed capital funds by the corporate parent, or indirect investment in seed funds via corporate venture funds. As may be expected, objectives include providing windows on early stage technologies; for example, one company invested in a health informatics fund in order to place representatives on the board of the seed fund to gain competence in the field. Another reason for investing is to access 'deal flow'—that is the opportunity to participate *directly* in subsequent rounds of funding beyond the seed capital stage. This was aimed at investing more directly in later stage technologies should they appear to be strategically important for the corporate parent. Clearly then, the goals of pharmaceutical firms' investments in new ventures are fundamentally different from those of professional venture capital firms. The goals of corporate venture funds are largely strategic, focusing on technology and potential new products, whereas the goals of venture capitalists are (rightly) purely financial.

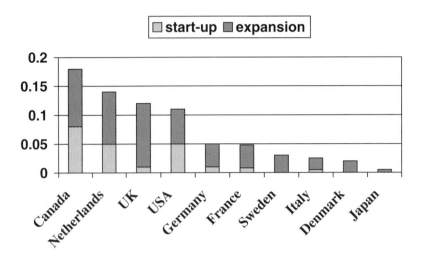

FIGURE 12.3 Venture capital as a percentage of GDP, 1997. Sources: CVCA (Canada), NVCA (USA), MITI (Japan), OECD (other nations).

BOX 12.2 Andrew Rickman and Bookham Technology.

Andrew Rickman founded Bookham Technology in 1988, aged 28. Rickman has a degree in mechanical engineering from Imperial College London, a Ph.D. in integrated optics from Surrey University, an MBA and has worked as a venture capitalist. Unlike many technology entrepreneurs, he did not begin with the development of a novel technology and then seek a means to exploit it. Instead, he first identified a potential market need for optical switching technology for the then fledgling optical fibre networks, and then developed an appropriate technological solution. The market for optical components is growing fast as the use of Internet and other data-intensive traffic grows. Rickman aimed to develop an integrated optical circuit on a single chip to replace a number of discrete components such as lasers, lenses and mirrors. He chose to use silicon rather than more exotic materials to reduce development costs and exploit traditional chip production techniques. The main technological developments were made at Surrey University and the Rutherford Appleton Laboratory, where he had worked, and 27 patents were granted and a further 140 applied for. Once the technology had been proven, the company raised US$110m. over several rounds of funding from venture capitalist 3i, and leading electronics firms Intel and Cisco. The most difficult task was scale-up and production: 'taking the technology out of the lab and into production is unbelievably tough in this area. It is infinitely more difficult than dreaming up the technology.' Bookham Technology floated in London and on the Nasdaq in New York April 2000 with a market capitalization of more than £5bn, making Andrew Rickman, with 25% of the equity, a paper billionaire. Bookham is based in Oxford, and employs 400 staff.

Venture Capital

Whilst there is general agreement about the main components of a good business plan, there are some significant differences in the relative weights attributed to each component. A survey of venture capitalists in North America, Europe and Asia found major similarities in the criteria used, but also identified several interesting differences in the weights attached to some criteria (Table 12.1). The criteria are similar to those discussed earlier, grouped into five categories:

1. The entrepreneur's personality.
2. The entrepreneur's experience.
3. Characteristics of the product.
4. Characteristics of the market.
5. Financial factors.

TABLE 12.1   Criteria used by venture capitalists to assess proposals.

Criteria	European (n = 195)	American (n = 100)	Asian (n = 53)
Entrepreneur able to evaluate and react to risk	3.6	3.3	3.5
Entrepreneur capable of sustained effort	3.6	3.6	3.7
Entrepreneur familiar with the market	3.5	3.6	3.6
Entrepreneur demonstrated leadership ability*	3.2	3.4	3.0
Entrepreneur has relevant track record*	3.0	3.2	2.9
Product prototype exists and functions*	3.0	2.4	2.9
Product demonstrated market acceptance*	2.9	2.5	2.8
Product proprietary or can be protected*	2.7	3.1	2.6
Product is 'high technology'*	1.5	2.3	1.4
Target market has high growth rate*	3.0	3.3	3.2
Venture will stimulate an existing market	2.4	2.4	2.5
Little threat of competition within three years	2.2	2.4	2.4
Venture will create a new market*	1.8	1.8	2.2
Financial return >10 times within 10 years*	2.9	3.4	2.9
Investment is easily made liquid* (e.g. made public or acquired)	2.7	3.2	2.7
Financial return >10 times within 5 years*	2.1	2.3	2.1

1 = irrelevant, 2 = desirable, 3 = important, 4 = essential. * Denotes significant at the 0.05 level.
Source: Adapted from Knight, R. M. (1992) 'Criteria used by venture capitalists', in Khalil, T. M. and Bayraktar, B. A. (eds), *Management of Technology III: The key to global competitiveness.* Industrial Engineering & Management Press, Georgia, pp. 574–583.

Overall, the study confirmed the importance of a bundle of personal, market and financial factors, which were consistently ranked as being most significant: a proven ability to lead others and sustain effort; familiarity with the market; and the potential for a high return within 10 years (see Box 12.2). The personality and experience of the entrepreneurs were consistently ranked as being more important than either product or market characteristics, or even financial considerations. However, there were a number of significant differences between the preferences of venture capitalists from different regions. Those from the USA placed greater emphasis on a high financial return and liquidity than their counterparts in Europe or Asia, but less emphasis on the existence of a prototype or proven market acceptance. Perhaps surprisingly, all venture capitalists are adverse to technological and market risks. Being described as a 'high-technology' venture was rated very low in importance by the US venture capitalists, and the European and Asian venture capitalists rated this characteristic as having a negative influence on funding. Similarly, having the potential to create an entirely new market was considered a drawback. In short, venture capitalists are not particularly adventurous, as the examples of Chiroscience and Autonomy demonstrate. (Boxes 12.3 and 12.4).

12.5 Growth and Performance of Innovative Small Firms

We discussed innovation strategy and the positioning of small firms in Chapters 3 and 4. Here we examine what is known about the subsequent growth and performance of innovative small firms.

There has been a great deal of economic and management research on small firms, but much of this has been concerned with the contribution all types of small firms make to economic, employment or regional development. Relatively little is known about innovation in small firms, or the more narrow issue of the performance of NTBFs. As demonstrated by the preceding discussion, almost all research on innovative small firms has been confined to a small number of high-technology sectors, principally microelectronics and more recently biotechnology. A notable exception is the survey of 2000 SMEs conducted by the Small Business Research Centre in the UK. The survey found that 60% of the sample claimed to have introduced a major new product or service innovation in the previous five years.[19] Whilst this finding demonstrates that the management of innovation is relevant to the majority of small firms, it does not tell us much about the significance of such innovations, in terms of research and investment, or subsequent market or financial performance.

Research over the past decade or so suggests that the innovative activities of SMEs exhibit broadly similar characteristics across sectors.[20] They:

- Are more likely to involve product innovation than process innovation
- Are focused on products for niche markets, rather than mass markets
- Will be more common amongst producers of final products, rather than producers of components
- Will frequently involve some form of external linkage
- Tend to be associated with growth in output and employment, but not necessarily profit

BOX 12.3 Mike Lynch and Autonomy.

Mike Lynch founded the software company Autonomy in 1994, a spin-off from his first start-up Neurodynamics. Lynch, a grammar school graduate, studied information science at Cambridge where he carried out Ph.D. research on probability theory. He rejected a conventional research career as he had found his summer job at GEC Marconi a 'boring, tedious place'. In 1991, aged 25, he approached the banks to raise money for his first venture, Neurodynamics, but 'met a nice chap who laughed a lot and admitted that he was only used to lending money to people to open newsagents'. He subsequently raised the initial £2000 from a friend of a friend. Neurodynamics developed pattern recognition software which it sold to specialist niche users such as the UK police force for matching fingerprints and identifying disparities in witness statements, and banks to identify signatures on cheques.

Autonomy was spun off in 1994 to exploit applications of the technology in Internet, intranet and media sectors, and received the financial backing of venture capitalists Apax, Durlacher and Enic. Autonomy was floated on the Easdaq in July 1998, on the Nasdaq in 1999, and in February 2000 was worth US$5bn, making Lynch the first British software billionaire. Autonomy creates software which manages unstructured information, which accounts for 80% of all data. The software applies Bayesian probabilistic techniques to identify patterns of data or text, and compared to crude keyword searches can better take into account context and relationships. The software is patented in the USA, but not in Europe as patent law does not allow patent protection of software. The business generates revenues through selling software for cataloguing and searching information direct to clients such as the BBC, Barclays, BT, Eli Lilly, General Motors, Merril Lynch, News Corporation, Nationwide, Proctor and Gamble and Reuters. In addition, it has more than 50 licence agreements with leading software companies to use its technology, including Oracle, Sun and Sybase. A typical licence will include a lump sum of US$100 000 plus a royalty on sales of 10–30%. By means of such licence deals Autonomy aims to become an integral part of a range of software and the standard for intelligent recognition and searching. In the financial year ending March 2000 the company reported its first profit of US$440 000 on a turnover of $11.7m. The company employs 120 staff, split between Cambridge in the UK and Silicon Valley, and spends 17% of its revenues on R&D.

The limitations of a focus on product innovation for niche or intermediate markets were discussed earlier, in particular problems associated with product planning and marketing, and relationships with lead customers and linkages with external sources of innovation. These topics were discussed in Part III, but a number of issues are specific to smaller firms. Where an SME has a close relationship with a small number of customers, it may have little incentive or scope for further innovation, and therefore will pay relatively little attention to formal product development or marketing. Therefore SMEs in such dependent relationships are likely to have limited potential for future growth, and may remain permanent infants or subsequently be acquired by competitors or customers.[21–23]

BOX 12.4 Chris Evans and Chiroscience.

Chiroscience Plc is one of the three biotechnology firms founded by the microbiologist/entrepreneur Chris Evans. Evans, Ph.D. and since OBE, formed his first new venture, Enzymatix Ltd, in 1987, aged 30. His business plan was rejected by venture capitalists, so he was forced to sell his house for £40 000 to raise the initial finance. Subsequent finance of £1m. was provided by the commodities group Berisford International, but following financial problems in the property market, the company was divided into Celsis Plc, which makes contamination testing equipment, and Chiroscience, which exploits chiral technology, the basis of which is that most molecules have mirror images that have different properties, essentially a right-hand sense and a left-hand sense. Isolating the more effective mirror image in an existing drug formulation can improve its efficacy, or reduce unwanted side effects.

Chiroscience was formed in 1990, other directors being recruited from large established pharmaceutical firms such as Glaxo, SmithKline Beecham and Zeneca. The company was floated on the London Stock Exchange in 1994. This was only possible because in 1992 the Stock Exchange relaxed its requirements for market entry, and no longer required three consecutive years' profits before listing. The biotechnology company applies chiral technology to the purification of existing drugs and design of new drugs. Chiroscience has three potential applications of chiral technology: first, and most immediately, the improvement of existing drugs by isolating the most effective sense of molecules; second, the development of alternative processes for the production of existing drugs as they come off-patent and finally, the design of new drugs by means of single isomer technology.

Chiroscience was the first British biotechnology firm to be granted approval for sale of a new product, Dexketoprofen, in 1995. This is a non-steroidal anti-inflammatory drug, based on a right-handed version of the older drug ketoprofen. The drug is marketed by the Italian firm Menarini. Chiroscience has been involved in a number of collaborative development and marketing deals. In 1995 it formed an alliance with the Swedish pharmaceutical group Pharmacia, to develop and market its local anaesthetic, Levobupivacaine. It also forged a more general strategic alliance with Medeva, the pharmaceutical group which performs no primary research, but specializes in taking products to market.

Biotechnology stocks are more volatile than most other investments, and it is difficult to use conventional techniques to assess their current value or future potential. Expenditure on R&D in the initial years typically results in significant losses, and sales may be negligible for up to 10 years. Therefore there are no price–earnings ratios or future revenues to discount. For example, in its first two years after flotation Chiroscience reported cumulative losses of £3.7m., due largely to research spending of £12.4m. Nevertheless, Chiroscience has outperformed the financial markets, and most other biotechnology stock. The company was floated in 1994 at 150p, and quickly fell to below 100p. However, by December 1995 shares had reached 364p. As a result, Chris Evans's personal fortune was estimated to have reached £50m. by 1995.

In January 1999 Chiroscience merged with Celltech to form Celltech Chiroscience, which subsequently acquired Medeva to become the Celltech Group.

The new company has some 400 research staff, an R&D budget of £51m. and adds much-needed sales and marketing competencies with a sales force of 550. Celltech Group is three times the size of Chiroscience, and reached a market capitalization of £3bn in 2000. It is one of the few British biotechnology companies to gain regulatory approval for its products in the USA, and the first to achieve profitability.

Moreover, an analysis of the growth in the number of NTBFs suggests that the trend has as much to do with negative factors, such as the downsizing of larger firms, as it does with more positive factors such as start-ups.[24]

Innovative SMEs are likely to have diverse and extensive linkages with a variety of external sources of innovation, and in general there is a positive association between the level of external scientific, technical and professional inputs and the performance of an SME.[25] The sources of innovation and precise types of relationship vary by sector, but links with contract research organizations, suppliers, customers and universities are consistently rated as being highly significant. However, such relationships are not without cost, and the management and exploitation of these linkages can be difficult for an SME, and overwhelm the limited technical and managerial resources of SMEs.[26] As a result, in some cases the cost of collaboration may outweigh the benefits[27] and in the specific case of collaboration between SMEs and universities there is an inherent mismatch between the short-term, near-market focus of most SMEs and the long-term, basic research interests of universities.[28]

In terms of innovation, the performance of SMEs is easily exaggerated. Early studies based on innovation counts consistently indicated that when adjusted for size, smaller firms created more new products than the larger counterparts. However, methodological shortcomings appear to undermine this clear message. When the divisions and subsidiaries of larger organizations are removed from such samples,[29] and the innovations weighted according to their technological merit and commercial value, the relationship between firm size and innovation is reversed: larger firms create proportionally more significant innovations than SMEs.[30] The amount of expenditure by SMEs on design and engineering has a positive effect on the share of exports in sales,[31] but formal R&D by SMEs appears to be only weakly associated with profitability,[32] and is not correlated with growth.[33] Similarly, the high growth rates associated with NTBFs are not explained by R&D effort,[34] and investment in technology does not appear to discriminate between the success and failure of NTBFs.[35] Instead, other factors have been found to have a more significant effect on profitability and growth, in particular the contributions of technically qualified owner managers and their scientific and engineering staff, and attention to product planning and marketing.[36]

In short, most of what we have discussed in this book about managing innovation is relevant to innovative small firms, but more research needs to be done on how to manage the particular problems they face. As we have argued throughout the book, we believe that there is a generic core innovation process which represents management 'best practice', but that this has to be modified in different organizational, technological and market contingencies. In the specific case of small innovative firms, best practice would include scanning the external environment and developing appropriate relationships with sources of innovation and lead users. However, different contingencies will demand action. For example, a study of 116 software start-ups identified five factors that affected success: level of R&D expenditure, how radical new products were, the intensity of product upgrades, use of external technology and management of intellectual property.[37] In contrast, a study of 94 biotechnology start-ups found that three factors were associated with success: location within a significant concentration of similar firms, quality of scientific staff (measured by citations) and the commercial experience of the founder.[38] The number of alliances had no significant effect on success, and the number of scientific staff in the top management team had a negative association, suggesting that the scientists are best kept in the laboratory.

12.6 Summary and Further Reading

In this chapter we have explored the rationale, characteristics and management of new technology-based ventures. Typically an entrepreneur establishes a new technology-based venture primarily to achieve independence, and venture capitalists will aim to make a five- to tenfold gain on their investment within five to seven years. There are important similarities in the organization and management of corporate ventures examined in Chapter 10. Both require a clear business plan and strong product champion or entrepreneur who must identify the opportunity for a new venture, raise the finance and manage the development and growth of the business. Thus the individuals involved in internal and external new ventures are likely to have similar backgrounds, levels of education and personalities: they tend to be highly motivated and demand a high level of autonomy.

The main differences between the two types of entrepreneur are the need for affiliation and interaction, and the degree of political and social skills needed. Corporate entrepreneurs seek higher levels of affiliation and need greater social skills than their independent counterparts. This is because the corporate entrepreneur has the advantage of the financial, technical and marketing resources of the parent firm, but must deal with internal politics and bureaucracy. The external entrepreneur must raise finance and develop functional expertise, but has the advantage of independence and managerial and technical autonomy. Both types of new venture represent an opportunity to grow new businesses based on new technology.

There are many books and journal articles on the more general subject of entrepreneurship, but relatively little has been produced on the more specific subject of new technology-based entrepreneurism. E. B. Roberts's *Entrepreneurs in High Technology: Lessons from MIT and beyond* (Oxford University Press, Oxford, 1991) is an excellent study of the MIT experience, although perhaps places too much emphasis on the characteristics of individual entrepreneurs. For a broader analysis of technology ventures in the USA see Martin Kenny (ed.), *Understanding Silicon Valley: Anatomy of an entrepreneurial region* (Stanford University Press, 2000). Ray Oakey's *High-technology New Firms* (Paul Chapman, London, 1995) is a similar study of NTBFs in the UK, but places greater emphasis on how different technologies constrain the opportunities for establishing NTBFs, and affects their management and success. For a review of recent research on the broader issue of innovative small firms see 'Small firms, R&D, technology and innovation: a literature review' by Kurt Hoffman *et al.*, published in *Technovation*, **18** (1), 39–55, 1998.

References

1   Roberts, E. B. (1991) *Entrepreneurs in High Technology: Lessons from MIT and beyond*. Oxford University Press, Oxford.
2   Martin, M. J. C. (1994) *Managing Innovation and Entrepreneurship in Technology*. Wiley, New York.
3   Massey, D., D. Wield and P. Quintas (1991) *High-Tech Fantasies: Science parks in society, science and space*. Routledge, London.
4   Westhead, P. (1997) 'R&D "inputs" and "outputs" of technology-based firms located on and off science parks', *R&D Management*, **27** (1), 45–61.
5   Henderson, R., A. B. Jaffe and M. Trajtenberg (1998) 'Universities as a source of commercial technology: a detailed analysis of university patenting 1965–1988', *The Review of Economics and Statistics*, 119–127.
6   Mowery, D. C., R. R. Nelson, B. N. Sampat and A. A. Ziedonis (2001) 'The growth of patenting and licensing by U.S. Universities: an assessment of the effects of the Bayh–Dole Act of 1980', *Research Policy*, **30**.
7   Peters, L. S. and H. Etzkowitz (1990) 'University–industry connections and academic values', *Technology in Society*, **12**, 427–440.
8   Kassicieh, S. K., R. Radosevich and J. Umbarger (1996) 'A comparative study of entrepreneurship incidence among inventors in national laboratories', *Entrepreneurship Theory and Practice*, Spring, 33–49.
9   Butler, S. and S. Birley (1999) 'Scientists and their attitudes to industry links', *International Journal of Innovation Management*, **2** (1), 79–106.
10 Lee, Y. S. (1996) 'Technology transfer and the research university: a search for the boundaries of university–industry collaboration', *Research Policy*, **25**, 843–863.
11 Seashore, L., K. D. Blumenthal, M. E. Gluck and M. A. Stoto (1989) 'Entrepreneurs in academe: an exploration of behaviors among life scientists', *Administrative Science Quarterly*, **34**, 110–131.
12 Samson, K. J. and M. A. Gurdon (1993) 'University scientists as entrepreneurs: a special case of technology transfer and high-tech venturing', *Technovation*, **13** (2), 63–71.
13 Oakey, R. (1995) *High-technology New Firms*. Paul Chapman, London.
14 Drucker, P. F. (1985) *Innovation and Entrepreneurship*. Harper & Row, New York.
15 Withers (1997) *Window on Technology: Corporate venturing in practice*. Withers, London.
16 Harding, R. (2000) 'Venture capital and regional development: towards a venture capital system', *Venture Capital*, **2** (4), 287–311.
17 Binding, K., C. McCubbin and L. Doyle (1998) *Technology Transfer in the UK Life Sciences*. Arthur Andersen, London.
18 Tidd, J. and S. Barnes (1999) 'Spin-in or spin-out? Corporate venturing in life sciences', *International Journal of Entrepreneurship and Innovation*, **1** (2), 109–116.
19 Small Business Research Centre (1992) *The State of British Enterprise: Growth, innovation and competitiveness in small and medium sized firms*. SBRC, Cambridge.
20 Hoffman, K., M. Parejo, J. Bessant and L. Perren (1998) 'Small firms, R&D, technology and innovation in the UK: a literature review', *Technovation*, **18** (1), 39–55
21 Calori, R. (1990) 'Effective strategies in emerging industries', in Loveridge, R. and Pitt, M. (eds), *The Strategic Management of Technological Innovation*. John Wiley & Sons, Chichester, pp. 21–38.
22 Walsh, V., J. Niosi and P. Mustar (1995) 'Small firms formation in biotechnology: a comparison of France, Britain and Canada', *Technovation*, **15** (5), 303–328.
23 Westhead, P., D. Storey and M. Cowling (1995) 'An exploratory analysis of the factors associated with survival of independent high technology firms in Great Britain', in Chittenden, F.,

Robertson, M. and Marshall, I. (eds), *Small Firms: Partnership for growth in small firms*. Paul Chapman, London, pp. 63–99.

24 Tether, B. S. and D. J. Storey (1998) 'Smaller firms and Europe's high technology sectors: a framework for analysis and some statistical evidence', *Research Policy*, **26**, 947–971.

25 MacPherson, A. (1997) 'The contribution of external service inputs to the product development efforts of small manufacturing firms', *R&D Management*, **27** (2), 127–143.

26 Rothwell, R. and M. Dodgson (1993) 'SMEs: their role in industrial and economic change', *International Journal of Technology Management*, Special Issue, 8–22.

27 Moote, B. (1993) *Financial Constraints to the Growth and Development of Small High Technology Firms*. Small Business Research Centre, University of Cambridge; Oakey, R. (1993) 'Predatory networking: the role of small firms in the development of the British biotechnology industry', *International Small Business Journal*, **11** (3), 3–22.

28 Storey, D. (1992) 'United Kingdom: case study', in OECD, *Small and Medium Sized Enterprises, Technology and Competitiveness*. OECD, Paris; Tang, N., L. Peng, A. Agnew and O. Jones (1995) 'Technological alliances between HEIs and SMEs: examining the current evidence', in Bennett, D. and Steward, F. (eds), *Proceedings of the European Conference on the Management of Technology: Technological innovation and global challenges*. Aston University, Birmingham.

29 Tether, B. S. (1998) 'Small and large firms: sources of unequal innovations?', *Research Policy*, **27**, 725–745.

30 Tether, B. S., J. J. Smith and A. T. Thwaites (1997) 'Smaller enterprises and innovations in the UK: the SPRU Innovations Database revisited', *Research Policy*, **26**, 19–32.

31 Strerlacchini, A. (1999) 'Do innovative activities matter to small firms in non-R&D-intensive industries?', *Research Policy*, **28**, 819–832.

32 Hall, G. (1991) 'Factors associated with relative performance amongst small firms in the British instrumentation sector', Working Paper No. 213, Manchester Business School.

33 Oakey, R., R. Rothwell and S. Cooper (1988) *The Management of Innovation in High Technology Small Firms*. Pinter, London.

34 Keeble, D. (1993) *Regional Influences and Policy in New Technology-based Firms: Creation and growth*. Small Business Research Centre, University of Cambridge.

35 Westhead, P., D. Storey and M. Cowling (1995) 'An exploratory analysis of the factors associated with survival of independent high technology firms in Great Britain', in Chittenden, E., Robertson, M. and Marshall, I. (eds), *Partnership for Growth in Small Firms*. Paul Chapman, London, pp. 63–99.

36 Dickson, K., A. Coles and H. Smith (1995) 'Scientific curiosity as business; an analysis of the scientific entrepreneur', paper presented at the 18th National Small Firms Policy and Research Conference, Manchester; Lee, J. (1993) 'Small firms' innovation in two technological settings', *Research Policy*, **24**, 391–401.

37 Zahra, S. A. and W. C. Bogner (2000) 'Technology strategy and software new ventures performance', *Journal of Business Venturing*, **15** (2), 135–173.

38 Deeds, D. L., D. DeCarolis and J. Coombs (2000) 'Dynamic capabilities and new product development in high technology ventures: an empirical analysis of new biotechnology firms', *Journal of Business Venturing*, **15** (3), 211–229.

Part VI

ASSESSING & IMPROVING INNOVATION MANAGEMENT PERFORMANCE

In this final section we briefly review the main themes explored in the book, and draw them together into a simple framework for reviewing and assessing innovation management in any specific organization. We adopt the concepts of auditing and benchmarks as aids to learning and improvement, and conclude with a short checklist of questions as a self-assessment exercise.

Part IV

ASSESSING & IMPROVING INNOVATION MANAGEMENT PERFORMANCE

Chapter 13

AN INTEGRATIVE APPROACH TO INNOVATION MANAGEMENT

13.1 Key Themes

Throughout the book we have tried to focus on a number of key themes surrounding innovation management. We can summarize these as follows:

- Learning and adaptation are essential in an inherently uncertain future—thus innovation is an imperative
- Innovation is about interaction of technology, market and organization
- Innovation can be linked to a generic process which all enterprises have to find their way through
- Different firms use different routines with greater or lesser degrees of success. There are general recipes from which general suggestions for effective routines can be derived—but these must be customized to particular organizations and related to particular technologies and products
- Routines are learned patterns of behaviour which become embodied in structures and procedures over time. As such they are hard to copy and highly firm-specific
- Innovation management is the search for effective routines—in other words, it is about managing the learning process towards more effective routines to deal with the challenges of the innovation process

We have also argued that innovation management is not a matter of doing one or two things well, but about good all-round performance. There are no, single, simple magic bullets but a set of learned behaviours. In particular we have identified four clusters of behaviour which we feel represent particularly important routines (see Figure 2.2):

- Successful innovation is strategy-based
- Successful innovation depends on effective internal and external linkages

- Successful innovation requires enabling mechanisms for making change happen
- Successful innovation only happens within a supporting organizational context

In the strategy domain there are no simple recipes for success but a capacity to learn from experience and analysis is essential. Research and experience point to three essential ingredients in innovation strategy:

1. The *position* of the firm, in terms of its products, processes, technologies and the national innovation system in which it is embedded. Although a firm's technology strategy may be influenced by a particular national system of innovation it is not determined by it.
2. The technological *paths* open to the firm given its accumulated competencies. Firms follow technological trajectories, each of which has distinct sources and directions of technological change and which define key tasks for strategy. We identify five generic trajectories in the book.
3. The organizational *processes* followed by the firm in order to integrate strategic learning across functional and divisional boundaries.

Within the area of linkages, developing close and rich interaction with markets, with suppliers of technology and other organizational players, is of critical importance. Linkages offer opportunities for learning—from tough customers and lead users, from competitors, from strategic alliances and from alternative perspectives.

In order to succeed organizations also need effective implementation mechanisms to move innovations from idea or opportunity through to reality. This process involves systematic problem-solving and works best within a clear decision-making framework which should help the organization to stop as well as to progress development if things are going wrong. It also requires skills in project management and control and parallel development of both the market and the technology streams. It requires attention to managing the change process itself, including anticipating and addressing the concerns of those who might be affected by the change.

Finally, innovation depends on having a supporting organizational context in which creative ideas can emerge and be effectively deployed. Building and maintaining such organizational conditions are a critical part of innovation management, and involve working with structures, work organization arrangements, training and development, reward and recognition systems and communication arrangements. Above all, the requirement is to create the conditions within which a learning organization can begin to operate, with shared problem identification and solving and with the ability to capture and accumulate learning about technology and about management of the innovation process.

13.2 Learning to Manage Innovation

As we suggested, developing innovation management involves a learning process concerned with building and integrating key behaviours into effective routines. Such a learning process can be assisted by inputs to the learning cycle through:

- Experience sharing, learning from and through the experience of others of both success and failure
- The introduction of new concepts, new ideas about tools and techniques
- Experiment, trying different approaches to the basic problem of innovation management
- Structured reflection, examining and reviewing how innovation is currently managed

Benchmarking can help learning in several ways—in particular it offers a powerful motivator for change since unfavourable comparisons are hard to ignore. But it can also offer valuable clues about how to manage key processes in different fashions. Such learning can come not only from direct comparisons between similar firms but also between firms in different sectors carrying out broadly similar processes. For example, Southwest Airlines has achieved an enviable record for its turnaround speed at airport terminals. It drew inspiration from watching how industry carried out rapid changeover of complex machinery between tasks—and, in turn, those industries learned from watching activities like pit-stop procedures in the Grand Prix motor racing world.[1] In similar fashion Kaplinsky reports on dramatic productivity and quality improvements in the health-care sector, drawing on lessons originating in inventory management systems in manufacturing and retailing.[2]

But perhaps the most valuable component of benchmarking is its use as a framework for structured review and reflection on how the organization currently performs. Such auditing does not necessarily have to be done in comparison with another organization but can usefully be done against normative models of good practice. A number of examples are now in place covering areas like quality management where the Baldrige Award in the USA, the Deming Prize in Japan and the European Quality Award all use sophisticated benchmarking frameworks.[3, 4] The approach has been extended to a number of other domains—for example, many companies are now benchmarking their software development processes against a capability/maturity model developed by the Software Engineering Institute at Carnegie Mellon University.[5] In the UK a framework for benchmarking and auditing manufacturing performance has been developed and is now being offered as a national service, with special emphasis on assisting smaller firms improve their performance.[6, 7]

This approach has considerable potential relevance for the practice of innovation management and a number of frameworks have been developed. Back in the 1980s the UK National Economic Development Office developed an 'innovation management tool kit' which has been updated and adapted for use as part of a European programme aimed at developing better innovation management amongst SMEs. Another framework, originally developed at London Business School, is now being promoted by the UK Department of Trade and Industry.[8] Other frameworks cover aspects of innovation management, such as continuous improvement and product development.[9, 10]

In each case the purpose of such auditing is not to score points or win prizes but to enable the operation of an effective learning cycle through adding the dimension of structured reflection. It is the process of regular review and discussion which is important rather than detailed information or exactness of scores.

13.3 Measuring Success

The problem with audit frameworks and benchmarks of this kind is that they often provide an indication of *how* a system and its components are performing but they fail to take into account the final piece of the puzzle—why are they successful? For example, in the total quality field in the USA much interest has been shown in the self-assessment framework surrounding the Malcolm Baldrige Award, and many firms have used this benchmarking and assessment framework to improve their quality performance. However one of the winners, Florida Power and Light, whilst undoubtedly doing many of the right things, was none the less forced into receivership; this prompted the addition of a performance category to the assessment framework.

In reviewing innovative performance we can look at a number of possible measures and indicators:

- Measures of specific outputs of various kinds—for example, patents and scientific papers as indicators of knowledge produced, or number of new products as indicators of product innovation success[11]
- Operational or process measures, such as customer satisfaction surveys to measure and track improvements in quality or flexibility[12]
- Measures of strategic success, where the overall business performance is improved in some way and where at least some of the benefit can be attributed directly or indirectly to innovation—for example, growth in revenue or market share, improved profitability, higher value added[13]

We could also consider a number of more specific measures of the innovation process or particular elements of it. For example:

- Number of new products introduced over past three years and percentage of sales and/or profits derived from these new products due to them
- Number of new ideas generated at start of product innovation system
- Failure rates—in the development process, in the marketplace
- Customer satisfaction measures—was it what the customer wanted?
- Time to market (average, compared with industry norms)
- Cost of product versus sector trends
- Quality versus sector trends
- Manufacturability versus sector trends
- Testability
- Disposability
- Man-hours per new product
- Process innovation average lead time for introduction
- Number of new processes installed and type over last three years

- Measures of continuous improvement—suggestions/employee, number of problem-solving teams, savings accruing per worker, cumulative savings, etc.

The point is, once again, not simply to collect data but to use these measures to drive improvement of the innovation process and the ways in which it is managed. As the quality guru, W. Edwards Deming, pointed out, 'if you don't measure it you can't improve it!'

13.4 Auditing Innovation Management

Having established in this book some of the factors which appear to influence success and failure in innovation in the experience of others, we can begin to develop a tool for assessing innovative performance in organizations. We can construct a simple checklist of factors and assign a score to each of them so as to develop a profile of innovation performance. So, for example, an organization with no clear innovation strategy, with limited technological resources and no plans for acquiring more, with weak project management, with poor external links and with a rigid and unsupportive organization would be unlikely to succeed in innovation. By contrast, one which was focused on clear strategic goals, had developed long-term links to support technological development, had a clear project management process which was well supported by senior management and which operated in an innovative organizational climate would have a better chance of success.

An example of such a scale might be:

1 = innovation not even thought about, rarely happens
2 = some awareness but random and occasional responses, informal systems
3 = awareness and formal systems in place—but could still be improved
4 = highly developed and effective systems including provision for improvement and development

What to Look For

In carrying out auditing of this kind there is clearly no such thing as an absolute score. Nonetheless it is possible to develop a number of indicators which give some underpinning to what will otherwise be rather subjective judgements about the innovation management capability of a company. For example, a firm which spends 10% of its turnover on R&D is likely to be better on resourcing innovation than one which does no R&D at all.

Table 13.1 lists some key questions which can help begin the process of auditing innovation management capability. The responses to these questions describe 'the way we do things around here'—the pattern of behaviour which describes how the organization handles the question of innovation. These represent the tip of an iceberg but can help focus attention on areas where there is room for further development and where more detailed questions need to be asked.

TABLE 13.1   Outline innovation management audit.

Key areas in innovation management	*Questions*
(a) Does the organization take a strategic approach to innovation?	1. How does innovation strategy link formally to corporate strategy? Do organizational practices reinforce the exploitation of technological opportunities?
	2. How do we compare to the competition in product, price, quality, delivery, level and composition of R&D, patents and publications, other benchmarks? How do we learn from the competition?
	3. How does innovation strategy link formally to corporate strategy? Do organizational practices reinforce the exploitation of technological opportunities?
	4. What are the potential opportunities and threats emerging from advances in key technologies? What are the implications for corporate skills, markets and organizational practices?
	5. What potential innovative advantages (disadvantages) derive from the national (local) environment? What action is being taken to benefit from foreign systems of innovation?
	6. In which broad technological trajectories are we active? What are the implications of the above for the tasks of innovation strategy?
	7. What are our technological competencies and where are they located in the firm? Are they effectively linked to each other, and to other corporate functions?
	8. How are R&D expenditures evaluated?
	9. To what extent do people in the organization understand how innovation helps it compete?
	10. How well is the innovation strategy communicated?
(b) Has the organization established effective external linkages?	1. Do we have clear criteria for identifying and selecting potential alliance partners?
	2. Do we identify and work with lead customers to innovate?
	3. Do we segment and manage our suppliers according to our objectives?
	4. Do we have clear policies for outsourcing, licensing-in and licensing-out technology?
	5. Do we include all relevant individuals and organizations in our network?
	6. Do we seek to develop and maintain formal and informal knowledge networks?
	7. Do we use exploratory techniques such as Delphi and Scenarios to help to identify future trends?
	8. Do we specify and communicate our education and training needs to local and leading providers, and provide appropriate support?
	9. Do our links with government provide early warning of relevant regulation and promotion and mechanisms for responding and communicating?
	10. Are all our financial stakeholders involved in major new programmes to promote their understanding?
(c) Are there effective implementation mechanisms?	1. Do we systematically search for new product opportunities? How? Is product innovation planning linked to the overall business strategy?
	2. Do we work with early or advanced users?
	3. Do we have a system for selecting product innovations in

the face of competition alternatives? Is this a formal or informal process?

4. Is there a formal procedure for reviewing progress against a series of 'stage gates'? Is this used in practice or are there alternative 'short cuts'?
5. Is there sufficient flexibility in this system to cope with small 'fast track' options?
6. Is there early involvement and concurrent working within the product development system?
7. Do we use cross-functional teams or other arrangements for improving integration?
8. Do we use different project management structures for different projects (functional, matrix, heavyweight team, etc.)?
9. Do we invest in team development?
10. How far do we know about and use formal tools and techniques (e.g. QFD, computer-based aids) in our product development process?

(d) Does innovation take place in a supportive organizational context?

1. Is there top management commitment and support for innovation? How is it expressed?
2. Is there a clear shared sense of strategic vision and ownership of the business plan?
3. Are key individuals recognized and supported in this organization?
4. Is communication effective? Does it operate vertically and horizontally and in two-way mode?
5. Are there adequate rewards and recognition for innovation?
6. How far is the workforce involved in innovation? Are there formal mechanisms for finding and solving problems which people use? Are these linked to monitoring and measurement systems to guide improvement?
7. Does the organizational structure support or inhibit innovation?
8. Do we have a supportive climate for new ideas—or do people have to leave in order to carry them forward?
9. How far is there effective teamwork? Is there investment in team-building?

(e) Is this a learning organization with regard to innovation management?

1. Are there formal mechanisms in place to capture and share learning? How do they operate?
2. How do we capture learning from projects and feed it into future practice?
3. How far do we seek to learn from the experiences of others in managing innovation? Within our sector? Outside our sector?
4. How well do we keep up with new thinking and concepts in innovation management? What channels are used—books, papers, Internet, courses, etc.?
5. Is training and development a priority issue? How well does it compare with the sectoral average?
6. Are there formal procedures to help people find and solve problems and record the results of their improvement activities?
7. Is there a framework for monitoring and measuring how well innovation projects run? How often is it reviewed?
8. How well is knowledge shared across the organization? How often do we reinvent the wheel or repeat the same mistakes?
9. Do we take the opportunity to learn from and share experiences with other organizations?
10. Do we seek to help develop learning in our supply chain?

Using the Framework

Table 13.1 provides a framework and a brief checklist of questions which might enable an assessment of innovation management to be undertaken. It is not exhaustive, but it does indicate the balance of facts and subjective judgements which would need to be considered to make a realistic response to the question 'how well does this organization manage innovation?'

The format of the particular tool is not important; what is needed is the ability to use it to make a wide-ranging review of the factors affecting innovation success and failure, and how management of the process might be improved. Some of the uses to which it could be put are as a:

- Audit framework to see what you did right and wrong in the case of particular innovations or as a way of understanding why things happened the way they did
- Checklist to see if you are doing the right things
- Benchmark to see if you are doing them as well as others
- Guide to continuous improvement of innovation management
- Learning resource to help acquire knowledge and provide inspiration for new things to try
- Way of focusing on subsystems with particular problems and then working with the owners of those processes and their customers and suppliers to see if the discussion cannot improve on things

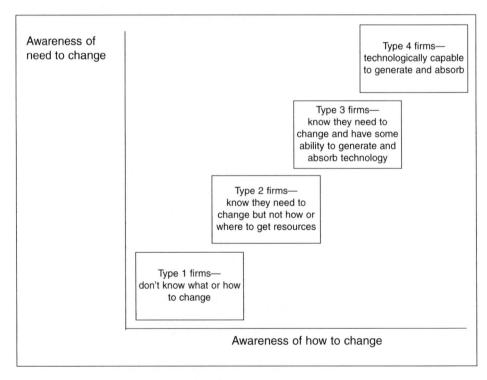

FIGURE 13.1 Distribution of innovation capability.

13.5 What Kind of Innovator is Your Organization?

We can represent the different positions resulting from such a simple audit in diagrammatic form as in Figure 13.1 and identify a number of 'archetypes' of innovation capability.

Such an approach gives the possibility of a quick 'snapshot' to focus attention and create the commitment to improvement. In the end the question is not of how well you scored on the self-assessment audit but rather of using the information to help the learning process for improved innovation management. We have repeatedly said that innovation is complex, uncertain and almost (but not quite) impossible to manage. That being so, we can be sure that there is no such thing as the perfect organization for innovation management; there will always be opportunities for experimentation and continuous improvement.

References

1 Shingo, S. (1983) *A Revolution in Manufacturing: The SMED system*. Productivity Press, Cambridge, Mass.

2 Kaplinsky, R., F. den Hertog and B. Coriat (1995) *Europe's Next Step*. Frank Cass, London.

3 Garvin, D. (1991) 'How the Baldrige Award Really Works', *Harvard Business Review*, Nov./Dec., 80–93.

4 Povey, B. (1996) *Business Process Improvement*. M.Phil. thesis, University of Brighton.

5 Paulk, M. *et al.* (1993) *Capability Maturity Model for Software*. Software Engineering Institute, Carnegie Mellon University.

6 Voss, C. (1994) *Made in Britain*. London Business School.

7 Voss, C. (1999) *Made in Europe 3; The small company study*. London Business School/IBM Consulting, London.

8 DTI (1994) *Innovation—Your Move*. Department of Trade and Industry.

9 Bessant, J. and S. Caffyn (1997) 'High involvement innovation', *International Journal of Technology Management*, **14** (1), 7–28.

10 Oliver, N. (1996) *Benchmarking Product Development*. Working Paper, Judge Institute of Management Studies, University of Cambridge.

11 Tidd, J. (2000) *From Knowledge Management to Strategic Competence: Measuring technological, market and organizational change*. Imperial College Press, London.

12 Luchs, B. (1990) 'Quality as a strategic weapon', *European Business Journal*, **2** (4), 34–47.

13 Kay, J. (1993) *Foundations of Corporate Success: How business strategies add value*. Oxford University Press, Oxford, 416 pp.

INDEX

3M 28, 46, 48, 49, 121, 123, 280, 293, 337

ABB 318
absorptive capacity 251
acquisition of technology 198, 224, 252
Adaptech 217
adoption of innovations *see*
    implementation, diffusion
Adplates 21–2
advanced manufacturing technology
    (AMT) 47, 191, 268
AEA 229
aerospace 15, 213
Agouron Pharmaceuticals 225
Airbus Industries 101–2, 212, 213–14
airlines 116, 213, 375
Allen, Tom 328
alliances 197–240
    learning through 229–37
    managing 233
    patterns 217–21
    problems with 202, 232
    rationale 198, 200
alpha testing 263
Atlshuller, Genrich 293
Amazon.com 4, 16, 22, 28
Ansoff, I. 70
Apple 58, 192, 229, 249
Arcangeli 216
architectural innovation 12, 23
ARM Holdings 180
asynchronous optical communications
    (ASOC) technology 3
AT&T 72, 169, 256, 315
attitudes *see* culture
audit 272
    current performance 266

innovation 376–81
automation 128, 190
automotive sector 5, 13, 74, 112, 124, 126,
    220, 257
autonomy 366
Azko 223

background technologies 124
banking 4, 19, 116, 176
BASF 88
Bayer 361
Belbin 334–5
Bell, Alexander Graham 12, 315
Belussi 216
Benetton 5
benchmarking 47, 66, 96, 97–9, 106, 168,
    244–5, 271–2, 375
Berenson 128
best practice 20, 367
beta testing 263
biotechnology 18, 116–20, 131–2, 143, 319,
    355, 359
BMW 172, 236, 297
Bodley 262
Boeing 101, 212, 213, 217, 285
Boisot 291
Bookham Technology 3, 362
Boston Consulting Group 27
Bower, Joseph 146
BP 227, 286
brainstorming 193
British Airways 22, 204
British Gas 301, 303
BT (British Telecom) 127, 176
Burgelman, Robert 83, 297, 308
Burns, Tom 318
business plans 296, 356–64

business process re-engineering (BPR) 47, 120, 264, 285–6, 341, 342
business-to-business (B2B) supply 204
buyer behaviour *see* users' needs

Cadbury Schweppes 283
Cambridge 281, 349–50
Canada 87, 319
Canon 58, 121, 122, 229
capabilities see competencies
capital, venture 361, 362, 363–4
Cash, J&J 253
Caterpillar 217
Celltech 180, 226
Ceramides 178
Chandler, A. 158
Charterrail 302
Chiroscience 367–8
Christensen, Clayton 14, 26
Chrysler 15, 144, 334
Cisco 124
CITER 323
Citibank 5
Clark, Kim 254, 261, 327
codification 225–6, 291
collaboration *see* alliances
collective efficiency 322, 324
communication 338–9
compatibility 186–7
competencies and capabilities 54–5, 66, 81, 120, 134, 200, 227–8, 280, 286–7
competition 70, 75–6, 96–7, 222–4
complete spin-off 303–4
complexity 18, 41, 43, 66, 70, 74, 111, 113, 165, 187, 225
  adoption 184–5
  commercializing 181–5
component innovation 12, 23
computer-aided design (CAD) 261
computing sector 74, 78, 156, 367–8
concept
  developing 246–7
  testing 247, 249
Concorde 15
consortia 209–11
Consumers' Association 171
continuous improvement 6, 73, 329–33
Coombs, Rod 237, 292
Cooper, Robert 41, 247, 249, 255, 258, 272
cooption 212
copyright 178, 179
corporate ventures 279–309
  assessment 295–7
  definition 279–82
  development 294–5
  identification 290–7
  internal 304–7

managing 287–9
reasons for 282–7
structures for 297–304
Cosworth 253
Covisint 204
creativity 55, 193
CRL 211, 223
C-space 291
culture, innovative 128, 299, 304, 336–8
customer requirements *see* users' needs
customer testing 263

Daimler Chrysler 204
Davidow, William 194
DEC 131, 258
Dell 30
Delphi method 193, 244
Denmark 91
design 6, 13, 55, 58, 73, 98, 112, 168, 249, 257, 262
  rights 179
development funnel 254
differentiation, product 76, 166–70
diffusion of innovations 163, 185–94
direct integration 299
Direct Line 4
disruptive innovation 14, 175
Dodgson, Mark 251
Dosi, Giovani 112
dot.com companies 119
Doz 212
Drucker, Peter 38, 360
dual ladder 337
DuPont 141
Dutton Engineering 333
dynamic capability 269
Dyson, James 313, 326

e-Bay 3, 28
E-business 28–9
Edison, Thomas Alva 9, 37, 44
education *see* training and education
electronics 86, 88, 115, 116–20, 131, 318
Eli Lilly 208, 225
emergent properties 324
Emerson, Ralph Waldo 38
EMI 100, 101, 186, 302
Encyclopaedia Britannica 22
enterprise resource planning (ERP) 329
entrepreneurship 152, 282–3, 351–3, 353–6
environment, scanning 52, 70, 243
  creating 290–5
  external 293–4
  internal 291–3
Ericsson 125, 129, 227, 332
ESPRIT 211
e-stops 29

Europe 80, 86, 94, 99, 103, 143, 151, 220
evolutionary models 42–3
expeditionary marjeting 182
experimentation *see* learning
extended firm 251
external scanning 39, 293

failure
   alliances 229, 231
   new product 48–50
Fanning, Shawn 313
fashion, management fads 47, 75
Fibernet 3
financial performance, impact of innovation on 4, 17, 37, 356–64
First Direct 4
Fisher Price 303–4
flexible manufacturing systems (FMS) *see* advanced manufacturing technology (AMT)
focus groups 247
Ford 15, 28, 144, 169, 198, 204, 253, 260, 323, 334
forecasting 71, 128, 185–94, 244–5
France 89, 184, 235
Fransman, Martin 78
Freeman, Chris 38, 112
Fuji 228
Fujimoto, Takahiro 327
Fujitsu 202
funnel, product development 254
fusion *see* technology fusion

gamma testing 263
Gardiner, Paul 38, 58
Gates, Bill *see* Microsoft
GEC 54, 154, 155
General Electric (GE) 17, 30, 217, 316, 318
General Motors (GM) 15, 17, 204, 283, 316
Genetech 178
genome, human 178
Germany 86, 88, 89, 98, 123, 184, 235, 314
Gerstner, Lou 317
GICN 302
Glaxo 228, 367
globalization 26–7, 85, 141–4
Globetronics 207
Granstrand, O. 158
Grossman, David 317
groups *see* teamworking
Groves 260
Guinness 226

Hall, Richard 128
Hamel, Gary 15, 66, 120–3, 129, 134, 182, 195, 202

heavyweight product manager 126, 261, 327
Herve Thermique 217
Hewlett Packard 28, 48, 256, 292
Hill, Terry 273
Hoffman, Kurt 130
Holti 335
Honda 5, 65, 74, 121, 123, 127, 202, 236, 247, 256, 327
Hoover 39

Iacobucci, Dawn 195
IBM 8, 17, 18, 27, 49, 72, 78, 100, 101, 156, 178, 256, 316, 317,
ICI 155, 208, 302
ICL 212
ideas, generation of 290–1
Imperial College 281, 300, 349
implementation 40, 49, 56–8, 59, 70, 80, 250, 265, 267–9
incremental innovation 13, 112, 147, 329
incubators 351–3
independent business units 302–3
India 26
individuals, role of 325–8
information and communications technology (ICT) 26–8
information technology (IT) 18, 43, 57, 67, 113, 116–120, 130, 143, 267
innovation 340–2
   definitions 38
   intangible 13
   management of 45
   models of 41–2, 44
   resourcing 55–6, 66
   sources of 112–13
   success and failure 51
   types of 6–13
integrated business teams 299
Intel 131, 180, 182, 217, 258, 284
intellectual property rights (IPR) 178, 179–80
   see also copyright; licensing, patentsinternal scanning 291–3
Internet 3, 16, 27, 191
interorganizational networking (ION) 324, 325
intranet 217, 291, 366
intrepreneurship *see* corporate ventures
invention versus innovation 39, 54
ITT 154, 155

Jaguar 198
Japan 18, 20, 86, 97–9, 126, 129, 205, 209, 220, 235, 281, 296–7, 327
Johnson and Johnson 359
joint ventures *see* alliance
just-in-time (JIT) 331

kaizen 329, 332, 333
Kanter, Rosabeth Moss 318
Kay, John 70, 80, 83
keiretsu 216
Kingfisher 204
Kirin 208
Kleinschmidt 249
knowledge
  -building 148–50
  management of 65, 112, 119, 183, 287,
    291–3
  networks 143
  sources of 79–80
  types of 101, 111, 202, 221, 225, 234–5
knowledge manager 292
Kodak 12, 24, 100, 227
Korea 94, 95, 99
Kotler, Philip 194, 272
Krubasik, Edward 317

lastminute.com 16, 28
Lawrence 255
lead users 248
lean production 98, 205, 322, 331–2
learning
  through alliances 229–37
  through corporate ventures 285, 287,
    304–7
  evaluation of 146
  organizational 40, 46, 58, 99, 106, 137,
    269–70, 287, 339–40, 374
  cycle 270
  tools 270–2
lens, ophthalmic 3–4
Leonard-Barton, Dorothy 125–6, 195
Lewis, Jordan 237
licensing 99, 207–8, 285
  pricing 179–80
light emitting diode (LED) 10–11
life cycles, technological, market and
    product 12, 42, 165
lightbulb 9–11
Linux 218
Lorsch 255
Loveridge, Ray 83
Lynch, Mike 350

McDonald's 319
Malaysia 94
Mannesman 17
Mansfield, Edwin 146
markets 163–96, 244
  business 172–5
  consumer 171–2
  friction 58
  maturity 166
  segmentation 170–5

Marks & Spencer 204–5, 238
materials 6, 86, 116–20
Matsushita 100, 121, 180, 228, 281, 295, 329
measures of innovation 376–7
Medical Technology Partners 361
Merck 180
mergers and acquisitions 198, 224, 252
MetalSite 204
Microelectronics & Computer Technology
    Corporation (MCC) 209, 210
Microsoft 116, 131, 180, 182, 202, 217, 227,
    307, 316
mid-term plans (MTPs) 333
Midland Bank 174
Mindscape 72
Minolta 228
Mintzberg, H. 70, 319
MIT 98, 147, 328, 349–50, 368
Mitsubishi Chemicals 208
models of innovation 41–2, 44
Mondex 174
Morse 39
Motorola 16, 227, 238, 293
Mowery, David 112
MP3 23, 24–5
multimedia 22, 306–7

Napster 25–6, 313
national systems of innovation 42, 66, 85,
    106
Natural History Museum (NHM) 299
NatWest Bank 174
NCR 72
NEC 123
Nelson, Richard 106, 112
Netherlands 86, 89, 173
networks 28–30, 43, 143, 187, 214–17, 324
  emergence 322–4
Neumann 335
'New Economy' 119
New Medical Technologies 361
new product development 20, 41, 54, 255,
    284, 325
'new sciences' 141
new technology-based firms (NTBFs) 130,
    131–2, 349–50, 353–64
new venture division 300–1
new ventures department 300
Nightingale, Paul 120
Nike 30
Nippondenso 198, 208
Nishiguchi, T. 205, 238
Nissan 5, 257
Nokia 17, 227, 317
Nonaka, I. 58
Nortel Networks 289
Novartis 361

Noyce 260
NTT 226
nurtured divestment 303

Oakey, Ray 354
observability 187
organization
  change 157, 267–9
  culture 336–7
  development (OD) 267
  learning *see* learning
  memory 287
  knowledge *see* knowledge
  networks *see* networks
  structure 151
outsourcing 203
Oxford Instruments 5
Oxford University Press 306–7

partnerships 204
Pascale, Richard 74
patents 37, 66, 99, 103–4, 225, 351, 355
  costs 181
  legal requirements 178–9
  measures of innovation 351, 376
Pearson 72
personal computer (PC) 177
Pfeffer 313
pharmaceutical sector 20, 66, 74
Philips 49, 121, 201
Pilkington 28, 100, 325
Pisano, Gary 66, 69, 81
Pitt, Martyn 83
planning 264
Polaroid 12
policy improvement 332–3
Porter, Michael 38, 69, 83, 106
post-project reviews 270–1
Prahalad, C.K. 66, 120–3, 129, 134, 182, 195
Preussag 17
process innovation 5, 19, 37, 50, 248, 264–9
product development *see* new product
    development
  differentiation 76, 165, 166–70
  leadership versus follower 77, 100
  life cycle 5
product mapping 247
profit impact of market strategy (PIMS) 167
profitability *see* financial performance
project
  management 46, 261
  resourcing 19, 250–4
  selection 250
  success and failure 16
prototypes 114, 120, 164, 262
Psion 227
publishing 21–2

Quaker Oats 303–4
Quantel 5
quality function deployment (QFD) 168–9,
    262, 338
quality management 4, 47, 167, 331, 339, 375
QXL 3, 28

radical innovation 7, 103
reduced instruction set computing (RISC)
    177
re-innovation 58
relative advantage 185–6
reputation *see* brands
research and development (R&D) 250
  consortia 209–11
  expenditures 359–60
  funding 66, 87, 146–7
  location 66, 125, 138–44
  selection 66, 149
Rickman, Andrew 362
RISC (reduced instruction set computing)
    177
risk *see* uncertainty
Roberts, E. 295, 353, 358
robotics 128, 190
Rolls-Royce 293, 301
Rosenberg, Nathan 112
Rosenbloom, R. 83
Rothwell, Roy 29, 38, 43, 58
Route 128 349, 355
routines, organizational 20, 45, 46, 59,
    263–4, 339–40, 373
Rover 202, 236
Rumelt, Richard 65

Samsung 49
Sapsed, Jonathan 127
Sayles, L.R. 297, 308
scanning, environmental 52, 70, 243
scenario planning 193–4
Schnaars 128
science-based firms 115, 141
screening 248–9
sectoral patterns of innovation 42, 112–16,
    219
segmentation 164
  behavioural 177
  technical 177
semiconductor sector 79, 130, 350
service innovation 4, 5, 7, 41, 116
Shanklin, William 194
Shell 8, 17, 286
Siemens 303, 317
Silicon Valley 106, 349–50
Silver, Spence 313
Singapore 95

size of firm and innovation *see* small firms
Skandia 292
skills *see* training
small firms, innovation by 19, 40, 42, 67,
    81–2, 105–6, 112, 129–32, 156, 318, 349–70
SmithKline Beecham 6, 367
software 116–20, 130–2, 219, 307, 375
Sony 130, 180, 201, 297
Southwest Airlines 5, 375
special business units 301–2
stage-gate model 255, 258, 259
Stalker, George 318
strategy 52–5, 59, 65, 226–7, 246, 263–4
    incremental versus rational 69, 280
    positioning 66, 78, 148–50
    concept 246–7
    control 153
    planning 153
subcontracting 203–7
success and failure 16–17
    alliances 229, 231
    new product 48–50
    new venture 304
Sumitomo 207
superstars 129–30
suppliers, relations with 113, 132, 182, 199,
    203–7, 248
support organization 264
sustaining innovation 176
Swann, Joseph 9
Sweden 86, 91, 92, 125, 184
Switzerland 86, 89, 91–2, 143
SWORD approach 246
SWOT analysis 72, 75
Symbian 202, 227

Taiwan 94, 95
Taylor, Frederick 323
teams/teamworking 257, 258, 315, 319,
    323, 334–6
technological trajectories, paths 66, 69, 79,
    111–35, 141, 374
technology
    acquisition 198, 224, 252
    codifiability 225–6, 291
    complexity 18, 41, 43, 66, 70, 74, 101–2,
        112, 113, 165, 181–5, 187, 225
    diffusion 185–7, 291
    forecasting 192–4
    fusion 12–13
    implementation 40, 49, 56–8, 59, 70, 80,
        250, 265, 267–9
    life cycles 12, 42, 165
    marketing 175–81
    transfer 163, 250–4
technology product matrix 133, 134
Teece, David 55, 66, 69, 81, 100, 107

telecommunications 8, 39, 71, 193, 220, 303,
    315
Tesco 124, 204
test marketing 263
Texas Instruments 180
Thomson 17
Thorn 223
Tidd, Joe 262
time to market 5, 203–4, 256, 319
Toshiba 180
total quality management 338, 340–1, 342
Toyota 5, 48, 126, 324, 329
training, education and skills 112, 269,
    328–9, 339–40, 353–5
transaction costs 198
trialability 174
TRIZ system 293
TRW Inc. 128
Trust 231–2

UK 89, 205, 352–3
UK Medical Ventures (UK) 361
UMIST 83, 201
uncertainty 18, 45, 65, 74, 146, 184, 198, 284,
    373
Unilever 173, 178
universities 131, 215, 223
    incubators 351–3
unlearning 270
USA 20, 39, 78, 86, 99, 103–4, 119, 178, 204,
    205, 209, 220–1, 296–7, 352–3
users' needs 17, 58, 163, 245, 249
Utterback, J. 14, 18, 23

Vancom Zuid-Limburg 336
venture capital 359, 361, 362, 363–4
Virgin 316
virtual organization 251, 324
visions 127, 258–60, 315–17
Vodaphone 17
Von Hippel, E. 203, 256
Voss, Chris 98, 107, 267

Walker, David 54
Webster, Frederick 194
Western Union 12
Wheelwright, Steven 254, 261
Whiston, Tom 272
Wittington, Richard 83
Woodward, Joan 319
Worldwide Retail Exchange (WWRX) 205

Xerox 97–8, 100, 130, 140, 256, 332, 350

Yahoo! 16

Zeneca 155, 223, 225, 229, 367